Power

Books by Adolf A. Berle

Adolf A. Berle

POWER

HARCOURT, BRACE & WORLD, INC., NEW YORK

To the memory of

my mother, Augusta Wright Berle, and her New Englander's
belief in the power and providence of God;

and of

my father, Adolf Augustus Berle, who opposed the absolutist
power of property in the United States as his father had opposed
autocratic power in Germany during the revolution of 1848

Contents

Contents

BOOK TWO
Economic Power

Contents

Contents

BOOK FIVE
International Power

Contents

Contents

BOOK SIX

The Decline of Power

Acknowledgments

In one sense, acknowledgments should be made to almost everyone I met in the past half-century. But this would merely mean that I am thankful to have lived in a great, tragic, and dangerous time and for opportunity to encounter its power problems at many levels.

Chiefly I am grateful to my wife, Dr. Beatrice Berle. She did far more than encourage. She juxtaposed, sometimes in a single day, microcosmic problems of power tossed up by her Harlem clinic with the phenomena of vast power problems presented all the way from the White House to lesser centers.

Thanks also are due to my brother and friend, the Honorable Rudolf P. Berle, whose lifelong devotion to town and county government gave me access to an unrealized (and still largely unexplored but increasingly important) stratum of power.

To my friend Henry Allan Moe, President of the American Philosophical Society, I am indebted for insight into the steady interplay between idea systems and power.

I am under great obligation to Mr. William Jovanovich, presently head of Harcourt, Brace & World, for his ranging and passionate interest, without which I would have abandoned this adventure.

Finally, I am indebted to my secretary, Miss Margaret A. Poole, who has struggled with the endless work of transcribing and retranscribing and organizing this manuscript.

ADOLF A. BERLE

Power

Prologue in Pergamum

1. Fulcrum of World Power

Let us make a rendezvous with Zeus. It could be made anywhere. I choose his altar at Pergamum, just inland from the Aegean coast of Asia Minor.

You may ascend the acropolis at Pergamum on foot, following a dusty path as it slabs up a half-desert hillside and comes out on a rocky peak. The mountaintop has been flattened by centuries of human labor. Great platforms have been made; they were once covered by palaces, fortresses, and temples. On a great esplanade is the fabled altar of Zeus, god of power, whose secrets we now seek.

Pergamum was once the strong capital of a Mysian city-state that grew to a great kingdom. Its Hellenist despot kings maintained themselves through centuries, holding power against barbarian Gauls and Persian armies; at one time it held under subjection a good part of Asia Minor.

The armies of Alexander the Great had conquered the region and after his death set up the Seleucid Empire—and Pergamum survived. The altar of Zeus we now visit may have been set up in 226 B.C. when the invading Gauls were defeated; but it was rededicated, fantastically sculptured, after the battle of Magnesia in 190 B.C. At that time, Pergamum had become a fulcrum, with which the balance of world power was changed by its king, Eumenes II. Fearing the imperialism of the Macedonians now become emperors, Eumenes had prevailed on the island kingdom of Rhodes to call in the Roman legions. They had come, conquering Macedonia and, thanks to Eumenes, crossing the Dardanelles without opposition. Roman and Macedonian-Seleucid forces met at Magnesia. The battle was won, not by the Roman legions, who were unable to solve the Macedonian phalanx, but by Eumenes' cavalry. With that victory, power over the eastern Mediterranean and the land bridge between Europe, Asia, and Africa passed into Roman hands—and Pergamum had done it. (In 1967, the United States, confronting the Russians as Arabs fought Israel, got a glimmer of understanding of the significance of that land bridge.)

For the following half-century, Pergamum was perhaps the most brilliant kingdom in the Mediterranean world. Second only to that of Alexandria, its library was the greatest. Its sculpture rivaled that of Athens in the age of Pericles. Its temples reflected its worship of power. Spontaneously, it is said, Pergamum deified its kings, as later it deified Roman emperors, leading Saint John the Divine to describe Pergamum (in the Book of Revelations) as "the seat of Satan."

Its freedom, of course, was doomed. About sixty years after Magnesia, the last Pergamese king bequeathed his country to Rome, to become the "Province of Asia Minor," leaving only memories. Its name survives in English today in a corrupted word, "parchment," since Pergamum had first learned to use sheepskin as writing material.

Perhaps more than any other single acropolis, Pergamum expresses the power cult. Hence our rendezvous. Standing on the esplanade of Zeus, one looks eastward over the rolling hills and plains of Mysia. A thousand miles away rise the staggering Caucasus Mountains, end of the world, where chaos began. Once, that chaos had been everywhere on the face of the earth, subdued, not extirpated, by Zeus himself.

2. Zeus against Chaos

It is time to call in a guide and interpreter.

Hesiod was the son of a seafaring Greek trader who, like many retired traders, wound up as a farmer—in Boeotia, north of Athens. The poet son, who inherited part of the farm, tended sheep on Mount Helicon. He may have been a contemporary of, but probably lived somewhat later than, Homer. Almost certainly he went to the temple of Delphi, dedicated to Apollo. He claimed inspiration from the Muses—that is, from Apollo's entourage. But he was no stranger to power. According to tradition, he died in a grove sacred to Zeus. His poetry, notably the epic *Works and Days*, competed for favor with the *Iliad* and the *Odyssey* as late as the eighteenth century. Passages in his *Theogony* give perhaps as good an interpretation of the emergence of power in men's affairs as we are likely to have. Mythology, to be sure, but mythology is shorthand for an immense amount of prehistory.

"Verily, at the first," says Hesiod, "Chaos came to be." This Chaos was universal, slow-moving, unceasing, devastating, chilling, destructive disorder. Earth appeared; Chaos brought forth black night. Earth, having produced the starry heavens, lay with Heaven and produced Cronus. Cronus "hated" his lusty sire. He perhaps opposed chaotic disorder—the text is obscure. In turn,

5

Cronus lay with Earth. Their son was Zeus. Cronus hated and sought to destroy him even before his birth.

The miscegenated family into which Zeus was born includes mythological symbols of all kinds of known disorder, and perhaps some forms our race no longer remembers. Thunder, lightning, fire; one-eyed giants; monsters; earthquakes—"of all the children that were born on earth and heaven, these were the most terrible." Terrible because unpredictable and incalculable, as though someone had stirred up genetics with hideous result. These monsters must have typified much of life. Natural forces, animal forces, subhuman forces, all hostile, all unpredictable, all untrammeled.

Presently Zeus joined battle with the whole irrational horde. He began by plotting against his father. With instinctive psychological accuracy, he bound and castrated Cronus—perhaps to end further production of monster progeny. Seizing thunderbolts from one of the Titans, he used them against the Titan tribe. His enemies were the irrational one-eyed Cyclopes, giants with a hundred arms and fifty heads, half-nymph goddesses with fair cheeks and the body of snakes, fifty-headed hounds of Hades eating human flesh—the whole race of horrors. These, with the offspring of Cronus, made war on the "gods, givers of good," of which Zeus was the first. Victorious at the end, Zeus and his cohorts drove them all to Tartarus; "There by the counsel of Zeus who drives the clouds the Titan gods are hidden under misty gloom, in a dank place where are the ends of the huge earth. . . . And there, all in their order, are the source and ends of gloomy earth and misty Tartarus."

Hesiod's collection of myths is a poetic account of power emerging out of meaningless chaos, becoming the antithesis of the parent anarchy and disorder. Zeus's classic battle with the Titans amounts to just that. (In the twentieth century, we also draw meaning from allegory; Freud is a notable example.) Zeus personified power, its vices as well as its usefulness. Because he used power to bring a measure of predictability, and therefore order, he became supreme.

Chaotic forces are not always in captivity. Some are loose in the twentieth century. They may be as near as the horrible potentialities of human personality. We saw them released at Belsen and Auschwitz in Nazi Germany; in the torture camps of Stalin; in the klaverns of the Ku Klux Klan in Mississippi; in riots in Newark and Detroit; in the dark corners that deface all societies everywhere. Zeus could "contain" chaos; he could not eliminate the possibility of its return. He could imprison the progeny of Cronus in distant spots, "hidden under misty gloom." But, Hesiod notes, they are still alive, however guarded by trusty warriors.

Power, raw and terrible, was preferable to chaos. This is still true. So the great altar of Zeus dominated the citadel of Pergamum. Its acropolis had been a citadel of order through a chaotic time and in a chaotic world.

Power had done this; and the Pergamese worshiped it.

3. The Challenge of Metis and Apollo

Hard by Zeus's altar on the Pergamum acropolis lie ruins of the temple of Pallas Athena. Pallas Athena signified wisdom and the results of thought; she could reason, a capacity not given to Zeus.

Hesiod produces a second allegory essential to our study. He tells that Zeus lay with Metis (she signified thought). Earth and Heaven warned him against this: Metis was, they said, wiser than the gods. Her offspring could challenge him and he had best be on his guard "to the end that no other should hold royal sway over the eternal gods in place of Zeus; for very wise children were destined to be born of her." So Zeus swallowed Metis, as Cronus had once attempted to devour him. But thought could not be destroyed. Pallas Athena, Metis' daughter, exploded, fully armed, from the head of Zeus; and thereafter, in an odd love-hate relationship she became his favorite daughter—favorite because essential; suspect because she qualified his royal sway.

The allegory dramatically expresses one of the laws of power. Thought and reason can challenge power. It is, apparently, im-

7

possible to kill or constrain thought and reason. It is, of course, possible to kill the thinker—but his thought remains; it cannot be wiped out. Pallas could not be destroyed, even by Zeus, or anyone touched by her—for example, Prometheus. Nor can power, if it is to survive, do without thought, wisdom, reason, and knowledge. So it must live with their challenge while using their product. Though brute power can exercise itself only within the range of a direct weapon—of a pistol or a machine gun, of a guided missile or the diameter of a nuclear explosion—at a minimum, to transcend the range of a man's fist, there must be enough knowledge to put together the weapons, be they swords or rockets. To achieve that, Pallas is needed; she was, among other things, a warrior goddess and "saviour of armies." But force alone does little. Power, to exert itself and accomplish intended ends, requires organization and the recruitment and services of other men, most of whom must act beyond the range of the power holder's personal presence. Such men have to be willing to obey instructions; and do so even when they are not under immediate threat. The most elementary organization requires a central core of ideas, and these must set up a measure of loyalty running from servant or subject to the power holder. That requires some alliance between power and reason. The advice Hesiod says Earth and Heaven gave Zeus was not far wrong; thought is indeed more powerful than the gods. Zeus could not hold unqualified rule once Pallas was conceived. Equally, he could not hold sway without her.

The myth outlines the endless paradox of contest between power and its companion idea system; the endless love-hate between king and priest. The alliance is at once essential and uneasy. Ideas and knowledge threaten the power holder; the priest continually threatens the king. The power holder steadily fears, often contests with, the thinker; frequently he tries to destroy him. On his side, the thinker plots against the power holder; the priest seeks to make himself king. Victory of either over the other is self-destructive. The two forces must coexist. Each is essential to the other; neither can exercise both functions.

So Pallas stands on the Pergamum acropolis next to Zeus. The myth gives no indication of what either thought of the other. Perhaps it does not matter. Power without ideas reduces itself all too rapidly to chaos—the monsters appear again. But if reason merely destroys power, it ceases to perform its function—once more chaos creeps forward.

Pallas, I think, may never have felt fully at home on the Pergamese mountaintop. Certainly you would not go there to meet her, though even there she had many followers, like Galen, the Physician, who worked out theories of medicine, surgery, and philosophy while serving as doctor with the gladiatorial school.

More likely you would find her at the Parthenon, her own temple, crowning the Athenian acropolis. If one comes into it late on a sunlit afternoon after long ascent, the peace of its perfectly proportioned beauty brings one closer to heaven than any other point on earth. Here was her capital and her kingdom. She had struggled against Poseidon to endow it with olive trees. No pacifist, she had given it means of defense. She was a great woman, as well as a practical and cosmic mind, who had worked with Hephaestus and taught men the crafts by which they came down from caves to build their homes; a noble friend, too, instructing Hercules as he went forth to his labors, and Eurynome, daughter of Nisus, for whom she sought unsuccessfully to find a loving husband; powerful enough to struggle with Ares, the God of War.

Beyond all else, she was a lady in the great sense of the word, wise and gracious, mature and considerate. One thinks of women dowered with her gifts of stateliness and womanhood: of Eleanor Roosevelt in her all-embracing sympathy; of the clear-eyed, steel-minded humanitarian Jane Addams; of Josephine Boardman Crane, seeking and endowing arts, music, beauty; of Julia Isham Taylor, liberating Henry Osborn Taylor in his search for the medieval mind; of certain matriarchs behind stormy Latin-American republics, bringing order where there was none.

In the Parthenon you may still find Pallas Athena, courteous as a hostess, great in her thinking, generous in her hopes, knowing that her followers are not her creatures but must follow the thinking of their own minds, and the philosophies of their own conception. She would visit Pergamum: the record of the city suggests she did. But the city belonged to Zeus.

For another moment, we must gaze across the Aegean Sea. We

will keep Hesiod's guidebook as we discover a third ever-present element in the exercise of power. Its divinity is Apollo, god of the lyre, father of the Muses, symbol of artistic force. It was claimed for Hesiod that he was a personal friend of the Muses. His greatest effort, perhaps, was a hymn describing how Apollo resolved to make his lovely template at "Crisa beneath snowy Parnassus, a foothill turned toward the west," where Delphi stands today. If Homer and Hesiod and their friends could make allegories, so can we. As Pallas was Zeus's favorite daughter, Apollo was, perhaps, his favorite son. Where Pallas dealt with reason, calculation, and thought, Apollo dealt with inspiration and intuitive impulses revealing design and beauty. He symbolized the truth that emotion and revelation can give insights beyond the range of logic.

At Delphi, if anywhere away from Delos, Apollo might be found. He himself had had to conquer one of the last of the monster enemies of his father on the way there—though that serpent-monster was fostered in hate by Hera to take revenge on Zeus for conceiving bright-eyed Pallas. On the crag overlooking the gulf, Apollo laid the foundations of his temple, there "to receive the tribes of men that gather to this place," especially to "show mortal men my will." Even its ruins still speak to men.

Historically, power has always sought the assistance of the arts. Why, it is difficult to tell. Attempt at alliance nevertheless has been constant; one finds it wherever one encounters power. As in the power relation with the idea system, the alliance is uneasy. Artists, poets, musicians serve their intuitions, and because they do are not easily ordered about. Princes have tried to induce into their service sculptors, like Benvenuto Cellini; painters, like Leonardo da Vinci; architects, like Christopher Wren; musicians, like Pablo Casals; poets, like Robert Frost. (In these cases, the princes were, respectively, a Borgia pope, Alexander IV; a French king, Francis II; an English monarch, George III; an American president, John F. Kennedy. Julius Caesar sought to win over the poet Catullus, and Chinese emperors sought the services of the artists who have left us some of the most beautiful pictures in the human record.)

Hesiod would explain all that rather clearly. For some strange reason men wish to know, not only that they can survive, but what life they shall lead. Cretans, guided to Parnassus by the music of Apollo's lyre and stirred by his spirit, asked quite simply, "Tell us now how we shall live." They were asking more than how to make a living on the Mediterranean slopes. Their question has been repeated throughout history. It is cried out aloud in the mid-twentieth century. It cannot be fully answered intellectually. Any reply must speak to the heart no less than to the head. Even power holders know that; indeed, they feel it themselves: the use of power is itself an art.

Aphorisms aside, we find power associated invariably with two external forces: a system of ideas and, more hesitantly, a system of art. One of the fascinations of the study of power lies in the fact that artists and thinkers, will they, nill they, never fully accept power. Yet they are never fulfilled except under conditions only power can create.

4. The Uneasy Balance

We have tasted the poetry of power, choosing an acropolis in Asia Minor to do so. Let us now leave poets and deal with harder facts of history.

Power, wielded by its holders, was a developed fact when known history begins. In his remarkable book *African Genesis*, Robert Ardrey adduces evidence suggesting that organized power exists among animals. It may therefore precede the emergence of man. Prehistoric drawings in caves by the Loire and in Spain show hunters harrying beasts of strength and swiftness until one hunter can come in for the kill. Such organization connotes a leader, able to make a plan, give orders, cause them to be carried out, and quite probably at the end divide the kill among the group. Power, held by leader, captain, chief, or king, is evident in the earliest known archeological traces.

Evident also is the fact that an idea system, represented by priest, shaman, or sage, stands by the side of each power holder. Force may have established his military or civil rule, but it is invariably paralleled by or intertwined with a structure of ideas, usually embodied in religious doctrine and edicts, and maintained by faith in its laws and fear of its judgments. Jacques Henri Pirenne, in his *Panorama de l'Histoire Universelle,* maintains that Egypt was born as tiny nomadic bands stabilized themselves in the Valley of the Nile. All peoples have passed through some similar process. Stabilization, requiring communities to live in specific territories, gave birth to the political organization from which we draw our present "states." Primitive communities were always under the protection of a god equivalent to Hesiod's Zeus, though terrestrially governed by a chief or king. Always associated with him was a priest. The king with a growing organization under him needed power; he decided on and carried out action and maintained discipline. Alongside him the priest and a hierarchy under him elaborated a system of relationships, practices, and moral judgments assumed to be required by the gods and were the repository of knowledge.

George de Santillana, in his book *Origins of Scientific Thought,* has sifted out and collected such material as is available on the prehistoric origins of science. In history's dawn they are found chiefly in priestly records and practices. We do not know what may have been in the minds of priests; in making their observations, they may merely have been ritually serving a god. But, while doing so, they made amazingly accurate observations of the movements of the sun and stars and carried them forward from generation to generation. Thus emotional religion was accompanied by remarkably detailed knowledge. The geographic calculations of Ptolemaic Egypt and the astronomy of the Mayan Empire in Central America excite the admiration of modern scientists. Pallas Athena supported Zeus; priest-savants supported the king-chieftains.

In early life I was attorney for the nineteen Indian pueblos that today survive in New Mexico. My task was to determine the landholdings they had been granted by the Spanish Empire. At the close of the Mexican-American War in 1848, the Treaty of Guadalupe Hidalgo included a clause by which the government of the United States agreed to maintain the rights of the inhabitants in the area ceded to it by Mexico. The problem was to find out what these rights were, and approximately the boundaries of pueblo-Indian occupation. I lived with these Indians for a time. At Pueblo Santo Domingo, not far from Santa Fe, the tribal council held a meeting at my request, at which I explained the data I needed. After consultation, their tribal historian was called in, aided by a young acolyte destined to succeed him when he died. He was, clearly, a tribal priest, although the Catholic church of the pueblo—originally imposed by Spanish conquest—nominally carried out the religious functions. He recited the tribal history in the form of an epic poem carried forward by oral tradition by the appointed priest-historian. Annually, it was brought up to date, adding each year's events. When it came to the area of recorded history, where I could check, it proved remarkably accurate.

Akkadian, Sumerian, and early Chinese communities must have had somewhat similar "libraries" of knowledge, transmitted orally until writing became available. There has always been, it seems, a dual apparatus: a power mechanism and a knowledge system. And the two are not the same.

We would like to know more about the organized art mechanisms, but that must await studies not yet adequately made. I find it difficult to believe that Apollo and the Muses were not on hand in ascertainably separate organization. But art does not easily organize itself institutionally and perhaps leaves less recorded imprint of its early structure. Yet it certainly demonstrates its presence in architecture, craft designs, statues big and little; and in drawings and paintings, of which unfortunately few survive.

History tells something else of importance today. It records how uneasy the coexistence is between the power system and the idea system. The priest could often oppose his ideas to the king's desire for unlimited use of power. In the sixteenth century before Christ, after the Hyksos nomads had been expelled from the

13

Egyptian kingdom, a new empire emerged. Its founder-king, Amasis, established the religion of Ammon of Thebes, whose high priests stood next the throne but contested for power. A century later, when a queen, Hatshepsut, became regent, the high priest made himself prime minister and virtual chief of state. In the following century, Amenophis IV, better known as Ikhnaton, came into square conflict with the religious establishment of Ammon. He therefore caused himself to be recognized as an incarnate god. Then he could give orders to the priestly system. Temporarily, the device worked. When he conquered Assyria (its Zeus was Shamash, the sun god), he announced that Shamash was the same as Aton, whose incarnation he was; so that he held both godships. Then he endeavored to decree monotheism, existence of a single god—himself—superseding all others, ruling by kindness and love, not by armies quartered on the people. It would be interesting to know the thoughts of this remarkable monarch. He may have been a saint, or merely a matter-of-fact politician as well as a brilliant general, cynically collecting and merging godheads as a means of power. Churches and idea systems have considerable capacity to make subjects behave as they wish. Men who might resist the soldier or the police might still obey the injunctions of a priest. Or Ikhnaton, as many power holders in that situation have done, may have believed his own propaganda.

But a companion constant in history is the fact that where the priest takes over power or, alternatively, where the king takes over the religion, the system explodes or decays. Ikhnaton's did on his death. Once a power mechanism begins to twist it, the religious or other idea system no longer commands adherence. In the twentieth century, we have seen Joseph Stalin endeavor to set up the doctrine by fiat that acquired characteristics can become hereditary. He backed a Soviet scientist, Trofim D. Lysenko, the promoter of the notion. Well, power can decree a dogma, and perhaps men can be made to swallow it, but power cannot make acquired characteristics hereditary, and empiric evidence presently will establish that fact. Then the knowledge and the conclusion drawn from it will cease to be valid. Power systems attempting to rely on invalid knowledge are bound to get into trouble.

Conversely, when the priest becomes power holder, he fares little better. Power invariably involves dealing with realities. The priest-become-king cannot impose the absolutes of his religion on the affairs of the day. He must adjust to the fact that soldiers can go only so far; that an economic system can support only so many people; that men, armies, and the forces of production do not come into existence merely because he asks the gods to provide them. In the realm of the spirit, the priest's claim and range may be unlimited. In the realm of actuality, his power is not. So he must compromise with circumstances. But if he insists that his compromises are decreed by God or are inherent in absolute scientific knowledge, his idea system becomes worthless. If he fails to compromise, he is led to attempt the impossible, and his power system is defeated.

The king cannot for long be high priest; the religious leader cannot for long be ruler. The two callings are incompatible. If there are exceptions to this rule, I have not encountered them.

Before leaving it, let us take a last glance from the Pergamese acropolis. Near the altar of Zeus is a temple dedicated to a then living Roman emperor, Trajan, made god by decree. The Roman Senate had betrayed an irrational desire to deify the first emperor, Augustus Caesar, in his lifetime. That wily and wise statesman knew enough to refuse, but the Senate did it to him shortly after his death. Thus the Roman god-emperor dogma began. Pergamum knew it of old and swallowed it whole. The city is counted as one of the centers of the god-emperor cult. In fact, merging the Roman imperial power system with the Roman religious idea system did not work well. The religious system rapidly deteriorated—so much so that three centuries later the religion of a Galilean Jewish thinker overturned the Greco-Roman gods altogether, shunting them into the cloudland of mythology and poetry.

The esplanade below the altar of Zeus overlooks ranges of Mysian hills softened in afternoon by blue mists. Thunderheads float away to the southeast. Zeus has left Pergamum—possibly seeking his old abode in the Caucasus Mountains whence Prometheus stole his fire. Perhaps human power-holders-become-gods and cult-emperors offended him. Mythical monsters and Titans emerged again in the Turkish valleys in the form of released human hatreds. They have proved as cruel and irrational as when Zeus fought them in prehistory.

Chaos and its monsters, defeated, contained, but not destroyed, still could erupt in human affairs. In time they destroyed not only Pergamum but the Roman Empire and several succeeding empires, leaving only ruins behind.

Nor are these monsters contained today. When the last of the empires left the land bridge between Europe, Asia, and Africa, hatred stalked the area. In June, 1967, the result was a brief war between its occupants, two branches of the Semitic race. Temporarily contained by Israeli force, disorder is still present, frightening and perplexing the world.

Pergamum survives as an insignificant Turkish village. Its peasants look up to the ruined acropolis and down to the Mysian plains, scene of ancient victories. They see neither the one nor the other. The altar of Zeus has crumbled; its god power has left it. Yet, examining the scattered stones, a traveler can still find all the elements that once made it a power center and fulcrum of world history.

Overture—in the Twentieth Century

1. Power: A Desire and a Social Necessity

Power and love are the oldest known phenomena of human emotions. Neither wholly yields to rational discussion; poets have as good insights as philosophers. Libraries are full of books about love. The literature of power is surprisingly scant. Perhaps it is natural that power comes off second best. Love is intensely personal and might be expected to interest everyone. Power, though also personal, is most dramatic when intensely political; its political aspects overshadow the personal dramas it causes.

Inevitably, the closing decades of the twentieth century will witness great increases of power and the proliferation of its uses.

Population growth, the increasing volume and complexity of economics, and the propensity of people to gather in great urban areas will call out power as matter of course. Empty roads need few rules and fewer traffic officers; congested highways multiply both, calling on police power to prevent chaos. Repeat this in analogy a thousand times and we have a fair forecast for the coming years.

Conversely, increasing congestion intensifies each man's search for individuality and distinction. One avenue by which men set themselves apart from their fellows is by seeking possession and use of power—be the level high or low. A Kennedy will pursue the American presidency no matter the peril. A teen-ager will organize a gang in the city streets, make war on a neighboring group, or perhaps merely smash plate-glass windows. H. G. Wells called this the queer human desire to astonish and impress one's neighbors. It accounts for a good deal of low-level activity, just as it accounts for a great deal of high-level politics.

Current American thinking has regarded power as a dirty subject, and desire for its possession a naughty emotion. When disciples of the late C. Wright Mills use the phrase "the power elite," they intend no compliment. When analyses of Communist systems are objectively written, they are likely to be less complimentary to socialist power holders. The general Anglo-Saxon attitude toward power is one of distrust and dislike accompanied by reluctant and rationalized appetites.

Appeals for and to power are, nevertheless, continuous. Reformers endeavor to solve any situation, from civil rights for Negroes to better distribution of national income, by calling for its directed use. All-out radicals demand popular revolution under dictatorships only faintly qualified by being "of the proletariat." It is easy, of course, to quip that power is an evil thing in your hands, though beneficent in mine; but the problem lies deeper. In point of fact, an element of power is essential to every human development above the level of Robinson Crusoe on his island. But power, wherever found and at whatever level, is capable of abuse. It is, therefore, dangerous to both society and individuals subject to it. Need for it is obvious, while knowledge of its control is only rudimentary. That knowledge will have to be acquired within the next ten or twenty years. The subject will not be remote, philosophical, or esoteric. It will be the most practical problem confronting all developed countries, and all people in them.

When the greatest single study of power on record—Niccolò Machiavelli's *The Prince*—was written, the subject seemed comparatively understandable. Machiavelli dealt with simple princely dictators of Renaissance Italian city-states. A modern Machiavelli has to follow power endlessly divided, subdivided, maintained, and applied through thousands of institutions. The subject has thus become more complex. Yet it is the same story. The basic problems are essentially the same despite a multitude of conceptions and organizations not known at the time of Lorenzo de' Medici and Cesare Borgia. Modern aspirants to power usually lack the drama and dash of the Renaissance; a twentieth-century American Cesare Borgia, seeking to seize a state like Massachusetts, as likely as not may hold the unromantic office of commissioner of motor vehicles or secretary of a Communist party organization. Drama would be higher if he also had the title and panoplied office of a prince like Cesare or a ducal field marshal like Wellington or Marlborough. Still, what he loses in drama he may make up in power. Major American administrative officials may well come to have more direct control over more human beings than did any Renaissance despot at his zenith.

And we *are* learning the subject. In the United States we have made a discovery. We are coming to understand, slowly, that property and power are essentially the same substance—though in different phases of distribution. Fragmented power tends to become property. This has been the norm of American development. Property aggregated tends to generate power. Property changes its form and aggregates its power elements as great collectives, like corporations, increasingly carry on production, whereupon state power is increasingly called in to assure that the power-driven economic system runs smoothly, and does, more or less, what most of the American public wants it to do. In result, power elements, private and public, are building up in America at a surprising rate. They are doing this because, in general, the public wants certain results and is willing to accept the risk of power required to get them. So far as I can see, no one really wants to reverse this trend, though some groups want greater participation in it. It does mean, however, that the country will increasingly have to deal with the dynamics of power and with its control if American democracy is not to change both its content and its form.

Human instincts parallel the social need. Most men want a measure of power, and the fundamental drives behind power are essentially personal and emotional. Ceaseless dramas, large and small, result. The poetry is epic, not lyric, and I have not hesitated to draw on poetic material where apposite. Political scientists and sociologists are the best analysts of structure, but poets still have the deepest insights into personality. Both will be needed in this study, which is also, unavoidably, a study of men.

2. Power and Property

In the twentieth century, half the world bolted to Communist systems of power in violent revolt against nineteenth-century systems supposedly based on property. While this was occurring, the non-Communist world had been discovering that its industrial organization turned increasingly on economic organization, this being, on analysis, a different system of power. The revolutions, wars, political arrangements, and novel economic doctrines of the late eighteenth and early nineteenth centuries were chiefly aimed at breaking up, defending against, or reducing power systems. Power certainly had not been an unknown phenomenon. Both the feudal system and its predecessor, the Roman Empire, had been overt power structures. So had the monarchic nationalist regimes emerging in Europe and Asia from the sixteenth century. Variations in power systems have, of course, been continuous. They chiefly reflect the extent to which power is concentrated (emperor or king) or diffused (among smaller kingdoms, chieftains, lords, seigneurs, guilds, and so forth). The Renaissance drew a contrast between the conception of power personally embodied in a ruler and power as abstract force capable of being given or withdrawn by the will of the church, or from officials by free republics, or perhaps by operation of moral law.

This poses the first difficulty in considering power. It is both subjective—an aspect of human experience—and objective—a fact in society. Like love, it can be intensely personal. Or it can be vastly and diffusively inclusive. In its personal aspect, it is a subject for poets and psychologists. In its general aspect, it is a continuing phenomenon of history, politics, and human organization.

It is also a universal human experience. Few individuals have not had and exercised some of it, if only in microscopic degree, at some time in their lives. A mother with her children, a father with a family, an elder in a group of juniors have held it in appreciable measure. Certainly no one has failed to be subject to one or another form of power during most of the waking hours of his life.

One may question Professor Alfred Adler's insistence (differing from Freud) that power, more than sex, is the prime determinant of human personality. Few, nevertheless, would deny that it is an almost invariable component. The Freud-Adler dispute we cannot pursue; psychoanalysis is still in its infancy. Poets and novelists may grant us insight, and the study of men may in time give us knowledge. In this book, our task must be to synthesize observed phenomena, drawing in some measure on history. Then we may have a sporting chance of discovering how this human instinct has been and can be used in human affairs.

The twentieth-century revolutions toward—not away from—power are not quite as surprising as might appear. The nineteenth century was dominated politically by British thought. In economics, Adam Smith had written a majestic tract, carried forward by David Ricardo, reaching climax in the philosophy of Herbert Spencer and the doctrines of John Stuart Mill. These, perhaps reacting to the violences of Bourbon monarchs, the French Directoire, and the Napoleonic era, came perilously close to

21

making a deity out of absence of power. So far as economics was concerned, they considered that the ultimate, supreme, and most beneficent regulator of affairs was a balance reached through and maintained by the "hidden hand" working through the "open market." Not only was that government best which governed least, but in economic affairs no interference or regulation could produce good results, if, indeed, it could produce results at all. That state of affairs which emerged automatically from wide competition in all fields was, and must be, the best obtainable. Mill carried the doctrine to extremes; though in the latter part of his life he conceded that a state might intervene to the extent of providing elementary schools for children and he made a few other grudging admissions. Western economic and political thinking seventy-five years ago refused to accept power within a nation except for the elementary end of preserving public order. In the United States, through the first decade of the twentieth century power was almost a dirty word to political and economic philosophers.

The human results of this line of thinking were highly unsatisfactory to many people. *Laissez faire* and the open market might, and almost invariably did, produce slums, child labor, degeneration, shocking conditions of work, disease, starvation. Uneasily, suspicion grew that complete refusal to accept the power of the state or society to interfere did not mean that power was not present. It merely left power in the hands of owners of property. Worse yet, denial of the power principle was not real, but sham. Refusal to permit outside power to deal with child labor or wages did not mean refusal to call on state power for protection of real estate from invasion or of property rights from interruption. A state that (under Spencerian and Millsian doctrine) could not provide a minimum wage at subsistence level could nevertheless hang thieves, dispossess tenants, break up labor unions, or fire on desperate mobs. Economic life, it seemed, was based on counters of property, preferably widely diffused. The result, according to Adam Smith and Herbert Spencer, should have been balance. Factually, the state, the police, sheriffs, soldiers, and courts seemed needed to maintain the integrity of those counters against assaults resulting from imbalance.

To anyone on the wrong side of the economic table there was no absence of power; the property counters seemed to conjure up plenty of it for their defense. Karl Marx in his London exile claimed just this as he flitted from volume to volume in the British Museum. It remained only for Lenin to cap the climax. He enthusiastically accepted Marx's theory of social economics and he contributed the pile-driving force that made it into a political system. His life was spent in elaborating methods of seizing power, means of maintaining it, and ways of centralizing it in a single dictatorship.

The result was a cosmic joke. Discard the counter of private property and the motivations and temptations that go with it, said Marx, collectivize everything in a state organized for that purpose, and a new classless society will emerge, splendid in achievement. Lenin's Russian soviet state, giving effect to the doctrine, substituted monopoly of power for the monopoly of property denounced by Marx. The profit motive, a factor of property, was not allowed, though ambition and the desire for power were not inhibited. Presently it became obvious that the two motives were suspiciously alike. If anything, ambition and the power desire could produce results more savage than property and the desire for profit. It had not then dawned on anyone that property and power might be the same phenomenon in different phases of development.

Yet that appears to be the fact. Precisely when a feudal or military ruler began to regard his duchy or his march as a basis of property one cannot tell. It was a psychological change. But happen it surely did. Until relatively recently, certain English peers had power to nominate rectors of churches within their baronies. Nominees were willing to pay for the appointment, so this was profitable. Presently the power of appointments to "livings," as they were called, became salable; they were bought and sold and quoted, and were classified in English law as real property. Milovan Djilas in his famous book, *The New Class*, points out that Communist officeholders in Yugoslavia already consider that they have superior claim to their positions in the power hierarchy. Suggestions have been received that a like process is going on in the Soviet Union. Particular slices of power are increasingly becoming identified with and attached to particular groups of men, if not as yet to individuals. It is a short step from this identification in a power system to new forms of counters, readily recognized as a variety of property.

Creaming the jest, the non-Communist Western world has been moving through an intense period of industrialization. One of the results has been the emergence of great collective economic organizations—corporations, public and private—notably in the United States. These increasingly reduce the nominal property owners (stockholders) to claim holders, while the actual management of the physical assets and intangible organization falls into the hands of directors and managers. If the power systems in the Communist East begin to exhibit symptoms of spawning property, industrial property systems of the West begin to show signs of turning themselves into power systems. Each regime, saying it will ne'er consent, gives in.

It looks, therefore, as though most of the world will live in and organize its affairs around systems that have elements of both property and power. The property element has been studied, re-studied, inventoried, reduced to statistics. The power element has not. Both the East and the West need to know a great deal about it.

3. Power, Property, and Science

We here survey power in the latter half of the twentieth century. The perspective of the writer and the reader alike is thus determined. The writer sees what he can from where he stands—in this passionate, pulsating, perilous Renaissance tossed up by the twentieth century. The contemporary reader will do the same; he takes off from these pages into the same world in which they were written. But if someone chances to read it twenty or even fifty years later, his point of view will have changed; the river of history will have moved. Man can look as far backward as history will permit—the past is prologue. If he can look forward, uncertainly, it is thanks to that body of knowledge we call "science." Scientific observation establishes what are usually called "laws." These carry a presumption that (within their field) what happened yesterday or in Egyptian times will continue to happen five or five thousand years hence. Sumerian, Egyptian, and Mayan priests followed the sun, its equinoxes and solstices. They assumed its phases and courses would continue, if not eternally, at least for uncountable eons. Through poetry and legend, they interpreted their astronomical laws as religious doctrine: the sun god must die at its nadir; he must be reborn as the new ascent begins. (This is why the Western world celebrates the feast of Christmas or rebirth in the winter solstice; why in many, if not all, religions, the schedule of rituals, sacrifices, festivals was made out for years ahead.) To a scientist, to look backward implies that he also can look forward.

I propose a somewhat similar attempt here. This connotes acceptance of the scientific point of view. It somewhat violates the current thinking of most historians, who insist that the story of the past, however factually accurate, offers scant base to forecast the future. All the same, few historians would assert that there cannot and will never be a philosophy of history or ultimate derivation of laws of historical development. They merely deny that any reliable philosophy now exists, and assert that at present no historical laws can be reliably derived. Some disagree. A great historian, Jacques Pirenne, writing a justification of his epic *Great Currents in Universal History*, observed: "Most of the great crises of history result from misunderstanding of these elemental historic laws. If statesmen have not taken account of them, this is because historical evolutions are extremely long, extending over many centuries, and in consequence peoples often have no knowledge of the sense of historical evolution which guides them." [1] Pirenne, perhaps, goes farther than most in believing that continuing, if not eternal, principles can be spelled out from history.

1. Preface to *Panorama de L'Histoire Universelle*, by his son, Jacques Henri Pirenne, Neuchatel, Suisse, Editions Baconniere, 1963, p. viii. (Translation mine.)

Clearly it is one thing for historians to say they do not know that such principles can be ascertained; it is quite another to assert that they do not exist.

Historians commonly look backward and tell what they see, leaving forecast to others. Scientists move into that gap with some degree of assurance. They endeavor to ascertain principles and to derive laws as valid for the next year or the next millennium as they were in the past. They are the last to claim that the principles and laws they try to discover and state are immutable. Later studies are sure to modify or discard today's conclusions, but all scientists are committed to the proposition that they exist and will continue to be effective, if not for eternity, at least for incalculable periods of future time. Some even suggest that such prophecy can be carried much farther than has yet been attempted. A symposium of scientists, entitled "Man and His Future," was convened in 1963. To it, René Dubos pointed out the tacit agreement of many participants that by using a proper scientific approach "almost everything one can imagine possible will in fact be done, if it is thought to be desirable," and added, a bit plaintively, "sheer diversity of views concerning what constitutes the good life led one of them to conclude that the only possible social policy for science as well as for human institutions was 'piecemeal social engineering.' " [2] He claimed history as his authority for the proposition that human institutions cannot be allowed merely to drift if they are to survive. Science and scientists, Dubos concluded, must take to heart questions deeply concerning human beings, giving greater weight to human values as they formulate their technical problems, thereby integrating physical science with the living experience of man.

At present the scientist, peering into tomorrow's millennia, is direct heir of the Egyptian and Mayan priests who observed the sun and the stars. But he is also first cousin to Max Weber, whose pioneer book, *Theory of Social and Economic Organization,* defined sociology as science's attempt to understand social action and thereby "to arrive at a causal explanation of its course and

2. *Daedalus,* Winter, 1965, p. 231.

effects." [3] Weber considers power a dominant factor in social organization, that all conceivable qualities of man and all conceivable combinations of circumstances may put him in a position to impose his will in a given state of affairs. It may be merely for an instant—as when a capable or assertive individual takes command in an emergency, tells people where to go and what to do, and, having met the occasion, subsides. (This experience has happened to virtually everyone.) To be lasting, power involves what Weber calls "imperative control," meaning that the person is in a continuing situation, big or little, making probable that the orders he issues will be obeyed.

Whether we look back with historians or forward with scientists or inward with poets, we find power, located in individuals, as a constant, unvarying factor in every phase of organized society. Invariably there are power holders who somehow attain a position making it probable that their commands will be carried out. The area of that probability may be tiny—the mother giving orders to her children—or large—an Eisenhower commanding the expeditionary forces in World War II—or vast—a dictator like Joseph Stalin giving orders to officials, Communist party functionaries, and police throughout a continental empire. There are all ranges in between. All of us are familiar with a great number of power structures. Many are normal features of daily life: a traffic officer at a crowded corner; an administrative official dealing with an income-tax return; the head of a town zoning board; the division chief in a corporation office; the governor of an American state. It is accurate to say that every person living in an organized community spends his whole life in a series of power structures. In some he holds power; in others he obeys.

An exception (it is a mighty one) is the operation of his tastes and his dreams. No power can wholly dominate the recesses of a man's mind. Attempts have been made to invade this silent area, some with a measure of success. Yet it is difficult to command men to think as a power holder wishes, or to prevent them from receiving from outside charges of information, thought, or emotion. These give rise to inconvenient or (to the power holder) dangerous

3. Glencoe, Ill., The Free Press of Glencoe, 1964, p. 88.

ideas. Most intelligent and certainly all successful power holders
know that the secret operations of a man's mind ultimately will
guide the man's action. So the power holder seeks also to use influence. He enlists (if he can) the service of men who can appeal
to the thoughts of their contemporaries and will persuade them
to agree with the power holder's decrees. If the power holder can
also convince his subjects that he is priest, lawyer, philosopher,
or fount of science (both Stalin and Mao Tse-tung endeavored to
do exactly this), and so add influence to power, so much the better.

This, too, is constant in history and forecast.

4. Power and Apprehension of Reality

A frustrated government servant, exiled at the age of forty-four,
lived penuriously outside Florence from the year 1513. There he
wrote *The Prince*, a detached treatise on the method by which
dictatorial power was got or held. He hoped it would get him a
new job in the Florentine government, then dominated by his
enemy Lorenzo de' Medici. His study has endless fascination. For
one thing, his analysis of power discards any element of morality.
Not, of course, that appreciation of some sort of "goodness" was
absent; Machiavelli urges "good laws" because "there cannot be
good laws where there are not good arms and where there are
good arms, there must be good laws." "Good laws" apparently
were those that prevented the prince from being hated by the mass
of the people. If a political party necessary to the prince's power
was corrupt, it must be humored and satisfied; good works would
be useless. Hatred, Machiavelli noted, is gained as much by good
works as by evil (a comment of interest to contemporary Americans).

The prince's business was to adopt whatever system served
his power. This might suggest some accommodation to the prevailing feelings of his subjects, but they must be strictly accommodations of expediency.

What Machiavelli did have was a powerful sense of the necessity of order. Hence his admiration for Cesare Borgia, illegitimate son of Pope Alexander VI. He, with his father's backing and his own mercenaries, hammered the Romagna into a single system, crushed the Colonna and Orsini factions, took the duchy of Urbino, and "designed to become Lord of Tuscany." Cesare was pretty well along with it when his pope-prince father died, and he, being ill, was unable to dictate the successor. Machiavelli's admiration went further than applauding Cesare's skill in seizing territory. He approved of the fact that Cesare brought order into the territory by eliminating local conflicts and suppressing brigandry and crime (other, of course, than that sanctioned by himself). Power is always preferable to anarchy; tyrannical order is less noxious than chaos. When there is a power vacuum, it will inevitably be filled. In such a condition, any individual capable of doing so is bound to take power; if it lies in the streets, he must pick it up. Cesare Borgia was doing so, and Machiavelli fully approved.

The Machiavellian state contemplated no one in it capable of denying authenticity to the prince's acts. That was not allowed, and not because, as elsewhere, the prince had divine right, or was put there by God, or claimed priestly authority. He was there because he could take and hold. A prophet like Nathan, condemning David for the rape of Bathsheba, would have had short shrift from Cesare Borgia. There was no effective system of law or morals to which such a prophet could appeal; certainly none strong enough to influence Duke Cesare.

But a major consideration has been left out. Without a system of law or morals, there is no way by which institutions can be built or power transmitted. True, the son of a prince had a reasonable stance from which he might seize his father's power; but no institutional organization made this automatic. In contemporary France and Spain, things were somewhat better organized. Monarchy then was a respected tradition, supported (if we accept Jacques Pirenne's analysis) by the age-old body of Roman law and custom carried forward by the Catholic church and undergirded by a substructure of civil service. It is not ac-

cident that Renaissance Italian despots regularly sought to inter-
marry or otherwise ally themselves with the French or Spanish
monarchies, invoking an institutional security their own states
did not provide. Even Napoleon Bonaparte, become emperor of
the French, sought the same result when he divorced his Creole
wife and married Marie Louise, daughter of the institutionally
supported Emperor of Austria, and to get it done made alliance
with the Catholic church.

In justice to Machiavelli, he was not attempting a theory of
power; he was writing a manual of Renaissance politics. Fifty
years after his death, *The Prince* was condemned by Catholics
and Protestants alike precisely because it made no adequate bow
toward any moral system. Two centuries after the essay was written, it began to be taken seriously—as it still is. Disregard of a
moral system in pursuing a political objective is an accepted
dogma of Leninist Communism in half the world and a tacit
practice in most other parts.

There is a danger, I think, of taking Machiavelli more seriously
than he intended. It is insisted, perhaps rightly, that his manual
was adopted as doctrine by nation-states from the eighteenth
century on. I think the theory open to question. What his doctrine
did do was perhaps more causative. It outlined rules of action
for power holders who were not princes but businessmen. Within
their scope of operation, nineteenth-century American and
European tycoons, moguls, and captains of industry followed
them pretty closely. Their successors, the twentieth-century heads
of great corporations and enterprises, even now struggle against
this legacy. They are quite aware that there is a gap in the theory
attributed to Machiavelli—and the precise gap is failure to
integrate their now enormously powerful institutional economic
machines into some moral framework of society.

Enough here to make a single observation: a power organization, be it country or corporation, government or school, cannot
long maintain itself unless it is supported by a more or less choate
and accepted system of ideas and values. Historically, such
systems have usually been carried forward by religion—though
there is no reason why they need not be rationalist, as is Com-

munist dogma. The point is that without such a supporting structure, power is ultimately self-defeating. Either the power holders go mad and are unable to transmit power to a successor or their naked power, unsupported by an idea system, with its lay or religious priests, becomes hideous and breaks up.

It is quite another proposition to say that power is inherently evil, dangerous, or useless. Actually, power is an essential ingredient at every level of human organization. Organization is essential, indeed automatic, whenever human beings live together. The larger the communities, the more organization is needed. In a country like the United States, with 200 millions of population, much of it crowded into urban regions, life itself depends on organization. And organization requires and generates power. Bertrand Russell long ago noted this, and observed, "The larger the organization, the greater the power of the executive." Organization invariably increases some individual's power in direct relation to its size.

Organization of a community may comprise a totalitariat—all fragments of it being subordinated to a single central power holder. Or it may be divided and decentralized into an endless number of groups, each having a degree of autonomy. Political scientists call this "pluralism." The word merely means that many organizations are used and many of the decisions in each organization may be made without securing approval of a central authority.

Power, I hold, is governed by the same laws in any situation, great or small, and wherever found. The principle holds in a pluralist as well as a centralized society. The head of a big manufacturing corporation or of a local bank, within the area of his capacity to make decisions and give orders, is, though less spectacularly, in the same position as a head of government. The scope of his power is tiny compared with that possessed by Cesare Borgia or an American president. But, to the extent he has any, the same rules apply. If his power is not supported by a system of ideas and morals, two results, as for a Borgia despot, are certain for him. He himself deteriorates, loses touch with reality, becomes irrational, and in extreme cases goes to pieces. Also, his power is

31

presently destroyed. Tycoon and dictator are bound in the same death knot. Stalin, having established absolute power, at the end of his life was contemplating a new blood purge and was building (and perhaps believed) a paranoid picture of a plot by Jewish doctors which was to serve as an excuse. Stalin may have been helped, or at least allowed, to die by an entourage fearful for their own lives. Henry Ford's despotic rule over the vast industry he had built was, at the end, not dissimilar. He too indulged illusion of absolute power within the range of an economic empire. His intuitive action became impulsive, arbitrary, and, finally, irrational. What had been genius in earlier years became irresponsible dictatorship. Senior subordinate executives with great responsibilities found themselves dispossessed overnight. On Ford's death, the entire organization had to be rebuilt. Neither in Stalin's case nor in Ford's did the fault lie with power as such. It lay in the lack of any element keeping the power and its holder in reasonable relation to surrounding life and, by consequence, in reasonable relation to what could and could not be done.

The cases of Stalin and Ford can be duplicated endlessly. These were spectacular because the organizations they headed were world-famous. Most readers know from personal experience that the same phenomenon appears less dramatically in heads of families, chiefs of local political organizations, executives—that is, power holders—of any kind. It may not be true that the gods make mad those whom they wish to destroy. Absolute power holders, nevertheless, big or little, do become mad and have been destroyed with wearying frequency.

In consequence, we must consider the relationship of power to a companion idea system which the power holder accepts formally or sincerely. It may take the form of religious doctrine or of philosophy capable of giving lifeblood to the institution by which power is transmitted. Unlike Friedrich Nietzsche, we shall find that power is rarely, if ever, a force by itself. Nietzsche, like the Marquis de Sade, who anticipated some of his doctrines, ended in a madhouse—the only possible result of a religion of power for its own sake. The interplay between power and its institutions and the idea system and its impact—the continuing duel between

Zeus and Metis (Thought) and, after her, Pallas Athena (Intellect)—is constant. It is evident today in American political and organizational life at almost every level.

For the past half-century, since attending the Versailles Peace Conference of 1918–1919, I have had occasion to think a great deal about power and from time to time to observe it at fairly close range. Desire to ask questions of power becomes passionate. This is the justification for the present volume.

1

The Laws of Power

Preface

Power is a universal experience; practically every adult has had a measure of it, great or small, for a brief moment or for an extended time. The rules here given may be tested by applying them to any such experience.

Five natural laws of power are discernible. They are applicable wherever, and at whatever level, power appears, whether it be that of the mother in her nursery or that of the executive head of a business, the mayor of a city, the dictator of an empire.

They are:

One: Power invariably fills any vacuum in human organization. As between chaos and power, the latter always prevails.

Two: Power is invariably personal. There is no such thing as "class power," "elite power," or "group power," though classes, elites, and groups may assist processes of organization by which power is lodged in individuals.

Three: Power is invariably based on a system of ideas or philosophy. Absent such a system or philosophy, the institutions essential to power cease to be reliable, power ceases to be effective, and the power holder is eventually displaced.

Four: Power is exercised through, and depends on, institutions. By their existence, they limit, come to control, and eventually confer or withdraw power.

Five: Power is invariably confronted with, and acts in the presence of, a field of responsibility. The two constantly interact, in hostility or co-operation, in conflict or through some form of dialogue, organized or unorganized, made part of, or perhaps intruding into, the institutions on which power depends.

I

Power Invariably Fills Any Vacuum in Human Organization

1. Order against Chaos

The phenomenon that a power vacuum is always filled by a power holder, or a number of them, is constant throughout the history of society. The reasons are not as obvious as the fact. Two of them are clear enough to note here.

The first is the need for order—at any level of society. Peace is a social necessity. Lacking it, individuals or larger elements in a situation fly apart, seeking to find place in some order of things where they can live, work, or enjoy themselves without being despoiled or interrupted. Professor George Catlin, of the University of Chicago, stated the proposition concisely in *The Story of the Political Philosophers:* "To maintain peace has been the justifying function of coercive government, despite all its tyrannies, since the days of the Pharaohs." [1] The human need of peace leads to acceptance of such government—at any level from school to empire.

The second operative cause proceeds from the emotional make-up of men. Instinct for power exists to some degree in everyone. As of all human instincts, it is stronger in some than in others, though never wholly absent. In any situation in which power has failed and is in abeyance, some individual is certain to take it, appropriating as much as he can. Often he will encounter others on the same search; then he must either conquer them or secure their adherence, usually by offering hope of a share of power in the structure he proposes to create. The process may be rational and studied. This occurs when the organizer of a party (or a revolution)—himself a power holder—recruits adherents from among possible rivals by promising them positions in the government he hopes to establish. It may work itself out dramatically or without assigned place in the elementary combinations one finds among children in a schoolyard, among students or members of a university faculty in a campus dispute, or in a political-party clash. We have all seen it happen.

Because power is essentially personal, the underlying social reasons can never be divorced from the factor of personality. Drive for power may be mere instinctive aggression. It may be desire to put into effect some principle of idealism or of order. It may proceed from selfishness and ambition or from altruism or inspiration. Mixture of motives is almost certain. The dominant motive will reflect itself later as the power holder announces, sincerely or falsely, the idea system or philosophy by which his power is justified and accepts—or creates—the institutions by which power is exercised. This we will turn to later. Primarily, the naked and entirely natural fact of the power instinct must be bracketed with the desire to overcome, and be protected against, anarchy.

When a vacuum occurs at any level of a power structure, the

1. New York, Tudor Publishing Company, 1947, p. 760.

immediate result is to throw power downward to the next lower institutional echelon. When imperial power is destroyed by conquest or revolution, its component parts go on functioning. In their spheres, regional chiefs exercise the power of the previous chief or overlord. In commercial organization, the same is true. In a business empire dominated by its organizer through a holding corporation whose head was suddenly struck down by illness, leaving no successor and a divided board of directors, power over its subsidiary corporations was at once assumed and exercised by their operating executives almost without a break. In the smallest unit —that of the family—elimination of the family head leads at once to assumption of his functions by the strongest remaining member of the family group.

At the Paris Peace Conference in 1919, we watched the phenomenon of the Communist revolution in Russia. Lenin's coup had destroyed the central government, as its armies had been battered to pieces by Imperial Germany. The provincial governments of Czarist Russia had never been strong; many of them went to pieces. Whereupon great parts of more or less choate Russian units organized themselves as "governments." At one time some forty or fifty existed within the confines of the old empire. One of them was remarkable. I recall receiving a communication from the "Russian Soviet Railway Republic." It had taken over and represented a substantial part of the Trans-Siberian Railroad, running roughly from the Volga River to Vladivostok. Its operating officers and workers considered that they had as good a right to power and political standing as anyone else; no one else was giving orders, and, for the moment, they had organization and reality. Accordingly, they proclaimed the "Railway Republic." They established their capital at one of the principal railroad stations along the line. To the operating head whose orders they were, more or less, prepared to accept, they gave the title "president." They constituted a cabinet of Ministers to whom were assigned the various administrative tasks previously discharged by the railway executives and officials. Thus this fragment of the Czarist organization that formerly ran the railroad erected itself into a politically autonomous unit. Of course it did not last. The Soviet government in Moscow rapidly filled the power vacuum throughout most of the old empire and re-established the central authority. But during the lacuna power was in abeyance outside Moscow, and devolved on local organizations.

At Paris in 1919 as a member of the staff of the American Commission to Negotiate Peace when World War I ended, I was occupied with information coming from the Balkan and mid-European countries. Part of the area had been subject to the dying Turkish Empire, in whose outer territories was a high degree of sporadic disorder. In the nineteenth century, much of it became autonomous or independent, and the Balkan region became a diplomatic cocking main for the Great Powers. Czarist Russia and Italy intrigued against Hapsburg Austria; Balkan chiefs of state intrigued against each other. The growing power vacuum in this part of Europe led to attempts and counterattempts by neighboring kingdoms to expand and protect their territories. This situation culminated in the Balkan wars of 1912 and 1913, the assassination at Sarajevo of Archduke Franz Ferdinand of Austria in 1914, and the outbreak of World War I. At the time of the Versailles Peace Conference, the Austrian Empire had fallen and its troops had been expelled from this region. The Soviet Union, laboring in the throes of Lenin's revolution, was temporarily out of the picture. Neither France nor Great Britain was prepared to annex the area; Italy's ambitions to take over some of it were partly frustrated by Woodrow Wilson's insistence on self-determination of peoples. The Versailles Conference formally recognized and enlarged the Kingdom of the Serbs, Croats, and Slovenes that had been proclaimed in December, 1918. The effect was to add to already independent Serbia the bordering Croatian and Slovenian provinces formerly part of defeated Austria. In form, this was a direction to the conflicting elements in Yugoslavia to establish their own central power. In fact, it was an invitation to numberless conflicting local elements to fight it out among themselves.

Milovan Djilas, a Yugoslav Communist who presently became second-in-command to Communist dictator Marshal Tito (Josip

Broz) and later was imprisoned by him, was eight years old at the time of the Versailles Conference. His autobiography, *Land Without Justice*, gives a devastating picture of youth in a small Serbian town. The tale is of meaningless cruelty and violence, internecine strife, killing without reason or rational result. Croat fought Serb; Turks and Armenians fought both. Catholics fought Orthodox Christians; Mohammedans struggled with all of them. Clan fought clan. Village fought village. Murder was the reciprocal of torture. Fear was unending. Djilas tells us what it looked like: "Everything is at war with everything else: men against men, men against beasts, beasts against beasts. And children against children, always. And parents with children. The guerrillas fight the Austrians, and the latter persecute and oppress the people. The spirits strive with humans, and humans with the spirits. . . . Certainly strife is one side of life. But there comes a time when only strife is the order of the day, as though there were nothing else in life." [2]

Whatever progress may have been made toward filling this power vacuum after World War I—and there was some—was demolished by World War II. Nazi intrigue before the war broke out, invasion by Italian armies in 1939 and Nazi forces after June, 1941, followed by guerrilla warfare as they retreated, shattered any fabric of order. It is not difficult to understand why, when World War II came to an end, one of the contending partisan leaders—Marshal Tito (a Croat) or Colonel Draja Mikhailovich (a Serb)—was bound to attempt domination of the country. With British support, Tito succeeded. He captured and promptly executed Mikhailovich, and established a Communist dictatorship which he maintains at this date. Had something of the kind not occurred, local captains undoubtedly would have set up local tyrannies, valley by valley, area by area, fighting each other until some chieftain obtained power enough to bring about a tolerable stability.

In April, 1965, an illegitimate government, established by a group of army officers, governed the Dominican Republic through a civilian junta headed by Donald Reid Cabral. A dissident group

2. New York, Harcourt, Brace & World, 1958, pp. 71–72.

of army officers revolted on April 24, nominally to re-establish the government of the former duly elected but deposed president, Juan Bosch. Their revolt immediately liberated a force move organized by three Communist groups—Communists claiming support from Fidel Castro in Cuba, Communists claiming to follow Moscow, and Communists claiming to follow the Peking line. Within forty-eight hours Santo Domingo City became a murderous cockpit. The Reid Cabral government disappeared. None of the contending factions was immediately able to reduce the other; anarchic civil war broke out. Indications suggested that the Moscow-Castro Communists had entered the fray; the situation indeed was made to order for such a move. Given the nearby presence of the Russian-oriented Communist government of Cuba, with a contingent of Soviet soldiers, Russian weapons, and 250,000 Cubans under arms, and Fidel Castro's stated intention and capacity to move, there was little chance the power vacuum within the Dominican Republic would long remain unfilled. President Lyndon B. Johnson thereupon ordered a powerful American force into the country, filling the power vacuum with a provisional government of his own choosing.

On the night of November 9, 1965, New York City was blacked out by failure of electric power. This occurred at 5:27 P.M.; traffic was at its peak. This traffic is directed at street intersections in large part by red and green lights. On their failure, such crossings became minor vortices of chaos. Almost at once, individuals appeared whose chief qualification to act consisted in their assertiveness and possession of a flashlight. Where Nineteenth Street (westbound, one-way) crosses Third Avenue (north and south) one such volunteer—he may have been twenty years old—moved to the middle of Third Avenue and took charge. He had no authority. Everyone nevertheless obeyed him as faithfully as if he had been a uniformed policeman. For the moment, he took and held power—and used it to combat chaos. He obviously enjoyed it and was successful. Similar incidents occurred all over the sprawling city.

The incident bears analysis. Self-appointed, the power was

momentarily illegitimate. It was recognized, and thus became legitimate on the instant. This was an alternative to chaos, and the only alternative there was. Nothing else showing, the boy's power was accepted. Equally, he was exercising the power within accepted standards—he was facilitating movement of traffic in a manner approximating the custom of the city under normal conditions. He was meeting the obligations of the situation and following institutional lines. Simultaneously, the drivers—who knew the situation as well as anyone else—followed his instructions. They were accustomed to a philosophy of traffic direction, the boy was carrying it out, the necessity was obvious. Microcosmic though it was, all power elements were instantaneously combined, and the power became real.

Compulsion to fill a power vacuum occurs at any level of social organization. The phenomenon is not limited to international affairs, as in the case of the Dominican Republic in 1965, or to breakdown of organization, as in Yugoslavia in the closing days of World War II and in New York City when the lights went out. It occurs in any form of organization.

A group of affiliated corporations constituted what is sometimes called a "business empire." It consisted of a group of insurance companies built by a genius emerging from the co-operative movement in the United States. It included a life-insurance company having outstanding stock owned by a co-operative fire-insurance company—which had no stock outstanding and for practical purposes was controlled by its directors. The organizing genius was president of both. The directors of both companies, in all ultimate matters, followed his decisions. His ascendancy was moral rather than institutional; they trusted him. He caused a holding company to be organized. The fire-insurance company exchanged its stock in the life-insurance company for stock in the holding company having power to elect one-half its directors. The holding company then sold to the public a class of stock having the right to elect the other half of its board. With the capital raised by this sale, the holding company bought control of several other large insurance companies. The combined empire had total assets of perhaps half a billion dollars. The genius became president of the holding company, which now could elect the directors of the subsidiary companies. But control of the holding company was divided equally—between directors representing the stock held by a mutual company and directors representing the class of stock held by tens of thousands of scattered public shareholders. The organizing personality was suddenly incapacitated by a stroke. Like many power holders, he had contemplated the fact that he was growing old, was not immortal, and that power must pass to other hands. But, like most power holders, he had recoiled from the task of choosing a successor, and there was no crown prince. No one had been developed, equipped, or was able to step into his place.

His incapacity created a power vacuum in a vast congeries of operations. The bottom of the pyramid felt the shock last; the controlled, or subsidiary, insurance companies had their own directors and managements. Their functioning was not interrupted, though they ran the hazard of being displaced, depending on where power came to rest in the holding corporation. But at the top, the holding corporation was in peril. Half its directors represented the mutual company; the other half, the public stockholders. Because the vote was equally divided, neither could elect. Momentarily, there was no presiding genius.

A vice-president of the most powerful subsidiary decided this was his opportunity. He canvassed the directors of both the mutual company and the largest subsidiary life-insurance company. The mutual company had no stockholders, was completely independent, and owned half the holding company's stock. It elected him its president. He was able to induce the directors of the subsidiary life-insurance company to elect him its president likewise. In combination, this gave him power to choose half the directors in the holding company—who were all higher officers of the mutual and the subsidiary life-insurance corporations. Their careers could now be vitally affected by his decisions as president of these two companies, even though one of them was subsidiary to the holding company. Aspiring to power, he immediately discharged all the senior officers in the life-insurance company who might conceivably either rival him in that company or aspire to headship of the holding company. Like Mohammedan princes of old (and sudden acquirers of power generally), he summarily disposed of all dangerous competitors within that part of the empire he now administered. The action appears to have been instinctive, but it was predictable. The stake—almost complete power over a commercial empire with assets of half a billion dollars—called out the same elementary reactions one expects to find in politics, or indeed in most forms of organization.

He at once sought election as chief executive of the holding company. This would give him full control of the empire. By this time, however, the opposition of the directors representing the public stockholders—half the voting power in the board of the holding company—had crystallized. They had no particular interest in being executives of the empire. They did have responsibility to many thousands of stockholders whose investment, running into millions of dollars, they were expected to represent. One of them called together the public directors, secured agreement that they would vote as a unit, and then pointed out to the aspirant that the holding company would be deadlocked unless agreement was reached. He felt that the directors representing the public investment could hardly accept dictatorship over the empire by an obscure president of one of its subsidiaries. He laid out the lines of an understanding. It included electing to the boards of the subsidiary companies representatives of both classes of directors of the holding company and seeking the services of a neutral outsider.

The public directors had been entrusted with power to protect a group of investors; they received and expected to receive only nominal salaries; but they had been given power to discharge a responsibility and intended to do so. The resulting meeting of the two sides became essentially an affair of diplomacy. Neither group had the weapons, legal, financial, or moral, to dominate the other. Both were acutely aware that the business operations of the commercial empire must continue and not be jeopardized. In confrontation, a solution for the immediate future was reached by consent, and a third party, representing both groups, became head of the holding company.

These illustrations, diverse in character, make the point. In each a power holder ceased to exist, leaving a vacuum. In the Dominican Republic, this occurred through an army rebellion. Vacuum in the republic created chaos likely to be filled by outside power. It was in fact filled momentarily by the paramount power of the United States as President Johnson acted, fearing lest a Russian-Cuban combination would fill it instead.

In the Yugoslav case, the central power had decayed and had then been destroyed by war, so that not only the central government but also the remaining fragments of local organization had been torn apart. This is the picture Djilas gives of Montenegro after the end of World War I. It was repeated when the Serbian group supporting the Yugoslav monarchy was ground to nothing, first by the German-Italian invasion and its defeat, and later by the guerrilla struggle between Tito and Mikhailovich. The vacuum was filled by the dictatorship of Tito, backed at the time by the diplomatic support of Britain and later by the forces of the victorious Soviet Union.

In the case of the commercial empire, vacuum was brought about by the disability of its chief and the absence of settled succession. Had the situation been allowed to continue, anarchy would have resulted. The void was filled by agreement between two rapidly organized forces, one an ambitious man dominating a fraction of the organization and seeking to take over, the other a group of directors finding a natural leader and negotiating a working arrangement.

Every reader has encountered analogous, though perhaps less dramatic, situations in his own experience. When normal processes of distribution of power break down, someone steps in, gives directions, and takes charge until the police or other established authority arrives to take over. The individual may do so because he is that kind of person—has, in common phrase, an "instinct for power"—or he rises to the situation because he feels an obligation to the people suffering from danger and confusion around him. Momentary anarchy induces assumption of power, whether in high politics or local circumstances. In my experience this invariably occurs.

And it is so predictable, indeed, that production of chaos is a standard method used by designing politicians as an avenue toward their assumption of power. The Leninist revolutionary handbook outlines the usefulness of doing this as a precondition to Communist revolutions, though revolutionary Communism has no monopoly on the method. It is used by the Students for a Democratic Society (SDS) in their attacks on American universities. In Brazil in 1936, President Getúlio Vargas connived at disorderly risings by groups espousing the fascist faith, and possibly also by Communist groups. When these had achieved a certain momentum, fear of anarchy rose. He then dissolved the Congress, proclaimed himself and was accepted as sole leader, occupied the entire power fabric, and held dictatorial position until 1945.

In 1961, his pupil, João Goulart, became president of Brazil through the fluke resignation of the duly elected president, Jânio Quadros. He then encouraged mutinies in the army and navy. His people endeavored to stimulate risings in the slums around Rio de Janeiro and other cities. He was prepared to declare himself dictator, and was prevented from doing so only by an immense popular rising backed, in its final stage, by the bulk of the Brazilian army.

Unhappily, chaos is never too far away. As Hesiod observed, Zeus could imprison its forces, not extirpate them. The more highly organized the community or civilization, the easier it is for some small part of the machinery to disrupt the fabric. The strike of a comparatively few policemen in Boston, Massachusetts, in 1919 left that ordinarily law-abiding town at the mercy of hoodlums and looters for a night, and damage was grave. A metropolitan center could be reduced to disorder by the acts of a few men. On the advice of his old friend Senator from Massachusetts Winthrop M. Crane, Governor Calvin Coolidge called out the militia and restored order. (The reputation he then gained led to Coolidge's nomination and election as vice-president of the United States and his automatic succession to the presidency on the death of Warren G. Harding.)

One need not have strong imagination to forecast the result if a nuclear bomb were to explode near any city. The most habitually orderly and law-abiding population has within it some elements whose conduct is kept within bounds only by external restraint—that is, by the presence of power. They emerge when power no longer is there. They subside only when it returns— unless they or one fragment of them sets up a tiny power system and takes over. If not immediately filled by the power institutions and institutions of the community, some boss gangster, usurper, or vigilante committee will occupy the field.

It is the genius of power to find and fill the vacuum whenever it occurs in human organization.

2. The Birth of Power

Power is brought into existence by the coalescence of three elements: men, a philosophy, and a group capable of organization into institutions (however rudimentary).

Birth may occur with implosive speed. The genesis of the Christian church, according to the account given in the first two chapters of the Acts of the Apostles, is the classic illustration: a tiny group of disciples in an upper room, remembrance of the teachings of the dead Christ, a brief speech by Peter, a preorganization meeting to choose a successor to Judas, a pentecostal irruption of spirit, and the prompt and lasting welding of an organization with Peter at its head.

Most of us have seen small organizations come into being less sublimely, whether insignificant, as in the founding of a club, or important, as in the launching of a political movement. Review of any such experience will show the three elements always present. A few men, including some with an instinct for power (usually dominated by one), meet in agreement on a common idea. Purpose becomes evident to attempt its realization. At the behest of the man with the strongest instinct for power, the group organizes. The process frequently occurs on battlefields after a military formation has been shattered and the strongest remaining individual remakes an organization out of the survivors. An excellent example was the birth of the power structure that in time became the government of the Soviet Union.

In *The Seven Pillars of Wisdom*, Lawrence of Arabia (who later preferred the name T. E. Shaw) recounts the formation of the government of Syria near the close of World War I. He had been sent to organize Arab underground rebellion against Turkey, then ruling the region. Working with a Hashimite prince, Feisal al Husein, he had brought together a substantial force of desert-dwelling Arabian irregulars, who harassed the Turkish armies and lines of communication while General E. H. H. Allenby, heading a British expedition, invaded Palestine and moved into Syria. Lawrence had honestly pledged to his Arab friends that they would have self-determination. They, and he, interpreted this to mean independence in case of victory. As the Turkish armies crumpled, Lawrence became suspicious, believing the British and French empires would take over the territory themselves. (Though he did not know it, his suspicions were justified. The British and French had partitioned the territory into "spheres of influence"; Syria had been allotted to the French.) Consequently, as the British armies approached Damascus, Lawrence detached part of his irregular force and with it rode toward Damascus ahead of the British troops. His plan was to expel the Turks and organize an Arab government before the British could move in and set up their own administration. He was able to enter Damascus three days before the British forces arrived. As the Damascenes rejoiced in their liberation from Turkey, he caused Emir Feisal to be proclaimed king. He organized a cabinet, appointing ministers to take care of public utilities, police, foreign affairs, and the elementary functions of government. He set up a rudimentary council. In result, a more or less organized government commanding local acceptance greeted the incoming British

troops, assigned them quarters, and dealt with the them as welcome guest-allies, not as conquering governors. British orders
apparently did not cover this contingency, and in any case it
would have been dangerous business to displace a native Arab
government while relying on Arab forces.

Lawrence's move coalesced an amorphous situation into a
power structure able to withstand anything except superior military force, and the resulting government survived. The group
composed of Damascenes, local leaders, and Arab chieftains of
the irregular forces could immediately be brought into elementary organization, generating the reality of power—sufficiently
so, in fact, to maintain an independent government of Syria for
many months. It was, of course, doomed in the long run. Following the lines of their agreement, the British acquiesced in the
landing of a French army, and the Clemenceau government had
little interest in the independence of Syria. Presently, the famous
Light Camel Division was sent to capture Damascus, as it did, ex-
pelling Feisal. Yet, while it lasted, the power structure brought
into existence by Lawrence maintained itself against all rivals and
went under only when defeated by the arms of a strong European
military state.

Lawrence went to Paris in the spring of 1919 to urge the
Arab claim of independence—and Feisal's claim to a kingdom—
before the Paris Peace Conference. He explained briefly what had
happened. His account in *The Seven Pillars of Wisdom* corre-
sponds to what he then said. The philosophy of his action was
Arab nationalism. It had high acceptance in Damascus. The instinct to take power was Feisal's, supplemented by Lawrence and
his officers. The combination immediately fused into a local government.

This is an instance of power at inception—where an organization first comes into being. The process is not materially different
when an election causes a change of president and party in the
United States and a new government must be put together. Here
the institutions are already organized and in being, and a phi-

losophy or idea system has been pounded out in the course of an election campaign. The individual leader has been selected by the democratic institutions of the country. The incoming president, nevertheless, must bring together and organize a top group which thereafter will give orders to the organized departments and presumably also give leadership to the Congress. In brief, he must take power. This the president-elect must at once set about doing. He has a little (but not much) time—the business is not quite instantaneous. Before he takes office, hordes of ambitious, power-hungry or place-seeking men strive to present their claims for office and preferment. Rapidly he selects a group of a few dozen at most, arranges them as he plans to organize, presently announces their appointment to Cabinet or other posts of institutional headship. They become an interim organization even before the president-elect is inaugurated, swears them in, and holds his first Cabinet meeting.

I have never been present at the accession of a king, but probably the process is much the same. Certainly the history of the accession of James I to the crown of England following the death of Queen Elizabeth displays similarity. James Stuart's mother, Mary Queen of Scots, heir to Elizabeth's throne, had been beheaded by Elizabeth's government. Her son's arrival in power can scarcely have been regarded without apprehension by Elizabeth's former adherents. Her most trusted adviser, Robert Cecil, had thrown his weight to recognition of James, following the institutional lines of the English monarchy, and had mobilized much of the Elizabethan organization to accept him. James naturally brought with him intimates of his own. Fusion of the elements into an effective power organization for the government of England followed swiftly. Like instance occurred on the occasion of the so-called "Glorious Revolution" of 1688, when a disgusted court and country threw out King James II and invited William of Orange and his consort, Mary, to take the throne. Sir John Churchill (later Duke of Marlborough) had been an honest servant of King James, but now played a part like that of Cecil at Elizabeth's death. He had a harder task because the institutional line of succession had been ruptured. William was a Hollander, tenuously claiming right through his wife. Churchill assured himself that William would accept the now settled Protestant and nationalist philosophy of England. On that basis he brought about control by William and Mary of the institutions of the country, enabling William to become not only titular king, but also actual holder of the royal power.

Implosive process of organization appeared in the United States in February and March of 1933. President Herbert Hoover had been defeated in the election of November, 1932; Franklin Roosevelt was president-elect. Problems normally involved when administrations change would have been present in any case. They were vastly expanded by the completeness of the economic crash that in March, 1933, brought the currency, credit, and commercial functions of the United States to a catastrophic halt. The government about to be formed had not merely to take over existing traditional institutions, but also to extend them and improvise new ones in vast fields of economic organization traditionally considered no function of the federal government. President Roosevelt achieved added organization and power structure before the Congress of the "hundred days" recessed. The substance of that structure remains intact to this day.

Swiftly or gradually, a power structure comes into existence as men with an idea system set up new or take over existing institutions. Normally, power is allocated through operation of the existing institutions—a president is elected, cabinet ministers appointed, key posts in Congress or Parliament are filled. Institutional processes place individuals "in power." This does not mean they really have it, but, rather, that they have a license to take it. They must establish their personal grip and control over the institutions they head. Any newly chosen executive of a corporation, chief of a government agency, even classroom teacher, realizes this fact at once. Until he organizes his personal position, he is impotent. Connecting the power position with the idea structure and with his subordinate officers and perhaps with outside allies is his first task. When the combination is made, a power structure exists and he is able to use it.

3. The "Power Form"

Coalescence of three elements—assertive men, an idea system, and a group capable of organization—generates power, be the measure small or great. It thereupon attains reality and assumes form. It has an impact on its environment. To borrow a philosopher's word, it achieves *Gestalt*. (Had the word "image" not been overused, abused, and misused, it might be applied.)

The *Gestalt* of power establishes itself in many ways, tangible and intangible. Preponderantly, it must exist in the minds of men affected by it at the time. Any subject of the Roman Empire in its great days knew that Roman power existed; he sensed what it was, though he might have little knowledge of its boundaries, its institutions, or the men at its head. It was a "thing." It had a center in Rome, or perhaps at the habitual place of administration chosen by the emperor. Some notion existed of the Pax Romana, an overriding force that limited or extinguished the independent use of local force. Sense also existed of its institutions. Probably foremost among these were the Roman armies, but there were also governors, judges, quaestors, and, pervasively, taxgatherers. Physically it was demonstrated by construction of cities, fortified towns, roads, temples, arenas, and, later, baths. These tended to be similar throughout the empire. A man passing from Lutetia (now Paris) in Gaul to Numidia in Africa would find buildings with which he was familiar. Roman power impact would be heavy or light depending on the level of organization and complexity of the local country and the tenacity of its own power structure. The Romans made relatively little impress on highly organized Egypt (albeit some) and powerful impress on weakly organized Gaul. I think the choate power form was as readily apprehended by realization of its control as by observation of its physical construction. Men must have known it even when, through ignorance, they might not have been able to name the ruling Caesar or understand whether a local temple was dedicated to Mercury or to Apollo.

Americans today visiting countries ruled by totalitarian regimes feel the form of their power organization at once—as do travelers from these countries to the United States. An American on entry reports to the immigration police, is allowed to enter and perhaps move about freely; but he never loses consciousness of the fact that his major movements are watched and known to the local authorities. They can lay their hands on him at any time. Visitors from Communist countries arriving in the United States present their papers and are allowed entry. Invariably their next question is when and where they should report to the local police. Presumably they discover that they do not have to do so; do not even present a passport when registering at a hotel. Gradually it dawns on them that American authorities have little interest in what they do. Their emotions are mixed; they are in a strange country, obviously a great power, but whose power form is wholly different from the power form they left behind.

Noticeable also is the fact that American and European cities are differently put together. Paris and Moscow evidence at once that their development is severely planned. New York and Chicago, aside from their street gridirons, appear to have been developed as illogical collections of individual expression. This or that great bank or corporation chose to build a skyscraper here; others followed suit. But the meanest of streets lie hard by. Occasionally a group of builders representing a single plan and will create islands of related architecture (for example, Rockefeller Center or Lincoln Center in New York) in otherwise unplanned messes of bricks and mortar. Yet, for some reason, the American city holds together. Oddly, it provides as well (or as badly) for most of its population, as do the closely controlled towns in Eastern Europe—neither having achieved a first-rate result. American cities depend on an enormous degree of consensus upon a common core of ideas, and the American power structure reflects that reality. Communist power structures and their resulting cities depend on a central order-giving institution whose fiats are accepted by and in any case enforced upon the population. Difference in form results from the difference in concept and the consequent difference in the power structure itself.

The form of the power structure probably also in some measure guides contemporary culture—literature, art, communication. This may be a systematic power object—as, in Rome, Augustus Caesar, through his genial informal agent Maecenas, subsidized poets (notably Horace and Vergil) and struggled to achieve for Rome some of the glory earlier attained by ancient and now Roman-conquered Greece. Even permissiveness may be relied on, with highly varied results. Norman Mailer, with his *The Naked and the Dead* and *The American Dream,* Robert Frost, with his New England poetry, Thornton Wilder, with his plays and novels, serve as illustrations in contemporary United States. At a lesser altitude, power form goes far to determine the content of schools, notably in the elementary grades. Anyone who has visited a grammar school in America and its counterpart in Poland or Russia is struck, first, with their similarity; second, with their difference. Both are compulsory—that is, expressions of power; both are supported by the state; from both, the state exacts minimal standards. Yet there is essential difference, not only in content, but also in attitude. An American child is thought to have been offered an opportunity and is expected to make what he can out of himself. A Soviet, Polish, or Hungarian child, though he is treated with exemplary kindness and consideration, is expected to emerge as a useful servant of the state to the extent of his capacity and fitness as determined by the educational authorities.

More familiar illustrations lie readily at hand, capable of being checked by any reader. The *Gestalt* of a Roman Catholic congregation visibly differs from that of a Methodist or Presbyterian. Contrast appears in architecture, in customs of meeting and worship, in the relationship of the members to each other and, most obviously, in their relation to the priest or pastor. All parish churches are, of course, tiny power institutions. They produce in small measure the phenomenon observable in power structures as great as France or Germany, the United States or the Soviet Union.

I suspect—I am not able to prove—that another element enters the scene whenever the three elements of power—men, an idea system, and an organization—have coalesced and created a power organism. That element may be called, vaguely, "culture"—the body of habits, of unconscious assumptions of thought and manner of expression, that power holders and the community affected by them alike have accumulated from environment or heredity. Subjects of power familiarly respond more readily to power holders of their own background. This is why a Hitler sought local Quislings for client rulers when he conquered neighboring countries; why the Roman Empire often governed through client kings. Results of power always have to be expressed through its subjects; their habits of thought invariably enter the *Gestalt*. Later we must examine the power dialogue with the people affected by it. Through it, contemporary culture enters the structure and, modified and modifying, determines power's ultimate form and product.

II

Power Is Invariably Personal

1. The Power Instinct

"Of the infinite desires of man, the chief are the desires for power and glory," wrote Bertrand Russell, in *Power: A New Social Analysis*, thirty years ago.[1] He considered that the fundamental concept in social science is power—in the same sense that energy is the fundamental concept in physics. Further, he believed that power was the same whatever tools it used or forms it took. It might express itself through wealth, armament, civil authority, influence on opinion, military command, or top position in an economic pyramid. Like energy, it continually passes from one form to

1. New York, W. W. Norton, 1938, p. 11.

another; it is useless to isolate it. Power has recently been defined as "the capacity or ability of an individual or a group of individuals to determine the behavior of other individuals or groups in accordance with his own wishes." Endless methods attempt to accomplish this—naked force, use of faiths, loyalties, and interest, and the probability that a great many people will usually act as anyone having the power position wishes. In larger aspect, power is the capacity to mobilize the resources of a group or a society to attain statist goals.[2]

Power is an attribute of man. It does not exist without a holder. Impulse to have it is included in the kit of instincts, emotions, and qualities of every normal person; and every normal person has had and exercised a measure of power. The span may be as tiny as that exercised by a mother over her children or as great as that wielded by a despotic emperor, or any measure in between. A dominant child in a playground, student in school, a subordinate in an office, businessmen, soldiers, tycoons, politicians, and prime ministers have made use of power in small or great situations. Power is not merely a universal instinct. It is also a universal experience. The reader will immediately think of illustrations in his own life.

It follows that abstract definition of power—as though it existed independently of a man—cannot take us far. Power in the abstract does not exist. As abstraction, it is a potential—not a social—fact. It becomes fact only when a man or woman following his inborn instinct takes and uses it. This is why power is invariably individual.

Part at least of its usefulness, its glory, its terror comes from that fact. In the hands or mind of an individual, the impulse toward power is not inherently limited. Limits are imposed by extraneous fact and usually also by conscience or intellectual restraint. Capacity to make others do as you wish knows only these two limitations. Either you cannot or you consciously decide that you will not. The teacher's order will not carry far beyond her schoolroom and she knows it. Circumstances have settled that. Or

2. Dow Votaw, *The Six-Legged Dog: Mattei and ENI: A Study in Power,* Berkeley, Calif., University of California Press, 1964.

perhaps she can cause her pupils to do something she desires but is constrained for some reason by her own choice not to do so. For example, she may believe it immoral, as undermining the school in which she works, or that morally she should respect the autonomy of her fellow teachers in their classrooms. A Latin-American dictator can perhaps give orders within the confines of his territory; but his area of power is externally limited by geographical boundaries. He may have power to order his guard to kill an enemy—as the late Generalissimo Rafael Trujillo was in the habit of doing in the Dominican Republic. Or (unlike Trujillo) he may be governed by a system of morals and ethics in which murder is not allowed. This is an internal limitation.

Limitations are always present—else the world would be worse off than it is, and its condition in all conscience is troublesome enough. Where a power holder has no internal restraints—that is, no intellectual or moral system stopping him—his power is limited only by the circumstances in which he is placed.

One may see this any day on any city street. A few juveniles have formally or informally collected into a gang. Invariably there is a leader. There are some things they cannot do because a policeman is there. This is the extraneous limitation. Within that limitation, what they will do is determined by limitations in their own heads. An anarchic juvenile will stop nowhere except when he meets the police; plate-glass windows have been smashed on the streets of New York, old men have been beaten to death in Brooklyn parks, youngsters have been stabbed or assaulted "just for kicks." These are assertions of power, unlimited by internal restraints and encountering no adequately opposing circumstances.

Normal individuals have a high content of internal restraint based on the system of ideas and morals in which they were brought up or to which they agree. Power holders know this; hence their concern with systems of ideas and of morals. To extend power beyond the sweep of their fist, they must foster a situation in which the people within scope of their power act predictably, will follow instructions, will maintain a degree of order. If need be, of course, order can in limited measure be produced by force. The mother knows that, in case of ultimates, she can spank her smaller children. She can do this only occasionally; domestic order must hold together most of the time without that resort. Because of this as well as because of moral conviction, she tries to instill principles of obedience, consideration, regard for orderly life. So, in different application, does every power holder in great or small affairs.

The power instinct appears connected with a group instinct for a degree of workable order. Both may have animal sources. Scientists have been studying this, though their conclusions are far from definitive. Konrad Lorenz, in *On Aggression,* suggests the existence of the power instinct and says that corresponding flock, pack, and group organization and order is widespread in animal life. Robert Ardrey popularizes some scientific conclusions in two books: *African Genesis* and *The Territorial Imperative.* My own view is that the power instinct in men carries forward inherited attributes that must have appeared long before the evolution of man in his present form. The point is not ready for decision. For us, the relevant fact is that every human individual possesses some fragment of the instinct, and every group appears to have a sense that it must develop some framework of corresponding organization.

2. Power as a Personal Attribute

Power is invariably personal. However attained, it can be exercised only by the decision and act of an individual.

This is not current dogma, still less the prevailing propaganda stereotype. Attribution of power is often made to an institution—the power of a nation-state, of a corporation, of a church, of a bank, of a professional association, of a newspaper, of a political party. Or power is attributed to an unorganized group—to a "class" of some kind, upper or lower, to the "proletariat," to the "intellectuals," the "press," the "masses," the "people," the "Blacks." Sociologists recently have developed a twilight zone.

They discover "elites," and speculate on their power. The late C. Wright Mills was the most conspicuous among these, and imitators follow in his path. By taking various blocs of statistics, they discover a relatively small group who have higher positions, greater education, or greater wealth. These are then entitled a "class" or an "elite group." To them, power is ascribed.

The facts do not bear out these assumptions—which, indeed, have little behind them but years of uncritical repetition.

No collective category, no class, no group of any kind in and of itself wields power or can use it. Another factor must be present: that of organization. The collective group must put itself together, must develop formal or informal structure, must establish stated or unstated rules by and through which power to decide and act is assigned to someone and, as a rule, distributed through a hierarchy of subordinates.

Without this organization, whatever its common interest or background, no collective group can or ever does act. History and contemporary politics are littered with illustrations of unorganized groups, whose members have had much in common, ignored or ridden over roughshod or sometimes destroyed by individuals having power derived from groups that did have organization. Lacking it, there is no effective exercise of power, quite simply because there is no individual or hierarchy of individuals who can exercise it.

When one speaks of the power of a collective group—a state, a corporation, a political party, a trade union—the phrase is shorthand. It conceals the fact that the group had achieved an organization, had conferred decision-making power upon, or at least its exercise by, certain individuals formally or informally recognized as power holders.

This observation is essential in an era that has swallowed whole the theory of the "ruling class." The theory (to be examined later) has a colorable basis. At every time in history and under all circumstances, certain qualities are especially needed in society. To be a power holder at all requires a certain collection of qualifications. A relatively small group may comprise most of the men who have these qualifications, and from such a group

63

most power holders will emerge. In feudal times, noble birth or military capacity, and sometimes both, were required. Today, for example, a level of intellectual equipment, usually formally bestowed by a university or occasionally achieved informally by self-trained men, is an almost essential attribute of becoming a power holder of senior rank in most categories of organization. From the group of men possessing the needed qualifications, therefore, power holders are usually drawn, or made, or make themselves. But it would be silly to say that holders of university degrees constitute a "ruling class." It may have been true in the nineteenth century when Karl Marx wrote *Das Kapital* that wealth was an essential qualification for power holding. But it is one thing to say that and quite another to suggest that a group or class having certain attributes exercised power. More often than not, though their members have parallel or similar attitudes or interests, they are fiercely competitive, fight among each other, are unable to organize and unwilling to designate power holders.

Rulers may predominately be drawn from classes. Classes do not rule. Power holders may be drawn from elites. Elites do not exercise power.

Elites and classes may have influence. This is an entirely different affair. The sentiments or opinions of a particular category of people may and often do affect the decisions and actions of the men who have power. Their conceptions, their value judgments, their desires, their emotions about the world in which they would like to live may be and often are extremely persuasive. But they can be blocked by a simple decision of the power holder not to act along these lines—to do nothing, or to do something different. The group, whatever it is, if seriously offended, may be stimulated to organize and oppose—to become a power structure. Consequently, views that may represent its body of sentiment are taken into account. But this is far removed from power to decide and cause others to concur.

3. The Effects of Power on Personality

The personal quality of power introduces an element baffling scientific analysis. The power process itself follows definite laws. But since power is made effective through individuals, the personality of the power holder is always a factor—and the content of personality is a vast unknown. What happens to the power holder, how he uses power, what he does with the control he can exercise or the events he can cause to happen may be surmised by theorists, or apprehended by artists and poets, but thus far it eludes scientists. Few men know themselves well; still fewer express what little they do know—power holders perhaps least of all.

For one thing, power holding is itself an emotional experience. The greater the power, the greater the impact. It may indeed be a shattering experience, especially when suddenly acquired. I have observed the fate of a good many men elevated from obscurity to positions of power in government and in business. Some men go to pieces under the experience. One of the first impacts is realization that the obligation of power takes precedence over other obligations formerly held nearest and dearest. A man in power can have no friends in the sense that he must refuse to the friend consideration that, power aside, he would once have accorded. He may be under all manner of debts of gratitude to an associate, but may be compelled to refuse that man's son appointment to a job. He may know that his children need the best of time and attention, but yet must neglect the desires and duties of fatherhood. If the power is great and demanding, it can strip him, layer by layer, of the fabric of his life. He may break under its pressures. Or he may sustain the obligations of power while he has it, and on leaving it come to disastrous end by suicide or nervous breakdown, as did the great American public servants James Forrestal and John G. Winant. Or he may grow in tolerance and capacity, blossoming under the experience.

The effect of power on its holder is unpredictable. Woodrow Wilson once observed that when he appointed a man to office, he never knew whether he would grow or swell—this was the mildest of comment. Fiorello La Guardia said savagely that when he appointed a man to a judgeship, he never could tell whether his head would develop or his buttocks. Men who have ascended to power gradually, or have been vaccinated by previous experience, are in a safer position than those suddenly thrust into it. Power, like love, forcefully introduces itself into personal development. Though power is a universal experience, power holding becomes romantic in upper reaches. Like it or not, there is more interest in what happens to a president or a prince than to a school principal. For this reason, the drama of a Napoleon or a John F. Kennedy engages more attention than that of the mayor of a city or the head of a business. Yet the rules of power are the same in all cases, as is the fact that it affects the personality and that its impact on the power holder can rarely be foretold.

Tolstoy—and no one has analyzed the personal nature and effect of power better than he—may have provided one explanation. In those chapters of *War and Peace* analyzing the failure of Napoleon's 1812 campaign against Russia, he makes a cardinal point. A man in power can cause events to happen—at short range. He commonly does so to execute a longer-range plan, aiming to bring about a series of events leading to a result he has in mind. Short-range events do occur as directed. The long-range result may be entirely different. This led Tolstoy to the conclusion that while historical forces do not control immediate events, they implacably dictate results quite apart from the power holder's will. Intelligent power holders learn this almost at once. Failure to do so would, and frequently does, lead them to live in a world of illusion, in which realities ultimately impose themselves, often in a manner quite contrary to the conception of the power holder. I remember President Franklin Roosevelt's stubborn desire not to allow his country to be involved in World War II if he could help it. My journal quotes his explanation of his aversion. Once involved, he said, we start on a course "whose end results none of us can foresee."

One impact of power holding on the holder is his discovery that the power act, the direction of an event, causes surprisingly unpredictable consequences. What it signifies to the men affected —a matter determined by their emotions and minds—is ultimately more causative than the thing done. That causation cannot be controlled; certainly not by him. The power to cause an event has scant relation to capacity to control the feelings and opinions of men about the thing done, or assure their adhesion to a larger plan.

The instinct for power consequently is likely to have more reach than grasp.

4. The Fallacy of "Class Power"

Denial of the existence of class or elite power cuts into an immense body of political dogma which has dominated affairs at least since the *Communist Manifesto* of 1848. It lays ax to the assumed trunk of some political structures, especially those of the Marxist world. It requires revision of some nascent theories of modern sociology. It is not a proposition to be advanced lightly, or to be ignored.

Classes, to be sure, are real. They exist. True, they are ill-defined. In any society, there are groups, large and small, whose members have a high common factor of common experience. The common factor may be that they are all of considerable wealth, or they all have a university education, or they all work in factories, or they are all poor; or, though diverse in wealth, education, and standing, they are Catholic, or Protestant, or Jewish, or Negro, or white. In each case, the factor of common experience is sufficiently great that on the basis of that experience they can communicate with each other. The group can develop a sense of identity. It can distinguish itself from the population around it.

The factor of common experience is higher as the group is smaller and as it is based on a recognizable common interest. We say "recognizable" because by itself the fact of common interest is not enough. The members of the group must realize that their interest is common. Not only that, they must be willing to accept, maintain, and defend that common interest. This is not to be taken for granted. Plenty of statistical groups have been worked out, groups whose members all have had property, an accepted position in the community, and so forth. Analysts point to a clear common interest in maintaining and defending their property or position. Yet on examination it turns out that the group members do not accept the analysis or know that the interest was common, and, so, are divided against each other even to the detriment of their common interest. It is one thing to say that the factor of common interest is there. It is quite another to say that a "class" necessarily exists because of that fact. The psychological element is necessary as well as the economic or political or racial fact.

Assume that the common factor of experience and common interest are present, and also that each member of the group knows consciously or vaguely that his interests are the same as those of the other members of the group. With that, psychologically he does feel himself a member of an aristocracy, or of an educated class, or of a minority group, or of a working class, as the case may be. At that point, the needed elements are present. Given a common medium of communication, a "class" exists.

Parenthetically it must be noted that the presence of all these elements, and especially the psychological factor, is frequently assumed to exist when it does not. Socialist doctrine was brought to America, in large measure, by exiles or immigrants from Europe. Attempt was made to appeal to American workmen as members of the "working class" or "proletariat" and to communicate with American farmers as agricultural toilers, that is, as a variety of peasant. Nineteenth-century dogmatic socialism called for class action by workers and peasants. But in America neither workman nor farmer accepted the class label. The workman knew quite well he had a job in a factory, but he did not, on that account, consider that he was a member of the proletariat. He could understand quite easily why membership in a labor union would fatten his pay envelope and improve his working conditions. He did not understand that his business was to advance the interests of the proletariat as against the propertied classes. In blunt fact, though conditions might have suggested he was a proletarian, his basic conception was that he was merely at one stage of a longer road. He hoped not to die a proletarian; certainly he did not intend his son to be one. So the American labor movement never became a revolutionary socialist political movement, as was the case in most of the European countries. Nevertheless, European analysts, many of them quite well informed, continue to speak of the "American working class" as though it were real.

Why the hypnotic attraction of the notion of "class" or "elite" power? Few of us have not felt it at one time or another. Probably the reason is simple. Most of us tend to attribute responsibility for unpleasant realities to a mysterious "they." "They" may be plutocrats or aristocrats, Communists, fascists, or other undefined conspirators. The late Senator Joseph McCarthy almost paralyzed the United States by playing on this sentiment. His Communist "they" came to include almost every intellectual group in the United States, from the Jesuit priest-editors of the magazine *America* to Protestant clergy, the State Department Foreign Service, intellectuals generally, and, of course, the known Communist propaganda apparatus. He merely imitated the Communist dogma itself, whose "they" classifies as exploiters not only property owners and businessmen, but also liberals and right-wing socialists. C. Wright Mills's *Power Elite* is a similar exercise. He lumped successful administrators and army officers of all kinds with administrators of big business, creating the impression that all were in a conspiracy to hold the American public in subjection. The French philosopher Pierre Joseph Proudhon had made the same mistake more than a century before when he denounced all property as "theft" and by inference all property holders as thieves.

A simple observation indicates the fallacy. Let any reader of these lines ask himself, when he conceives the existence of any "they," whether he considers himself (or ever has considered himself) in it. He will find that he never does or has. He is always out of it. The "they" never becomes a "we." Invariably when a man speaks of "we," he thinks of himself as a member of an organized body, never a member of an indefinite or inchoate group, even though it may have common attributes or experience.

No group, no class, comes into recognizable existence automatically. Elements in common are likely to bring about common experience. Common experience does bring about the possibility of wide communication. From that communication may develop a body of common feeling. From this there can emerge a psychological acceptance of the desirability of defending the common interest—this is, "class consciousness." But because all this can happen is no guarantee that it does or will happen.

Every group is not a "class"—actually, no one has yet defined "class." In the United States, for example, there is a category of educated men—let us say, college graduates. There may be, possibly there is (though I have not encountered it), an amorphous sense of unity within this group. Yet within it there would be found a large number of members whose income would place them in the lower, middle, or upper-middle class. A smaller number would be men and women of affluence, members of the "wealthy" class. If one were to base classes upon income, one would find among college graduates at least four alleged "classes" —lower, middle, upper-middle, wealthy. Almost any class line that can be drawn intersects or overlaps some other class line. The theory of "class" is always arbitrary in making divisions; quite frequently the divisions are artificial. Assumption that any individual is in one class as distinct from another has little behind it. He may be in several classes at once—as a college graduate may be an impecunious white-collar clerk. Whether he considers himself a member of the lower middle class defending lower-middle-class interests or considers himself one of the educated elite— of which he is also a member—depends on what he himself thinks. A blue-collar worker may consider himself an Italian-American or a man saving a grubstake in order to go into an independent business. Something else is needed to classify him. There must be an emotional focus causing him to identify himself with others having one feature of his experience. That requires an intellectual job, done by someone, that tends to unify the group. Classes, therefore, are made, not born. When made, they do not have power. They are merely strata which can perhaps be organized, can then choose representatives and delegate power to chosen or self-chosen representatives. Until this occurs, classes have about as much power as, let us say, the quite identifiable sector of the American population that has red hair.

The reality is that groups with common experience can more easily be organized than others. The smaller the group, the easier the task. Even so, organization is not only not automatic, it is not easy. For example, one per cent of the American public—that is, about 2,000,000—control more than twenty per cent of the personally owned wealth of the United States. If economic interest makes an upper class, here is one. In the United States, the members of this statistically visible class do not know each other. They may have a common interest in property. Probably they have a type of common language. The factor of common experience is high. They would tend to read the same newspapers, to be interested in some of the same ideas. But, as a class, they have never met; they have never organized; there is no board of trustees or directors; they have no president or acknowledged leader. So they do not have power. They are merely a congeries of individuals, each of whom has a tiny measure of power in his own particular sphere.

There are (in 1969) about 26,000,000 holders of stock in American corporations. These may have a common interest. Not only have they never organized, but their influence is essentially negligible even in the tangible focus of their interest, that is, the corporations whose stock they own. From time to time attempts have been made to organize the shareholders of America. They have invariably failed. Anyone who speaks of the "power" of the individual shareholders of the United States is talking nonsense. Every expert in corporation finance or administration knows it.

Contrast this with the power of "organized labor" (not, be it noted, "labor," but "organized labor"). Workmen, factory workmen especially, do have a high factor of common experience. Under stimulus of propaganda, organizing teams, and so forth, and

71

a certain amount of compulsion, they can be brought into communication and brought together. They can be induced, or perhaps coerced, to organize. They then can grant power to represent
them to specific individuals. This has happened in the United
States, where 15,000,000 American workmen (out of a total labor
force of more than 70,000,000) belong to labor unions which
recognize a central group of executives as their leaders. These,
affiliated through the AFL-CIO, entrust a very few executives with
power. Note, however, that power is held by individuals, vested in
them by labor unions. It is not the power of the "working class"
or of "labor" generally. What developed was power in the hands
of leaders of labor unions. These are not a statistical aggregate.
They are not economic "models." They are individuals heading
tangible institutions. They are individual leaders of small or
great district unions, leaders of industry-wide unions, or leaders
of the central labor organization.

Classes, however delimited or defined, are important in this
study not because classes have power, but because they are potential fields of organization. By sheer organization, power can
perhaps be lodged in or obtained by specific individuals. Potentially, power can be developed, though there is no certainty
that this will occur.

The fact of class does, to be sure, exert influence. Power can
be developed or expanded only on the basis of a system of ideas.
When endeavor is made to bring an organization out of a class,
the system of ideas must be one that appeals to its members. Their
common experience, their common interest, will dispose them to
accept this system of ideas in place of that. Aspirants for power
have this in mind. The idea system they profess will not be acceptable if it threatens the common interest of the group in question, though even that is not wholly certain. Property-holding
groups *might* be willing to organize themselves around a set of
socialist ideas—if their minds ran that way. This has happened
often enough to demolish the idea that property or economic
interests always determine the action of a group. All the same, a
first assumption would be that the group would more readily re-

ceive ideas that protected their interests than those that did not.

We need not carry the discussion further here. On close examination, the theory of "class power" appears absurd. There never was any evidence of it. Factually, classes more often than not are never organized at all, do not exercise any power, never delegate any power, cannot act even when their disparate members may desire to do so.

5. The End of Power

The power of any man—or men—invariably ends in time.

Death may end it, as where a man holds hereditary office during his life or when he dies in office. Hereditary offices are rare in the twentieth century, and become rarer as kingdoms and empires fall. Offices held for life are more familiar. The United States is accustomed to federal Supreme Court justices and judges to whom life tenure is granted to guarantee their judicial independence. Even in such office, custom, convenience, and legal institutions often cause and assist retirement—that is, encourage voluntary renunciation of power before death as strength ebbs.

Death aside, men leave power in one of three ways: they voluntarily resign or abdicate it, their term of office expires, or they are expelled by means not contemplated in the institutional structure—by revolution, usurpation, or foreign conquest. In the last case, they are, in current phrase, "illegitimately" displaced, and painful re-creation of an appropriate institution must legitimate the incoming power holder.

Intentional renunciation of power commonly occurs in one or two situations. It may be contemplated by the institution conferring power. Practically all governmental institutions face the possibility that a man may leave office and they provide for the choice of a successor. In lesser institutions such provision may not exist. One of the established American institutions is the family. When husband and wife separate, one of the two taking the children, no provision is, or perhaps can be, made to fill the gap. A separation agreement or divorce decree may place authority and responsibility in the hands of one of the two; even so, a period of extreme difficulty usually occurs. Leaving power voluntarily, especially where there is no ready means of providing a successor, may well produce a chaotic condition. Consequently, resignation or renunciation is itself a dangerous act—the degree of danger being measured by the degree of probable ensuing chaos or conflict.

Shakespeare's tragedy *King Lear* is the classic statement of the case. Commonly regarded as a drama of filial infidelity, in fact it is almost a political treatise. In Elizabethan England, the power of the king was the chief, if not the only, binding element holding the country together. It must have been still more so in the legendary periods described in Holinshed's *Chronicles of England, Scotland, and Ireland* and in Geoffrey of Monmouth's *Historia regum Britanniae* (composed about 1135), on which Shakespeare drew for his plot. Conceive, then, what it meant to his kingdom when Lear, at the opening of the play, expressed his "darker purpose"—his intent to divest himself "both of rule, interest of territory, cares of state"—and split his country between Goneril and her husband, the Duke of Albany, and Regan and her husband, the Duke of Cornwall. Lear himself proposes to keep the powerless crown:

> Ourself, by monthly course,
> With reservation of a hundred knights
> By you to be sustained, shall our abode
> Make with you by due turns. Only we shall retain
> The name and all th' additions to a king.
> The sway, revenue, execution of the rest,
> Beloved Sons, be yours. . . .[3]

This was a plain ticket to trouble. By the rules of power, what presently happened to Lear was his own fault. Specifically, he had committed a crime of the first order against his kingdom, as his fool systematically points out:

3. Act I, Scene 1.

Thou hadst little wit in thy bald crown when thou gavest thy golden one away. If I speak like myself in this, let him be whipped that first finds it so.[4]

The sister duchesses were surely unkind to their father; but they had the problem of defending against foreign invasion and local conspiracy. Lear, with his hundred-knight escort, became an embarrassment; his empty title made difficult their sway. The tale is rough, grievous, and unhappy—but Lear, by deserting his kingdom, had asked for it. At the play's end, the Duke of Albany, who effectively had gained power, proposed re-establishing the institution, if not the reality, of kingship:

> For us, we will resign,
> During the life of this old Majesty,
> To him our absolute power.
> You, to your rights . . .[5]

But Lear was dying, and the conquering Duke grimly sets about the business of arranging that the riven state shall be sustained. The moral is that the holder of power must not desert it.

A similar illustration occurred in 1961 when the then President of Brazil, Jânio Quadros, unexpectedly and unaccountably abdicated his office. Elected by a large popular majority, he had vigorously attacked the tremendous task of reorganizing a vast country wracked by corruption and inflation. After ten months in office, without notice, he suddenly resigned. Though the institutional apparatus for filling the presidency was present, he chose a moment when the Vice-President, João Goulart, was visiting Communist China. Quadros knew better than anyone else that Goulart had only minority support, was distrusted by the army as well as by great parts of the population, and was rather openly ambitious to become dictator. The inevitable result of the resignation must be to throw the country into confusion. Probably Quadros hoped for a popular demand that he himself take over dictatorial power to avoid chaos. It is impossible to believe he did not realize the momentary crisis he was about to create.

4. Act I, Scene 4.
5. Act V, Scene 3.

In countries less gifted than Brazil the result might have been civil war; it is a tribute to its people that they resolved the crisis with a minimum of disorder. Their verdict on his abdication of power was not spontaneous popular demand that he become dictator. It was an amazed conclusion that he had betrayed his followers, his country, and himself in abandoning his high office. His flight to Europe and voluntary exile was the logical sequence. To the country, of course, the result was a period of confusion, ended by its adherence to the institutional succession when Goulart returned and by its attempt not to permit gravitation of power to him to a dangerous degree. When, somewhat later, Goulart made his own attempt to carry out a revolution, he was displaced by a convulsive popular reaction eventually supported by the Brazilian army.

Voluntary abandonment of power creating chaos is properly considered a major offense. The reason is obvious. Achievement of power—by whatever means—sets up a relationship between the power holder and those affected. That relationship cannot be ignored, humanly or politically.

In 1967, there was wide demand that, having (rightly or mistakenly) assumed wide measure of power in Vietnam, the United States should forthwith and unconditionally withdraw. One result would have been to surrender the South Vietnamese to the uncontrolled and far from tender mercies of the Viet Cong and the North Vietnamese government of Hanoi. This included considerable probability, judging by past tactics, that many thousands would promptly be killed or exiled. Neighboring states whose policy had been based in part on the existence of nearby American power might well have suffered. My own conviction is that unconditional withdrawal would have raised cries of condemnation even greater than those directed against American participation in South Vietnam.

The government of Belgium in 1960, seeking to divest itself of the burdens and dangers of ruling its African Congo colony, arranged for overhasty evacuation of that huge territory, leaving power in the hands of a shaky government with dubious capacity to rule. Far from gaining encomiums for its generous anticolonialist move, the Belgian Cabinet was roundly denounced for a political blunder causing thousands of deaths, dislocation, and civil war—specifically, for abandoning power without making adequate arrangement for its replacement.

These illustrations can be paralleled in lesser situations. A man who has made himself indispensable to an organization, corporation, university, or club who abdicates his power without arranging for a successor is not a hero but a deserter. He has failed the first law of power: it must protect against chaos. In great affairs, ensuing events may well destroy him.

Perhaps the most famous abdicator in history was the Roman Emperor Diocletian. In A.D. 305, he retired to a magnificent palace-city he had built in Dalmatia, surrendering his power to the four sub-emperors with whom he had governed the Roman world. Personally, he survived this better than might have been expected—he was allowed to live out his life in comparative peace. But his immediate family and children, including his favorite daughter, were systematically hunted out and murdered by his successors, and the empire was rent by civil war. His abdication was "respected" because he had made arrangements for devolving power on institutional successors. They were in fact almost adequate—but not sufficient to protect his family or his empire. The price of voluntary abandonment of power without adequate arrangement to vest it in someone else can be high.

Power holders are expected to defend their power and to defend the institutions that vested power in them. They are allowed to retire if the institution vesting power in them requires it. When expelled by operation of their institutions, they may, having lost the political battle, retire and more or less gracefully accept their successors. This happens when a British cabinet is defeated in Parliament. It resigns, recommending to the monarch that another government be formed, or that Parliament be dissolved and the country proceed to a general election. An institutional expulsion from power has occurred—but institutional provision is made for succession, and quiet retirement is no act of political wrongdoing.

The case is quite different when a power holder is attacked, let us say, by a revolution, rebellion, or foreign force. Then he must defend to the limit of his capacity. He may be defeated, but he must not leave. His attackers may, and ordinarily do, have a successor power holder in view who will take power if they win. This is not, however, the entire story. In winning, they have damaged the institution by which power was vested—and the new power holder necessarily has less capacity to govern. He is, in the modern phrase, "illegitimate."

Turning again to Shakespeare, one finds Richard II, whose arbitrary incapacity first exiled Bolingbroke, son of John of Gaunt, Duke of Lancaster, and eventually caused a movement of the barons against him. These in time took young Bolingbroke as their chief. Their movement succeeded. Richard II was defeated and forced to abdicate. Bolingbroke, crowned as Henry IV, promptly arranged the murder of Richard, lest his existence become the focal point for a new civil war. Whereupon Henry IV—a worthy king in Shakespeare's book—nonetheless pays the price for overthrowing the institutionally lawful king of England. The Bishop of Carlisle forecasts it:

> And if you crown him, let me prophesy,
> The blood of English shall manure the ground
> And future ages groan for this foul act.
> Peace shall go sleep with Turks and infidels,
> And in this seat of peace tumultuous wars
> Shall kin with kin and kind with kind confound.
> Disorder, horror, fear, and mutiny
> Shall here inhabit, and this land be called
> The field of Golgotha and dead men's skulls.[6]

So it proved. If force makes kings, any force would do. Bolingbroke, now king, laments the breach of order through the two following plays. Dying, he calls in Prince Hal, later Henry V, and says:

> God knows, my son,
> By what bypaths and indirect crooked ways
> I met this crown, and I myself know well
> How troublesome it sat upon my head.

6. *Richard II*, Act IV, Scene 1.

To thee it shall descend with better quiet,
Better opinion, better confirmation.
For all the soil of the achievement goes
With me into the earth. It seemed in me
But as an honor snatched with boisterous hand. . . .
        And now my death
Changes the mode, for what in me was purchased
Falls upon thee in a more fairer sort. . . .

But he counsels Hal to keep the enemies and tempestuous friends busy with foreign quarrels

that action, hence borne out,
May waste the memory of the former days. . . .
How I came by the crown, O God, forgive,
And grant it may with thee in true peace live! [7]

Damage to the institution of the crown survived even Prince Hal. Richard III (Crookback) in due time seized it (Shakespeare accepts his murder of all the legitimate heirs to the throne), to be defeated in turn and killed by the Earl of Richmond. We must take Shakespeare's view of history. Though playwright, his tracing of the penalty of aborting the institution of power, in fact, is better than any political scientist's. No less true also is his conception (in *Richard II* and both parts of *Henry IV*) that time and acceptance of deserts of power eventually either create a new institutional base or cure the lapse of the old. Revolutionary governments, accepted when able to fill the obligations of power, presently become legitimate.

When a power holder is illegitimately expelled, two offenses take place. One is the inability of the power holder to defend his position. Weakness is itself a blot on a power holder's escutcheon. The other is the crime involved when an opponent endeavors to seek power outside the accepted institutions. He may be more moral than the legitimate power holder. His attack may be wholly justified by the defaults, omissions, or abuses of the man he seeks to displace. Yet in success as well as failure, he must answer for the offense of wrecking the institutional base on which power rests—and the advance of chaos caused thereby.

7. *Henry IV, Part II*, Act IV, Scene 5.

The problem is not confined to Shakespeare's history. In Latin-American republics, overthrow of a constitutional government by force is just such an offense. Even when the result is to place men of great rectitude in power, they are still responsible; if they seize power by force, so can anyone else, and the country is in greater danger of chaos because of that fact. Only where they are able to convince both themselves and the people of the country that the government overthrown was itself guilty of seizure of power—that it abused, rather than fulfilled, the institution it headed—are the revolutionary successions really justified—until passage of time and general acceptance legitimates their seizure.

Tampering with power outside the institutions on which it is based may occasionally be justified. But, prima facie, it is a political offense.

6. The "Post-Power Syndrome"

Except in rarest fortune, power leaves men before their lives are over. Men are chosen for office; their term expires. They are heads of universities or other institutions; the day arrives when they must give way to younger successors. They are executive officers of great corporations; the time comes for retirement, compulsory or dictated by circumstances. They may be heads of families; their children grow up and assume independence. In all cases, the moment of voluntary or involuntary separation occurs.

Consequence to the personality of the power holder is emotional and immediate. If he has held power of reasonably high estate—for example, important government office—the sensation is about that of walking out a window and landing three floors below on a brick walk. He will, as a rule, deny that it made a difference. Yet, yesterday he went to his office, was saluted by respectful subordinates, sat at his desk, and was enthralled by a stream of problems and events. He had no need to ask what to do with his day—the day engulfed him. His importance was not in question—all manner of decisions were to be made. He was a conduit through which flowed an electric current of institutionalized power. Years of habit accustomed him to its stresses and flow. Today he is disconnected from the current. He must decide what to do with himself; little happens to him unless he makes it. If by luck he has left public life for a private power position, there is some filling of the vacuum. Even so, the largest decisions in business or private life are puny compared with the problems of and the decisions required in any government office. They tend to bore him.

He is not yet accustomed to being out of power. Intellectually, he tells himself that what he said yesterday guided the actions of many, while what he says today is merely one opinion among thousands. Then, news media sought to find out what he was doing, what he was thinking, what he was likely to do tomorrow. Now, they briefly seek to extract indiscreet revelations about his previous job—and thereafter pay little attention to him. Desperately, perhaps, he may seek to call attention to himself in some fashion as occasions permit, though the occasions grow steadily rarer.

Men suffering this post-power syndrome sometimes do strange things. In my opinion, a mantle of oblivion, or at least of kindly tolerance, should be drawn over the next few months of their lives. They must re-establish a position requiring someone to heed what they say or do. Some men, appreciating the dangers of the post-power period, travel abroad for a time. Theodore Roosevelt on leaving the presidency explored parts of Africa. Some universities, including Wesleyan and Harvard, have established research or study fellowships with generous stipends with which for a year or so former officeholders can withdraw, think, and perhaps set down lessons drawn from their experience. Professors lured from campuses to government office return to their teaching. In all cases there is danger that the men may be lured into making speeches, writing articles revealing confidences of other power holders, or taking part in public discussion outside their field of competence. During the post-power syndrome it is desperately easy for men to make fools of themselves.

Few escape two emotions. One is gnawing bitterness that their hour of greatness is ended, combined with a desire somehow to

81

get back. Another is a feeling of hostility to their successors in power and the groups these gradually build around themselves. This is not rational. Successors may (they do not always) have the friendliest sentiment toward their predecessors; they may even think of ways and means of giving scope for some of their talent. But no one can revisit an office he formerly occupied without a vague sense that it has been deserted, or even subverted, though he realizes there is no reason for feeling so. Probably the worst thing he can do is to return to the scene of his former triumphs, though many succumb to the temptation.

Machiavelli was dismissed in 1512 when the Soderini government was thrown out by the Medicis. After a brief imprisonment, he was interned on his own farm. In the evenings he "put on garments regal and courtly; and reclothed appropriately, I enter the ancient courts of ancient men where, received by them with affection, I feed on that food which only is mine and which I was born for, where I am not ashamed to speak with them and ask them the reasons for their actions; and they in their kindness answer me." [8] Meantime, he sought re-employment with the Medicis, and seven years after leaving office got his foot in the door. In time, he was called back for minor jobs. It is said that he dropped in from time to time at his old office to give opinions and counsel, often unasked. Machiavelli had the post-power syndrome badly indeed.

It was for him, as for most men, a period of difficulty, and was followed by a period of attempt to put down in lucid language the lessons of his office. Many men try this, though not all succeed. In Machiavelli's case, it made him, albeit posthumously, famous. He is a contemporary of all of us. The president of a great university who chose many others for presidential position told me he always gave them one bit of advice: read *The Prince* at least once a year. Machiavelli's pen proved infinitely more causative than his power.

We need not go back to the sixteenth century to find examples of the post-power syndrome. Theodore Roosevelt, on his return

8. Giuseppe Prezzolini, *Machiavelli*, New York, Farrar, Straus & Giroux, 1967, p. 162.

from Africa, increasingly resented the successor he himself had chosen, President William Howard Taft. He intrigued against him, splitting the Republican party. Heading the Bull Moose campaign, he ended the long era of Republican rule. Men high in the administration of Franklin Roosevelt took refuge chiefly in writing their memoirs. Examples need not be limited to men who have left high office. Plenty have left lesser office—in politics, business, or academic life. They are present in every community.

The post-power syndrome should be a passing phase. Sooner or later the former power holder convinces himself that he is no longer important as a decision-maker, and that if he is to be important at all, it will be because of private or personal achievement. Then, if not crushed by the realization (and this sometimes occurs), he attacks a new life with perspectives not available to most. A surprising number of former power holders have made their greatest contributions after their days in office are ended, as writers, planners, or counselors. One of them was John Quincy Adams, president of the United States from 1825 to 1829. Two years later, he accepted nomination for and was elected to the far humbler office of member of the House of Representatives, an office he held for seventeen years, effectively devoting much of his energy to prevent extension of American slavery and to promote scientific knowledge through the Smithsonian Institution.

Great Britain and America, especially, owe a great deal to such men—men to whom power was not essential and who could overcome its druglike habit. They were strong enough to subject their power instincts to their philosophy.

III

Power Is Invariably Based on a System
of Ideas or Philosophy

1. A Precondition of Lasting Power

Two ingredients of power are inseparable. One is an idea system, a philosophy. The other is an institutional structure transmitting the will of the power holder. Without an idea system, institutions cannot be constructed and certainly cannot endure. Without institutions, power cannot be generated, used, or expanded.

I am convinced that a philosophy or idea structure is a precondition of formation of any organization—that is, it precedes the coming into existence of power in any form or at any level. This cannot be proved. Instances may exist in history where the development of an organization and its power occurred simultaneously with the development of a set of ideas. Such instances, if they do exist, must be rare. Typically, the power structure, however new, adopts an idea system already known and accepted.

One of the clearest known illustrations of a power apparatus coming into being and adopting a pre-existing philosophy was the famous Mayflower Compact, designed to order the colony the Protestant Pilgrims were about to set up in New England. So apt is it that I cannot forbear to quote Governor William Bradford's record of it in his *History of Plimoth Plantation:*

I shall . . . begin with a combination made by them before they came ashore, being the first foundation of their government in this place; occasioned partly by the discontented and mutinous speeches that some of the strangers amongst them had let fall from them in the ship—That when they came ashore they would use their own liberty; for none had power to command them, the patent they had being for Virginia, and not for New England which belonged to another government, with which the Virginia Company had nothing to do. And partly that such an act by them done (this their condition considered) might be as fine as patent, and in some respects more sure.

The form was as followeth:

In ye name of God, Amen. We whose names are underwritten are the loyal subjects of our dread Sovereign Lord, King James, by ye Grace of God of Great Britain, France and Ireland, King, Defender of the Faith, and so forth, having undertaken for ye glory of God and advancement of the Christian Faith, and honor of our King and Country, a voyage to plant the first colony in the northern part of Virginia, do by these presents solemnly and mutually in the presence of God, and of another, covenant and combine ourselves together into a civil body politic for our better ordering and preservation and furtherance of the ends aforesaid; and by virtue hereof to enact, constitute and frame such just and equal laws, ordinances, acts, constitutions and offices from time to time, as shall be thought most meet and convenient for the general good of the colony, unto which we promise all due submission and obedience. In witness whereof we have hereunder subscribed our names at Cape Cod, the 11 of November in the years of the reign of our Sovereign Lord, King James of England, France and Ireland the 18th and of Scotland the 54th. Anno Domini 1620.

All elements were present in this microcosm: threatened power vacuum, danger of anarchy, desire to advance religion, intent to set up a system of laws and institutions for that purpose and to "order" and assure the "general good" of the prospective colony—and the presence of a man, Bradford, who kept the record and had an instinct for power.

The *Mayflower* band already had its philosophy—the Christian faith, the democracy of a Protestant congregation, and the concept of English common law. The institution they created commanded loyalty because it filled a plain need on the basis of a philosophical consensus. It did not attempt to add novel conceptions—novel, that is, to the people involved. Additions of new conceptions to idea systems on which power is constructed may and often do take place later. Historically, power systems are usually—perhaps always—built on pre-existing structures of ideas. The *Mayflower* example shows an exalted group, brought together precisely because they had been practicing a new religion. They had already worked out a philosophic framework; their need was to make it valid through an institution. They could not have done the latter had the former not been present.

Descending from the sublime to the sordid, we find the same elements in any power organization. A gang in New York or Chicago will operate under an acknowledged leader. Though they usually do not write it out, they set up a philosophy of loyalty to the "chief" and prescribe obedience to his orders as an avenue for deriving profits from the gang's organized activities. Unlamented "Dutch" Schultz in New York maintained a gangland empire on this basis for some years in Prohibition days; it is reliably reported that Cosa Nostra does so today. Elevated to a political doctrine, this becomes the *Führerprinzip* expounded by Adolf Hitler. The leadership principle has been praised and justified by some philosophers, notably Friedrich Nietzsche. He contended that a successful conqueror of power by the very fact of his conquest shows himself superior to the men around him. Himself a superman, unbound by rules, his will makes rules for all others, who best attain themselves by conforming to it. More, apparently, can be built on that strange philosophy than one likes to suppose. Using it, Hitler was able to create a powerful organization capable of seizing, first, the German state and, later, most of Europe.

The leadership principle (it may be at the bottom of all power if one goes back far enough in prehistory) is, all the same, too limited, perhaps too coldly selfish, to long attract or hold many adherents. To enlarge an organization—let alone build it to national proportions—ideas must be included capable of attracting recruits and engendering loyalty to the organization as well as to the man. Hitler did that by adding to his philosophy the doctrine of Nordic supremacy. In the United States in the twentieth century, the secret society of the Ku Klux Klan included in its ideology a dogma that its members were ordained to protect Protestant white society from corruption by Negroes, Catholics, and Jews, and to safeguard the purity of Southern womanhood. Between 1920 and 1930 it actually achieved domination of the politics of several American states. The Nazi idea system, like the Ku Klux Klan, bore heavily on negative emotions—hatred, fear, race antagonism. To attract recruits, it sought warfare with other groups. This automatically limited the number of people to which it could appeal, but engaged the emotional support of its adherents.

Of great interest is the philosophy developed over more than half a century on which Communist power was successfully organized in 1917. One of its primary appeals unquestionably was—still is—negative: the doctrine of the class war. Fear, hatred of, and revenge upon groups supposed to be or to have been oppressors was an operative part of it. Greater drawing power lies in its conception that under Communism all property and economic operations (first of the Communist state, eventually of the world) are to be administered for the benefit of the "people"—proletariat, workers, and peasants—assumed by Communists to be the great majority in any country.

Small institutions as well as large require an idea system. A successful country club cannot be organized and run without the thesis that the club will be a pleasant place to while away leisure time, and that leisure, friendly sport, and exercise are "good things." An American commercial corporation has a philosophy relative to its operations. Its staff, like its stockholders, believes that its production of goods and services is useful in itself, entitled to be compensated by profits, and that, through dividends, salaries, and wages, these profits will be shared. Elementary though it is, this central core of ideas is sufficiently attractive to induce men to form and work for a corporation, to bring about investment in it, to carry on its operations, and to expand them to enormous size.

Illustrations need not be multiplied. A central idea system will be found in every organization, schoolroom or university, concert orchestra or church, neighborhood association or political party, labor union, army, or empire. No power holder heading any of these institutions could hold it together without such a core of ideas.

2. Limits Imposed by the Philosophy

The constituting philosophy of a power system necessarily limits the exercise of power by the head of the organization based on it. This is inescapable. Action known to be contrary to it at once weakens and may destroy the organization on which the power is based and by which it is transmitted. Adolf Hitler, rising to power on the doctrine of Nordic supremacy, and claiming Jewry as an enemy and threat to Nordic life, could not have announced his conversion to Judaism or have married a Jewess. Many of his adherents would at once have become his enemies.

A measure of opportunism in applying the philosophy may get by—if the power holder is strong enough. Joseph Stalin proclaimed fascism and Nazism as the chief enemies of his Communist Soviet state. When he considered it expedient, he made the famous nonaggression pact with Hitler of August 23, 1939. The Stalinist machine survived, but it lost adherents in many parts of the world, and perhaps weakened Stalin's dictatorial hold even on parts of the Soviet Union. But by 1939, Stalin had become more than a mere chief of Communist institutions. He had undertaken to be, and was accepted as, a kind of high priest, like a deified Roman emperor. To some extent he could "reinterpret" —that is, change—Communist doctrine. Combined with his control over the army and the secret police and with his argument that the move was justified to safeguard the Soviet state, he could make the deviation acceptable. In fairness to Stalin, it must be added that he had twice sought some sort of understanding with the Western powers and had been rebuffed both by France and by the British government of Neville Chamberlain. Absent this combination of circumstance, the Hitler-Stalin Pact might have been fatal even to Stalin's power. It is not easy to escape the limitations of the philosophical framework.

Tension in some measure always exists between the power holder heading the institution and the men loyal to the idea system holding his institution together. Invariably, situations arise where the opportune thing to do does not correspond with the idea system. Invariably, the men in power consider that the interests of the organization as a power apparatus—and, incidentally, their own positions—must be the overriding consideration. Given the choice between conforming to the philosophy at sacrifice to the effectiveness of their apparatus or their own prestige and strengthening their machine and their position, pressure is strong to do the latter. Conflict is neither as crude nor as dishonest as might appear. A pope might quite honestly consider it better to compromise with an antireligious Nazi regime than risk complete destruction of the Catholic church in great areas under Nazi military and police control. A politician in a country dedicated to freedom of information might quite honestly consider suppression of a piece of news more desirable than allowing it to come out and weaken the political effectiveness of his government. Problems rarely present black or white alternatives—especially when, as frequently happens in international affairs, other men's lives may be endangered. Men with power to decide find their philosophical principles in conflict with their estimates of pragmatic result. No one put it better than Machiavelli. To him, getting and keeping power was the first consideration—but a prince must *seem* to act in accord with accepted notions of "goodness." "A prince, and especially a new prince, cannot observe all those things which are considered to be good to men, being often obliged, in order to maintain the state, to act against faith, against charity, against humanity, and against religion."

Undoubtedly, a power holder can violate a core of ideas for a time without being found out. But once the policy of violation becomes clear, the institution he heads turns against him. Such a situation occurred in Brazil in 1964. The president at the time was João Goulart. He had been elected vice-president, had acceded to the presidency on the resignation of Jânio Quadros, and disliked the limited power held by a constitutional president. He therefore sought to carry out a *coup d'état*—as his mentor and predecessor, Getúlio Vargas, had successfully done in 1936. This was contrary to the historic and then ruling philosophy of Brazil, on which its republican institutions had been constructed. (The Brazilian army, for example, took an oath to defend the public order and constitutional institutions of the country—as Goulart himself had done when he became president.) Increasingly, he maneuvered to divide the army and to put himself in a position where he could dissolve the Congress and move to assume absolute power. But he operated crudely, with the result that, first, a popular movement built up against him and, then, the army moved in to prevent his *coup*. Had he stuck to the philosophical rules, he would have maintained his presidential position throughout his term.

I conclude that the philosophy underlying power institutions is ultimately determinative. A power holder must conform to its general lines, making only limited sacrifices to expediency, else his institutions become useless to him, they break down or he becomes their prisoner and is eventually displaced.

Unless, of course, he is able to change the philosophy itself. To do that requires intellectual as well as organizational leadership. It can happen. Fidel Castro did so in Cuba in 1959. He had successfully conducted a revolution against the then dictator, Fulgencio Batista, in the name of democracy, free elections, free institutions. He had gained the support of most of Cuba, and of the democratic governments in the Western Hemisphere, including the United States. Arrived in power in 1959, he at once set about transforming Cuba into a Communist state, taking about two years to do it. He concealed his objective until the end of 1960. By that time he had destroyed all the elected democratic institutions and had built up Communist-dominated institutions in the university, the army, the militia, the press, and most of the labor unions. Even so, he probably would not have succeeded had he not called in the assistance of the Soviet Union to supply money, arms, and, in 1961, troops. From then on, he became, in name as well as in fact, a Communist dictator, jettisoning with appropriate scorn the democratic philosophy by which he had risen. Since the philosophical change-over was far from complete, he had largely to rely on force and terror—his firing squads were busy, and his concentration camps full—but he was successful. The cost in human life of changing a philosophy may come high.

The principle that the power holder is limited by his idea system is not restricted to princes and dictators. It is valid universally. A university president may find himself displaced if he violates the ideology on which his faculties are organized. A corporation president, when he takes a secret profit for himself as part of a corporate deal, is likely to be displaced as soon as the fact is known. This happened in the case of a president of the Chrysler Corporation in 1963. Catholic priests cannot marry; a Protestant clergyman cannot have an illegitimate child; a judge (no mean power holder in a given sphere) cannot be caught taking a bribe or yielding to the orders of a politician. If the principles are notoriously violated, either the power holder must go or he must subvert and change the institutions by which he holds his place.

IV

Power Is Exercised through, and Depends on, Institutions

1. The Necessity for an Apparatus

Power is invariably organized and transmitted through institutions.

Top power holders must work through existing institutions, perhaps extending or modifying them, or must at once create new institutions. There is no other way of exercising power—unless it is limited to the range of the power holder's fist or his gun. But in that case it is completely impermanent—if only because from time to time he has to sleep.

Institutions through which power is exercised as a rule are the institutions by which power is conferred—that is, by which the power holders are chosen. Occasionally, these institutions are overthrown and their choices are displaced by action contrary to the established institutional procedure. This result may be accomplished by conquest, *coup d'état,* or revolution. In either case, and in any event, new power holders must at once take over the old or set up new institutions if they wish to make their power effective.

A few years ago, three university professors, Richard C. Hodgson, Daniel J. Levinson, and Abraham Zaleznik, tackled the riddle of power. Their motives were practical. Two of them taught business administration and organizational behavior at the Graduate School of Business Administration at Harvard. Their business was training men for executive positions in business corporations. The third was a psychologist-psychiatrist at Harvard Medical School. They did not use the word "power." They were studying the "executive role" (power holders in business are called "executives"). Because no executive can do much alone, they assumed, correctly, that each executive had several sub-executives around him, and entitled their study *The Executive Role Constellation.*[1] They approached it as scientists do a laboratory problem, by exhaustively analyzing a single small organization. They chose to study the executive administration of a mental hospital. Choosing a hospital for examination may seem strange, and the director of research felt it necessary to explain. The premise was, he said, that human problems in organization represent deeply rooted aspects of man's condition. They deserve careful investigation in *any* setting, because "Human control of organizations and events is possible through the increased understanding that follows painstaking study and research."[2] In simple terms, the rules of power are likely to be the same in mental hospitals and corporations, golf clubs and governments.

Examining their hospital, they found that the place was operated by an institution. At the top was an executive—a power holder— under whom were two second-echelon men. These constituted the

1. Boston, Mass., Harvard University, Division of Research, Graduate School of Business Administration, 1965.
2. *Ibid.,* p. vi.

executive "triad" and were holders of authority within the institution. The researchers did not commit themselves to the proposition that a similar "constellation" of power holders would be found in all institutions, though one gathers they thought it likely. (In my own travels through many types of institution, from the White House to New York City Hall, from corporation offices to academic faculties and tiny committees, I have never encountered one without a top group, though they were not always a triad and did not call themselves "constellations." Formally, through officers or executive committees, or informally, in operations, the fact always was present. Frequently there were more in the second echelon—the vice-presidents—and the top group might be a shifting one.)

The three professors considered that the top group—to use their term, the "executive constellation"—might be dislodged or otherwise ended. In that case, power dropped from the power holders at the top to a loose, flat, meaningless nonentity of the aggregate. By "aggregate," they meant a number of third- or lower-echelon men endeavoring to act together as a "band of brothers." Such aggregates are without structure. They are rarely able to meet outside pressures or to mobilize effort. They are usually short-lived. The researchers reached a tentative but accurate conclusion that power holding by an aggregate is a transitional stage. Another power holder or constellation is bound to emerge. The conclusion is sound, though the process is more complicated. A group or aggregate cannot exercise power. In it is an element of chaos. Someone struggles against that chaos. He contends for power, gets it by express or tacit authority from the group, and takes the real as well as the formal headship of the institution in question—mental hospital, corporation, tribe, or government—and a new administration begins. The top executive seeks to assure his own ascendancy. The lower-echelon men accept it or rebel. The rebels either succeed or are squashed. The power apparatus gradually comes into balance—and the institution proceeds on its way.

These are the findings in brief summary. I have omitted a considerable amount of jargon. (A characteristic of much modern research has been a strange yearning to construct a new vocabulary, as children in school invent a secret language. This does not invalidate the conclusions.) The study of the mental hospital might have been written by Machiavelli. The individuals were building their own future along with the future of their hospital. They held medical instead of feudal titles—apparently it makes little difference whether a power holder is called doctor or duke.

The study illustrates, in miniature, the working of the larger propositions here laid down: power is always refuge from chaos; power is always personal; power is always exercised through institutions. Power is not exercised by "an aggregate," group, or class; rather, the group or class is the context from which the power holder emerges.

2. The Emergence of Institutions

Institutions grow up, emerge, are developed, or are consciously organized both to transmit the will and accomplish the plans of power holders and to direct and confine the use of power toward predetermined ends.

There are, so far as I know, only two classes of power holders: those considering themselves subject to no control or check except outside circumstances and those claiming authority to exercise power on behalf of someone else or some group for the purpose of achieving results determined or desired by them. In the latter case, the power holder claims to hold power under formal or implicit mandate, and the institutions become instruments, not merely to accomplish his will, but also to assure that his will shall be exercised in accordance with the mandate. They may also include procedures for modifying, altering, or changing the mandate, or for displacing and replacing the power holder himself.

Whether they purport to control the power holder or not, institutions inevitably exert influence over him. He must take them into account in everything he does. Failure to keep them in working order, violation of the feelings of his subordinates in these institutions, action contrary to the philosophy or idea system that holds them together weaken their effectiveness. In extreme cases this may lead to revolt. When a power holder dies or vacates his position, the institutions of power he has used invariably undertake to determine his successor—though they may not be successful.

On Alexander the Great's death, deep in the heart of Asia, the chronicler Arrian records, his army staff at once assembled and allocated his power; his army was, of course, the primary instrument through which he held and exercised sway. The army had not conferred power on Alexander—he had attained that by succession from his father, Philip of Macedon, through the institutions of Macedonian royalty. But he owed the huge conquered empire to his army. He ruled it through them, though for local purposes in each country Alexander required his armies of occupation to adopt and make use of the local institutions they found. On his death, the army assumed—as matter of course—the task of arranging for succession. Actually, they divided the empire between the principal generals—some of whose dynasties maintained themselves for several centuries.

Such developments are automatic. They occur through the necessities of the exercise of power. Power holders know this well and, if rational, take account of the fact. If they lose contact with or comprehension of their power institutions, they are rapidly replaced, in fact if not in name.

The twentieth century has seen accelerated development of both absolute and authorized power, and of institutions corresponding to each group. It is fashionable to divide the world into nations governed by dictatorships under totalitarian organization and those governed by constitutional or representative governments. The distinction is sound, but does not carry as far as supposed. Dictatorship increasingly becomes involved with, and presently dependent on, its institutional frame. Increasingly, the dictator becomes "responsible" to the institutions—first as matter of policy and efficiency, and presently as matter of established practice that crystallizes into a form of constitutional law.

Such evolution produced British democracy out of Plantagenet, Tudor, and Stuart despotisms. It is apparent in the Soviet Union in our own time. Two decades after Stalin's tyranny, the Central Committee of the Communist party and the Presidium are able to depose and choose Soviet power holders, as they chose Khrushchev in 1953 and deposed him in 1964.

Institutional control of power is not limited to governments. Business organizations are no less subject to it. In America, there are two principal forms of business organization: individually owned business, wherein, theoretically, the owner is absolute and can do with it what he wills; and large corporations, whose stockholders elect directors who in turn choose officers with a mandate to run the business, for the stockholders' profit. The individual owner, nominally absolute, nevertheless has to hire officers and employees. In time he comes to consider their views, if only to avoid the trouble and expense of replacing them. Ultimately, an "organization" takes shape, and despite his supposedly absolute rule, its members influence the owner's policy. Not infrequently, they, or some of them, come to be the real power holders. A corporation has institutional organization from the outset. In it, under law, stockholders are *not* permitted to give instructions. (In large corporations the aggregate of "stockholders," like the "people," is an abstraction—they cannot act.) They can elect a board of directors, which selects the principal officers or "management." The management—that is, the power holders—organizes a hierarchy through which the chief executive officer delegates power to department heads and subordinates. Thereupon all the institutional processes come into action. The power holders' "mandate" calls for maximizing profits for shareholders. The management and organization want increased growth and correspondingly greater power, pay, and status. They may interpret their mandate as operation for greatest immediate profit, or for greatest growth (as did David Sarnoff in the early history of the Radio Corporation of America), which may mean slender dividends, at least for a time. This can be acceptable; it is rarely challenged. But let any member of the organization use the fragment of power delegated to him for his personal profit at the expense of the corporation—say, by collecting kickbacks or secret commissions —and the whole institution is weakened. Eventually, the institution must end the abuse of delegated power or go to pieces.

For these reasons, the care and feeding of institutions is a primary concern of any power holder.

His first preoccupation is with the mandate on which the institutions are constructed and through which they confer power on him. Mandates evolve with conditions and therefore have to be flexibly interpreted. Loyalty to the mandate from the men at every level in the institutions has to be preserved. Involved in this is the fidelity the power holder himself must demonstrate, both to the institutional mandate and, within its terms, to the individuals constituting the institution; and, it must be added, fidelity to the conception or spirit of the institution as well as to the mandate. When the institution is unable to fill the changing or expanding requirements of its essential purpose, it may have to be changed. Dealing with this problem is one of the reasons—perhaps the chief reason—for the power holder's existence.

3. The Relation between Institutions and Power

Power may be personally won; it may be a trophy of the strength, conquest, or cunning of its holders. There is little need to discuss this occurrence. Not much could be added to Machiavelli's chapter in *The Prince* discussing new dominions "which have been acquired by one's own arms and ability." I cannot forbear, however, quoting his sardonic conclusion that innovators in the power field succeed ill when they depend on others "but when they can depend on their own strength and are able to use force, they rarely fail. Thus it comes about that all armed prophets have conquered and unarmed ones failed . . . it is necessary to order things so that when they [men] no longer believe, they can be made to believe by force."

Machiavelli's observation is sound. Existing institutions aside, the simplest and swiftest method of organization is by force. My first experience of the process was in the Dominican Republic after President Wilson had ordered its occupation in 1915 by the United States Marines. Upon landing, Admiral William B. Caperton had been appointed governor general. His orders gave him a free hand, except that the civil courts of the country were not to be interrupted. His first executive orders destroyed all other institutions. The Dominican Congress was adjourned sine die. The press was placed under censorship. The general orders of the Governor General were to have the force of legislation. The Admiral's staff officers were appointed to posts roughly corresponding to the previous cabinet ministries; they, with the approval of the Governor General, were empowered to staff these departments by appointees of their choosing. Courts-martial flanked the civil courts. In a word, the organized administration of the republic was dissolved and replaced by the military institutions of the United States Marine Corps. Their basis was force. Parenthetically, one result may be noted. When, in 1924, the Marine occupation was withdrawn and the government turned over to newly constructed Dominican national institutions, these were so weak that six years later an ambitious officer in the Dominican Guardia, Rafael Trujillo, using force under his command, easily made himself dictator of the country.

Plenty of adventurers have taken power—in great and small affairs—in our time. Probably it is done every day by juvenile gangsters in city and rural slums and every year by ambitious officers in weak African states. A teen-ager possessed of a gun may terrorize an area, briefly bending part of it to his own will. Petty raiders in districts of "violence" in the South American republic of Colombia, where institutions of national order have never ruled, take power in just that way. These are sporadic instances. Nevertheless, most power in the later twentieth-century world has been and is given through operation of institutional structures. Such operations confer power on individuals at the top and determine hierarchical delegation all the way down to the lowest ranks, through secondary chiefs, administrators, bureaucratic heads, and their deputies, agents, and subagents. They enable power holders in each echelon to exercise power within the range assigned them. Institutions perform a double function: they confer power and they are the instruments by which it is used. Achievement of power normally is accomplished by winning the designation of the institutions accepted as having the power-conferring function.

A large and complex state necessarily has many institutions, simultaneously operated. In monolithic organizations like the Soviet Union, the army, the courts, the police, the economic administrators all acknowledge a single, order-giving chief. In countries like the United States, where power is essentially suspect, there is no single national power holder, and many institutions are autonomous—hence the overworked word "pluralism." The American Constitution itself contemplates three autonomous governing institutions: the executive—including the military establishment—headed by the president; the judicial system, at whose apex is the Supreme Court; the legislative system, called the Congress, which in turn delegates power to its committees and confers power on their chairmen. In the United States, all these function in a country whose endless minor institutions, political and private, choose their own chiefs and have wide autonomy. There are great and small corporations, banks, universities, ecclesiastical organizations, engines of mass communication and entertainment such as newspaper chains, broadcasting companies, and moving-picture syndicates, with lesser, independent concerns. It would be found on examination and without exception that every institution, whether part of the government or distinct from it, is a mechanism for conferring power on individuals and assuring with more or less success that their use of power shall be effective.

A conqueror in his field of power—gangster, head of a revolutionary movement, *caudillo*, dictator—lacking institutions will at once set about creating his own unless he finds existing ones and is able to take them over. On a tragic day in October, 1917, the power of the Russian Empire lay in the streets of Petrograd. With some hesitation, Lenin and his group assumed it. Kerensky had collapsed. The army and police were in mutiny and complete disarray. A friend of mine, the late Wladimir S. Woytinsky, was eyewitness to the disintegration. Lenin hastily appointed people's commissars, assembled people's courts, constituted revolutionary committees and local soviets, liquidated the institutional remnants of the Kerensky regime, and began to set up the germs of the current institutions of the Soviet state.

Often as they have appeared, nevertheless, the creation of new institutions after naked conquest is unusual. Power is commonly attained by president, pope, or king, by corporation executive, university head, county official, schoolteacher, or parent, through the operation of existing institutions. Underlying this attainment there is usually an element of personal conquest. The man or woman had to secure the award of the position—whatever it may have been—by the institution, and more often than not struggled against others to get it. (Even parents are not wholly immune from a degree of struggle.) Institutions accord power; to secure institutional action in their favor individuals must work to bring it about.

4. Personality and Organization

The fact that any power structure is institutional raises a conflict between it and the development of personality. Such conflict is endemic. It will never be wholly resolved. Power and the operation of its institutions must in some measure prevent individuals from doing as they please. Friction between individuals who seek to act against or outside the scope of functioning institutions and the organization is perpetual.

Volumes of ink, tons of paper, have annually been expended in America and Europe on the plight of the individual. He, it is said, lives in a structure of power or "organization" that prevents him from "being himself," prevents him even from knowing what he "himself" is or should be. So, the complaint goes, he is a lost soul living in a world he never made (in that, perhaps, he is lucky but does not know it), giving him little opportunity in thought or circumstance to realize his true self. An essay in a brilliant book by Dr. Paul Goodman, *People or Personnel: Decentralizing and the Mixed System,* blames the individual's "sentiment of power-lessness" for much of this. Conservatives, liberals, and extreme leftists alike appear to believe in "top down" management. This, according to Goodman, leaves dedicated individualists no recourse but anarchism. The youngster of today complains that he does not have the opportunity to be a "person"—he becomes "personnel" or an "organization man." The theme is repeated endlessly in modern novels.

It is easy, though not enough, to dismiss these complaints by debating points. We can point out that a student with no idea of himself is highly unlikely to "find" himself. Obviously, if there is no organization of some kind, no individual is likely to exist very long in a rather heavily populated world. Food, shelter, reading and writing materials must come from somewhere. A man dropped by parachute into the Sahara Desert is entirely free to develop himself, but probably destined to die in about five days. Individuality needs some system of supply, however modest. These, though unsatisfactory, are unanswerable arguments. They do, however, develop a fundamental premise that appears to be universal. Human life of necessity involves two simultaneous elements: personal entity, and social structure permitting such entity to survive. The history of civilization is in part the search for frameworks of society providing for both elements.

Within any framework a boy or a girl, a man or a woman, may —indeed, must—be *both* person and personnel. There is no escape from this; the problem is one of balance between the two. When the boy gets a job, he enters an organization; he becomes "personnel"—if the term is useful. The organization assigns him a specific function, tiny or great, depending on his position. His capacity to choose what he will do at any moment is heavily limited. He must fulfill his function or he becomes useless to the organization and loses his job.

Simultaneously, nevertheless, the job assigned him gives him a degree of power. He may—or may not—assist his fellows. He may—or may not—watch the process of which he is a part and suggest improvements or changes. He may—or may not—analyze the procedures. Almost without exception, he may—or may not—influence the segment of workers in the organization with whom he is thrown into contact. These are tiny measures of power. Like all power, it can be exercised only within the limit of circumstance. But in this respect, the humblest laborer—he has a little of it—shares the frustrations of the most powerful emperor, who likewise finds himself limited by reality.

More imperturbably, outside the organization any individual is free to think, probably to read, usually to discuss. This is true in some measure even in the most violently totalitarian societies. After the Hungarian Revolution of 1956, many defeated students crawled under the barbed wire to asylum in Austria. They had successfully revolted against the Communist government in Hungary but had been crushed when Soviet armies entered the country. Various European and American organizations undertook the care of many of them, arranging for their education in Western Europe. One of these was the Collège de l'Europe Libre, an American-supported institution near Strasbourg which offered to East European refugee students education to the extent of its capacity. There I met a good number of these Hungarian refugees. A surprising proportion spoke and read English. I asked how they had learned it. They answered that the Hungarian Communist regime had forcibly required students to learn Russian as a second language, and to read immense doses of Stalinist propaganda. As protest, the students studied English at night. They worked out a crude organization under the noses of the Hungarian Communist commissars for securing books, magazines, and materials. In minuscular degree, each had used the power over his own thinking, and of association with his fellows, to develop himself, and, along with it, to develop means of communication and organization capable of overturning the Hungarian Communist state, though they

103

were rapidly defeated when the Soviet armies entered Budapest. If that could be done in a ferocious police state, American youngsters can scarcely plead lack of opportunity.

Looking upward, the individual may indeed be oppressed by the weight of the organization of the corporation by which he is employed, or of the administration of the labor union of which he may be a part, or of the bureaucracy of a government department in which he works, or, more generally, by the limitations imposed by American mores. Looking around or downward, as a mother may look at her family, a teacher at her classroom, a jobholder in a craft, he discovers that he has, or can achieve in some degree, a measure of power itself. Looking inward, his range of choice is limited only by his imagination and mental capacity. He can think, he can dream. (It was an aphorism of the late Professor George H. Palmer, of Harvard, that dreams are dangerous—apt to be fulfilled.) In human fact, a man or woman, a youth or girl, combining the possibilities of his circumstance with the possibilities of his thought, always holds a measure of power, capable of expansion.

Unrestrained, this measure of power may, in fact, produce a degree of chaos. In factories, machines can be sabotaged. The occupation governments set up by Nazi armies in Europe discovered this rapidly enough. The plants did not produce to normal capacity. Workers in them refused to make the choices necessary for efficiency; some made choices that smashed the machines. Any system—production, government, social—becomes increasingly vulnerable as it becomes more highly organized. The smallest group may throw the whole affair into shocking disarray. A few thousand longshoremen could, and did, tie up the eastern ports and a fair proportion of the economy of the United States at the close of 1964 and in the opening months of 1965. A few thousand striking elevator and building employees made great parts of New York almost uninhabitable in 1935. In both cases, relatively small organizations—the longshoremen's union and the building workers' union—had handed power to chosen leaders; these used it to tie up large sections of economic activity until their demands were satisfied.

In the longshoremen's strike of 1964, the leaders negotiated a settlement. The men declined to accept it, chiefly because, as one news reporter noted, they were accustomed to having this kind of stoppage when contract-negotiation time came around. They preferred demonstration of their power to prompt acceptance of what was, concededly, the most favorable labor contract ever negotiated on their behalf.

The conclusion must be that order—the first premise of civilization—requires establishing a balance between personal interest in unlimited realization and community interest in adequate organization. Balanced they must be. Unlimited personal expression means anarchy. In modern society, others are always parties to the proceeding and may have to pay for the consequence or contribute to the organization that feeds the anarch. This side of jungle isolation, life is not lived in dissociation from other people, from some sort of community. Conversely, no organization of any kind, be it family, government, army, or corporation, can hope to maintain itself without a steady influx, through new personalities, of new conceptions, facts, and ideas, extending or changing its working scope. This is part of evolution. To maintain themselves, institutions must evolve, and especially in the twentieth-century renaissance, must explode into new fields of science and technique.

In little as in great, Zeus needs both Pallas and Parnassus. The tiniest power holder accomplishes little for himself and less for anyone else unless guided by some system of ideas and some conception of esthetics. In little affairs as in great, the organization f power becomes significant and lasting only to the extent that acknowledges its antithesis in wisdom and in beauty.

5. Mandate and Institutional Organization

Even absolute power holders and their institutions usually claim to act under some authority or mandate. Probably they find it easier to build a co-operative, obedient organization by doing so. But the source claimed by absolute authority usually is not reachable—or, at all events, not readily available for consultation. Their word alone attests where they got power, and what they are authorized to do. In earlier centuries power holders familiarly claimed a mandate from God. Genghis Khan, whose thirteenth-century empire covered much of Europe and Asia, did so; he claimed God had given him the entire earth—all resistance was contumacious and criminal rebellion. Virtually all kings, princes, and princelings, down to the end of the eighteenth century—some of them throughout the nineteenth—asserted divine right. Absolutists find it convenient to claim a mandate from God—few, if any, are in a position to disprove or get an effective ruling on the point.

Following the French Revolution and the American Revolution of a few years earlier, and harking back to ancient Greece and Rome, governments began to claim that they held a mandate from the "people." When honestly made, the claim was supported by a vote or other evidence of popular will, transmitting through a constitutional convention, legislative body, or other institutional procedure the desires of so much of the people as were in a position to have a viewpoint and cared to express it.

Factually, during much of the French Revolution there were periods when the chief power holders had little behind them but the capacity to organize a mob, terrorize the constitutional convention, and, during the period of its intimidation, exile, imprison, or kill their enemies or opponents. Marat did exactly that, hiring hoodlums for his massacres in 1792. Danton and, later, Robespierre claimed to be acting for the "people of France" and used mob force to terrorize the National Assembly. In both cases (spectacularly in that of Robespierre), when at length a small group of men with arms sufficient to oppose these mobs upset them, the "people" were surprisingly acquiescent—even glad of their downfall. While each lasted, his power was virtually absolute. Neither survived because neither was able permanently to dominate existing institutions or create new and substantial institutions for consolidation of power. (Factually, too, the

106

"people"—a statistical figure in a census report—is as much an abstraction as is God. Unless institutional means make it possible for them to register common desire, determine a mandate, or confer authority, they are an impotent element.)

More recent absolutists have claimed authority and mandate from "history." This equates to the medieval claim of power by the grace of God. Apparently the theory is that history is an omniscient, omnipotent, eternal validating force. Power holders working in accord with its laws are supposed to survive and flourish; those opposing are quickly defeated or eliminated. We need not discuss the theory; sufficient to say that no one can confront history, asking whether this or that government holds her mandate. She is thus a convenient sponsor.

The soundest claim that can be put forward by any absolutist is necessity: he took power to overcome chaos. In some situations in life, absolute power is essential to carry on a necessary function. A mother is absolute in her nursery. She is so because she is there. Only she can do, or require, what has to be done. Volumes of jurisprudence have been written to suggest that she has authority because the state authorizes her to bring up her family; any mother will recognize this as rubbish. The state, it is true, may take her children away from her; some states do. Communist China attempted to do so within the past few years, though the practice has been modified. But unless that happens, the nursery, however rudimentary, is hers, and she must manage it.

Division between absolute and authorized power appears in religious institutions. Both the Catholic church and the early Mohammedan churches claim mandate from the direct instructions of God, transmitted through an incarnation (in the case of the Catholic church) or an inspired prophet (in the case of the Mohammedan). The heads of these institutions were authoritarian. They were not "representatives," authorized to act by any existing human institution, though popes are chosen by the College of Cardinals with the help of divine inspiration. The Protestant revolutions of the sixteenth century brought into being Christian organizations whose officers and heads were chosen by the lesser clergy and the laity; they were responsible to earthly congregations which authorized them to act and thus become representative of bodies of human beings seeking God, rather than God's vicars on earth speaking for Him. The respective institutions of Roman and Greek Orthodox Catholicism, on the one hand, and, let us say, Wesleyan Methodists, New England Congregationalists, and Quakers, on the other, reflect the difference. Communist institutions, developed in the last half-century, perhaps more closely resemble those of the medieval Catholic church than any other single model.

Authorized, or representative, power must develop institutions along the lines of a mandate which purports to grant this authority. Like absolutist institutions, these unquestionably seek a degree—perhaps a high degree—of conformity so that the authorized power holder's will may be effective. But institutions claiming to act through mandate must also attempt to assure that the power holder's will shall be limited by, and carried out for, the purpose of fulfilling the mandate. Practically, they must also make possible the enlargement, change, or interpretation of his mandate as changing ideas or circumstances may require. Provision must be made for legislation, since change, in a mandated institution, can scarcely be made merely because a power holder has changed his mind, or wants something new or different. This means setting up some system of checks, if not balances. The "government of checks and balances" set up by the American Constitution was neither a new invention nor an American aberration; it recognized realities. Division of power is built into any power system that is not absolute.

6. Institutions as Instruments for the Delegation of Power

Power is vested in holders by delegation from the supporting institutions. The will of the power holder is transmitted and executed by delegation to subordinates.

Delegation may be from the bottom up—as when a group of citizens in a town meeting chooses a board of power holders (selectmen) and gives them power to carry out instructions agreed on by the group. In the United States, the federal government is said to have "delegated powers," delegation having been made by the several (and at the same time sovereign) states when the American Constitution was adopted and by the thirty-seven states subsequently admitted to the Union.

Equally, institutions are arrangements to delegate power from the top down. The power holder authorizes officers, senior, subordinate, and of lower rank, to exercise specific fragments of his power. Each recipient is expected to extend, but not to limit or divide, the power conferred on him from the top. His task is to use his authority to carry out and express the policy—that is to say, the interpreted will—of the power holder from whom he got it. Otherwise the machine breaks up. Power, like capital (of which power is a form), must be parceled out and put to work through delegates and functionaries. It must yield a return, as capital must yield a profit or an interest rate, in the form of increased capacity at the top to decide, govern, make its will effective. If the recipient of delegated power marches off with it and deals with it as if it were his own, the central power holder loses part of his effectiveness.

A widely held theory maintains that organizations—kingdoms, empires, government departments, corporations—grow in strength to a certain point; then, inevitably, they become static, begin to decay, and eventually break up. I am not convinced this theory is wholly valid, though a good deal in human experience backs it up. If valid, one of the reasons may lie in this phenomenon of "interest rate" yielded by delegated power. In a growing, powerful state, each institution commands the allegiance and co-operation of its staff, each member of which has had some fragment of power delegated to him. It follows the will and endeavors to accomplish the purposes of the central power holder. Central power is thus extended by delegation to subordinate officials. Comes a day in which conviction, enthusiasm, and obedience begin to fail. Officials become comfortable, seeking to hang on to their jobs and little else. Or, worse, they seek to make of the fragment of power given them a tiny, independent possession of their own. Then the institution breaks up—and is eventually sunk by some other organized group which supersedes it. At fragmentation point, there is a power vacuum. And, as we have seen, power vacuums are promptly filled.

It is not clear to me that every organization or institution must necessarily reach a static plateau and thereafter begin to decay, though in history no human organization or institution has lived forever. Some, nevertheless, have lived a long time—the Catholic church for nearly two thousand years. Perhaps we can leave to philosophers the problem of the eternal life of institutions. Enough to note here that power must be delegated in order to be extended, and that each fragment of power—handed downward through any organization—must yield a dividend of increased power to the central authority. When it does not, the central power holder must meet the issue or suffer.

In 1951, the United States was engaged in a war in Korea. As president, Harry S Truman was commander in chief of the armed forces of the United States. By his authority, General Douglas MacArthur commanded the American forces in the theater of operations. The war was a United Nations military action designed in due course to end a threat to peace set up when the Communist regime holding power in North Korea organized an army and moved south, intending to seize the southern half of the country. A difference of opinion developed between the General and the President. Truman's policy was to treat the conflict as a "limited" war; he did not wish it to extend beyond the borders of Korea. MacArthur was painfully aware that the North Korean forces were supported by two Communist empires, the Soviet Union and Red China, both bordering on North Korea. Munitions were supplied from across these borders. North Korean troops when defeated in battle found refuge in China, and were retrained, reequipped, and regrouped to attack the U.N. forces anew. He wished to be free to extend his operations, particularly in the air, to attack enemy positions beyond the boundaries of Korea proper.

As he approached the Yalu River, Communist China, without formally declaring war, poured in armies of its own. The General was prepared to accept the risk of full-scale war with Communist China. President Truman, as commander in chief as well as civilian president, was not.

General MacArthur, whose power was delegated, remained militarily within the limits of his delegated power. But he used his position—which was eminent—and his popular following in the United States—which was significant—to put political pressure on Washington. He issued policy announcements not cleared through the Defense Department. He corresponded with members of the Congress. It is difficult to avoid the conclusion that he aimed to force the President to carry out a policy desired by himself. Had he succeeded, the result would have been more than a personal defeat for President Truman. It would have been a substantial rupture of the institution of the presidency.

President Truman's dismissal of MacArthur resounded like a thunderclap. It had repercussions in American universities as elsewhere. My own classes at Columbia were divided. I pointed out to them that in a time of troubles only the president of the United States can lead the country out; no single army officer, whatever his rank, standing, or reputation, can possibly do so. (During the Civil War, General George B. McClellan at one time indulged a fantasy that he, not Abraham Lincoln, was the God-appointed leader to preside over the country's destiny; fortunately, he never challenged.)

DeLesseps Morrison, former mayor of New Orleans, was appointed by President John F. Kennedy in 1961 to be United States ambassador and representative to the Council of the Organization of American States. This is a permanent international body, meeting in Washington, D.C. In some aspects, it resembles the Security Council of the United Nations. Ambassadors accredited to it are the mouthpieces of their governments; under American constitutional practice, an ambassador is the representative of the president of the United States, though he normally receives instructions from the Department of State. In Morrison's case, the reality was that his instructions were drawn in the Latin American Bureau of the State Department, headed by an assistant secretary of State for Latin-American affairs—a middle-echelon official reporting to a deputy undersecretary of State, an undersecretary of State, the secretary of State, and occasionally to the president. The Latin American Bureau is composed of lower-echelon officials, members of the Foreign Service having permanent tenure under a special statute—the Rogers Act. Presidents, secretaries of State, and assistant secretaries of State usually change with each administration. Foreign Service officers (barring misconduct) remain in the bureaucracy throughout their entire career. They therefore are closer to the bureaucratic organization than to any political appointee or elected official. They tend not to like the intrusion of politically elected or appointed officials in their fields of action. That tendency manifested itself in the case of deLesseps Morrison.

In his lively book, *Latin American Mission,* Morrison tells that he discussed a matter with President John F. Kennedy, receiving Kennedy's instruction. Returning to the State Department, he attended a staff meeting of the Latin American Bureau. The presidential decision was brought up for debate; the Bureau questioned whether it should be carried out. Morrison exploded. The President of the United States had decided the matter—why the debate? Bureau officials enlightened him. They were, they said, "protecting the President." "Against what?" asked Morrison. Against his own mistakes, was the answer. In practice, this meant, if they thought fit, overruling his decision. Morrison again exploded, and carried the point. (The incident later was reported to the White House. Such things are pretty likely to be reported sooner or later. President Kennedy immediately asked the names of the men involved. Morrison, who had to live with the State Department bureaucracy, prudently found means of avoiding disclosure.) What he had encountered was a case in which lower-echelon officials in a major American institution whose authority in this field came from the president proposed to use the delegated power as they, not as he, saw fit. The issue was minor but frightening.

When I was working in the Department of State in 1961, the great musician Pablo Casals wrote a courteous letter to President Kennedy, sending it, through the Puerto Rican government, to me for delivery to the White House. President Kennedy appreciated artists and musicians. He knew all about Pablo Casals' hostility to Franco's government in Spain. He wrote a warm, nonpolitical, personal answer, sending the letter through the Latin American Bureau to me for delivery to Casals. The Bureau scrutinized it, decided it should not go forward—and quietly filed it. The letter, after pursuit and a fight, was resurrected from its bureaucratic grave. The excuse for what had happened was that the courteous letter from the President to Casals might offend General Franco, complicating relations with Spain. Finally it was duly delivered. (The sequel was a historic evening at the White House when Casals, as guest of President Kennedy, played in the United States for the first time since American relations had been renewed with Spain after the Spanish Civil War.)

In neither of these cases could there be any question about the honesty of the bureaucrats. Unquestionably they thought they were choosing the best course for the United States. But in both cases they abused the fragment of power delegated them as lower-echelon members of the Department of State. They were not carrying out the policies of the President; they were carrying out their own. If they had serious question whether the President knew what he was doing, their proper course as public servants was to ask the Secretary of State to communicate with the President, state their concern, and ask that the instructions be confirmed. This was not done; in time, it forced reorganization of the Latin American Bureau.

Holders of delegated power, it must be added, also are often confronted with situations not covered by their instructions, or perhaps lying outside the scope of their power, which nevertheless have to be met. A loyal holder of delegated power will act, doing the best he can, and report to his superior as soon as practicable. A disloyal or ineffective one frequently will fade out, washing his hands of the affair, irrespective of what happens to the central

113

authority. Filling a power vacuum on behalf of the central power holder is often the best service possible.

It was an aphorism of my father's that there were two kinds of men who never amounted to anything: those who could not do what they were told, and those who could not do anything else.

V

Power Is Invariably Confronted
with, and Acts in the Presence of, a Field
of Responsibility

1. Responsibility and Dialogue

Power is invariably confronted with a field of responsibility.

This confrontation is a fact of life; it cannot be avoided. Those affected by power have feelings and opinions about it—however hazy or ill-informed. These cannot fail to interest the power holder. At the very least, he keeps informed about them. He enjoys favorable opinions or emotions; he dislikes or fears the unfavorable. A formal or informal dialogue emerges. Here fun and fear, humor and malice, drama and heroism, sordidness and hatred really reside, and here is where the final verdict is eventually rendered.

2. Organized and Unorganized Forums

The field of responsibility is itself a collection of tiny or great power organisms. Any member of a committee with more than seven members knows that cliques emerge. They may challenge the chairman or support him, but they move somewhat independently. As the size of any group grows, these organisms multiply. They are of all kinds, of all degrees of importance and experience, all manner of opinions, ambitions, idealisms, self-seeking.

For example, take any American congressional district. It will contain a couple of formal party organizations. These, as far as they go, organize and delegate power to their officers or to informal leaders. There is a newspaper circulating in the district; its administration is also a power apparatus. There may be neighborhood organizations, Elks clubs, chambers of commerce. There may be a school and students, a farmers' co-operative. In fact, there are all manner of groups. The business of a congressman representing the district is to maintain the support or conquer the opposition of as many of these groups as he can. Aggregated, they make up his "field of responsibility." His relations with the field become a continuous and running dialogue with many people, carried on in many ways. For that matter, each head of the smaller organizations in the district is carrying on a similar dialogue with his own field. The principal of the local school is dealing with his students, with their parents, with the board, with local emotions about everything from race relations to the curriculum of the school.

Recognition of the field of responsibility and the organization of an orderly dialogue between it and the power holder are, precisely, the qualities of democracy. A dictatorship does not admit its responsibility, does not, at least in form, accept a dialogue as important, and seeks to control its functioning as completely as it can. Even when the dictator does that, he nevertheless accepts its existence. He cannot do otherwise. He carries on a dialogue through his secret police and his propaganda people, rather than through argument; but the dialogue is there all the same. The feelings and emotions within the field are reported to him by his spies or his police rather than through open argument and expression of views. His answer may take the form of repression, of public announcement, of propaganda, or of measures designed to alleviate discontent or please his adherents, even though he declines to acknowledge interest in the views to which he responds. Where there is also an institutional means of dialogue, he may, outside that framework, use this indirect discourse. Even a president of the United States reads and reacts to opinion polls.

Institutional recognition of the field of responsibility and organization of some sort of dialogue is, however, the normal condition. Few institutions by which power is transmitted or conferred fail to include provision for some sort of forum (adequate or inadequate) wherein feelings, views, opinions, complaints, satisfaction, and desires can be expressed. Perfection, in organized form, should cover all the feelings and opinions excited by the power system, though, like any ideal, this is rarely accomplished in most such forms—parliaments, congresses, councils of state, committees, and the like, cover only a part. Around and beyond their margins are outlying areas not included in the formal dialogue.

In organized form—or by informal process—judgments are made, first, on the power holder and his action; second, and less often, on the adequacy of the power institution itself; third, more rarely (though it is happening at present), on the philosophy and idea system holding the institution together.

Organization and recognition of the field of responsibility and the resulting dialogue are essential tasks of power at any level. Governments maintain councils of state, parliaments, representative congresses, national assemblies. Heads of corporations have boards of directors, operating committees. Subordinate officers and bureaucrats have staff meetings. Schools have student committees or more formalized student-government arrangements. These are useful if not necessary to power holding. The information they transmit is essential to the formation of policy at any

117

level. They assist powerfully in creating an atmosphere of co-operation, helping to assure that orders will be carried out or laws enforced. The individuals charged with maintaining the power institution—be they family heads, school authorities, executives of business, officers of government—find this contact important. They rely on an idea system to create loyalty. Disapproval of acts, or of these ideas, causes demand for modification. If this is not met, the institution becomes less and less reliable. To hold power at any level involves constant attempt to overcome, adapt to, or meet continuously evolving and changing desires and opinions.

Danger exists when any substantial body of opinion is not involved in the dialogue. Any group having no means of expressing its views within an organized dialogue must either be quiescent or obstruct, demonstrate, or perhaps rebel. This, in fact, is what Southern Negroes began to do in the 1960's, and they led American statesmen, notably Presidents John F. Kennedy and Lyndon B. Johnson, to use federal power to compel their admission to the electorate, thus giving them participation in the organized dialogue between the federal administration and its people through the Congress.

Tension invariably exists between the organized dialogue within the field of responsibility and the outer fringes or elements not participating in it. The nonparticipating groups will either seek to enter the organized form—to vote for congressmen, to be represented on the board of directors, to have relations with the bureaucrat—or become opposed and eventually enter conflict with it. At the very least, they seek to have their views expressed and made known. In time, some organization outside the organized form will come into existence and will determine whether to seek admission or to change or overthrow the institution of power itself. In this last event, they become revolutionaries.

Institutional organization of the field of responsibility is successful in proportion to its coverage of the entire field, though it never can do so completely.

Even in systems refusing formal organization in whole or in part, there is steady evolution toward broader coverage. In the

Soviet Union, Lenin created and Stalin intensified a substantially absolute dictatorship. They nevertheless nominally organized the field of responsibility through the institution of the party congress and the top committee of the Communist party. Because both were under close control, the coverage was incomplete. Obviously, this did not prevent Soviet citizens from having views about men and affairs, though the dialogue was so limited that their views could not easily be causative—indeed, they could not be freely expressed. Yet, insensibly, the coverage broadened. Visibly after Stalin's death the Central Committee began to entertain a dialogue with its partisans. By 1964, it included and represented enough external views and opinions to be able to depose Khrushchev himself—and to cause Khrushchev quietly to accept its verdict. Currently the Central Committee increasingly acknowledges its own responsibility to, and maintains a wider dialogue with, the much larger Party Congress. The increase in political stability has been notable, though coverage is still small and great areas of unorganized opinion are denied admission to more formal dialogue.

Paradoxically, a verdict rendered in the field of responsibility is essential even to the most absolute of power holders. If it approves, his word is effective with little force or compulsion. He then has "authority," actual as well as formal. If it does not, his power is reduced; he must use compulsion, with immense waste of effort and usually with continually diminishing effectiveness. In a democratic state, the next election may displace him. In a non-democratic state, he may be eliminated by growing power combinations built up against him by his rivals or by men who fear for their own safety. This is a process apparently going on in Cuba today, where the absolute dictatorship of Castro is already limited by hostile power combinations within his own state.

3. The Processes of Dialogue

In the United States, where the organized field of political responsibility—the electorate—potentially takes in all the adult citizenry, private expression of opinion becomes of prime importance. The editor of a newspaper is a power holder in a small organization; his importance lies in the news and views he prints. These make or influence opinion, and that opinion can register itself politically through parties and the organized electorate. Any individual able to command the resources for a sound truck in the city streets, to scrawl chalk slogans on a blank wall, or to hire a hall and hold a meeting is attempting to do the same, and not infrequently succeeds.

This is done under full protection of constitutional law in America and most European countries, but it is done clandestinely or surreptitiously (and often effectively) in Latin-American, African, and Asian dictatorships. One suspects that even where no expression of opinion is allowed, silent satisfaction or bitterness in the minds of a silent population nevertheless ultimately determines events. As noted, each individual has power, though to an infinitesimal degree. When any great number of them use it against the institutional power apparatus of a country, its rulers are eventually lost, though causation is not easy to trace. No one knows how much Hitler's defeat was due to the bitter though silent disapproval of him and his measures by a substantial sector of the German army. Though not decisive—perhaps even minor—it certainly was a contributory element.

All manner of elements and organization enter the informal field of responsibility whether or not they enter its formal or organized dialogues. Impossible though it is to examine them in any detail, we may note a few. There is, for example, a great group of nonpolitical institutions constituting the so-called "intellectual" establishment. These deal within—or against—the system of ideas on which the institution's conferring and transmitting power is based. There is a rising sector of the intellectual establishment loosely known as the "scientists." There is the press. There are the churches, who pass or induce moral verdicts on power holders and power action. There are propagandists overtly or covertly pleading specific causes, splendid or sordid, as the case may be. All of them work within the field of responsibility, endeavoring to influence the use of power.

The field of responsibility is the high court of appeal. Its judgments review, influence, limit, and occasionally reverse the actions of power holders, and from time to time displace them.

The power holder can, and usually does, enter the field himself. He can use argument, persuasion, cajolery, inducement. He can use fear, favor, force, or suppression. He can succeed, for a time, in silencing all dialogue, as did Stalin, if we accept (as I do) Khrushchev's famous exposé of his tyranny at the Communist Party Congress of 1956. But once the power holder's field of responsibility really turns against him, he is lost, though the end may be delayed by rear-guard action.

Power, we have observed, is personal. Its possessor upholds it in the presence of a field of responsibility. Inevitably, the love or hate, the support or opposition developed through myriad tiny power organisms constituting the field react on him. It cannot be otherwise. I do not recall any situation, even before opinion polls were invented, in which a power holder was unaffected by the emotions operating in this field.

The greater the power, the wider the field of responsibility, the more intense is the impact on the personality of the man. It may not be true, as Lord Acton said, that power corrupts. Yet it certainly penetrates the emotional life of the power holder. For one thing, he is invariably at the center of this particular stage—large or small, as the case may be. He is not merely "expressing himself." He is putting on an act. In this drama, he must always be the star. News items about him assume more importance to him than the weightiest dispatch about events. The effect on the structure of his personality depends on his tensile strength, on his capacity to endure this kind of strain.

He may break under it. Many executives have had the experience of promoting a man from a lower power position to a higher one only to discover that, though capable in the lower place, he goes to pieces in the higher. As the ladder is ascended, pressures become greater. Chiefs of state are not immune. Probably such pressures ended Woodrow Wilson's career in 1920. He had mastered the power position of president of the United States during his first administration. In his second, as a war president, his power in America had reached its zenith, and victory in 1918 gave him the senior power position in the entire world. It was transiently institutionalized at the Paris Peace Conference in 1918–1919. Then, for a brief time, his word carried farther throughout the earth than that of any other living individual. By the spring of 1919, he had become ill and unhappy. On his return from the peace conference to Washington, he became increasingly stubborn, increasingly unable to deal with opposition, increasingly certain—as Samuel Eliot Morison observed—that "God and the people were with him." In September, 1919, he collapsed, and never recovered. The late Dr. Harold Wolff, after a lifetime of research at the Cornell Medical School, came to the conclusion that unendurable strain makes men vulnerable to disease. Wilson's illness—like Franklin Roosevelt's in 1945—was, I am certain, an illustration of this medical conclusion.

These were instances of supreme drama; lesser illustrations are more common. In 1933, a number of obscure men were suddenly propelled to positions of power. I was one of them and had occasion to observe. The human wreckage among that group was higher than most people know. Some men, happily, were not beyond repair; others never recovered. Suddenly acquired power had placed these men against a vast field of responsibility, setting up strains that some of them were unable to handle or, perhaps, endure.

One wonders what the personal reveries of a Plantagenet or Tudor dictator must have been. Shakespeare probably gives a better analysis than historians. His pictures of the breakdown of Macbeth, of Richard II, and of Richard III are more convincing than most historical studies. A power holder leads two lives: exterior, which history can trace, and interior, which can only be guessed at. With that interior life, the field of responsibility interacts. Elements in it love him or hate him, praise him or revile him, strengthen him or betray him, flatter him or tell the truth to him. These processes he feels rather than analyzes. Combined, they fortify or destroy him. He must keep his feelings secret, for he is required to play his part. Not for him to reveal that he may be frightened or in doubt, that he may be worried or brokenhearted. At least half his emotions he must keep to himself, since in action he must appear calm, measured, informed, resolute, worthy of confidence. The play must go on. Under the big or little spotlight, before his great or small field he must act the role.

And the part may be difficult. Outside the formal forums, like that provided by the Congress of the United States, the roles are notoriously ill-defined. In journalism, limits of propriety and practice are observed by most newspapers. In some areas, nevertheless, the limits break down, or, more accurately, are not recognized. The United States Supreme Court has ruled that normal laws of libel do not apply to a public figure—he is fair game for any statement or comment, however slanderous, mendacious, or scurrilous. Since pornography in large measure is no longer barred, scurrility has no nether limit. In and of themselves these abuses might not endanger the dialogue process. But when there is conscious and organized intent to create hatred, to whip up emotion designed to produce violence, danger does exist. Carried from journalism to television, the nether limit of uncontrolled dialogue can be as base as the capacity for human depravity. Human passion can from time to time become uncontrolled. To this a power holder cannot respond reasonably, though if gifted with a sense of humor and a witty tongue he may be able to deflect its force. If violence is ultimately released, he has little recourse except force.

Passions released in 1967 by the Vietnam war, probably exacerbated by the intrusion of foreign propaganda and psychological warfare into the field, gave illustration that when established limits are passed, the dialogue process itself breaks down. When it breaks down altogether, force from somewhere follows.

4. The "Intellectuals"

Of many elements active in the field of responsibility, one group is especially interesting at all times. This is the group loosely known as "intellectuals."

The name is not a definition. Anyone can nominate himself a member of this group, and a great many do. For practical purposes they may be described as those individuals who by occupation engage in study and expression of views—about anything of interest. Their claim to being "intellectuals" is based on the assumption that prior study and thought give weight to the opinions they express. I, for example, can claim to be an "intellectual" because I have studied, taught, and written books based on my studies. Intellectuals commonly have an academic background or its equivalent. Many—perhaps most—have had memberships in teaching faculties; a considerable number are journalists, magazine writers, or perhaps have been research men in government and great corporations. Their experience supposedly entitles their views to higher respect than the casual opinions of untutored men on the street. The importance of intellectuals is derived from the fact that because of this background many will accept their views. In all countries, an intellectual community exists; in highly developed countries it is large and growing. Technical civilization requires a large general staff of scientists and technicians merely to maintain itself, and a still larger one if it is to continue its material progress. The larger the population and the greater its awareness, the more social and economic problems must be dealt with. These require a growing group of economists, social scientists, and lawyers, and growing development of the less well-based disciplines—political science, education, sociology, and behavioral techniques. Finally, as the possibility of the admission of an entire population to a measure of higher education is accepted, large increase in the size of faculties of universities and of secondary schools becomes inevitable.

Modern government depends, and increasingly must depend, on

the work of intellectuals—notably academic intellectuals. Separated from the inflow of scientific, economic, and sociological knowledge, and from possibility of reasoned action based on it, any national power structure is sure to deteriorate. Certainly in time of war, such knowledge and its expansion are essential to national defense. In time of peace, governmental mechanisms are likely to decay.

Men do not live by social or physical science alone; they also demand entertainment, inspiration, and interpretation. Novelists, dramatists, musicians, artists of all media enter the field and are comprehended within the group.

Inevitably, this disparate group becomes important in the field of power responsibility and its endless dialogue. Many of them write or teach; their views are constantly before, and may even have weight with, their readers or students. Technical and scholarly publications are usually available to them, extending in greater or less degree to the general press. From among them are drawn commentators, members of radio forums, lecturers at local and national meetings, and advocates at legislative and other meetings. Like the clergy (the oldest division of the intellectual community), they are always writing, drawing, or talking. This is their job.

Their contributions fall into four main categories.

They formulate and dramatize problems of all kinds, and some of them put forward measures for their solution.

They criticize existing and proposed measures, evoking continuous discussion of them.

They suggest changes in or additions to the institutional power structure.

They may, and from time to time do, criticize, attack, seek to reform or to overthrow the tenets of the idea system on which prevailing institutions are based. In extremes, members of this community may become nihilist, repudiating the existence of any idea system or institutional expression of it. If successful, their activities create chaos, paving the way for some new power system to move in.

Aggregated, the influence of the intellectual community in any power structure is great. At times it may be determinative. The ablest revolution-maker of our time, Lenin, considered that a major objective of true revolutionaries must be to secure the "transfer of allegiance" of the intellectuals from the non-Communist to the Communist system. He ranked such change as of equal importance with undermining and subverting such organizations as the army and the police.

Lenin's observations were, it is true, tribute to the political effectiveness of intellectuals rather than recognition of the intellectual process itself. True intellectuals secure and evaluate evidence, arrive at conclusions, and follow where their minds take them. This is the last thing wanted by totalitarian and dictatorial systems. Once in power, they attempt to wipe out free-thinking intellectuals lest the operation of their thought attack their own crystallized idea systems and the institutions of power they immediately construct. A totalitarian power holder claims to be also priest and truth holder; he admits as little competition as possible. When Nazi-Fascist power was regnant in Europe— from 1935 to 1945—the best brains in Europe survived only in exile. Dr. Alvin Johnson, head of the New School for Social Research in New York, was able to organize a University in Exile with an incomparable faculty, later headed by Dr. Max Ascoli, from just such refugees. Neither Hitler nor Mussolini, Mao Tse-tung, or Stalin could be safe were such men allowed free expression in his country.

The intellectual community is a vast, deep, and fertile source of insights and ideas. Power at any level can make its members, or some of them, useful and effective. Unhappily, the intellectuals are often plain pushovers for politicians and propagandists, in power or out. Within their fields of competence they have unlimited expertise in analyzing, studying, and solving problems, in exposing error and pretense, in forming opinion. Segments of their community nevertheless are afflicted by a weakness: being intellectuals, they consider it part of their function to have and express opinions on the issues of the time. Not without justification, they consider they are better able to make an informed judgment than the uninstructed public. As members of an elite, they believe they have a duty to make their views known, taking part in the endless dialogue between power holders and their field of responsibility. Their weakness lies in the fact that the issues on which they have and express opinions frequently lie outside their competence.

A French social analyst, Jacques Ellul, brilliantly and accurately pointed this out in a book called *Propaganda* (published in English translation in New York in 1965). He was writing chiefly about France, but his conclusions are apposite to other countries, including the United States. The greatest of philosophers—for example, Bertrand Russell—or of scientists—for example, Linus Pauling—may know little or nothing about the situation underlying the Vietnamese war, the occupation of the Dominican Republic, or the defense of Israel. Proceeding from the sound premise that all war is horrible, they conclude that any war should be immediately stopped. If asked whether the slaughter of, say, a million men in Vietnam or a hundred thousand in the Dominican Republic as result of failure to intervene would be a good thing, they would instinctively react against it with equal horror. Withdrawal from Vietnam, for example, could easily result in consigning thousands of South Vietnamese to prompt death. Failure to move in the murderous fighting in Santo Domingo in 1965 (where the death toll had already reached three thousand, and the slaughter seemingly had no limits) involved responsibility for its unlimited continuance. Power holders sometimes have to choose between horrors. It is quite possible that intellectuals demanding withdrawal and nonintervention might sincerely consider the results of conquest or revolution worth the lost lives. The point is that the large sector of intellectuals advocating withdrawal or nonintervention was not making or equipped to make that calculation.

The assumption—with which I agree—is that only by free debate in the field of power responsibility is the truth likely to emerge. That is why free speech and free expression are of the utmost importance. Yet it also explains why mere statement of point of view by any sector of the intellectual community need not, and perhaps should not, command immediate assent. Debate and counterstatement are essential. First-rate intellectuals recognize this; they are anxious to have the debate go on for its own sake as well as for direct dialogue with the current holders of power. Less gifted sectors of the intellectual community do not accept this conclusion. Like ultramontane Catholics in the nineteenth century, these take the view that "error has no rights." In an amateur way, they even attempt the use of force—sit-ins, teach-ins, claques, and the like—to prevent opposing viewpoints from being heard. At this point, the actors in the debate cease to be intellectuals; they are endeavoring to use a low form of power. Properly considered, they lose their intellectual union cards. The world did not cease to move because Cardinal Bellarmine, the Inquisition, and conservative Catholic intellectuals forced Galileo to say that it was static.

An able power holder—be he president of a corporation or president of the United States, dean of a faculty or head of a legislative committee—seeks to maintain contact with intellectuals active in his field of responsibility. If he can establish a fertile dialogue with them, his resources become immeasurably expanded. If he cannot do so, he is less able to command assent, and consequently more dependent on cold power. He will recognize that political opponents, in his country and abroad, will endeavor to interpret, indeed to misinterpret, that dialogue. Intellectuals surrounding the late President John F. Kennedy established a singularly useful relationship with him, and particularly for him. Upon his death, the Kennedy family broke with President Lyndon B. Johnson; perhaps because of that fact many of these intellectuals withdrew from a co-operative to a hostile position, from which Johnson's administration suffered severely. Ironically, the chief cause given for the breach—the Vietnam war—was an attempted fulfillment by President Johnson of a commitment made by his predecessor.

If power holders are required to take account of intellectuals as a major element in their fields of responsibility, it is also possible that the intellectual community may be required to take account of developments in their own lesser fields. Certainly each has such a field—the teacher with his classes and with the academic public, university heads with their community, scientists and technicians with the groups listening to their conclusions. Audit of their own successes and failures, of the results of the positions they take, might be sobering.

Let us take a single illustration: that of Harvard University. Harvard is the oldest and perhaps the greatest university in America. Its original field of responsibility was primarily Massachusetts and New England. Some forty years ago it undertook with substantial justification and the highest motive to become a "national university" (the phrase is its own). Let us consider certain results.

In 1910 the Massachusetts public-school system was perhaps the best in the United States. In that year, Harvard organized a School of Education—designed specifically to train teachers and administrators in public education. The school is today recognized as one of the greatest of its kind in the country. But by 1967, the Massachusetts school system had dropped from first in the United States to the bottom half of the list—somewhat, but not much, ahead of Mississippi. Again, in 1910 the administration of the state government and of its courts and its localities ranked well toward the top. Lawyers sought to have their cases tried in Massachusetts rather than in the federal courts. Administration was incorrupt and by prevailing standards very efficient. To Harvard's Political Science Department was presently added a glorious institution— the School of Public Administration, first known as the Littauer Center, renamed after 1963 for the late John F. Kennedy. Its academic work is recognizably outstanding. Meanwhile, unhappily, the administration of the State of Massachusetts became a byword for incompetence, if not corruption. The consciousness of superiority prevalent in Cambridge may have isolated Harvard from its immediate field of responsibility; but whatever the case, it is undeniable that the state deteriorated while the university enhanced its position.

Participation in any field of responsibility—the precise quality of intellectuals—involves duties and responsibilities as well as rights and privileges. This is doubly true when intellectuals seek or attain positions of power, as they frequently do. An intellectual—for example, a university professor—may and frequently does accept public office. Once in it, he must during his period of power holding lay aside intellectual pretension. Thought or expertise in his field has infinite range. Power requires an infinite series of compromises. He must make terms with the institution whose head he has become. Its bureaucracy, settled habits, and perhaps brute weight resist major change of ideas and practice. Unless, or even if, dictator, he must accept limits in action he would not recognize in thought. He is part of a government, private or statist, and that government is already committed to policies—commitments the intellectual in office must respect even though he may want to change them. Rarely will he agree to all its intended ends. Even in the highest ranges of action he is walled in by reality: the resources he commands are perhaps not adequate to fulfill his purposes; the authority of companion agencies must be observed and is beyond his control; the assistants he has and men through whom he must work may be less competent than he and have their own ideas. In making decisions, more often than not he must choose between evils, presumably selecting the lesser but rarely following his own thought. Meanwhile, he is required to uphold and maintain both the structure and the overriding policies of the institution through which his power is derived. Gradually, he may alter both—but during the process he must engage in operations many of which run counter to or even offend the principles of his thinking. Honest intellectuals in power positions draw a sharp distinction between their thinking and their action. They learn even to accept rejection of their advice by the men superior to them in the power structure.

Returning from power position to the intellectual community, unhampered by power, intellectuals are once more free. They can propound their own opinion, hoping to make it public opinion and thereby influence, guide, or control the power structure itself. This is part of the process of dialogue within any field of responsibility. Opinion and advocacy in the political field cannot claim the prestige and authority accorded to statements of conclusion by responsible scholars within the field of their competence. Standards for scholarly statement require that it be limited to the scholar's field. Humility requires acknowledgment that any apparent truth may be proved wanting by further thought and experiment. Political expression, oftener than not, involves condemnation or support of policy based on judgment not capable of scholarly verification, not unmixed with appeals to emotion and interest, tools scholarship must reject. Bertrand Russell the political advocate and propagandist cannot claim in that field the authority validly held by Bertrand Russell the philosopher and social analyst.

Professor André Cournand, a Nobel Prize-winning French scholar who has spent his life at the Columbia University medical school, has devoted much thought to a possible code of ethics for scientists. One of his suggestions has been that intellectuals engaging in political dialogue outside their professional fields should clearly disassociate these efforts from their professional pronouncements. As individuals, they have a right to argue for any opinions they choose. As scientists, they do not have a right to endow any statement with the prestige of their expertise unless it falls within the field and conforms to the standards of their scholarly competence.

That distinction being made, there is no reason why intellectuals should not enter any field of power responsibility the dialogue implies. There are indeed many reasons why they should do so. Increasingly it is clear that no power structure, be it government, corporation, university, or other organization, can safely exist if cut off from the knowledge of the intellectual community whose learning is relevant to the power structure. This is strikingly true in the realms in which science and economics are apposite. Defense of a nation as well as fulfillment of constructive projects for the improvement of civilization are impaired, or perhaps destroyed, when their organization is disconnected from the resources and innovations of academic thought.

The artist-intellectual is perhaps subject to less limitation. Artists, poets, musicians, novelists speak only for themselves. Acceptance of their product is required of no one; it must be derived from the reactions of those who see their painting or sculpture, read their poetry, listen to their music, or find insight and inspiration in their fiction. They are rarely members of a power structure, except as they may chance to become museum directors, editors, symphony conductors, or theater managers. Their ethic, like their art, is inherently personal. Diverted toward entry into power operations, the fabric of that ethic is weakened.

5. Foreign Invasion of the Field of Responsibility

Invasion of national fields of responsibility by other countries is standard international practice. "Propoganda," "political warfare," "psychological warfare" are among the names given to such incursions. Their objective is to set up currents of opinion and organization designed either to influence national power holders or to overthrow them. The practice is ancient; certainly it was highly developed in Europe in the sixteenth and seventeenth centuries. Religious movements were then active in most, if not all, European countries. They could be and were used by foreign governments to support or oppose aspirants for national power in those countries or to influence the power apparatus, national or local.

The same process goes on today. The weaker a country and the less well organized its field of responsibility, the more effective such external incursions can be. On December 9, 1966, the New York *Times* carried an excellent article by C. L. Sulzberger reviewing politics in Central Africa. The Chinese Communist government had renewed its activities in a number of the new states on that continent. By skillful use of small but passionate political movements there, it could, and in one or two countries temporarily did, establish ascendancy over their local power holders. That fact did not necessarily mean conversion of these movements or of many men in them to the current Chinese version of Marxism-

Leninism. It meant that they had set up and caused organization of currents of opinion tending to force local power holders to follow the Chinese diplomatic line.

The United States, for practical purposes, has never effectively attempted such measures. Its policy has been that of information, by radio, through the Voice of America, and intellectually, through the establishment of American libraries. For the rest, it has left the field to independent contacts—the press, exchange of students and professors, and making available academic material. The operating motives leading to these alliances may be admired, and few would wish to dispense with any of them. The political effectiveness of the American procedure is not so clear. There was no particular advantage in allowing Russian and Chinese propaganda to plaster the semantic label "imperialist" on the United States. Still less reason existed to allow them to stamp on Latin America a popular stereotype that the United States had become wealthy and prosperous by draining Latin-American production through the capitalist system into an American maw— the claim being demonstrably false. In France it made less than sense to allow some propaganda centers, one of them commanding the great name of Sartre, to give currency to the proposition that in 1950 the United States had "baited" North Korea into attacking South Korea for the sole purpose of bringing about an American war of conquest. (The fact was that the Soviet Union sponsored a North Korean army of sixty thousand, armed it with one hundred Russian tanks, inspired a surprise attack, and was surprised and shocked when President Truman resisted.) Unstated truth is no adequate defense against either big or little lies.

One of the duties of a power holder in dealing with this field of responsibility is therefore to assure that he is informed about the forces working within it. If a newspaper with wide circulation were to be bribed to conduct a campaign of special pleading for some commercial interest, a duty would exist to make that fact known. If a current of foreign propaganda is active, this also is relevant information. In both domestic and foreign affairs, individuals and organizations active in the dialogue of responsibility should know, have a right to know, perhaps have a duty to know,

133

what the real motivations operating within the field actually are. Actors in the field of responsibility and the dialogues carried on in it are effective or ineffective, trustworthy or untrustworthy, in large measure to the extent that the field is well informed about motives.

VI

The Higher Criticism

1. Critique of Power

Application of the five laws of power set out here provides a basis of critique alike for power, power holders, and entrants into the dialogue of responsibility. In major or minor degree, participants in the dialogue are themselves exercising power, and some of them are aspirants for a greater measure of it.

When opposition to the power system arises, it is important to know what the objection really is.

The complaint may be that the system is inadequate—it does not replace chaos, does not overcome disorder, does not govern.

Complaint may be the personal inadequacy of the power holder —in which case the remedy is to replace him.

Or the complaint may be that the institutions by which he governs are badly formed, badly organized, or unsuccessful in action. In that case, the problem is to expand, reorganize, or otherwise change the machinery.

More deeply, objection may be to the basic philosophy underlying the institutions of power. It may be felt that ideas have been outmoded, conceptions of justice no longer hold, the institutions do not deal with the objectives or seek the goals or answer the problems of the contemporary subjects of power. Then, the answer must be to bring forth new idea systems, fuse them into the old institutions, or, if these are inadequate, destroy them and construct new ones. This is the content of revolutionary dialogue.

Or the difficulty may lie in the very dialogue carried on with the field of responsibility. New ideas and changing conceptions may not find adequate expression, or, if expressed, they may not be adequately heard. Power then becomes increasingly divorced from the current of ideas and its use increasingly inconsistent with the conditions it is expected to create or undirected toward the events it should control.

Any reader can apply the rules to any existing political controversy. He can determine whether new personalities introduced as heads of existing institutions will solve the dispute. He can determine whether additions to existing institutions should be made. He can discern whether the underlying contention is that the philosophy of the institutional structure has been rejected. He can even satisfy himself whether in such rejection an alternative is presented—or whether nihilist chaos is the obvious result. Of this last, a good deal has appeared in later literature—for example, in Herbert Marcuse's *The One Dimensional Man*, Hegelian reasoning modified by Freud, excluding any ethical system whatever. In contrast to these he might read Professor James H. Meisel's brilliant essay *Counterrevolution: How Revolutions Die* and study his grim fear of "anarchist totalitarianisms" without even the therapeutic possibility of a lonely prophet set out by Max Weber.

Anarchist nihilism as a result of an abused dialogue can indeed briefly occur. But not for long. Power invariably takes over, using any tools at hand, and is promptly accepted as alternative to the irrational and unpredictable cruelty of chaos. It is the precise business of the power dialogue to avoid such lapses. Fashionable as it is to decry use of force, there are conditions in which force power providing a predictable society is preferable to no social organization at all.

Only when some such analysis is made can the endless dialogue produce manageable issues and lead to meaningful results. It is not enough to object. It is necessary to know what the objection really is, to focus upon issues, to determine what changes should be made. The value, if any, of this study chiefly lies in suggesting that standards of power critique are possible.

2. The Godlike Dialogue

Power, we have seen, inescapably faces a field of responsibility. In that field, dialogue, formal or informal, recognized or unrecognized, invariably emerges. Power's attitude to such dialogue perhaps determines not only its continued fact, but also its historic significance. The greatest, and perhaps the oldest, attribute of power is its acceptance of this dialogue with those subject to it. The history of civilization could, in good part, be written around that theme. The phenomenon is unending—as new as each morning's press and as old as prehistory.

Its conception reaches its finest as well as one of its earliest expressions in the Book of Job. The beginning is obvious fantasy: no God would wager the happiness of a follower with any devil, even a fallen angel like Satan; this is literary device to pose the question.[1]

Job had asked what transgression he had committed, why he

1. The closing passages of the great poem are confused, its text is corrupt, and the speeches of the young rebel, Elihu, are clearly a late interpolation. The drama's greatest speech, beginning "Where wast thou when I laid the foundations of the earth? declare, if thou hast understanding," though attributed to the Lord, properly reconstructed should, I think, be taken as that of Satan impersonating the Lord (as he sometimes did).

should be afflicted, what injury he had done to any man. His prayer was that the Almighty should answer. A diabolical voice from the whirlwind overwhelms him:

Where wast thou when I laid the foundations of the earth? declare, if thou hast understanding.

Who hath laid the measures thereof, if thou knowest? or who hath stretched the line upon it?

Whereupon are the foundations thereof fastened? or who laid the corner stone thereof;

When the morning stars sang together, and all the sons of God shouted for joy?

Or who shut up the sea with doors, when it brake forth, as if it had issued out of the womb?

When I made the cloud the garment thereof, and thick darkness a swaddlingband for it,

And brake up for it my decreed place, and set bars and doors,

And said, Hitherto shalt thou come, but no further: and here shall thy proud waves be stayed?

Hast thou commanded the morning since thy days; and caused the dayspring to know his place;

That it might take hold of the ends of the earth, that the wicked might be shaken out of it?

It is turned as clay to the seal; and they stand as a garment.

And from the wicked their light is withholden, and the high arm shall be broken.

Hast thou entered into the springs of the sea? or hast thou walked in the search of the depth?

Have the gates of death been opened unto thee? or hast thou seen the doors of the shadow of death?

Hast thou perceived the breadth of the earth? declare if thou knowest it all.

Where is the way where light dwelleth? and as for darkness, where is the place thereof,

That thou shouldest take it to the bound thereof, and that thou shouldest know the paths to the house thereof?

Knowest thou it, because thou wast then born? or because the number of thy days is great? . . .

Shall he that contendeth with the Almighty instruct him? he that reproveth God, let him answer it. (38:4–21; 40:2)

Great as is the poetry, this must have been the voice not of God but of the fallen angel, Satan, taunting the impotent man. It denigrates Job to nullity. It is the dustiest answer ever given a justified question, an answer unworthy, unwise, disastrous if made by an earthly power holder to a subject.

Hope lost, Job submits:

> Behold, I am vile; what shall I answer thee? I will lay mine hand upon my mouth.
> Once have I spoken; but I will not answer: yea, twice; but I will proceed no further. (40:4–5)

Whereupon comes the authentic voice of God:

> Then answered the Lord unto Job out of the whirlwind, and said,
> Gird up thy loins now like a man: I will demand of thee, and declare thou unto me.
> Wilt thou also disannul my judgment? wilt thou condemn me, that thou mayest be righteous?
> Hast thou an arm like God? or canst thou thunder with a voice like him?
> Deck thyself now with majesty and excellency; and array thyself with glory and beauty.
> Cast abroad the rage of thy wrath: and behold every one that is proud, and abase him.
> Look on every one that is proud, and bring him low; and tread down the wicked in their place.
> Hide them in the dust together; and bind their faces in secret.
> Then will I also confess unto thee that thine own right hand can save thee. (40:6–14)

His manhood restored, Job speaks once more:

> I know that thou canst do every thing, and that no thought can be withholden from thee.
> Who is he that hideth counsel without knowledge? therefore have I uttered that I understood not; things too wonderful for me, which I knew not.
> Hear, I beseech thee, and I will speak: I will demand of thee, and declare thou unto me.
> I have heard of thee by the hearing of the ear: but now mine eye seeth thee. (42:2–5)

Job's friends rebuked him for his questioning. A satanic voice proclaimed his nothingness, condemning him to silence. The Lord appeared, proposing, not refusing, the dialogue, inviting Job's participation. In the command "gird up thy loins like a man: I will demand of thee, and declare thou unto me," and Job's acceptance of the challenge, the eternal dialogue presents itself.

The allegory postulates the demand of reason and power's unavoidable duty to meet it. Throughout all human history that demand is unvaryingly made; unless met, even godlike power stands on trial.

2

Economic Power

Preface

1. Power without Glory

Economic power arises with capacity to cause or to refuse production, purchase, sale, or delivery of goods, or to cause or prevent the rendering of service (including labor). Such capacity brings with it the power to impose conditions and prices on those who desire to employ labor, buy goods, or receive services, or to sell or work.

Most individuals have a fragment of this power, if only microscopic. Like all forms of power, it is personal. Force systems aside, each individual has the power to go to work or to stay home, to buy or refuse to buy, to produce (in some measure) or decline to do so. In deciding, each individual may act separately or may join with others. As a single person, what he decides has little appreciable effect. In combination, power grows—as in the case of a boycott or a strike. To bring about common action, organization is needed, be it a co-operative or a corporation, a labor union or a consumers' boycott.

Organization, in any form, brings into operation the standard laws of power. It sets up an institution. Each institution must bring about the choice of a chief or directing head and subordinate officers, vesting in them the capacity to direct, energize, or withhold activities of the organization—in other words, giving them power to decide. As in all institutions, there must be an idea system, explicit or implicit definition of objectives and principles, guiding use of the economic power thus created. By the same token, a field of responsibility, formal, informal, or both, invariably appears.

Economic power, like any other form, is "legitimately" exercised when its use is relevant to its function. The power of a labor leader is legitimately used when he organizes a strike or makes a labor contract for the purpose of benefiting union members. It is illegitimately used if he does so for the purpose of obtaining private gain. The power of a corporation is legitimately used when it produces and sells, let us say, motorcars, and seeks to make profits for its shareholders. It is illegitimately used when (as recently occurred) it employs its private detective force to shadow or harass a crusader for safety measures in its automobiles.

Zenith is reached when an economic institution attains monopoly in its field, particularly when the goods or services it monopolizes are important, if not essential, to the life of the community or customers it serves. Then, responsive to its own self-interest, the organization—in practice, the men vested with its power—can provide the goods or services within its control at any price or on any terms it chooses to dictate. Even then the power is no more absolute than in other fields. A corporation exercising a monopoly over a necessity of life might decide to refuse supply and liquidate. But it would then be in danger of seizure by the political state; or refusal to supply the market might stimulate organization of some different method of supply, unforeseen by the monopoly. These possibilities limit the decisions of the economic power holder. Limitations of this kind are observed in all power situations. The most absolute political despot must reckon with the possibility that, if his decisions are repulsively arbitrary, their result may cause rebellion or foreign war. A monopolist does not charge the highest price possible for his goods. There might be too few buyers. He selects the "monopoly price"—that price which, combined with the volume of goods he can sell, will give him the greatest profit—if his object is to make maximum profit for himself and his operation.

Tools other than compulsion imposed by the necessities of consumers are included in economic power. This is especially true where the economic institution has not ascended to the grade of monopoly. Its administrators must seek to persuade, attract, or induce people to buy, to want their goods or services. Advertising, "bargain" prices, flamboyant publicity, stealthy appeals to emotion, offering the prospect of enhanced social esteem, using fear of ill-health or personal repulsiveness, all may be employed. Even Communist states, whose economic operations are monopolist by doctrine, carry on propaganda in a fashion more or less comparable to commercial advertising prevalent in non-Communist countries. Power to command resources of television, radio, press, and billboard—or, in a socialist state, to carry on propaganda campaigns—carries with it the capacity to suggest, induce, or persuade where, perhaps, there is not means to compel.

More fundamental, though less obvious, is the capacity of economic power holders to affect the direction of affairs or enter new fields through "innovation." Heads of great corporations commonly have or can command capital resources which could be directed to increased production of old products but may be directed toward developing new ones. A few years ago, the Du Pont company discovered the possibility of developing a chemical product that could serve as a substitute for leather—just as a couple of decades earlier it had been presented with chemical products capable of being substituted for silk. In each case, it

145

had the power to develop and market the product or to refuse the operation. Its heads had, of course, to consider the possibility that, should they refuse, the process might be developed elsewhere. In each case, the company decided to go forward. The emergence of nylon changed the direction of an entire current of Far Eastern commerce. The development of the recently unknown substitute for leather could powerfully affect husbandry and the cattle industry from Argentina to Canada.

International oil companies are regularly presented with alternate geographic areas in which they may develop, or decline to develop, the resources of oil. The United States Steel Corporation, seeking iron ore and choosing from a number of sources, determined to develop the Sierra Bolivar mines in Venezuela—whereupon new cities in the Orinoco Valley resulted. Illustrations could be multiplied.

In economic life, every decision made affects, in some way, every life in the modern world. This is the peculiar quality of economics. The impact of economic-power decisions may be imperceptible or great, but it is always there. The woman who chose nylon stockings instead of silk (a choice she still has, though nylon has clearly won the campaign) affected the lives of silk growers in Japan, China, and Southeast Asia. Because the effects are often not immediately visible, economic power is still considered mysterious, though the mystery steadily grows less.

Decisions of this character rest, primarily, on the ability and will of a power holder to use capital in organizing new enterprises and to determine the time, place, nature, and scale of the development. Decision having been made, enterprises buy raw material, employ workmen, sell products. Neighborhoods, perhaps cities, grow up around them. Homes are constructed; subsidiary shops and other small businesses serve the new community. The aggregate of all decisions to supply new capital can determine the character, speed, and quality of the development of communities, regions, entire countries.

Less massive decisions of economic power holders may have effect, tiny as well as great, in their impact on the lives of great numbers of people. The determination of a great surgical-supply corporation, Johnson & Johnson, to use first-rate architecture in building its New Jersey plants went some distance toward preventing one area of that state from falling into the esthetic mess that disgraces much of its Hudson River border and of New York Harbor. Conversely, economic power holders built in the air space over some of the tracks leading to Grand Central Station in New York an ungainly, ill-featured skyscraper blocking the stately vista of Park Avenue. Millions who enter and leave New York are, by the presence of that eyesore, so much the poorer.

Though the public has at times been intrigued by spectacular villains, economic power holders rarely attract the attention of poets, playwrights, or novelists. The Venetian trader Antonio is not a great figure in Shakespeare's *Merchant of Venice*. Countinghouse men and entrepreneurs are occasionally depicted in Victorian and Edwardian writing—one must remember John Galsworthy—but these are exceptions. As a rule, businessmen and financial and economic statesmen receive notice and are dealt with only when they are associated with high political events and figures. Literature has always preoccupied itself with the personality of emperors, kings, princes, and generals. Skipping the middle position of economics and business, it today interests itself in the poor, the neglected, the rejected.

The reason, I think, is clear. Economic organization arises in response to the demands of its times and avoids conflict with them. Power holders do not usually struggle with individuals. In minor degree they affect the lives of faceless thousands—by collecting a price—in ways anything but dramatic. Someday economic power will find its way into literature, though it may require new forms of expression.

So we must treat of economic power without heroes, observing it for what it is, wondering, rather than describing, what effect it may have on the men who hold it. Until recently, indeed, the men themselves considered that their fate was determined not by themselves, but by the gods of the market. They were not struggling with destiny. They were shrewd or stupid, industrious or lazy, clever or unwise—therefore, successful or unsuccessful. So, no Schiller pictured them as he did the great Austrian general Wallenstein, or planned writing the drama of Louis Quartorze's chief of police, Marquis Marc d'Argenson. Even in the heyday of American plutocracy, when, if ever, economic figures were all-powerful, high drama passed them by. They felt no necessity to explain themselves. Literary art reciprocated their feeling.

I surmise this lacuna may not continue. The current world of huge corporations and their counterparts, government commissariats, steadily pushes economic power holders into the wider theater of politics and statesmanship. From it will come a period when men stand out from the machines they turn on or off and from the bureaucracies over which they preside. The significance of their decisions will become more apparent. They themselves will come to understand that verdicts on them will result less from balance sheets and income statements than from the impact of their power on human beings. Dialogue between them and their field of responsibility will become at once more acute and more orderly; they will emerge as human beings.

2. Diversity of Economic and Political Power Holders

Political and economic power at all times interact. They commonly do not merge. Politicians control the state; technicians hold economic power positions. Not often do either succeed in taking over the permanent decision-making function of the other.

Heads of institutions wielding economic power, whether state or private, do have a built-in tendency to invade and control part, and occasionally all, of the political power. At all times they seek to achieve, maintain, and extend conditions and privileges favorable to their operations and interests. Conversely, political power holders, to buttress their positions, have a propensity to reach for economic power, whether as an instrument of control or to deal with situations demanding remedy. Rarely, nevertheless, do the two power forces combine in a single institutional system or vest power over both forces in the same man or men. When merger does take place, the two forces presently tend to divide.

Theorists have sometimes argued that, in effect, the two power systems are the same; that economic power merely reflects forms of political organization. Others have insisted that the political state in essence is little more than an institution maintaining order for the benefit of the prevailing economic system. I do not think either conclusion justified, though each group can cite historical examples.

Communist states have united political and economic control during the last half-century, as did the fascist and Nazi states. Yet as I observe the scene, there has always been a division of function. The men of the state think of their function as apart from and senior to economic organization, even when they control it. The men operating economic institutions consider their function as different from and more limited than the government's, even when, as has happened, they are able to determine government policy. Each group from time to time considers it useful or even essential to dominate the other. Yet in essence they are different, and the difference lies in their picture of themselves. The political chieftain frequently feels he cannot dominate his government institutions or make them fully effective without subordinating some part of the economic institutions to his will; but he thinks of them as instruments to gain some larger objective. Economic heads find that their wealth, their position, or the capacities and range of their enterprise are threatened or limited unless they are able to secure privileges or overcome rivals by political means. But they think in terms of their enterprises rather than of a state. A continuous, frequently uneasy struggle for balance between the two forms of power seems to characterize the internal structure of most twentieth-century states, Communist and non-Communist alike.

Factually, when either the political or the economic power succeeds in fully dominating a state, the results may be disastrous. Exception may exist when extreme conditions—notably war— call for devotion of *all* forms of national resources and organization to a single purpose. Then all forms of power are willingly subordinated to a single objective of national will—as occurred in the struggle of Britain and, in large measure, America for victory in World War II. But willingness to pool all effort for a single imperative end rarely occurs. Once the pressure is lifted, and the single end no longer dominates the scene, division between economic and political power reappears.

Power holders, both economic and political, it must be admitted, may be cursed with the taste and ambition to hold the widest attainable measure of power for its own sake; to be order givers, dictators, princes; to force every tongue to flatter, every knee to bend. One can only guess the dark sources in the human psyche setting up such desire. Psychiatrists recognize, without explaining, the impulse. Economic power holders, no less than political chieftains, occasionally exhibit the condition, though their invasions of political power more often have been for limited ends. When such a situation exists, it does not matter greatly whether the institution conferring economic power is a privately owned wealth- or profit-creating apparatus, or whether it is a state or publicly owned economic instrument. The operative fact is that the man holding economic power dreams of empire with economic position as the base, and seeks to extend his capacity to enforce his will as far as he can.

High drama attended a recent thrust and counterthrust in Italy between economic and political power, each seeking control of the other. In that country, fuel and sources of energy are scarce. In 1926, Mussolini's government organized a corporation, entirely owned by the state, to explore Italy for oil and acquire interests in oil fields abroad. It was known as AGIP (Azienda Generale Italiana Petroli). During the fascist period, it had little success. At the close of World War II, its assets were put up for sale. There were no bidders, so the Italian government kept them. The Italian Republic gave to a young but ambitious man, by name Enrico Mattei, the unimpressive job of commissioner in charge. Luck attended his administration; he struck oil and natural gas in the Po Valley. At once he sought and got monopoly rights for the sale of petroleum and allied products for his organization—and was on his way. In 1953, he caused a law to be passed converting the corporation into a larger, more inclusive state-owned concern, Ente Nazionale Idrocarburi, known as ENI. Its oil properties and monopoly provided revenue in large amounts, of which Mattei, as head of ENI, had sole control. Its operations became far-flung, and presently grandiose. Cities were built by it in the Po Valley. It negotiated on even terms with the Soviet oil commissariat. Though, being publicly owned, the enterprise was essentially socialist in its property aspect, Mattei as its dominating power holder behaved much as did the elder Rockefeller in the halcyon days when he owned and dominated the Standard Oil Company. Mattei promptly moved to secure a larger share of statist power for the ENI monopoly.

Thanks to party divisions in the Constituent Assembly, the Italian government was weak. The Christian Democrats, who had a majority of the deputies, lost ground and, to save themselves, called the Nenni-led Socialists to join in a coalition. Pietro Nenni considered, probably mistakenly, that opportunities to introduce socialism were greater because of the state-owned monopoly operated by ENI. With Mattei's economic power, Nenni might become master of Italy, making it into a socialist state. But, by then, thanks to a powerful public-relations campaign, to careful handling of patronage, and to his own manipulation of economic power, Mattei, a member of the Christian Democratic party and now one of its leaders, had become a formidable opponent. "Probably no Italian government in the last ten years could have stood against determined Mattei opposition. So great was his influence with his own party, and so popular was he with the left, that only the most courageous or foolhardy of ministers would have tried to pull up on Mattei's reins," observes his biographer, Dow Votaw.[1]

By 1960, Mattei's power had become an Italian political issue. The Liberals, a small splinter party, presently came to hold a crucial balance of voting strength in the divided Chamber of Deputies. As a condition of its continued parliamentary support of the government, it demanded that Mattei be dismissed. On refusal, the Liberal deputies voted against the

1. *The Six-Legged Dog*, p. 111.

Cabinet. It fell—but Mattei stayed. By this time even the Socialists slowly began to oppose him, chiefly because to his economic power he had added substantial and dangerous increments of state power. They feared, probably rightly, that he intended to subvert the government itself. Issue was joined, with Mattei holding a slight edge. A confrontation loomed. Fate or fortune intervened: Mattei was killed in an airplane crash. At the time, he was apparently in a position to hold and extend his political power— as he had already concentrated in himself the vast and growing ENI monopoly economic power. He left no successor and no bureaucratic institution able to create one. The drama ended there.

In more constructive degree, somewhat similar phenomena have occasionally occurred in the United States. Mr. Robert Moses, an extremely able organizer, has spent his active life not only as holder of some formal government offices, but chiefly as simultaneous head of a series of great publicly owned economic enterprises chartered by the State of New York. Of these, five were large; taken together, their facilities constitute a group of immensely profitable partial monopolies financed by tax-exempt revenue bonds. One was the New York Power Authority, disposing of much of the electricity generated from the Niagara and the St. Lawrence rivers. Another was the Triborough Bridge and Tunnel Authority, operating several of the bridges and two of the tunnels which constitute the greatest conduits of traffic between the island of Manhattan and Long Island, Brooklyn, Queens, the Bronx, and Westchester.

Moses, a man of great ability and driving force, conservative in his prejudices, intolerant of opposition, adept at rough-and-tumble infighting, rapidly established himself as a power figure in New York political life. Unsuccessful as a vote getter (he was badly beaten when a candidate for governor of New York in 1935), his power base rested on the success and strength of the state-owned economic enterprises he headed and personally dominated. His patronage, freely used in connection with the New York Legislature and in New York City, was sufficient to assure that the enterprises he operated would be immune from legislative attack. Their charters gave him wide latitude in using the profits from these enterprises for other public works. He decided upon and was able to carry through the building of the Coliseum exhibition hall in New York as an offshoot of the Triborough Bridge and Tunnel Authority—though its connection with that enterprise is remote. His voice became powerful in the party councils of both Republicans and Democrats, and continued so until his retirement in 1967.

More often, economic power holders take a more limited view of themselves. The era of American plutocracy reached its zenith with the election of President William McKinley in 1900. No attempt was made to conceal the fact that he, a rather colorless man, was chosen by a small group of industrial and financial leaders. His secretary of the Treasury was Mark Hanna, a head of the steel industry who overtly represented the combined economic power of the then more or less choate plutocratic group of American banking and industrial magnates. Yet the American plutocrats of the day did not interest themselves greatly in government office. Rather, it seemed, they considered government a convenience whose favors, functions, and power were useful to their operations, but in which they did not care to participate. As I read the history of the time, they sought economic power less to achieve power over the state than to use elements of statist power to assist their then personally owned economic institutions.

Labor leaders of the mid-twentieth century take a similar view. Not many of them seek public office; only occasionally do they become members of party committees. Their main interest in politics is to assure that privileges their organizations have secured through legislation shall not be impaired, and that the operations of their unions shall not be interfered with. This does not prevent them from regular activity in the political area. They steadily support and forward social programs of which they approve, rewarding and punishing politicians and candidates. But thus far they have sought rather to use the state than to be the state. Whether these choices to limit extension of their power will continue as conflicts increasingly compel state intervention in economic affairs remains to be seen. They may feel impelled to put

153

their own men forward as candidates and officeholders; they have never yet done so.

Would their political role continue thus limited if the United States ever became a dictatorship, or brought all functions under a single controlling institution? Or is it the result of "pluralism," under which power, both economic and political, is divided among many institutions? It is impossible to tell. Mattei demonstrated that economic power could readily be made an avenue toward political power; James Hoffa, that control of a powerful union might excite desire for political power as well. The triggers that release unlimited ambition in men are still unknown. The late Sinclair Lewis, in *It Can't Happen Here*, described the rise of an imagined American fascist leader. Historically, nevertheless, economic power holding has not yet significantly released that ambition in the United States—and relatively rarely anywhere else.

Latin-American experience provides interesting and confirmatory comparison. Despite current shibboleth-stereotypes, the great landed oligarchs (few great Latin-American industrialists have yet emerged) have not as a rule sought to become dictators. They do seek to maintain their positions, their privileges, their tax exemptions. For that purpose, they do seek to influence political power holders, to assure that they will be let alone in their entrenched economic positions. By contrast, instances are many in which Latin-American army officers or government officials have sought not only to seize the state, but also to levy tribute on their country's economic institutions.

While the propensity of economic power holders to strive for total political power is rather less than the propensity of political leaders to seize economic power, politicians also tend not to rush into economic power. In the United States certainly, politicians' motivations tend to be limited by practical considerations. The United States is so vast, its economic institutions so complex, and their techniques so various that economic power holding is a hazardous adventure for political figures. To attempt control of General Electric or Du Pont, of United States Steel or General Motors, or to control and become responsible for the great labor unions is, therefore, politically unattractive. Extreme conditions calling for remedy may, and occasionally do, require that such concerns be brought into line or forced to conform to certain rules. Running them, however, is a job most sane American politicians seek to avoid.

I recall a fantastic night in March, 1933. A small working committee of which I was informal secretary was endeavoring to draw up a plan for reopening American banks, many of which were bankrupt and all of which were closed. A suggestion was made that the United States government take them over and at once reopen them as government institutions—thereafter operating all banks as publicly owned instrumentalities. I said I had no theoretical objection but I did not see that the incoming Roosevelt administration had the men, staff, organization, or expertise requisite to run them if we did take over. Nor was it necessary to make the attempt. It was better to keep them as they were, set up standards for their functioning, and assure that they conformed.

Politicians can run government. Bankers can run financial institutions. Under clear ground rules, economic organizations can serve the public and the state. Anyone attempting to be at one and the same time politician and banker or industrialist would likely fail at both. Pluralism does more than divide power. It divides functions as well, reducing power burdens to sustainable limits. Occasionally, personal ambition and energy—or anarchic circumstances—lead men to combine functions, placing themselves upon a pinnacle. Whereupon, implacably, the differing imperatives of the two forms of power undermine their position.

I

Prologue in History—the Bloody Dialogue

1. Competing Economic Myths

More ink has been spilled—and more blood shed—in the twentieth century over economic power than for any other single concept.

To some, discussion of economic power seems repulsively dull; to others, a fighting issue; to still others, a hopeless attempt to grapple with an incomprehensible fact of modern life. In part, perhaps, this last attitude results from the false assumption that economic power is an inscrutable mystery.

This thought has been shared not only by laymen, but also by first-rate scholars. A classic study in political science, *The Modern State*, by my old friend Robert M. MacIver, comes close to accepting this view. He asserts that political power is formally superior, but he believes that economic power in turn asserts its sovereign claims, saying: "Be off with you, my boy, and play with your caucuses and leading articles and historic parties and great leaders and burning questions and the rest of your toys. I am going back to my counting-house to pay the piper and call the tune." [1] For, he says, "Economic power is swift and untrammelled, spontaneous and endlessly variable. . . . Economic power can act at the nearest centre and turn wherever it will. . . . The economic network covers the earth with its unbroken strands, woven most thickly where civilization is most advanced." [2] Inevitably locked with the political state, economic power can never be made to coexist with political power; it rides through inequality to new inequality. Neither the economic order nor the political order can ignore the other, but "Economic power has many weapons and political power has few. Political power must fight in the open, economic power has the advantage of secrecy. Economic power, once established, has a single and definite aim, political power is composite and easily divided. Economic power can scarcely be corrupted, because what it seeks it seeks only for itself, because also there are scarcely any means of corruption but its own." [3]

This was written in 1926, before the analytic study of economic institutions—corporations, banks, labor unions, money and credit systems—had really begun. Typical of that period was the assumption that economic power was a pervasive abstraction. To struggle with it was a labor of Hercules. Like the nine-headed Hydra fought by Hercules, if one head was cut off, two more at once appeared. The mystery of economic power came, essentially, from the conception of the "market" as a hidden but all-powerful hand determining wages, prices, personal influence, interest rates, formation of capital, and its points of application.

The reality behind this was the fact of small-scale production and distribution, carried out by many millions of individuals and

1. New York, Oxford University Press, 1926, revised edition, 1955, p. 291.
2. *Ibid.*, p. 294.
3. *Ibid.*, p. 302.

small enterprise. Taken together, they created economic conditions, but no organization controlled them. These enterprisers were said to form a "class." Naïvely, it was assumed that the "class" had power, though the fact was that practically everyone in it was himself powerless. Forty years later, few would accept this view. No longer is economic power regarded as mysterious —any more than we accept forces of weather as mysterious, though they are not yet subject to control. Economists have observed, classified, and related the phenomena of economic power, just as phenomena in physics and everything else have been observed and analyzed. John Maynard Keynes began to analyze money, savings, and unemployment in 1930. I undertook examination of the modern corporation and published an analysis in 1932. The Federal Reserve Board had painstakingly sought to examine money and credit since 1914. It was beginning to publish discoveries and practical applications. President Franklin Roosevelt gave impetus to a more intense collection of statistics. Statistics are the raw material of economic analysis, and the United States now has as good a statistical system (despite imperfections) as any in the world.

In result, economic power began to lose the mysterious position assigned it in the closing period of the nineteenth century and the three opening decades of the twentieth. True, old emotions carried forward. They continue in some measure today. The pictures drawn by Proudhon in 1846, by Marx in 1867, and by Lenin and other Communist writers as the nineteenth century closed continued to dominate political thinking. Yet scientific attack chipped away at these conceptions, just as medical science was exploding the notion that plagues of smallpox and typhus were uncontrollable misfortunes sent by Heaven to chastise the human race.

Perhaps one myth—the theory of "class power"—has lasted longer. It still stalks the political scene. It is perpetuated in the volumes of contemporary sociologists such as the late C. Wright Mills. Certainly it is the main theoretical theme (though I think not the practical driving force) behind the revolutionary wars raging or threatening today in Vietnam, Laos, Cambodia, and Burma, and in fateful sproutings of guerrilla operations in Cuba and Latin America. Analyzed, as we have seen, there is no such thing as "class" power. Power, including economic power, is personal. Probably more progress has been made—up to a point —in controlling economic power than in any field but that of control of disease through medical science. Our grandchildren are likely to wonder why the dispute—just as we today blankly wonder why uncounted thousands of men in the late Roman Empire had to die in Monophysite wars, caused by religious controversy over whether God and Christ were of "one substance" or of "similar substance."

In ultimate analysis, economic organization deals with men's actual wants. Men want what they do want, not what some external force or influence thinks they ought to want. Included in the problem, therefore, are conflicts between the wants of some and those of others. They proceed from the inside of men's heads as well as from the needs of their bodies. Every man, woman, and child has the last word not on what he gets, but on what he wants or at least what he wants most. There is a high element of individuality in the business. Emotions can, of course, be stimulated. Tastes perhaps can be created. Psychologists can suggest; advertisers can induce; propagandists can manipulate an individual's desires—within limits, but only within limits. If there is mystery, it lies in human personality. There, science is groping. The mystery of the desires of the individual mind and heart and soul is quite different from the mystery of blind economic force. The former remains; the latter has begun to disappear.

We certainly do not now know everything about economics or its operation, or the power that can be derived from it. But it is safe to say that, forty years after Robert MacIver's classic observation, economic science has definitely placed economic power in a relation subordinate to political power. In substantial measure, it has reduced economic organization and its processes to the status of a tool. Strong and developed states use it. Mysterious, uncontrollable economic force is today feared, hated, appeased, or worshiped chiefly in those parts of the world we call "underdeveloped"—where political power is weak, unsophisticated, incompetent, or ill-trained.

What remains is a lingering, though violent, dispute resulting from obsolete theories of economic power, surviving after economic power itself has lost its magic. So-called religious wars survived long after men had learned that the Catholic church could coexist with Protestantism. The last decade of the Thirty Years' War (it ended in 1648) was a conflict of straight national impetus, though ancient theories were invoked as propaganda, when needed, by one or the other side.

2. The Bloody Dialogue

Drama reaches twentieth-century height in this conflict of theories of economic life. Wars going forward in 1969 have their overt source in that conflict. They equal in intensity and have exceeded in geographic scope the sixteenth- and seventeenth-century religious wars. Men fight to the death in Southeast Asia, in Latin America, in Central Africa because of this struggle over theory; hundreds of men monthly die and uncounted thousands rot in prisons and concentration camps in China, Cuba, mid-Europe, and (fortunately in declining degree) in the Soviet Union. "Wars of liberation," armed and maintained by the two principal Communist powers, are planned, organized, financed, and fought precisely on the basis of this conflict.

Theory rather than human well-being lies at the stated root of these struggles. In a number of cases—notably in Cuba—the actual human situation was better before than after the new regime imposed as a result. Certainly Czechs were better off before Soviet troops and agents compelled their highly prosperous and developed country into the Stalinist Moscow complex. Principle, not pragmatic fact, was the stated issue. The twentieth-century struggle rapidly overpassed the quarrels of social theorists and became bloodstained beyond belief. It continues today. Its se-

161

quence and effects jeopardize the peace of the world; it may even (though I think it will not) trigger the nuclear holocaust whose possibility darkens the brightest day.

Why this theoretical struggle? Its history would fill a library; we will merely glance at its salient points.

Put crudely, economic power resides in the hands of a man or men heading some organization able to stand between other people and resources, goods, or services they want or need. Such an organization can then collect a "price" from those getting and enjoying them. The process is at least as old as antiquity. Visitors to Istanbul are shown the island in the Bosporus said to have been occupied by the Greek Alcibiades; according to legend, he and predecessor pirates charged tolls to merchant ships passing through the narrow strait that leads to the Black Sea. In Europe, the heights overlooking the Rhine River are dotted with ruined fortresses from which robber barons once levied tribute on passing river commerce. Economic power in these cases was a result of military power. Exactly similar use of force is made by contemporary racketeers. A not-too-impressive gangster sends word to a businessman that his delivery trucks will be dynamited or his drivers beaten unless he pays. A fig leaf of disguise may be added—payment may be made for "guards" or "public relations," or by contract with a racketeering "labor union."

Later in history the same process included rendering by the toll collector of a really useful service. Many feudal lords did so. One such lived near Marburg in Germany, where a hill in the midst of a small valley is crowned by a fort. In the thirteenth century, a nobleman and his family, with some pretension to right, had occupied the hill, built the castle (in modernized version it still exists), and maintained a mobile group of armed men. He and his successors kept peace—of a sort—in the valley plain. They excluded outsiders; they could make it militarily difficult or expensive for raiding armies or neighboring lords to invade. They could guarantee a degree of security, so that farmers and peasants who sowed a crop had some assurance of reaping it. They could provide market places where merchants could safely sell their wares. They offered a degree of police protection and outside defense. It was worth its price and was paid for.

This was the economic content of "lordship" under the feudal system. The count or princeling considered that he had "lordship" (not "ownership") of the land. This meant, chiefly, that he could collect feudal dues, tithes, market charges, and crop rents from the occupants. In return, he gave a degree of protection. Perhaps from the very beginning (no one quite knows) the relationship between him and his vassals, sublandholders, peasants, or serfs was not based on consent. Neither he nor they made a "contract." He was there. They were there. He had military force; they had to make their living from the land. The arrangement crystallized. Lordship passed from the count to his son by inheritance. Peasant or farmer landholdings also passed from occupant to son—though a fee had to be paid to the lord to enter the inheritance. In time, ownership of real estate evolved out of this arrangement.

Until the nineteenth-century Industrial Revolution, production was primarily agricultural. Land was the chief productive property. Right to land—at first feudal, later private—gave its holder or owner the capacity and right to grow crops and sell them, just as ownership of a plant gives capacity and right to a corporation to weave cloth or manufacture machine tools and sell the product.

Some lands were more valuable than others because they had desirable products underneath. That tiny German valley mentioned earlier had an excellent slate quarry, useful for building material, and most of the houses were constructed of it. A Spanish valley, first owned by the Romans, had mercury, and its Rio Tinto mine in time became, and now is, private property. It has floated down the stream of history even to the present. But mining involves more than standing on top of the land and charging a toll. Organization and labor of some kind are required to dig out and make the product useful and salable. The supplier of that organization—the "capitalist"—presently emerged in possession of the production. He could charge a "price."

Later, as machines began to be developed, higher investments of capital were needed. Iron for machines had to be brought from the earth; a charge was made for that. It had to be manufactured into steel; a charge had to be made for that. It had to be delivered to the machine toolmakers, who fabricated tools from the most primitive to the most intricate, like today's computers. They also charged. The whole price system came into existence—less as a matter of racketeering than as a matter of exchange. Also, the growing necessity for capital brought a new element. The lord, the landowner, frequently did not have the means. He had to go to money men, to borrow, to sell participation, or to sell out altogether. In the process, a theoretical debate emerged, ancestor of the bloody struggle of today.

At bottom, the question was ethical. Who was entitled to the flow of wealth emerging from this system? "I am," said the owner of the mine, the factory, the plant. "I am," said the owner of any money gathered and loaned to or invested in these plants. "I am," at long last said the laborers—or at least someone claiming to speak on their behalf.

Lenders did not claim to own, but claimed the right to levy a charge called "interest." Owners claimed the right to charge a price for whatever they produced and the services they rendered. Anything over their current cost was "profit." "This I own," they said. Meanwhile, theorists got into the act. For one thing, the Catholic church in medieval times took jurisdiction and proclaimed an ethical doctrine. It made a number of points.

First, it said that "interest"—a charge for having provided money—was not only wrong but also sinful, the sin of usury. Interest was therefore outlawed by ecclesiastical law. Priests required their parishioners to confess receiving it as a sin, and imposed penance. A bishop, if he seriously cared, could hale the lender before an ecclesiastical court and punish him.

The "perfect knight" of the twelfth century was Sir William Marshall. He served under Henry II of England, fought Henry's son, Richard Coeur de Lion, when he revolted against his father, then served Richard after Henry's death. He was the hero of contemporary chivalry. A story is told about him. Riding through a forest, he discovered a boy and girl eloping. The elopement was itself irregular, but Sir William was accustomed to love affairs.

He offered them a lift. As they traveled together, he asked what they expected to live on. A horrid fact emerged. The boy had a certain amount of money and intended to lend it out at interest. Marshall at once withdrew his friendship. Helping a couple of eloping lovers was fair enough. But assisting a usurer, never! He turned them over to the nearest troops and went on his knightly way. That was the medieval view of moneylending.

Profits, gained by selling goods or services at a price, were different. They were allowed, without question. Merchant traders had been buying or manufacturing goods, taking them to markets, and selling them at a profit since the beginning of time. Outlawing them was impossible—nor did the church desire to do so. Instead, the church worked out a doctrine of "just price," considering it a sin to overcharge. The idea may have originated at the parish level. Most priests had seen bad crop years, and had seen men buy up food crops and hold them till famine impended. Then, of course, the "forestalling" merchant could collect a price dictated by hunger. Probably the doctrine was rarely effective. Price control at any time or under any theory is not easy—as Americans found out when prices were fixed in World War I and again in World War II. The "just price," it must be noted, did not exclude a profit—that was assumed—but there was an undefined limit beyond which the transaction was considered a sinful "enormity" in the opinion of the ecclesiastical authorities.

But the church never did touch the question of charges imposed on land—what today we call "rents." Feudal lords imposed these charges and continued to collect them when they ceased being political officeholders and became mere owners. The Catholic church itself had a feudal position: it was lord of a great many lands; it supported the system, and its churches and abbeys were supported by it. Of the three principal sources by which wealth is accumulated—interest, profits, rents—ecclesiastical law outlawed one—interest—vaguely attempted to regulate the second—price and profit—but did not touch the third—land rent.

Nor did it touch the companion question: pay for labor. Aside from a general theory that the laborer was worthy of his hire, the church left the question pretty much alone. Vaguely it as-

165

sumed that a laborer was paid about what he was worth as he
went along, and few questions were asked. Meanwhile, wealth
accumulated, as it has done pretty much throughout history. In
considerable measure, it followed and was the fruit of sheer military or political power. Kings, nobles, military leaders, captains
could take, could collect, could hold, and could keep because, and
as long as, they had power or were part of the power apparatus of
some major or minor ruler.

Came the religious wars, Protestantism, and abandonment of
ecclesiastical rule. Wealth could be accumulated without restraint.
Thence emerged the nineteenth-century revolution and the explosion of a new doctrine. Foreshadowed by Proudhon's savage
remark, "Property is theft," it was elaborated by Karl Marx, who
produced a theory. Everything in this world not put there by
nature must have been developed directly or ultimately out of the
labor of man. Therefore, Marx considered, all wealth was created
by laborers, past and present. Fundamentally, it belonged to the
laborers of this generation, as heirs of past generations of workers, going back to the beginning of time.

Obviously wealth was not in the hands of past laborers—they
were dead—and contemporary labor certainly did not possess it.
As Marx presented the question, it was simple enough. Throughout ages, economic power holders had paid laborers less than the
value their labor had created. That "surplus" value had been, was
being, taken from them and piled up as accumulated wealth in
the hands of very few. The property owner renting his land, hiring
out his money at interest, or owning plants and instruments of
production had acquired power to employ labor, paying less
than it produced, and, because he was owner, selling the product
for a greater price. The surplus value he was taking to himself.
He was in effect robbing the laborer-producer of this wealth of
part of his product.

So far Marx was talking economics. The other prong of his
doctrine was more direct and bitter. He considered the owners,
the capitalists, directly and personally responsible for the poverty of labor. It was to the interest of the capitalist-employer to
pay as little to the laborer as he could, thereby increasing the

surplus value he could pocket. This was, indeed, not far from the fact. When Marx was writing *Das Kapital* a century ago, child-labor conditions in England were as cruel, outrageous, and indefensible as one can readily imagine. Satisfactory answer never has been written, or can be written, to Marx's chapters documenting the hideous conditions in England in 1865 and 1866. He needed merely to quote the contemporary descriptions and the contemporary arguments for retaining them written by highly respectable British authors. His conclusion was that the individuals owning capital were guilty of direct robbery, and that these men connived at the continual creation of overpopulation so that starvation wages could always be paid. Deaths by starvation in London were in fact common; degradation of women and children was unlimited. Capital, Marx concluded, was "the capitalized blood of children"; it "comes dripping from head to foot, from every pore, as blood and dirt."

Meanwhile, Britain and other countries were growing richer and "along with the constantly diminishing number of the magnates of capital, who usurp and monopolise all advantages of this process of transformation, grows the mass of misery, oppression, slavery, degradation, exploitation." He prophesied that the system would collapse of its own internal weight. Particularly, he considered that literal bloodguilt rested on the heads of the bourgeois—a tiny, diminishing class. He advocated a war to root out and destroy that class—and its replacement by a Communist state, to administer for the benefit of the "people" all the economic processes previously carried on by these people.

In November, 1917, came news of the Communist *coup d'état* in Russia. Lenin, nurtured on Marx, had elaborated in Machiavellian style a technique of revolution and argued the need of destroying the capitalist classes. By accident of war and history, the first Communist government had come into power, not in a highly capitalist country (Marx thought it would come first in Germany), but in Russia, which had not yet effectively escaped from medieval feudalism. The Leninist government was faced with the task, not of liquidating a capitalist society, but of destroying an emperor, a court, a great number of semifeudal noblemen and boyars, and some rudiments of a capitalist industrial system barely getting under way. While doing that, Lenin made no bones about his mission to exterminate capitalism everywhere in the world; the Soviet Union was to be merely a beginning. But he, differing with Trotsky, who wished a general campaign for world revolution, believed Communism could maintain itself in Russia while continuously working outward, and was cautious about foreign adventure.

In 1922, Lenin was felled by a paralytic stroke. Presently he discovered Stalin quietly gathering to himself the reins of power; and Stalin, he believed, had a dangerous mania for unlimited conquest. From his deathbed he endeavored to mobilize the machinery of the Communist party and its governing committees against Stalin. A second, followed by a third, stroke reduced him to comparative impotence. His efforts failed—in any case, they were cut short by his death. At once Stalin seized the power of the Soviet state. Stalin's doctrine—like the doctrine of the Chinese Communist government today—amounted virtually to assumption that a state of indirect war existed between the Soviet Union and all non-Communist countries. They were, by hypothesis, imperialist, colonialist, and warmongering aggressors. Resources should be directed toward those countries where an "indirect war" could most easily produce victory and Communist revolution. Particular target countries should be selected against which indirect wars should be actively prosecuted. These became in due course the "wars of liberation" so widely heralded in Soviet communiqués in 1967. By "liberation" is meant, of course, destruction in them of any system other than a Communist one, with attendant liquidation by death, exile, imprisonment, or other means of all property owners—"capitalists"—and their children. One aim is to prevent the individuals thus liquidated from attempting by counterrevolution to overthrow the Communist regimes. Another is punishment for their bloodguilt in having derived benefit from the accumulated surplus value of production earlier robbed from workers and peasants, and for having thereby caused the degradation, starvation, and degeneration of uncounted proletarians.

This is the direct relation of our mid-twentieth-century warfare to the theory of economic power.

Lenin, Stalin, and Marx are dead. Meantime, in America and increasingly in Europe the "capitalist system," as it is still sometimes called, has come to bear only historical relation to the capitalism of a century ago. A new system has been developed in which the prosperity, if possible the wealth, of the laboring class is an almost essential precondition to the growing wealth of a country. The United States does not prosper if only the rich grow richer. It can thrive only as poverty is progressively abolished. To Marx, a degraded working class living in misery meant cheaper employees for the capitalist. To contemporary American corporations, underpaid and starved labor means a shortage of customers to buy motorcars, television sets, major and minor luxuries, not to mention the necessities of life. It would have been impossible to convince Marx of that; it is impossible to convince a doctrinaire, religiously inspired Communist of as much today. Yet in fact the interest of mass employers and employing organizations now is to have highly paid workers at all levels. In contemporary America, bankbooks as well as heartstrings suffer if there are great areas of unemployment and poverty.

Still less, perhaps, could nineteenth-century revolutionaries understand a later twentieth-century phenomenon for which corporations are directly responsible: the splitting of "property" into two levels. The new system *simultaneously* permits accumulation of physical property and widening dispersion of wealth. The progressive accumulation of property which Marx foresaw has indeed taken place beyond his wildest forecast—but in the hands of corporations, not individuals. At the same time, the wealth resulting from these accumulated hundreds of billions of dollars' worth of aggregated plants, machines, assets, mines, materials, and so forth has been fragmented and represented by many billions of shares of stock. These shares have been increasingly (though still quite inadequately) disseminated throughout an entire population. There were some 26,000,000 shareholders in the United States in 1969; the number steadily grows. Few of us would endeavor to draw a picture of the distribution of wealth in the United States in the year 2000. Yet it is likely that the number of shareholders will approach, if it does not overpass, 60,000,000, and many millions more will share through devices of distribution such as pension funds. Accepting the theory that "surplus value" wrung from labor is the source of all property, Marx could hardly have foreseen the increasing distribution of accumulated wealth through the device of the modern corporation, into pension funds, precisely to the workers by whose ancestors and present efforts it was produced. Marxian theory, converted now into a doctrinaire religion, thus is becoming fantastically obsolete.

One must concede that the process of accumulating capital throughout the nineteenth and early twentieth centuries had a vast content of cruelty and horror. Defense against Marx's assertion of bloodguilt can only be that few people took the time either to observe or, observing, to comprehend the system. Against that must be set the fact that year by year the record of Communist regimes is little or no better. The remedy prescribed and put into effect by Lenin in the Soviet Union, by Mao Tse-tung in China, by Castro in Cuba was seizure of all property and productive systems by the state—that is, take-over of economic power in all forms by government—whereupon the government at once appropriated all the "surplus value" it could secure and accumulated it as military establishment and state-owned capital. Government, it should be noted, was conceived here as an assumedly benevolent dictatorship, acting on behalf of the proletariat.

Economic power was accordingly placed in the hands of the same individuals who exercised political and military power. The result of that has been a period as bloody, terrible, and hideous as are Marx's descriptions of the capitalist system—if anything, perhaps slightly worse on the ethical side, because cruelties were consciously and intentionally inflicted. The "capitalist" or "bourgeois" classes found guilty by Marx were in considerable measure unconscious of their participation. Few, if any, among them considered they were in any position to change the system.

On the other hand, killing, imprisonment, cruelty, imposition of economic hardship, and stirring up of wars were conscious and deliberate policies of most Communist governments organized after 1917. Stalin had no hesitation whatever in starving 5,000,-000 Ukrainian peasants to death because they resisted his agricultural policy. In his purges of 1936–1938, hundreds of thousands of entirely innocent Soviet citizens were seized, tried, and exiled or executed in a meaningless counterrevolutionary terror. When Khrushchev succeeded to power on Stalin's death, there were probably 12,000,000 prisoners in Russian jails and concentration camps—and most of them had been there a long time. (To his credit, he released many, perhaps most, of them.) The Chinese Communists took power in 1950 and likewise fell to liquidating their opponents. The Peking government acknowledges the killing of over 1,000,000; outside students believe the number could be multiplied several times. A Communist government succeeded to power in Cuba in 1959. The dead still cannot be counted; but in a country of 8,000,000 they run into many tens of thousands. A half-million refugees and exiles from that unhappy country are presently in the United States; and it is currently reported that twenty thousand more are presently in Cuban jails. Clearly, if balance must be struck between the "capitalist" systems as they were in 1917, and have evolved since, and the Communist systems as they began in 1917, and have since evolved, the dishonors are at least even.

It is, to be sure, no defense for the old system to say to the new, "You are another." But the balance sheet does suggest that a country defending itself against having a new system imposed on it is neither irrational nor immoral. "Wars of liberation" are declared against other countries because they have failed to redistribute economic power as Marxian theory dictated. But Marxian organization seems not to prove more kindly, more evolutionary, more capable of innovation, freer, than the old. Economic power united to political and military power has not increased production sufficiently to permit much assistance to proletarian classes; it has not resolved questions of production. There has been little to distribute.

As in the old sixteenth- and seventeenth-century religious wars, Communist empires claim the right by guerrilla and military force to compel other countries to take over economic power and place it in the hands of politicians. Resistance to a "war of liberation" by the country involved, or by anyone disposed to assist it, is cried down by Communist propaganda and by intellectual fellow travelers as positive criminal aggression. Factually, "wars of liberation" have become as meaningless, as outrageous, and, to be blunt, as imperialist as were the campaigns in the religious wars. Those ended only because Europe, wounded, disgusted, having lost twenty-five per cent of its entire population, stopped in 1648 in sheer exhaustion.

Understanding of these two currents of contemporary history is indispensable in this prologue to our study of economic power. They result from the rise of one economic system in time rationalized as "capitalism," its challenge by a later system rationalized as "Communism," and struggles continuing today arising from rivalry between power groups speaking in the name of one or the other.

Essentially, both are obsolete.

This is scant comfort for those who lived in degradation and squalor or died in starvation or distress in the industrial towns of England and Europe, the stockyards of Chicago, the ghettos of Harlem, or the rural slums of Mississippi. Still less is it consolation for those who died in civil wars, concentration camps, or imposed squalor under the regimes of Joseph Stalin, Mao Tse-tung, and their disciples in smaller countries. Our task must be to understand economic power—its capacity to benefit as well as degrade, its honorable use, the danger of its abuse, the possibilities of its control. Neither classic capitalism nor the newer but aging Communism wrestled with this problem. Economic power existed; men dominant in both systems wanted it for themselves. In both camps, top men insisted that with economic power in their hands, their peoples would be better off—capitalist advocates claiming automatically beneficial, though inscrutable, workings of free-market processes; Communist zealots urging the benefits of the benevolently controlled designs of doctrinaire dictatorship. Both advocates were self-interested: capitalists wished to keep their property; Communists intended to keep their power. Both were logical.

Neither was right. Neither group knew enough to deal with the tasks it had set itself. Effective understanding of economic power, rudimentary even now, came somewhat later.

II

Taming the Market Gods

1. Assault on the Market

In 1874, John Richard Green published his *Short History of the English People*. He chronicled the rise of the younger Pitt just as steam was developed as a source of energy. He noted that the combination of steam with machinery had enabled Britain to become the greatest manufacturing country in the world, even during the Napoleonic Wars. Capacity to deal with the new currents of production and trade required, Green observes,

a knowledge of the laws of wealth which would have been impossible at an earlier time. But it had become possible in the days of Pitt. If books are to be measured by the effect which they have produced on the fortunes of mankind, the "Wealth of Nations" must rank among the greatest of books. Its author was Adam Smith, an Oxford scholar and a Professor at Glasgow. Labor, he contended, was the one source of wealth and it was by freedom of labor, by suffering the worker to pursue his own interest in his own way, that the public wealth would best be promoted. Any attempt to force labor into artificial channels, to chart by laws the course of commerce, to promote special branches of industry in particular countries or to fix the character of the intercourse between one country and another is not only a wrong to the worker or the nation but actually hurtful to the wealth of the state.[1]

The quotation tells as much about the England of 1870 as about the England of the second Pitt. The doctrine called for letting production, banking, and trade severely alone. Markets, in the stilted phrase of the day, effected the "optimal allocation of resources." The doctrine became dogma. It remained so through the second decade of the twentieth century; it still is revered in many quarters today. Senator Barry Goldwater became a candidate for the presidency of the United States in 1964 on a platform urging return to these principles. His ablest adviser was Professor Milton Friedman, of the Department of Economics at the University of Chicago, a school devoted to the now classic teachings of Adam Smith and John Stuart Mill. Goldwater's staggering defeat at the polls made clear that public opinion did not agree. Not many Americans, it seemed, wished to return to the rule of the market gods—if, indeed, those gods had ever really existed. It was the fate of the mid-twentieth century to dethrone the market gods in their turn; or, at least, to prove that their mystical power could be tamed. They are not under control today, though the fact of their eventual control now lies within the foreseeable future.

2. Scientific Technique—Economic Science

Two converging currents were responsible for the dethronement of the market gods.

1. Third edition, New York, American Book Company, 1911, pp. 792–793.

Scientific and technical advance was the first. In the century from 1826 to 1926 techniques emerged capable of increasing production faster than it could be distributed by the market system. Steam, and, later, electricity, turned wheels. Mechanical contrivances worked looms, cast and fabricated metal, stamped, turned, and assembled all manner of goods. Advances in chemistry were responsible for the manufacture of fertilizer; the production of goods multiplied. Before 1826, men lived, pretty much, by the product of sun, rain, and earth on land worked with human or animal muscles. In the century following the so-called "Industrial Revolution," muscle power became increasingly obsolete as energy was drawn from material found in the earth's crust. The twentieth century, probably about 1925, witnessed the crossing of a vast economic watershed. Behind lay a time when men and their forms of social organization were limited and conditioned by the amount of goods they could produce. Ahead, on the other side of the divide, human affairs were to be conditioned by the capacity of men and social organization to distribute the product of an advanced civilization that could, more or less at will, produce more of anything, at any time, than old-style markets were able to distribute. A phrase was coined describing the new phase—it is ascribed to Professor Rexford Guy Tugwell—"the economy of abundance."

All countries, all civilizations, did not and do not attain this technical ability. The gulf between the "have" and the "have-not" nations at bottom is based on their respective capacities to produce—though this is another story. For our purpose, it is enough to point out that capacity to increase production (for whatever reason) to any desired level knocked one prop out from under the market system. That system relied on the notion that the "market" was the best, indeed the only effective, means for distributing what product there was. It went to the human beings who could buy it.

But if power in some fashion can push up production and the supply of goods more or less at will, the case is different. When more food, clothing, shelter, and luxuries could be produced than market economics would absorb, the result was called a "surplus." Yet it was obviously an artificial surplus. Plenty of men and women clearly needed or wanted the product; but for immense numbers, the market system simply did not provide for their paying for and getting it. Enduring privation, suffering, hunger is one thing when there is no known way of providing products needed for their alleviation. Acceptance in the face of actual or readily available plenty is quite another; in fact, such acceptance is essentially irrational. More than irrational, it is dangerous, for under it some sort of social explosion becomes inevitable.

A second, no less powerful, current moved against the market gods in another direction. In classic fashion, human beings asked questions of the system. So, one may imagine, the legendary Prometheus questioned control over fire by the inscrutable Zeus. So, as we noted, Job asked questions of God. Questions in time dictate answers, and the twentieth century began to provide a few.

Plenty of abuse had been hurled against the market gods long before the quiet questioning of scientists. By the mid-nineteenth century, a current of European thought had observed their inhumanities. In 1848, Marx wrote the *Communist Manifesto*. This includes many ideas, but essentially it was not a question; it was a curse. As curses frequently do, it attracted romantics. It was not analytic; it damned the whole system. Marx's great disciple, Lenin, expanded the curse, while developing techniques for the system's overthrow. Like Proudhon and Marx, he localized the devils of the false gods—they were the owners of productive property, "bourgeois," or "capitalists." For half a century, Marx documented the horrors produced by the market system and its growing use or abuse of machinery and technical tools. Lenin elaborated methods of revolution. Between them, they proposed a new god—the "people," conceived by them as the proletariat—in whose sacred name their intended revolution would seize all productive property—indeed, all property of any kind—and would thereupon create a new system of production and distribution based not on markets but on a rationalized system imposed by political power.

Their theory did not study with great care the techniques and underlying problems involved in both parts of the system.

177

Marxians were, in fact, proposing a reversion. They were going back to the feudal economics of force. A dictator—in the name of the abstract "people"—would produce and distribute according to decrees he would lay down. It was assumed that the new regime would automatically take over and operate the technical and productive capacities developed by the market system, while its fiat would cause distribution according to a system it would work out. Force would compel, if enthusiasm did not motivate, both processes.

That the system rested on force is scarcely open to doubt. The Leninist handbook—and Marxist-Leninist doctrine today—explains that market civilizations must be taken over by violence. Absent blood and violence, they contend, no revolution is real. Jan Librach, in *The Rise of the Soviet Empire* (1966), documents the doctrine.[2]

Attack on the market gods is one thing. Taming them, using what they have to offer, is another. That current flowed strongly over a long period in England and the United States, bringing about an intellectual break-through in the decade from 1930 to

2. After destruction of all market institutions and, with them, the endless personal associations built on commerce and ownership—so it was thought— the nonmarket system of production and distribution based on the fiat of the political leaders and transmitted through institutions responding to their will could be made successful. The fact that market systems grow up in response to desires and wants of people did not, at least in early Communist phrase, matter very much. Rather rapidly, they learned. Considerable use of markets is made in the Soviet Union now. A large proportion of food reaches city consumers through quite conventional market processes, being produced by private operation.

I was in Venezuela in 1963 when President Rómulo Betancourt was making effective the great reform that today is transforming Venezuela, steadily attacking and alleviating area after area of its former misery. He was under political and paramilitary attack from the Marxist-Leninists the while. He was not killing; he was not plundering; he was not shooting landowners whose holdings produced food and goods. He was not expropriating foreign oil companies. He was merely taking advantage of this production (and increasing it by using his state) and setting up purchasing power so that product could flow toward need. Therefore, said his Communist enemies, his revolution was not "valid." Because he was using the economics of assent and not the economics of force, the most effective economic statesman of Latin America fell under the Communist curse.

1940. Its development is worth a book in itself. We merely indicate the salient lines of its emergence. Its full scope has not yet been attained. Combined with the technological explosion, the results of it suggest that channeling economic forces, rather than forcing men into arbitrary patterns, is the wave of the immediate future.

History was changed by this scholarly break-through in theoretical economic science. It came unheralded. No spectacular theories comparable to those in physics of Max Planck, Niels Bohr, and Albert Einstein indicated the transformation of economics from a speculative set of assumptions to empirically tested conclusions. No climax like the atomic bomb focused world attention. Yet since 1930 the face of the world has been altered by the realization that the supposedly uncontrollable processes of market economics could, in some measure, be guided and directed, stimulated or retarded. Possibility was opened that in another generation organized society can offer most human beings a tolerable level of life—so far as this can be attained by giving them enough goods and services to provide moderate comfort. Whether human beings will know what to do with this power when they have it is a different problem. No economic system can do more than provide materials for life, leaving to individuals and their social organization to build mediocrity or greatness, splendor or horror, on this material base. The change will offer the opportunity for men and women to make of life what they will. Their choice will be determined, not by economics, but by philosophy, religion, art, and morals.

Effective assault on the market gods began, typically, in scholars' studies. It is difficult to assign credit to any one man. Most scientific and scholarly break-throughs (even when an individual is named as a hero) result from the patient work of a good many men, working separately. After them come individuals who push thinking to the point of scientific discovery. Three men, out of many, may be mentioned here.

Thorstein Veblen, an American of Scandinavian origin, perhaps was the scholar who most energized varying speculations about market economics, setting up a highly sensitive field of intellectual action. A strange man, no less angry than Marx at the cruelties, wastes, and, indeed, horrors of the market economic system, he drove at the underlying motives and processes that seemed to make it work. He foresaw the effects and potentials of the technical revolution, though it was only beginning in the two decades (1900–1920) of his best work. He dreamed of a revolution based not on force, but on technocracy. If technicians ruled the economy, their capacity to organize distribution could produce results as beneficial as their capacity to organize production. He wondered about motives—why flamboyant wealth (he called it "conspicuous waste") was considered desirable and its attainment the reward of success. He suggested that, if the framework of possible economic organization was the amount of product, we ought to know something about national income. If social justice depended on distribution of income, we ought to know who got that income and why. If continuous increase in production were needed (and it was) and if this depended on capital, we ought to know where, how, and by whom capital was formed. In his moody, quarrelsome, sometimes even paranoid intensity, he antagonized everyone even as he fractured barriers of economic thought.[3]

Among his pupils was Wesley Clair Mitchell, later to become master toolmaker of economic analysis, professor at Columbia University, and, in 1922, organizer of the National Bureau of Economic Research. Departing from the then standard academic pattern, Mitchell endeavored to develop precise measurements. Much of what we now know about the economic system is the product of his workshop. Earlier contemporary scholars, notably Professor Frank Taussig, of Harvard, had refined the theories of market economy developed first by Adam Smith, then by David Ricardo, given philosophical underpinning by John Stuart Mill, and elaborated by Alfred Marshall. Mitchell's preoccupation, on the other hand, was with statistical events. What had been produced —of goods, services, or both? What prices had the market economy

3. See J. S. Gambs, *Beyond Supply and Demand*, New York, Columbia University Press, 1946, and D. F. Dowd (editor), *Thorstein Veblen: A Critical Reappraisal*, Ithaca, N.Y., Cornell University Press, 1958.

been prepared to pay for them? What wages did all categories of labor actually receive? What could they buy with these wages? What was the real value of the money received—as measured by what it could purchase?

And what was money, in any case? Was the dollar a thing of value because it could ultimately get for its owner a stated amount of gold, or because it could at any given moment buy a given amount of food, shelter, necessities, and luxuries? Mitchell was as sensitive as his old teacher Veblen to the irrational cruelties of market economy, but he rigidly refused to allow his sympathies to affect his factual findings. The tools he forged could be used by anyone—and are being used today.

A host of disciples followed him into the scientific (as distinct from philosophical) study of economics, changing it from a theology based on the gospel of Adam Smith to a discipline of measurement, description, correlation, analysis. A volume could be—some day will be—written covering the evolution of social-economic thought during this period. Enough to say that it will fall, probably, into two parts: the study prior to 1917 and its transition since then from philosophy to science and econometrics. That thought forged instruments, first, for audit of the work of the market gods, and presently for controlling them.

From 1920 on, political as well as intellectual battle lines were being drawn. They had been brought to climax by World War I. That conflict did many things—but one of them proved surprising. It forced wartime nonmarket control of economics on the governments of all the principal belligerents—Britain, France, Germany, and, in large extent, the United States. Despite the slaughter and horror of the fighting lines, their populations increased, and most of the people in these countries were, amazingly, better off under war-controlled than under market economics! The level of living was higher—especially for workmen and the least-favored classes—than it had been in time of peace.

The fact, of course, did not prove that market economics could be dispensed with. But it suggested possibilities, just as Wilbur and Orville Wright's first airplane managed to fly only for a few minutes but did indicate that flight was possible. If market economics could be controlled to take care of populations during war, the process might be used for less lethal purposes. At war's end, many men were exploring a new field of ideas and asking new questions of old gods.

John Maynard (later Lord) Keynes was one of these. Assigned as a young man to the British delegation to the Paris Peace Conference at the close of World War I, he worked on the Versailles Treaty clauses requiring Germany to pay "reparations." I first met him at that conference. Before the treaty was signed, Keynes was convinced that the treaty requirements were not only physically and economically impossible, but also might lead to a second world war. (As in fact they did, because they wrecked the Weimar government of Germany and led to the accession of Adolf Hitler.) Keynes resigned in disgust. Back in England, he turned to his pen. He first wrote *The Economic Consequences of the Peace*—a damning exposé. Of more importance, he considered methods by which market economics might be beneficially influenced, if not controlled—a pure heresy in the then academic world. Wholesale unemployment was blighting England; uncontrolled economics seemed to lead nowhere.

He selected for examination the difficult tool of money, credit, and monetary theory. In 1930, he published his preliminary findings as a *Treatise on Money*. For him, as well as others, it opened a new vista of thinking. In Keynes's own words, in his later book *The General Theory of Employment, Interest and Money*, "I was still moving along the traditional lines of regarding the influence of money as something so to speak separate from the general theory of supply and demand. When I finished it, I had made some progress towards pushing monetary theory back to becoming a theory of output as a whole." Pushing his untraditional line, he no longer asked questions of the market gods, but grappled with the whole problem. "A monetary economy, we shall find," he wrote, "is essentially one in which changing views about the future are capable of influencing the quantity of employment and not merely its direction." His book was, for him, "a long struggle of escape, and so must the reading of it be for most readers if the author's assault upon them is to be successful,—a struggle of escape from habitual modes of thought and expression. . . . The difficulty lies, not in the new ideas, but in escaping from the old ones. . . ." [4]

Effectively, he was pioneering the possible use of money and credit as weapon or tool to guide the market gods. "The authoritarian state systems of today," and here he was thinking of the Soviet Union, of Mussolini's Italy and Hitler's Germany, "seem to solve the problem of unemployment at the expense of efficiency and of freedom. It is certain that the world will not much longer tolerate the unemployment which, apart from brief intervals of excitement, is associated—and, in my opinion, inevitably associated—with present-day capitalistic individualism. But it may be possible by a right analysis of the problem to cure the disease whilst preserving efficiency and freedom." And he thought the new system of which he dreamed might be more favorable to peace than the old. He even believed that the ideas of scholars would bring about the change. "I am sure that the power of vested interests is vastly exaggerated compared with the gradual encroachment of ideas. . . . But, soon or late, it is ideas, not vested interests, which are dangerous for good or evil." [5]

As it proved, the statement was correct. As history would have it, Franklin Roosevelt's empiric attack on the uncontrolled market in 1933 preceded Keynes's fully mounted ideological assault in his *General Theory* by a couple of years. Convergence of the two, reduced, though they did not destroy, the power of the market gods in the West in some ways more effectively, perhaps, than Communist force economics proved able to destroy it in the East.

3. Subordination of Economics to Political Directives

Uncontrolled economics and the market gods meanwhile were being assaulted on the political front.

4. New York, Harcourt, Brace & World, 1936, pp. vi, vii, viii.
5. *Ibid.*, pp. 383–384.

Essentially, great bodies of men were unwilling to accept their impotence in the face of the blind market forces described by Adam Smith and exempted from human control by John Richard Green. Still less were they in a mood to accept the apparently eternal state of misery to which market economics and Malthusian theory consigned them. They organized, and proposed to control economic processes by political power, using force or laws or both, as the case might be. Socialist movements were in being or in formation all over Britain and Europe. Up to the beginning of World War I, they had not been successful. That war, however, besides introducing political control of economics for war purposes, also broke up old political forms. As World War I neared its end, climax became inevitable.

The crash came in Russia at the war's end, and its reverberations are not yet ended. The defeat of the Czarist armies and the singular incompetence of the old regime had reduced the Russian system to a shambles. Revolution against autocracy and toward democratic government took place in March, 1917. Communists, long in the process of organization under the leadership of Lenin, immediately went to work to seize all power—political, military, police, economic—in the Russian Empire. They did so the following November. In the next few years they were able to dominate every cranny of Russian economic life, and to eliminate all local market gods by putting in effect their measures of force control, for force control it certainly was. Presently, even Lenin thought it was not working too well. Without abandoning his theory of a political-economic dictatorship of the proletariat, in 1921 he permitted a degree of reversion to freer production, and sale of some products in open markets. This was called the "New Economic Policy," adopted less from conviction (Lenin was a highly practical man) than from expediency.

Upon Lenin's death, Stalin reverted. Force economics became once more the rule. Force was used less to destroy a supposed oppressive class (it had already been destroyed) than to compel conformity to Stalin's rules of forced production and distribution, forced labor and forced exchange. His concentration camps at maximum use held somewhere between twelve and fifteen million prisoners (nearly seven per cent of the Soviet population). Russian agriculture had been by law a serf system until 1867. In practice, it had remained such a system until 1917. The technical revolution had not really invaded Russia; in any case, industry developed before 1917 was largely dependent on monopolistic or other privileges granted by the Czarist state. The Bolshevik Revolution did not require as much change in habits of thought, work, and economic exchange as would have been the case in France, Germany, or Britain.

In Russia, the market gods were weak at best and retreated early. The Soviet regime could without too much difficulty accomplish reversion to the force economics of Oriental despotisms. It improved on the system; to be sure, it accomplished more in the process than a mere Asiatic restoration. In Professor Karl A. Wittfogel's words: "The agrarian despotism of the old society, which, at most, was semimanagerial, combines total political power with limited social and intellectual control. The industrial despotism of the fully developed and totally managerial apparatus society combines total political power with total social and intellectual control." [6] He called the result a "managerial apparatus society." Capital gathering and use, production, distribution, and exchange were dictated by power, administered through a bureaucracy and constrained to obedience by the police—the power arm of a dictatorial state. No market gods there!

Greater political climax, because world-wide, materialized in 1929 to 1933. Then market processes broke down almost everywhere. Though productive facilities were in being, their product could not be distributed under the current market systems of employment, wages, and distribution of income to individuals. Keynes's predictions were being fulfilled in Europe. In America, following a wave of prosperity and a speculative phase, the banking and money system collapsed. From 1930 on, President Herbert Hoover honorably, manfully, and mistakenly defended the proposition that market forces would presently reach a balance and again achieve prosperity in the United States.

6. *Oriental Despotism: A Comparative Study of Total Power*, New Haven, Yale University Press, 1957, p. 440.

Running against him in the campaign of 1932, Franklin D. Roosevelt advocated, and was prepared to exercise, political control over markets. He was elected by a landslide and took office on March 4, 1933. On that day, every American bank was closed. The economy of the United States had come as nearly as possible to a full stop. Conditions exhibited the nearest imaginable approach to chaos. Rightly, the American public expected the political state to restore order, creating new institutions, if need be, for the purpose. Rexford G. Tugwell, Raymond Moley, and I were expected to suggest and advise and furnish theoretical argument, as in fact we did. At my urging, the Reconstruction Finance Corporation was built into a huge capital-credit instrument designed to guide and to supply the immediate capital operations of the country. The Agricultural Adjustment Administration, devised by Tugwell, was aimed at setting limits to the catastrophic market situation in agriculture. Harry Hopkins converted a jerry-rigged federally financed relief program into a Civil Works Administration designed to provide jobs and pay for the unemployed, though the "market" for labor of all kinds was almost nonexistent. A little later the National Recovery Administration was worked out to set minimum wages, hours, and prices higher than the panic rates then current. Basically, the program was designed to create effective demand by distribution of money to those who needed it and by federal action to steer a substantial portion of the national income into the hands of the lowest-income groups.

Europeans later criticized us for a reason that will seem strange to Americans. We had, they thought, revolutionary conditions on our hands—why had we not used the opportunity and frankly jettisoned all the institutions of private market economy? The answer was simply that the distress and delay caused by that process would have been immense and the prospects for its success anything but good in a country with no acceptance of socialist thinking. Empirically, therefore, we sought to adapt settled American institutions and customs to a guided economy, using market prices where we could, controlling them where necessary. President Roosevelt, flexible in his approach, was quite unconcerned whether his field of responsibility called him "socialist" or "capitalist."

Roosevelt did not have the full benefit of the intellectuals' analyses. They then were only beginning. Compared with the economic knowledge and resulting tools every president and chief of state now takes for granted, those available to Roosevelt in 1933 were puny, though some intellectual break-through had indeed been made. So he, like Lenin, had to proceed empirically. Meeting problems as they shrieked for solution, he first imposed and used political controls over money and credit and later over prices and production. Adequate description is given in Arthur M. Schlesinger, Jr.'s *The Coming of the New Deal,* whose Prologue lists the measures of the "Hundred Days" between March 4 and June 16, 1933. Especially in the money and credit field, on behalf of the federal government, the President established political power over many of the principal levers of economic power previously held in private hands, and created, largely through the Reconstruction Finance Corporation, new instruments where necessary. He was to deal with other levers in the ensuing years. There is no need here to retell the long story. Sufficient to say that by the end of Roosevelt's first administration—that is, by 1936— few of the great economic levers were not ultimately in the control of the President and the Congress of the United States, though their use was by no means well understood. The market gods increasingly were seen to be less masters than potential servants of the politicians.

One unnoticed fact is worth underlining. This was Roosevelt's steady and continuing interest in developing economic tools. He gave continuous and constructive attention to developing statistical analysis of the American economy. Frequently during that period, I found him working with the various statistical offices. Owing to that interest, the United States now has perhaps the best continuing and up-to-date records of its economic progress and performance of any nation in the world. Not that its statistical system is perfect: continuous improvement is being made. Aggregated, nevertheless, it now gives a reasonable picture of what is happening in practically every sector, and provides a rational basis for determining why the performance is satisfactory or the reverse. Roosevelt's interest in developing this system is a glistening fact often lost amid the mass of narrative and interpretation of his administration.

Politicians in the United States undertook to use the work of the academic intellectuals, unlike the empiricism of Leninist and Stalinist force economics. Wesley Clair Mitchell's analysis and his figures, Simon Kuznets' quantitative statistics of cycles, which he had begun in 1926, John Maynard Keynes's theoretical correlations of money and credit to saving and spending, all entered the political process. Historically, Roosevelt's empiric attack on problems preceded the use of Keynes's theory; but the theory, complete in 1934, was rapidly drawn on to support his early solutions and began to influence the shape of continuing measures. The market gods were no longer treated with reverence. Rather, they were djinns to whom orders might be given. The problem was discovering what orders should be issued. Economic scientists were gradually discovering what these orders should be.

They are still doing so. No serious student of economics would contend that knowledge is adequate, but it already has reached a state permitting practical use. Though the break-through came in his time, more progress has been made since Roosevelt's death in 1945 than in the slightly over twelve years of his administration. Those of us who were with him in the New Deal look enviously at the Council of Economic Advisers, established in law by the Full Employment Act of 1946 and functioning continuously since then in Washington, at the Planning Commission operating in France, and at the economic tools in the hands of the British Cabinet and the government of the United States today. Political officers can choose their objectives and, with some measure of predictability, create and use economic forces to produce desired results.

In 1933, we had to guess whether economic levers could be used at all. Theorists believed they could be used, and we used their theories. Growing knowledge and experience have demonstrated not only that it can be done, but also that it can be done with a gradually growing degree of effectiveness and certainty.

The next generation may well see a completeness of economic control—a capacity to reach social objectives not defined by economics—through use of constrained market gods. And with it a vast accretion of economic power in the hands of government servants.

Should this occur, it will represent a solid and enduring advance in political-economic organization. It will provide a service of supply by which men and women increasingly secure what they *do* want—rather than are forced to accept what political power holders think they ought to want. In other words, they will be free to make their own lives. Precisely this was in Keynes's mind when he dreamed of preserving "efficiency and freedom" while curing economic disease, recognizing that ideas rather than vested interests (or perhaps police force) would then guide the next phase of civilization. In that condition, markets could reflect the ideals, values, and resultant choices of a population free to choose—a clean break from the earlier twentieth-century totalitarian concept.

III

The Realities of Economic Power

1. The Shifting Structure

The mid-twentieth century—the generation living now—has experienced one of the greatest shifts in economic power structure of which there is record.

In Communist countries, the political state took over by dramatic revolution, its bureaucracy supported by its police controls. In "developed" countries, the shift has been gradual but no less thorough. There the power has devolved in part on the state, but in greater part on the bureaucracies of the vast private collectives called corporations. At the turn of the century, personally owned banking systems (the Rothschilds in London,

Paris, Vienna, and Germany, and, in the United States, the House of Morgan and the House of Kuhn, Loeb & Company) controlled the capital supply and currency-credit system. Rich men owned and controlled most of the railroad, mining, energy, manufacturing, and other basic industries. In less than a half-century, the structure changed. Men and their families kept wealth, but lost their power.

Mere growth of these enterprises perhaps would have caused this in any event. Henry Ford no longer could effectively handle the Ford Motor Company; it became too big for personal dictatorship. No one man could possibly make the number of specific decisions involved in operating enterprises of this size. He had to delegate. This meant that his decision-making power increasingly became limited to hiring and discharging executives. Even that proved difficult. The corporate institution had to be tightly organized and staffed. Its internal organization ceased to be an unsystematic collection of owner's agents. Systematic division of function, the organization of resulting internal institutions, and their uninterrupted operation became essential. Otherwise, the large corporate enterprise would become chaotic. The result was the emergence of corporation bureaucracy—a new institution whose leaders exercised economic power.

A history and analysis of the process was written by Professor Alfred D. Chandler in 1962.[1] He studied the evolution of the administrative organization in a number of companies, notably Du Pont, General Electric, Standard Oil of New Jersey, and, later, Sears, Roebuck. He started with the proposition that if entrepreneurs act only like managers, concentrating on short-term activities, they fail both in their enterprises and as bearers of their role in the national economy. Staff as well as line institutions were needed. So, parts of the corporate organization had to be devoted to staff, to plan strategy and growth—that is, to determine long-term goals and how to accomplish them—accompanied by the design and structure of a line organization, by which large enterprise can operate. This was administrative in-

1. *Strategy and Structure: Chapters in the History of the Industrial Enterprise*, Cambridge, Mass., The M.I.T. Press, 1962.

novation on a large scale. Pierre du Pont had been studying the possibility of a structural model for the Du Pont enterprise as early as 1919, which was adopted in 1921. In 1920, in partnership with J. P. Morgan & Company, he took over control of General Motors, and promptly proposed and presently caused adoption of a bureaucratic organizational structure for that company as well. In the ensuing twenty years practically all major American corporations followed the example. They became bureaucracies, whose organizations developed and demanded internal—that is, managerial—in place of external—that is, ownership—direction.

Still greater shift, in my view, was caused by a more fundamental change. The sources, formation, habits, and location of capital itself were changing. Dr. P. T. Bauer, in *Economic Analysis and Policy in Underdeveloped Countries,*[2] underlined an important but little appreciated point on this. Whenever, he said, savings become compulsory, the power structure changes. The reason is that the creation and control of capital shifts to the hands of the compelling authority. This happened in both the United States and Europe. Factually, savings can be compelled when an enterprise achieves sufficient market power over the price of its product so that it can accumulate its own capital. To do this, it must achieve a size and position enabling it to collect a price for its product or service that yields more than mere owners' profit. The price can then include an additional amount, over and above distribution of dividends, which the concern can plow back, save, use for expansion or new ventures. These "savings" are compulsory—at the expense, of course, of the customers and consumers, who pay the price or go without.

2. Durham, N.C., Duke University Commonwealth Studies Center, Duke University Press, 1957, pp. 112–126, especially p. 124. Bauer was thinking primarily of savings compelled by taxation. But the same result occurs when an enterprise attains market power enabling it to collect from its customers an accretion to price which the enterprise accumulates as capital. Such power, like that of taxation, in Bauer's words (p. 124) "often greatly increases the power of particular groups of people over their countrymen, and it thus implies a restriction in the range of alternatives of those over whom the power is exercised."

Every American business enterprise attempts to attain this capacity. Small businessmen live modestly and plow back their profits. Great corporations do the same thing on a vast scale. When either successfully reinvests these undistributed profits, the yield from the new investment is added to the profits from the old. Compounding these "savings" over half a century or so, American corporations became not merely vast producers and sellers of goods, but also vast capital-gathering machines and reservoirs.

Savings also became compulsory by another route. Most modern countries adopted governmentally administered systems of "social security." Under them, compulsory contributions are exacted from employers or employees or both. Collected annually, these contributions are accumulated in government-administered trust funds. From these are paid employment benefits, sick benefits, and old-age pensions. But the huge reserves are available as capital. The future benefits are, in effect, required additions to the wages or salaries of the workers, but until required are withheld and piled up in trust funds.

In the United States, this government-compelled saving ("social security") was paralleled and is gradually being exceeded by companion, nongovernmental welfare and pension funds. Virtually every large corporation maintains such a fund for its own employees; some are industry-wide. Labor unions regularly demand the establishment or expansion of such funds as "fringe benefits" and make the supply of labor conditional on their maintenance. By 1968, the amount of private pension funds—compulsory savings—had passed $90 billion; the amount about doubles in each decade.

By compulsion, these savings are accumulated partly in governmental and partly in private trustees' hands. Power resulting from the amounts of capital so aggregated can, within limits, be exercised by the administrators of these funds.

All this is part of the "accumulation" process Marx accurately observed (and decried) in *Das Kapital*. His prediction failed to foresee that these accumulations would be independently held, leaving personal, family, and even corporate owners behind.

193

Institutions—corporations rather than owners, and aggregated governmental and private pension and trust funds—were the residuary heirs of the capital power. The immediate result was the rise of the government bureau and the corporate manageriat. They became and now are the primary holders of economic power.

The American and most European systems were, of course, coping (successfully as it proved) with a basic problem. Production required plants and organization of increasing size. To pay for these, enterprises needed to accumulate capital—administered by fewer managerial hands—not primarily to increase personal wealth, but because technical progress in mass production required it. At the same time, the trend toward distribution of wealth could be satisfied by public ownership or by distribution of stock as families multiplied and family fortunes were divided and as imperative demands, enforced by the power of labor unions, that workers get a growing share of production could not be denied.

The industrial economic system was thus required at one and the same time to accumulate capital for increased production and *also* to distribute wealth. With design, this was accomplished, partly through the action of government but chiefly through the device of the modern corporation. Corporations, like government, can accumulate property almost without limit. They can split the wealth represented by that property into millions of fragments called shares of stock just as government can distribute the product of public-sector investment in social benefit. The two together can make possible almost unlimited aggregation of property for productive purposes, and at the same time can make possible as wide a distribution of wealth as the community demands and as broad a division of production as its mores require. The process has shifted economic power from wealth holders to administrators of corporate property and managers of their operations, and to government bureaus.

2. State Investment as a Factor of Corporate Growth

With the growth of corporate power emerged a second influence presently attaining strength. A rising factor of required "investment"—let us call it that—came into being altogether outside, yet requisite to, the commercial system. A successful industrial and commercial system requires that a series of things be done—and paid for—though the product is not or cannot be sold and no market method exists for recapturing their cost.

Education is the greatest single item. Mass-production systems, if they are to work, require a reasonably literate, trained, and sophisticated population. Labor in any kind of plant must have a minimum capacity to read and write; unskilled labor has already been displaced by machines. More than minimal literacy is needed by industry for other reasons. Education is needed if population is to want—and buy and use—the products of the modern industrial system. Businessmen may want an educated public for humanistic reasons; but they *need* it for market reasons. Illiterates are poor consumers.

Education, as a rule, is not an advantageously salable commodity. Primary schools, high schools, universities cannot be operated at profit. Money spent for schools can rarely be raised by charging the pupils a price that will yield a profit. Part of the cost, of course, can be collected if the school charges tuition, paid by pupils' families farseeing enough to recognize that learning is an asset. Historically, however, few families have been prosperous enough to pay more than a fraction of the cost of their children's education. To achieve any widespread system, the state had to be called in, asked to levy taxes, and pay the expense. This was what economists call a "public-sector" operation conducted for the general welfare.

When the state levies taxes, it must use political power. Public officials entrusted with organizing, operating, and paying for public schools and state universities have power over the operation. They determine how money shall be "invested" in institutions whose product is education. The "investment," let us note, is highly profitable, though its returns accrue not to the power holders or the educational institution. Recent calculations of it have been made—one of them by Professor Theodore Schultz, of the University of Chicago. They indicate that "investment" in education of all kinds caused over twenty per cent of the increase in the gross national product of the United States since 1953. Society as a whole got the product, though it could not be recaptured and assigned as "profit" in any market place.[3]

Though the largest of public-sector items, education is only one of many types of investment that have to be made whose results cannot be recaptured on any other than the social balance sheet. As density of population grows, the proportion of public-sector investment almost certainly must rise. Sparse populations in the northwest of the United States can do with less than is needed in congested cities like Los Angeles, Chicago, and New York. Farming areas in Normandy and Provence can do with less than Paris, Lyons, and Marseilles. As life becomes increasingly sophisticated, populations need or demand more public-sector service: police, traffic regulation, parks and parkways, in-and-out access, medical and hospital care, sanitary and antipollution services. Above all, as men and women demand more from life esthetically, growing public expenditures have to be made.

Developed industry, indeed, imposes such investment. Technical advance in all fields is due to a great continuing effort in scientific investigation. Only part of this can be done at a recapturable profit—though that situation may vary. Currently, in the United States two-thirds of all scientific research is paid for by the federal government in one form or another.

Similar principles apply to other forms of public-sector ex-

3. See E. F. Dennison, *The Sources of Economic Growth in the United States and the Alternatives Before Us*, Committee for Economic Development, 1962. See also the presidential address of Professor Theodore Schultz to the American Economic Association in 1960. The Ford Foundation's pamphlet *Prospecting in Economics*, December, 1966, states a conclusion: "In recent years economics have come to recognize that investment in education—like investment in buildings and equipment—is a distinctive ingredient of economic growth" (p. 9).

pense. In every case a portion of current income is compulsorily taken by the state from its citizens. It is "invested" in operations believed necessary, whose benefit and productivity justify the expenditure but whose product cannot be recaptured by entrepreneurs or merchants. Because it cannot be appropriated by private investors, commercial institutions cannot (except occasionally) undertake activities as incident to their profit-making business. In 1968, slightly over one-fourth of the gross national product of the United States was taken in taxes by the federal, state, and local governments and expended by them on public-sector activities. The fraction varies slightly but not much. As the gross national product for the year 1968 totaled about $860 billion, it may be assumed that approximately $216 billion has been collected as taxes and spent by public officials. Much of this—for example, military and relief expenditures—is currently "consumed"—that is, leaves little permanent residue. But a great deal of it—education, health, public works—provides a lasting body of tangible or intangible capital assets whose effect is to add to the productive capacity of the community and its members. These are compulsory savings.

Public expenditures are made through an endless number of institutions—school boards, highway commissions, state education departments, housing administrations, departments of health, government scientific institutions, state universities, and so forth. Power thus devolves increasingly on hierarchies of officials, be they permanent civil-service bureaucrats or appointed or elected officeholders. Aggregated, this is a formidable subtraction from the economic power of nonstatist owners, private or corporate.

This growing public sector and the economic power corresponding to it interact forcefully with the activities of the "private"— that is, nonstatist—corporations which produce and sell services or goods. The two groups may not like each other. Bureaucrats distrust businessmen. Businessmen dislike bureaucrats as much as taxes. Yet they need each other and must work together. At the very least, each must reckon with the result of the other's activities. The decades following the end of World War II have seen an erosion of the relative power of the great corporations and financial institutions, despite their enormous growth in actual size, and the slow trend toward concentration of economic power in a few hundred of them. Literate corporation managers know that were public-sector expenditures stopped their plants would rapidly decline. Government men know that atrophy of commercial life would present them with grievous problems.

Even in nonproductive distribution, the necessity of a public-sector system is evident. Unless the "poor" are to be allowed to die of starvation (and they were as late as 1930), or blatant misery in the midst of plenty is to be allowed to go on, noncommercial or public-sector operations must flank the commercial or profit-making mechanisms. Modern businessmen understand this, Marx to the contrary notwithstanding.

Hence the vast change in economic-power location and structure in the mid-twentieth century. It is now shared by some thousands of federal and local political officers, a rather smaller number of private corporate managers and staffs, and the heads of a number of labor organizations. There remain a large number of rich and small private enterprisers (roughly 1,200,000 of them), though they are of far less significance. The first two groups carry on the overwhelming bulk of operations.

Though the operating heads of six hundred or seven hundred corporations in aggregate dispose of most of the nonstatist economic power, they are not organized. No one of them accepts the orders or instructions of any other. Side by side with them are dominant officials in towns, cities, counties, states, and federal agencies. Their number runs into tens of thousands, and they are drawn from all sorts and conditions of men. The institutions they head divide, rather than concentrate, the realities of statist economic power.

There is not, under American practice, an effective "establishment" in this field, either within or without the government. Combination of such power is not impossible; it could, and for some purposes perhaps should, occur. Thus far the pluralist system has prevented the attainment of permanent national-scale power by any single private individual or government officeholder or by any combination of them.

3. Power over Price

The first great power of corporate management is its capacity to determine the price for the products or services sold by it.

Corporate managers—as also managers of government enterprises—usually have this power. Economically, it is basic: out of the price they receive they have to pay the wages and salaries of their laborers and their employees, the cost of their raw materials, and their administrative overhead. Otherwise the enterprise must seek loans or subsidies, or shut down. In addition, the price must be sufficient so that they may accumulate capital, or the enterprise is likely to be static—it cannot grow. Besides that, they must, under a system of private ownership, collect profits out of which they must pay taxes and interest, and can pay dividends to stockholders. American corporations of any size must pay nearly half their profits as taxes to the government of the United States. The government thus is in effect a nearly even partner in every enterprise. Corporate managements want their profits to be as large as possible; consequently, they want their prices to be as high as they can collect for the volume they plan to sell.

Theoretically, in a capitalist system, enterprises are free to name any price they like. Actually, this power is limited. In great sectors of American industry (and, indeed, in most so-called "capitalist" countries), the government itself fixes the price. This is true of all transportation, of all public utilities, of most communication services (radio and television time are notable exceptions), and frequently of rents charged for housing. Where government price-fixing does not exist, the pricing power is partially limited by competition. Only a monopoly can set any price it chooses, and then only if the government does not intervene. An Arabian monopolist owning a water hole could charge any price he could collect from passing caravans, because they must buy or die of thirst. Modern industry rarely has comparable security.

Monopoly pricing power, except when regulated by government, rarely exists in America. Instead, under a system of large corporations, pricing power is reflected in a partial form known as "administered price." This means that some organizations—invariably big corporations—can maintain the price they fix for their production over long periods of time despite fluctuation of demand. Automobile prices, for example, do not change greatly from day to day. Some bargaining is possible. But dealers or middlemen from whom consumers buy must pay standard wholesale prices to the manufacturers. These roughly govern the price paid by the consumer—as every car buyer knows. The prices are not agreed on by the three major manufacturing corporations. Were they to do so, the Department of Justice would immediately institute criminal antitrust prosecutions. But the costs of manufacture to General Motors, Ford, and Chrysler are not far apart. They buy labor from the same union. The profit each expects to get is similar. So, except in emergencies (great numbers of unsold cars or the like), all three corporations come out with substantially similar prices. These do not greatly vary through each year. Advantage as well as disadvantage results. Consumers do not get a break from temporary conditions. On the other hand, workers in factories tend to benefit from more or less stable continuing employment.

In an industry dominated by one or two large companies, the administered-price effect is much the same. If I manufacture sugar, supplying, say, ten per cent of a market in which a far larger corporation supplies fifty per cent, the giant sets the price. My price is likely to "follow the leader." I cannot sell my sugar for more than the giant does—my customers would leave me and buy from him. But if I can sell my sugar at about the leader's price, I have no reason to sell it for less. Consequently, when the leader announces a price, I follow it. When he lowers, I must do so, or lose my market. When I try to approximate his increase, certainly I will come as close to it as I can. "Follow-the-leader" markets exist in most basic American industries.

These are examples of the administered price. Both indicate the substantial, though limited, pricing power of corporate managers, especially those of the largest in each market. Gardiner C. Means, in his book *Pricing Power and the Public Interest*,[4] contends that the political government should take a hand in regulating administered prices, basing its decisions on a rating of the usefulness of the industry's performance. The conception is interesting, its fulfillment difficult.

Government does take a hand in some circumstances. President John F. Kennedy, having helped to negotiate an acceptable wage contract with the Steelworkers union in 1962, found himself faced immediately after with an across-the-board price rise announced by United States Steel, whose "leadership" most other companies followed. He at once loosed all the political lightning he had—denunciation, investigation, search for possible antitrust violation. United States Steel promptly recanted. In 1965, President Lyndon B. Johnson, seeking to prevent inflation and after taking technical advice from his Council of Economic Advisers, moved politically against price increases by steel manufacturers, aluminum manufacturers, and copper producers, with measurable temporary success. Government is immediately concerned when major and unsatisfactory price increases are put forward; price increases are rarely popular. On their side, manufacturers who find the prevailing price level too low for comfort are not slow in demanding government assistance. They ask—and often get—subsidies, limitation of competing imports, government purchases, or similar relief measures.

On the government side, the system is as yet uncrystallized. All that can be said is that unsatisfactory prices—either because they are too high and customers complain or because they are too low and suppliers are in trouble—are likely to precipitate political intervention, though circumstances must be extreme to bring this about. Absolute power over prices is thus not in the hands of private corporations. But the power of corporate managers to set "administrative" price levels does exist, and has wide scope. Corporations with competent management obviously are not in distress. Certainly they have continuously been able to achieve comfortable profit margins, with comparatively rare interruption.

4. New York, Harper, 1962.

It is wholly uncertain that giving pricing power to government appointees, rather than leaving it with corporate managers, would be more satisfactory. Experience suggests that bureaucrats behave much as do private corporate managers. State take-over commonly eliminates competition; state commissariats or bureaucracies are monopolies. Private monopolies are relatively rare under the American system, but under socialist and Communist systems, monopoly is invariable. There the central-government bureaucrat has direct power, the bureaucratic plant manager less power than the corporation manager. As a rule, the government-owned enterprise does not charge lower prices than the private corporation. Its manager wants and takes all the profit he can get, to enhance the position of his bureau, and his own power with it, and therefore finds himself in conflict with the state. He turns profits back to the state if he must, but invariably he fights to keep and use them as capital in expanding his own commissariat. His claim is that the profit he is allowed to accumulate will eventually accrue to the public. The state insists that it will spend it on needed development (or perhaps defense), which will benefit all alike—there should be no conflict. In immediate fact, the bureaucrat (like the corporation manager) wants to keep it in his enterprise. State ownership does not resolve the price-profit conflict.

Pricing power, like any form of power, can be abused. Private corporations can and do set oppressively high price levels. There is, nevertheless, a deterrent. An angry public may appeal to its political government. And political governments do, in fact, intervene. On the other hand, if a government bureaucracy running a state-owned enterprise sets too high a price, customers have little recourse. They can appeal to the political state—but the bureaucracy is itself a powerful arm or expression of that state. Their practical recourse is not to buy, if they can avoid it—and this they do. Then, the bureaucratic, like the private, enterprise finds unsold goods piling up.

In economic fact, no single price stands wholly on its own base. It is part of a structure of prices. If out of line, it is likely to cause difficulty across the board. Unduly high prices for copper will force increased use of aluminum. Unduly high prices for food or shelter—both necessities—will cut down the purchasing power of individuals to buy clothes and luxuries; these go unsold as a result. This is particularly true where the level of personal income is low. State monopolies and nonstatist corporations alike have to cope with this fact. The pricing power is more limited when the enterprise is in private than when it is in public hands. In neither is it absolute.

4. The Power to Accumulate and Apply Capital

Corporation managers have, as we noted, capacity to accumulate capital—and their most creative single power is to invest that capital.

This power is both quantitatively and qualitatively formidable. For the calendar year 1964, for example, American corporations took in just under $69 billion in "profit." In addition to this item, they also recouped "depreciation charges"—that is, repayment of past capital investment—amounting to $34 billion. They paid out over $27 billion in taxes to the United States government and $17.2 billion as dividends (this was the stockholders'—or wealth holders'—share). For the year, they retained and accumulated the remainder—nearly $25 billion of their profit, plus the depreciation charges. Thus, after paying taxes and dividends, they had in cool cash about $59 billion (retained earnings plus depreciation allowances) available for "investment"—for direct application to expansion of old enterprises or the organization of new ones. This was for a single year.

The phenomenon of accumulation has excited criticism of the American system. Originally, it was directed against wealth holders—owners of corporate stock. These were erroneously assumed to have power to control these annual accumulations. Today the criticism is more often directed against the right of private managers, as heads of corporations, to hold the power of accumula-

tion and investment on this scale. Yet, socialist agencies and bureaucracies seek to achieve like power of accumulation; it is
singularly convenient. A socialist government, were it to expropriate all stocks and bonds, taking them away from their present
owners, would merely transfer the results of corporate accumulation (presently reflected in the steadily increasing value of stocks)
to accumulation in government-held funds. There is no reason to
assume that any other system would wish to end the power of
accumulation set up by the present American system. More likely
it would want the advantages of it for the new regime.

Drama certainly can attend power to apply capital. In 1958,
United States Steel executives were prospecting all sources of iron
ore in South America. They were compelled to do this because the
quality of American ore resources was beginning to decline, and
also because a development of American antitrust law made it
desirable to locate steel mills near the markets they serve. Mr.
Benjamin Fairless, then head of the company, projected construction of a steel plant on the Delaware River just below Trenton,
New Jersey. He contemplated the possibility that iron ore could
be imported to the plant by sea from South America.

One of his prospecting crews explored the lower Orinoco
Valley, not far from where its great tributary, the Caroní, brawls
in. Iron ore is not hard to find. But it must be of high quality and
must be near to transport (in this case, by sea), or the cost of
carrying it to the port of loading may increase the expense so that
the operation becomes unprofitable. This prospecting crew finally
looked at a range of low hills one hundred and twenty kilometers
or so from the Orinoco. Romance deepened at the end of their
work. They had spent the funds allotted to them by Mr. Fairless
and his committee; the time had come to abandon that particular
search. But the chief of the party was convinced that they were on
the verge of discovery. Overspending his allotment (at considerable
risk to his personal career), he centered on a group of hills and
presently selected one of them. Its name was Sierra Bolívar; it
proved to be, literally, a mountain of very high-quality iron ore
covered by a thin mat of jungle. He reported back; Mr. Fairless
had the reports evaluated and verified; the area and location

were determined. Development into an iron mine meant building a town and strip-mining facilities at the hill, running a railroad across the plain to the Orinoco, constructing docks and port facilities on the shores of that mighty river, and surrounding them with a small new city, Puerto Ordaz. It meant connecting that city with the Delaware River by a fleet of ore transports. It meant another substantial city on the Delaware in Pennsylvania—the whole to be a single integrated scheme connecting two continents. The project was carried out; it is in operation now.

The head of United States Steel had to cope with many factors. First he had to allocate many millions of dollars of capital accumulated in the United States to the plan. Then he had to secure the appropriate concessions and contract arrangements with the Venezuelan government—under Venezuelan law all subsoil minerals are the property of the state. There as elsewhere the right to run a railroad had to be secured from state authorities. He had no trouble on the American side. The American doctrine of private enterprise concedes just this power to initiate and carry out projects. Probably his main negotiations in the United States had to be carried on with the local authorities of the county in Pennsylvania where the Fairless steel plant is now located. He had to attract another business enterprise to provide housing for the employees of the new plant. This latter was supplied by Levitt Company, which bought, constructed, and resold houses in Levittown capable of accommodating the personnel of the steel plant and the associated activity that necessarily went with it. By European standards, the total project would be of grand-ducal proportions. Rightly, Mr. Fairless' name is attached to the Delaware River plant; rightly, Fairless himself is one of the heroes of the United States Steel Corporation. (Of interest is the fact that when Fairless retired as president of the company, his personal fortune was comparatively small. According to him, it was less than one million dollars.)

In the field of selecting investment and applying capital, private corporation managers are perhaps at their power zenith. They can survey the world and put it, or some of it, where they please. The bureaucrat or state commissar usually cannot. He has been assigned by his government to a specific sector of production. He has to go to the central administration, get increased authorization, and otherwise maneuver to "invest" outside the specified sector. It is precisely the relatively uncontrolled freedom of the private corporate manager to put capital where he will that excites the objection of Marxists—and perhaps they have a point. Untrammeled exercise of power to invest in one enterprise instead of another, to develop this area and not that, to produce this product instead of a different one, to extend service to one community, leaving out its neighbor, does not guarantee that human beings everywhere in the country are well supplied. The corporate manager says, "I go where I see a profit." A government, Communist or otherwise, at mid-twentieth century must say, "Our economic system must offer jobs, pay, goods, and services to substantially all our people practically everywhere." It will require its agencies to place investment where it tends to realize that end.

The struggle for power to apply capital thus involves a contest between two conceptions. One is the corporate manager's desire to make profits for his institution. The other is the notion that capital should be put where it is socially most needed to provide services, goods, jobs, as government power holders appraise need. At present, these conceptions coexist in the United States, but the corporate managers are far ahead. Probably the balance will change as conditions shift. Other countries may find other solutions suited to their own customs. Certainly no sound solution is reached through bloody dialogue and civil wars.

Contest over the power to apply capital apparently goes forward in any system. In June, 1966, the *Bulletin of Atomic Scientists* (which concerns itself with politics as well as science) devoted an issue to "China Today." Miss Audrey Donnithorne, lecturer in Chinese economic studies at University College, London, reviewed the policy of central economic control by the government of Communist China. One of its main targets is control of the rate, and direction, of "investment"—that is, formation and application of capital. An obstacle is "leakage" of capital away from state-planned fields and projects and bootlegging into individually chosen (though still public) enterprise. To accumulate and invest capital outside or in violation of the central-government plan is a crime in China. Apparently, nevertheless, heads of Communist-organized units, when they can gather a little capital, are tempted to steal it from the central planning authority and put it where they think it will be locally useful. From time to time they risk getting shot in order to do this.

Power holders in any enterprise, bureaucrats or businessmen, know their particular operation and situation better than any central-government bureaucrat or corporate administration. Each struggles to meet the needs of the enterprise he manages. Apparently each does this without, as well as with, hope of reaping a personal profit. A plant or division manager of an American corporation may find that his central management has allocated him a half-million dollars for plant improvement. He wants a million—that plant, that division, is his baby, and he wants it well fed. He invents all manner of dodges to circumvent the decree of the central office. He overstates normal "maintenance cost," he clandestinely puts the overage into plant development, enabling his plant to produce more. His salary remains the same, but he feels more important. In any case, the plant develops its own demands, and he responds. To managers, state or private, their plants are their lives.

The demands of institutions—in this case, plants—attain a reality of first importance in determining the decisions and actions of their directing power holders. Though the process is little understood, the reality is obtrusive. Institutions acquire a collective entity—one might almost call it personality. Plants require continuous care, repair, renovation, innovation. Their staffs must be held together, kept together, reinforced. The managing bureaucrat, like the officer in charge of a platoon, a division, or an army corps, knows these requirements, knows that unless they are met, the organization will decay; knows also that his leadership is at stake if he is unable to provide them. He sacrifices his personal interest to the imperatives of his organization, without which, indeed, his power declines. Understanding the "personality" of an economic institution is the first essential of managerial power. Multiply the process throughout the thousands of economic and productive institutions necessary in any society, and one begins to understand the imperatives of production. Add to this the necessity of co-ordination, so that the processes work together, and the necessity of power to achieve this result and the problems—as well as the realities—of economic power begin to emerge.

Historically, we have seen, the market gods are increasingly being brought within control of humanely exercised power through processes of politics. The American state is today developing a philosophy under which economic organization is expected to produce certain results. It is enabled to do so because increasingly it is learning a better means of controlling its operation than leaving it to the blind result of the untamed market.

The free market would have yielded power in any event. Left to itself, certainly since the advent of the large corporation, it would have produced sheer monopoly—destroying itself in the process. Uncontrolled market processes engender chaos, into which power automatically moves. In point of fact, the ultimate choice lay between the power of a monopolist, heading a huge corporation or cartel combination based on a philosophy of maximized profit, and state power, whose philosophy is to direct production, exchange, and profit toward the realization of some concept of civilized life. As between the two philosophies, the latter, as one might expect, was more attractive. Statist power, being greater, was able to displace or forestall monopoly power, the latter being the only relief from chaos offered by the free market.

This evolution is relatively new in the modern era. It is a twentieth-century product. Since World War II, for practical purposes, all countries capable of adequate organization exercise statist power rather than allow free rein to the verdict of the market place, though their methods run all the way from Communist totalitarianism to mild guidance of autonomous business corporations complemented by social legislation. For about thirty-five years, this has been the salient form in economic history.

Each country has changed and developed its system. Communist governments are cautiously experimenting with business autonomy. The magazine *East Europe: A Monthly Review of East European Affairs* for April, 1968, chronicles some of these changes in Czechoslovakia and Hungary. Countries like the United States and France move cautiously but steadily toward increased planning, accompanied by the directed use of credit. No country appears to desire to return to the altars of the market gods; their image failed in crisis.

If the use of power to control has not gone faster, the reason is plain. Definition of objective—a philosophy of what a civilization should be, and therefore what the state should do—is far from precise. It has not progressed as rapidly as our understanding of economics and its possibilities. So we are in a phase of transition. Power has been called in; institutions have vested it in men required to bring about certain effects, and they are apparently able (within reason) to do so. The philosophy of the use of economic resources is still in infancy, and therefore the dialogue between power and its field of responsibility is still confused and unclear. Nevertheless, it is in progress. The next generation almost certainly will see a surprising, and, I believe, healthy, advance.

5. The Power to "Innovate"

The technical ability of big economic organizations combined with the capacity to accumulate capital gives them the ability to introduce what economists currently call "innovations." That word meant not so much the initiation of new projects, like that of Sierra Bolívar, as the development of new processes and products made possible by technical and scientific developments and discoveries. A hotly debated question has been whether the characteristic mid-twentieth-century "big" economic organisms—corporations, as in the United States, mixed semipublic enterprises, as in France and Germany, socialist commissariats, as in Russia—have adequately carried out innovation and given their countries the benefits science has offered. Unquestionably, these organizations have the power—they "can." Enormous technical progress, a direct result of innovation, has certainly occurred. The issue is whether it resulted from, was merely accompanied by, or perhaps was hindered by, big organization. Implicit in this is the problem of what motives do lead to innovation and, with it, increased technical and economic development.

The largest organizations are governmental—the greatest (unhappily) being military. After these come the nonmilitary government agencies and commissariats. These are rivaled in size by the large American and European companies. All have high capacity for organizing talent for research, and most of them devote capital in large amounts to research and development. Their capacity to induce invention and innovation, to discover new principles, or to use new discoveries nevertheless may be no greater than the aggregated capacity of unorganized thousands of individual scientists, researchers, and inventors. It is impossible to prove the case one way or the other. What big organizations undoubtedly do have is higher power to develop. They have or can get capital. A decision taken in an executive office of a large corporation or a government agency can devote assets and assign trained men to development of innovation far beyond the capacity of any individual scientist or inventor.

Do they use this power? A debate in the *Quarterly Journal of Economics* discusses the point. In May, 1966, Professors Walter Adams and Joel Dirlam tested a hypothesis of the late Professor Joseph Alois Schumpeter that large firms with market power had greater incentive and greater resources to "innovate." Adams and Dirlam picked the steel industry as illustration. They came to the conclusion that despite the "big" organization and high capital resources of private steelmakers, they do not "innovate." The greatest recent technical change in the steel industry has been introduction of the oxygen process. It was developed and put into operation by a strong, though small, Austrian maker in 1952. Two years later the twelfth-largest steelmaker in the United States (McLouth) introduced the process to America. McLouth was followed by others in the ensuing ten years. The largest American steelmakers (United States Steel and Republic) began to use it only in 1963 to 1965. Adams and Dirlam therefore concluded that the larger and more powerful the concerns, the less incentive they had to take the risks of pioneering. The American steel giants, they thought, lagged behind the smaller steel producers in Europe.

To this Dr. Allan K. MacAdams answered, in the same journal in August, 1967, that the argument did not stand up. The giants had moved more cautiously, it is true; but they had merely awaited the inevitable improvements on the technological break-through and had innovated more cleverly. They had been more prudent in their timing. Adams and Dirlam replied vigorously, analyzing the operation. Their conclusion, simply stated, was that "It is the cold wind of competition, not industrial concentration, which is conducive to economic progress." Reduced to lowest terms, their thesis is that decision-making power oriented chiefly toward profit making does *not* stimulate innovation. The decision maker in a big corporation has to be emphatically kicked into it by fear that a competitor will outdistance him. Capacity he has; but the more secure he feels, the less motive he has to innovate. A monopoly would therefore be the slowest to move.

Let us compare the big corporation to the big governmental organization. No serious review of the latter's achievements in innovation has come to my attention. My observation has been that, in the nonmilitary field, government organisms do not innovate swiftly. They are, almost invariably, slow and timid. They can move, and in fact most of them do; but their progress is certainly not outstanding. They also need a propelling boot in their bureaucratic behind.

Sometimes they have it. The largest economic organisms are the military establishments. They probably are responsible for more technical and scientific innovation than either big corporations or nonmilitary government projects. It is at least possible that they are responsible for more innovation than all of the rest put together. True, in each country they are monopolies. Yet the kick of a different competition is continuous and emphatic:

other military establishments elsewhere in the world may outdistance them. So they act.

It is unpleasant to record but accurate to observe that the
greatest break-throughs of the twentieth century, even those ultimately applied to civilian use, have been developed by military
organizations and only later spun off and developed for peaceful
ends. The theory of the release of nuclear energy was the outcome
of individual research: one thinks of Einstein, Fermi, Bohr, Oppenheimer, and, before them, Planck. Motivation for scientific research was individual; these were men in classroom or university
studies. Nevertheless, the kick that pushed them into practical innovation was World War II. It induced President Franklin D.
Roosevelt to pick up the suggestion contained in Albert Einstein's
famous letter and to devote a then unprecedented amount of national capital to the "Manhattan Project," and to creation of the
nuclear bomb. Thereafter, through the Atomic Energy Commission, companion development was carried on. Emergence of the
hydrogen bomb, through work by Dr. Edward Teller (over the
opposition of Dr. J. Robert Oppenheimer), was caused by the
Pentagon, which rightly suspected that the Soviet Union intended
to create one.

Civilian use followed the military. As in the cognate case of
Alfred Nobel's development of dynamite (for war purpose), the
eventual civilian use of atomic power is likely to be infinitely
more significant than its military use. Historically, nevertheless,
the primordial motive was a search for weapons—a grim com-
mentary on how innovation is motivated. The case of atomic
energy is not exceptional. Use of airplanes for transport was
barely thought of before World War I. The push toward developing them came as a result of the war competition between the
German and the Allied military machines. Civilian innovation
began after the war. And greater push was given after 1938 when
war loomed again. The jet planes now used by millions for travel
were designed, developed, and paid for by the Pentagon during
and after World War II. Rockets and guided missiles—still not
adapted to civilian use—emerged later, as did the development of
space missiles. A continuing push was given by the Cold War to

competition between Soviet and American military organizations. Military competition, motivated by the desire to survive (and/or to dominate) appears to be a most powerful impulse toward what is innocuously called "innovation."

The conclusion may be drawn that power inevitably acts according to its constituted idea system. If profit making is the impulse, the motive to innovate is relatively weak. Under it, the greatest single push seems to be the desire to save or cut labor costs, especially where labor unions have power to exact high pay. A second push is fear lest some competitor may develop new methods. Otherwise, big industry would move slowly, if it did not remain static. But if threat from other nations is believed to endanger national welfare or national survival, then the power to innovate is used. This is a different idea system. Innovation then is required not for profit, but for national survival; or perhaps, as in the case of the space race, for national glory and prestige.

A day may come when national glory and national prestige, perhaps even national safety, are best established by a country's being the most beautiful, the best socially organized, or culturally the most productive in the world. Economic power would then be inspired by a new, greater, and splendid idea system engendering innovation to realize it. This inspiration, it seems to me, will increasingly become essential, if only because it will attract and engage capable men in the statist and nonstatist organizations of production. But that day has not yet come.

Quarrel with corporate managers now is not complaint that they are rich, but that their power is not adequately used or well-directed, and would be better used if placed in other hands. Socialist and Communist governments want corporate managerships and their economic power for themselves. Their leaders consider that they are or can become able to direct and operate great and complicated industrial systems with results more satisfactory to the public. They do not always succeed. Innovation by government organizations, outside the military field, has been slow—slower than by corporations that do not have monopoly position. The Communist administration in 1948 took over Czechoslovakia's highly advanced industrial enterprises. They ceased to develop. Drop in Czechoslovak productivity was steady and continuous. Twenty years later, it only begins to exceed the pre-1948 level. Military stimulus aside, socialist organizations seem even more sluggish in innovation than do big corporations.

6. Social Direction

The application of capital, plus innovation, goes far toward determining the next phase of civilization in the areas of its investment. Decisions as to where production shall be organized may cause cities to rise on empty land, or may exacerbate crowding in overfull urban areas. The decision to manufacture this product and push it into consumption through market channels may overfill wants of no great importance, leaving obvious needs unfilled. American industry today does not produce cheap houses, hence in 1967 it was possible to predict a dangerous shortage of acceptable shelter by 1970. The willingness to extend electric power or highways could bring about settlement of undeveloped regions. The decision to abandon internal-combustion gasoline engines and work out some different automotive device could not only, literally, change the atmosphere, but could also force modification of the world-wide petroleum industry. Such description could be extended, almost without limit.

Control of capital investment, accordingly, and requirement that it conform to some rational plan seem probable, if not certain, though this may be some distance off. France found it necessary to institute such controls when it set up the *Commission du Plan*, introducing a degree of order into the investment process. The United States could learn a great deal from its experience, and borrow some of its methods. This lies in the future, but may not be too long delayed.

The imperative arises from a visibly developing chaotic situation calling for power exercised through new institutions and giving effect to a new idea system. A breach in economic order has be-

214

come visible in many American cities. These are not functioning well—hence the cry for urban reorganization, urban redevelopment, and a changed base of urban finance. But rotting and overcrowded ghettos, inadequate housing and schools, and incapacity to pay for obvious necessary services are results rather than causes. They came about because breakdown or imbalance in production and distribution left masses of humanity inadequately attended and served. National economic capacity to rebuild or even eliminate slums and remedy conditions is certainly present, but is not being used for that purpose. Less dramatic breakdowns are beginning to appear in other contexts.

The obvious failure is perhaps more ideologic than economic. No adequate idea system has yet been hammered out establishing principles and priorities to guide the application of capital and technique to American needs. Behind this lies the fact that no American picture has been outlined of an affluent civilization. Yet some such picture is essential. Lacking it, no priorities but the grossest of needs can be determined, no plan can be adopted, no sound institutions for control can be constructed—and no orders can be given to the economic power holder able to apply capital and direct research, development, construction, production, and distribution.

Fortunately for the United States, a ferment of dialogue has begun. Gradually, it draws in thinkers, artists, architects, bankers, urban planners, even scholars and philosophers. Questions are asked of the existing system, and from the answers a consensus is gradually distilled. Initially, it focuses on the kind of production and service modern life demands. But consumption, in the final analysis, turns on the kind of life the consumers want. Aggregated, their wants are the material expression of their society and civilization. As its outlines emerge, the chief objectives that planning must forward will become plain.

Sooner or later, capital-development planning will become a national function, just as control of commercial money and credit is a national function in 1969. Economic power over capital application, presently held by corporate managers and administrators of certain government institutions, will then be guided by conscious national decision—that is, will be controlled by govern-ment power holders chosen by representative government and charged with bringing about a greater measure of economic order. These will maintain an orderly dialogue with the population the economic organization exists to serve.

7. Rich Men

As of now, in the United States and in Western Europe, the rich man has little power merely because he is rich. He does, never-theless, in certain fields have avenues to power not readily avail-able to poor men.

We noted that a power holder amounts to little unless he con-nects himself with effective institutions. He must master past institutions or must create new ones. The man of great wealth is in the same position. However large his bank account, he can do nothing with it but consume. He can build or buy palaces, amuse himself at Mediterranean or Caribbean resorts, become a figure in Monte Carlo, Miami, or Las Vegas. He can amuse himself by collecting books or purchasing bonds. He can give libraries or laboratories to universities and have his name put on them. He can receive the pleasant but powerless recognition of decorations, honorary degrees, and even titles of nobility. None of these things entitle him to make decisions affecting other men or to give orders (outside his household) with any likelihood they will be fulfilled. Even when he seeks to give his son a career in business, he must ask the assistance of acquaintances and friends who will give the boy a fair chance—and can give him little more. Beyond that, he can leave his son nothing but the ability to live without work and to waste as long as his wealth holds out. All of this does not add up to power.

So, if he wishes a power position, he must find it outside his bank account. He can, it is true, use the bank account to buy into, or possibly create, an institution. He can buy control of a small corporation. (Few rich men are left who are capable of buying individual control of really large ones.) He can undertake the management of that corporation. Then he can derive power from the institution—if, but only if, he is capable of handling it. Whatever power he has comes from the corporation or other institution, and from such intellectual or organizing skill as he may have—not from his wealth, which is largely irrelevant. He at once discovers that he is subordinate to the institution. It operates under, and in conditions accepted or laid down or directed by, the paramount political power. Then he is tested, not by the dollar value of his wealth, but by his performance as director or manager of the institution.

This is what wealth means in the United States and in the more or less democratic countries of Western Europe today. It is not true of wealth in the underdeveloped regions of the world. These are still accomplishing the transition from primitive agriculture to modern industrialization. Some of them are still in the phase of brute political power. Wealth in a Latin-American dictatorship is an attribute of the dictator or of his friends and associates. In these cases, true wealth is not the tracts of land or commercial monopolies the rich man holds. It is the dictator's power or his favor. In weakly organized countries, where the system allows free-market development, he may have a power position analogous to that of the American plutocrat a century ago, as long as his country accepts and permits it. Only history will tell how long these phases will last. They tend to be short.

My belief, contrary to that of many intellectuals, is that all systems will yield to the slow but steady evolution toward democracy. This is because, over the last two centuries, democracy has developed systems of economic development and government vastly more productive and more nearly stable than any other form of organization. Under them a degree of wealth is likely to be accepted because it results from productive institutions. But it is highly unlikely that wealth will run wild, as happened in the nineteenth century, precisely because a wide degree of distribution is essential to modern production. Power will remain with the administrators of production—wealth being a secondary result. And paramount power will remain in the political offices whose concern, at least in a democracy, must be with distribution.

There is, nevertheless, a major and dangerous exception. It obtrudes itself unpleasantly on the American and perhaps also on the British scene. Wealth does give the power to connect its holder with, or even to organize, political-party institutions and make himself a power holder, occasionally to make himself a chief power holder, in them.

In the past few years, the United States has seen its richest men emerge as contenders, sometimes successfully, for political power. In 1956, Mr. Averell Harriman, possessor of great inherited wealth, who had become governor of New York (no mean power-holding position), sought to become the nominee of the Democratic party for the presidency. In 1960, in the Republican party, Mr. Nelson Rockefeller, who had made himself governor of New York in 1958, challenged for the presidential nomination—a challenge he abandoned, perhaps too soon. Also in 1960, a young man, John F. Kennedy, backed by his father's huge fortune and using it for the purpose, succeeded in making himself the Democratic candidate for the presidency and was elected. All three were men of first-rate caliber. It is no disparagement to say that probably none of them could have attained the great power positions of either second or first rank had they been poor or of only moderate means. The process of using wealth to achieve power has been excellently described in Richard J. Whalen's biography of President Kennedy's father, Joseph P. Kennedy, *The Founding Father*. It has unpleasant overtones.

More closely analyzed, the exception may be only partly real. The technique of acquiring political power with money is comparatively simple. Money is used to hire organizers familiar with the local political machinery. These are dispersed over wide areas and strategically important districts. They cultivate relations with minor political leaders, holders of power positions in the political party selected as the avenue of approach. District leaders in great cities, county leaders in more rural areas are obvious recruits. American political parties do not have continuous war chests. Contributions are asked for political campaigns; these support the party organization in campaign time. Between campaigns, organizations languish. Then, any "angel" willing to make political contributions secures the friendship and eventually the allegiance of the district, county, or local leader, who must pay a modest office rent, carry on his correspondence—and, incidentally, pay his own bills. His precise problem is to keep a cadre of the party organization alive. This costs money, and there is no regular source of it. In consequence, the man of wealth can contribute, building a spreading group of allies. Once achieved, it can forcefully influence the party of a city or a state. On a large scale, it can affect party operations in an entire nation. The preconvention campaign that resulted in the nomination of Senator Barry Goldwater on the Republican ticket in 1964 was carried out in just this way, as was the Kennedy nomination in the 1960 campaign.

Even so, something besides money is needed. An individual financing a political campaign cannot merely by money unify a wholly disparate group. He has to work within a certain framework of ideas, or at least emotions. Senator Goldwater's backers appealed to a latent right-wing extremism. The Kennedy clan chose to organize the liberal democracy found among the urban populations of the country. Mere desire for power, unattended by an idea system, would not be enough. Money in both operations was an indispensable tool—but only a tool. The personality of John F. Kennedy and his own middle-of-the-road Democratic doctrine were supported by a hard-boiled personal entourage that gave point to the use of the great wealth possessed by his father. The vivid emotional right-wing coherence in the Goldwater campaign (unfortunately for Goldwater, it antagonized the Republican liberal center) was crystallized by the vivid appeal of the Senator from Arizona, himself an attractive individual. Inherently, the nominations of John F. Kennedy and of Barry Goldwater were secured by the same method. Money was an essential element in both results. Money, nevertheless, without the personality and the idea system of each would have been wasted. No rich man could, without more than money, have bought the power position either of the Republican nomination or of the Democratic election to the presidency.

An increasing measure of political power unhappily can be purchased by buying the service of mass media, especially television and radio. Here, wealth is essential. Television time, especially, is immensely expensive. If he can buy it, a rich man can publicize himself, or can push his pet ideas or publicize a favorite nominee, creating a body of sentiment later to be used for political purposes. The process necessarily presupposes that the rich man has some ideas, or has acquired some from advisers. Considerable use of this capacity is presently made in the United States by rich men emotionally involved on the extreme right and the extreme left. (Surprisingly, left-wing extremism finds a remarkable number of wealthy "angels.")

Less ambitiously, wealth may buy promotion and publicity for a play, a book, or a favored artist or actress. The late William Randolph Hearst is said to have provided a cinema career for his friend Marion Davies in this manner. Joseph P. Kennedy, the "Founding Father," used this avenue to introduce his three sons, John, Robert, and Edward, to their political careers. This power is limited. The actress or play put on the stage and the favored politician thus introduced have a chance, perhaps even a good chance, but not more. If the play elicits a yawn, the actress distaste, the politician distrust, the money is wasted.

The power, nevertheless, is appreciable, not because it is determinative, but because, lacking it, too many plays, artists, public servants, and ideas fail to be presented and never come within the range of choice of the American public. In many instances, talent and capacity do not emerge merely because money is lacking to present them. Rich men can provide resources for their presentation, and, because they can do so, can (if they wish) choose whether and what men, ideas, or artistic expression will or will not be offered. Obviously, no rich man has more than a measure of power in this area; yet the problem is major and unsolved in American organization. Better means of presenting ideas, men, artists for public judgment is needed than the favor of rich men.

Sooner or later—let us hope, sooner—the expense of both political and artistic presentation will be financed through other sources. Election campaigns should be recognized as part of governmental machinery and paid for by taxes. Art, plays, and other forms of expression should be financed partly by government, partly by foundations, as scientific research is financed at present. The rich man then would really become important. If a public agency did not do a good job (and it frequently does not), he could compete with it. In competition, his power in this respect could be immensely useful. Tycoons of the past generation—whatever their motives—did leave some great legacies of semipublic presentation. Andrew Carnegie provided libraries. John D. Rockefeller provided social and scientific foundations. The Duke family interests founded a great university, and the Mellons a great art museum. A later generation of Rockefellers provided a large part of the funds and organizing ability for the Lincoln Center drama, dance, and music complex and for the Museum of Modern Art in New York. In the next generation, rich men could become one of the alternatives to bureaucratic financing of these and similar ventures. Left wholly in their hands, the situation might become intolerable, but the usefulness of rich men as challengers to some other system might be great.

One other consideration may summarily be disposed of in this context. Rich men might hold a plutocrats' convention, might organize, might attempt to convert the brute force of their aggregated wealth into concentrated power. The possibility is theoretical only. No such organization has ever been, or could readily be, created. Rich men do not normally accept organization. No consensus on an idea system to support one exists or could easily be developed. Any institution of rich men would become a target for counterpolitical action so rapidly that it could scarcely succeed. In any case, were the wealthy to pool their aggregated power, each rich man would lose his. It would devolve at once on the heads of any apparatus they might set up.

8. The Individual Proprietor

Finally, in the United States, the small individual or family proprietary enterprise—as distinguished from large corporations

—is steadily shrinking as a factor. They still are there; more than a million of them exist in this country. Each proprietor has the capacity to make decisions within his own business; he can give orders to subordinates, ask prices for goods, determine what commercial venture he will enter. But he does not have power to determine the conditions around him. Under the legal system prevailing, he does not have great liberty to combine with other men similarly placed or organize with them to give greater power to chosen leaders. The antitrust laws prevent "combinations in restraint of trade."

What can he do? He can set the price of the product or service he makes or sells. But this is highly limited because he is likely to have competitors; individual small businessmen cannot, as a rule, exercise "market control." He can, within limits, determine what wages he will pay to his workmen and employees. He is limited, however, by the opposed greater power of labor-union leaders where, as in most areas, employees are unionized. He can determine from whom he will buy—but competition makes him buy the cheapest material available. More often, the materials he needs are supplied by only a few great enterprises. He can, and occasionally does with spectacular success, introduce and market some scientific or technical innovation. But he is limited by his need for ever larger capital—and, in any case, success thrusts him into the position of a corporation manager rather than an owner-entrepreneur. For practical purposes, economic power to the owner-proprietor of a business means that he is—but only within limits—boss in his own shop. Small enterprise does place the individual in a tiny power position—but the power is extremely narrow.

IV

Organized Labor and
Its Leaders

1. The Emergence of Labor Unions

Among the most spectacular power holders in the mid-twentieth century United States are the men able to offer or withhold the labor of workers. These are the heads of or dominant individuals in labor unions. Essentially, the power they wield is economic, though it can transcend normal economic limits. Some of these leaders, like James Hoffa,[1] head of the Teamsters Union, have

1. James R. Hoffa became a member of the International Brotherhood of Teamsters in 1934; he was then nineteen years old. Three years later, he became president of its Local Number 299. Passing through various posts, he became vice-president of the union in 1952 and president in 1957. In all of

dreamed of making themselves virtual masters of the United States. Many labor chiefs now rank in power with the men who at the turn of the century dominated American life because they could offer, or withhold, the crucially important supply of capital, and with the owner-magnates of great corporate monopolies in crucial commodities—oil, steel, farm implements, railroads—able at that time to influence policies of the United States government and collect tribute from the public for the benefit of their purses. Labor leaders today wield as much power, if not more, as any group of economic power holders has ever done in the United States.

The institutions by which this power is conferred and through which it is exercised are the labor unions. Each individual worker can, to be sure, work or refuse to work at his job. He has this individual power. It amounts to little. If he chooses not to work, someone else is likely to replace him. When he bargains with his employer for a raise in pay, his employer holds all the cards. Only when he can organize with others and prevent his employer from securing adequate labor except through him or his organization does the laborer meet his employer on more or less even terms.

This fact gave impetus to the formation of labor unions a century or more ago. Initially, they were rather elementary groups of workers in a single enterprise getting together and organizing for their common benefit. Specifically, they combined their individual power to work or refuse to work, with the hope

---

his posts, he demonstrated a liking for and capacity to use ruthless power. As head of the union, he used its strength to organize a substantial number of activities outside the teamsters' field. He had a personal staff of forty lawyers. He bluntly stated that he believed the economic operations of the United States could be regulated by control of transport, and he seemed sure that he could find ways around or through any legal obstacles. He successfully defended himself against a number of criminal charges, but he eventually was convicted of tampering with a jury and at the present time is serving sentence. Perhaps his real offense was seeking to unite the power of a country-wide union with political power. He convinced many of his opponents that, using union power as a base, he intended to construct a variety of political dictatorship, though until he writes his own autobiography the charge cannot be proved. It cannot be denied, however, that under his leadership truck drivers came to be among the best-paid workmen in the country.

that in combination they could require their employer either to meet their wage terms or to shut down his enterprise.

Almost at once they found need for doing more than merely withholding their labor until their terms were met. They had, effectively, to prevent anyone else—"scabs"—from substituting for them. Practically, this was done by force. The combining workers themselves or with allies "picketed" the enterprise from which they sought to withhold their labor. "Peaceful picketing" was, more often than not, a myth. Pickets, as a rule, were prepared to crack the skulls of anyone attempting to work in their place. Riots, small sieges, local conflicts frequently resulted. The Colorado Mine War of 1916 and the fighting at Herrin, Illinois, in 1922 were outstanding cases.

Such conditions in England, on the continent of Europe, and in the United States led social analysts to picture industrial society as in a state of permanent though intermittent civil war. Employers endeavored to prevent workers from organizing and imposing higher wage terms. Unions, syndicates, and similar groups used force to prevent laborers not affiliated with them from entering enterprises or plants they sought to unionize or from which they chose to withhold labor, and to compel unaffiliated laborers to join the ranks. At that time, wages and conditions of labor were low and debased, frequently leading to unspeakable situations. Marx described English conditions accurately in the closing chapters of *Das Kapital*. Upton Sinclair described American labor conditions in Chicago no less accurately in *The Jungle*, written in 1906. Society in general and government in particular rarely considered alleviation of these conditions as their business. The so-called "free market" was assumed by social theorists and speculative economists in universities to reach an equilibrium which, if not ideal, was nevertheless the means of the "best possible" allocation. As a result, labor and employers alike used force and counterforce in addition to their economic weapons of denying labor or wages.

These conditions are not wholly ended even in the mid-twentieth century. There are regions in the American South and there are areas in some agricultural states where matters have not evolved much further than the state existing fifty or seventy-five years ago. Employers in past generations, and in some areas now, were, and are, likely to be able to enlist the assistance of governmental authorities. Local police, sheriffs, courts, and occasionally the state militia could be used to "break" a strike or prevent organization of a union in any particular plant. Excuses were not difficult to find; labor organizations themselves were employing violence to prevent unorganized workers from supplying labor when a plant was "struck."

Given the conditions, however, it is impossible not to sympathize with the labor organizations, despite their undoubted use of illegal weapons. Employers also were using illegal weapons. But they often had ways of legalizing violence denied the opposite side.

Over a period of forty-odd years in the United States, labor unions became recognized, first as legitimate organizations, then as proper spokesmen to secure better pay for workers, finally as recognized legal bodies to which were granted specific legal privileges. The first great federal law in America codifying their status was the Wagner Act (the National Labor Relations Act) of 1935, subsequently revised to become the Taft-Hartley Act, in force today. Employers were required to recognize and "bargain in good faith" with labor organizations chosen by a majority of the workers in any plant or enterprise and to hold elections at which those workers could decide, if they wished, to select such organizations. Employers were deprived of certain legal means by which the authority of the police and the state had been conscripted to their side. Courts were limited in issuing injunctions against strikes. Antistrike injunctions had been a familiar weapon of employers; once an injunction was granted, the employer could legally use force and the police could jail the striker. A law of 1932 bearing the names of two famous Americans, Senator George Norris, of Nebraska, and Fiorello La Guardia, of New York, constricted the injunction practice almost to the point of forbidding it.

Before the Norris-La Guardia Act, almost any excuse could serve for the issuance of an antistrike injunction. In one case, a

coal enterprise was faced with a threatened strike. It had outstanding an issue of bonds, secured by mortgage on the property.
The company procured a bondholder to ask a federal court to
issue an injunction against the strike, on the ground that the
strikers might injure the mine, thereby impairing the bondholder's
security. On their side, labor organizations steadily attacked
judges and courts as being little more than the cat's-paws of employers.

A generation of this sort of infighting produced labor unions of
high organization and strong discipline. Heads of such unions developed a notable capacity to coerce their own members as well
as to prevent outsiders from moving into jobs. When, by the
Wagner Act, their status was recognized and employers were
obliged to deal with them, most unions were tightly knit, formi-
dably led, and closely controlled. Nominally their organization was
democratic. Their officers were chosen by vote of the members of
the union. But the power holders in most unions did not readily
tolerate opposition. Many were able to head off, deny jobs to, or
otherwise destroy any group of union members likely to vote
against them. There were and are exceptions; but successful opposition to the leaders of an established labor union is, on the
whole, rarer than a successful stockholders' proxy fight against
the management of a substantial corporation. As an institution, a
labor organization is an extremely efficient power apparatus. The
pyramided hierarchy of its officers and the tenure of its executive
committee and its senior power holders are well nigh invulner-
able. As in the corporate world, the top group in a labor union
chooses its own successors.

In their use of power they act, theoretically, because their
members so wish. Practically, the wishes of their members more
often than not are dictated by the top group. Labor power holders,
like power holders in other institutions, to be sure, endanger
themselves if they act contrary to the strongly held wishes of their
constituents. They then must enforce their will; the process may
be successful, but is likely to weaken their hold. Consequently,
there is a loose conformity between the application of power by
the top group in any labor union and the uncrystallized desires

of the union members. Yet, ordinarily, the top group tells the members what it thinks the members ought to demand; the members usually respond by wanting it.

Power holding in a labor union has the same psychological effect as any other form of power holding. The men in power want to keep and extend it. They also like the ego satisfaction resulting from widespread recognition that they do have power. Many of them like, and some approximate, the affluence, the luxury, the comparatively grandiose way of living and working enjoyed by power holders in the corporate and the political worlds. (Under the skin, power holders are pretty much alike, though some maintain an ascetic and nonluxurious life. For that matter, some Roman emperors insisted on sleeping on camp cots, declining the voluptuous life of their palaces.) Workmen, as a rule, do not grudge panoply and circumstance to their leaders. They consider these part of the apparatus of power—as they are. They also rightly recognize that the labor organization and its leadership is largely responsible for a salient fact in the United States: thanks to labor unions, in the past half-century most American workmen have moved out of downtrodden proletarian poverty into middle-class incomes and standards of living. Few who have lived through the earlier period, not only with knowledge of, but also in, conditions as they were a half-century ago, would refuse credit to the leaders of organized labor for assuring to workmen their receipt of a respectable share of the enormous increase in American productivity.

Some economists are not so sure of this, believing workers would have enhanced their position had there been no organization of labor power. I do not agree with them, though the point can hardly be proved either way. These economists contend that wages and conditions of work improve automatically as production per man increases. Conceivably, that might have happened; no one can now tell. But that is not how it did happen. As a result, powerful labor unions, led by tough, seasoned leaders, are an established part of the American power structure. Their leaders are among the most powerful men in the country.

2. The Changed Impact of Labor's Power

Unhappily for social and economic theorists, while labor organization was developing, the actual impact of labor power was steadily changing. Briefly, major strikes are now called not against employers, but against the public. Organized labor power has direct or indirect power over great sectors of the American public —and knows it, and uses it. This change was not as complete, and certainly not as well recognized, as that wrought by the corporate system in the nature of property and the resulting reduction to comparative impotence of the power of owned wealth. Yet it is, perhaps, more fundamental. In future, it may be a controlling alteration in the American structure.

Labor organization was, in theory, built to create and locate power—power to bargain with and to coerce an employer into paying higher wages and giving better labor conditions. Bargaining was conceived to be on an equal basis. Coercion could be exercised by strike, making it impossible for the employer to run his plant, just as the employer could coerce laborers by cutting off their jobs and pay. Originally, a strike exerted pressure by preventing the employer from making profits and inflicting on him financial loss. To avoid this, he negotiated with the power holders in the labor union, at length reaching an agreement. When employing enterprises were isolated and relatively small, labor power holders (if they had any sense) realized that an employing enterprise has to make a profit on its operations if it is to pay wages and keep the enterprise going. When the employer sells his product in a competitive market, there is a top limit to the price he can charge for the goods or services he produces. That sets an outside limit on the amount he can pay his workers for wages, labor conditions, fringe benefits. Within this range, the labor power holders asked for what they thought they could get. They usually did not try for a range of wages that would force the employer to shut down, to "price himself out of the market." Bargaining was real and realistic; a bankrupt employer

229

and a closed-down enterprise are of no use whatever to laborers, labor unions, or their leaders.

With the advent of the corporate system, conditions altered. In most industries, a small number of great corporations came to manufacture the bulk of a needed product or render the bulk of a needed service. Though not monopolies, these oligopolies had (within considerable limits) the power to raise their prices and collect them from customers. If all of them were negotiating with an industry-wide union, this fact could be useful. Their power to push up prices, though not unlimited, was great indeed. And where the public depended on their goods and services for their daily life, it must pay or perish.

This fact was a bonanza to organized labor. Labor power holders could demand much more than before. In the days of small business, the employer could plead that his costs were so much, the price he could charge was so much, and that the profit he made was so much. The amount of his profit was the upper limit of what a labor union could demand. But as the oligopolistic corporate system developed, the labor union could say, "We want more pay. Charge it to your customers. Put up your prices." Far oftener than not, this was done. Union leaders and corporation heads both know what they are doing. They are discussing what amounts they can take from the consuming public.

The results have been precisely, lucidly, and sardonically stated by Professor J. Kenneth Galbraith in a brief volume, *American Capitalism: The Concept of Countervailing Power.* He pointed out that an employer had little motive to oppose even unreasonable demands. The line of least resistance for him was to accede to union requests—and promptly raise his prices across the board. The ultimate result might well be price inflation—but that was not his business. The power of a labor-union head thus has a force and impact quite different from and far greater than that of a half-century ago. He is not taking part of the profit away from the employer—the employer can recoup that. He is demanding that the employer raise his prices and meet the demands of labor (and his profits) by collecting from the consuming public.

Union power to withhold labor, thus interpreted, became power to require the employer to levy a higher price for his product or service. When that product was widely used—steel or automobiles, for example, or a daily necessity like transportation—this meant levying a price tax on the entire economy of entire regions or even the country as a whole. As Galbraith observed, labor-union power holders assumed, rightly, that the corporation power holder would cannily raise prices so that his profits would be greater rather than less after he raised wages and prices.

Business during the past half-century has become increasingly affected with a public interest. Increasingly, in large sectors, the goods a great corporation manufactured or the services it rendered were vital, not only to its immediate customers, but also to everyone in the vicinity, or perhaps in the nation. Other enterprises and millions of individuals depended on their transport, their steel, their fuel, their milk, or their product. Deprived of it, great numbers of smaller dependent concerns must shut down. Charged a higher price, they must pay it. Pressure applied to any essential item in the vast economic machine that supplies America rather promptly translates itself into pressure on all parts of it.

A railroad strike, for example, goes beyond withholding labor from the railroad's employers and cutting down the railroad's profit. Without that service, in a relatively short time substantial areas may go without food. The wage claims of labor are directly made against an employer. Actually, they are levied against a large segment of the surrounding society. The employing enterprise, it is true, still has plenty of private interest in not having the labor power holder apply coercion to it. But essentially, the employer has become a conduit, transmitting the demands of the labor union to, and, in case of a strike, inflicting the impact of its coercion upon, a large sector of the consuming public. The coercive power of labor leaders has thus been expanded beyond the wildest dreams indulged by any of them a generation ago.

In New York City, transit is a nonprofit publicly owned municipal monopoly. A public agency, the municipally owned Transit Authority, operates the subway systems and surface buses that shuttle the denizens of the metropolitan area from their homes to work, shops, amusements, and back again. The popula-

231

tion of the city is about 8,000,000, of the metropolitan area about 15,000,000. Many of these millions are, and must be, daily in transit from one part of the city to another. Some thirty-four thousand workers are employed by the subway and bus systems. They are members of the Transport Workers' Union.

In 1965, the union was headed by a colorful old-line labor leader, Michael J. Quill. Wages and conditions of work were fixed by a contract between the Transit Authority and the union, expiring on December 31. Discussion of the terms of a new contract began between the Transit Authority and the union a month or so before the expiration date. The Transit Authority is under the legal duty to charge fares that will pay its expenses and bond interest. In 1965 it was running at a loss or, at any rate, not better than even. Mr. Quill opened the proceedings by demanding a thirty-per-cent increase in per-hour wages, a *four-day* week, and a variety of other benefits. He announced (it was customary with him) that he would strike the transit lines and shut down the city if his demands were not met *in toto*. This threat was dismissed as rhetoric. But the city of New York had just elected a new mayor, John V. Lindsay. Quill previously had had his private ways of doing business with the municipality of the City of New York, based on close acquaintance and political arrangements between himself and the administrations of Mayors William O'Dwyer and Robert Wagner. The outgoing mayor, Mr. Wagner, did not wish to negotiate a contract with the Transport Workers' Union binding the succeeding administration, but Mr. Quill did not wish to negotiate with Mayor-elect Lindsay. Exercising the dubious prerogative of a power holder, he insulted him publicly. As a result, serious negotiation had not even begun when the contract expired.

On January 1, all subways and buses halted, paralyzing New York. As had been foreseen, suburban and intracity traffic attempted to move in privately owned automobiles, thereby dumping thirty-five per cent more cars than usual into the city streets. As New York's Commissioner of Traffic, Henry Barnes, put it, the first few days were chaos; the next few, organized chaos; the third stage, organized confusion. Losses to business and workers unable to reach their jobs were estimated at more than $40,000,-

000 (but may have reached as high as $100,000,000) for each day of the strike.

The real issue, of course, was the fare to be charged by the Transit Authority for rides in subway or bus. The fare was fifteen cents per ride. Raising it to twenty cents would cost an average New York family seventy-five to one hundred dollars annually. Such an increase was the only visible source of revenue out of which union members could be paid their demands. Quill and the union power holders knew that; the coercive power of the union was precisely intended to produce the fare increase. Secondarily, no doubt, the strike was also designed to give Quill a momentarily spectacular position in history. (This is one of the little vanities of labor leaders as well as other power holders, and not the least of the dangers inherent in any power system.) The case was not that of an employer who could go bankrupt and out of business. It was a case where withholding labor from an essential service virtually held a huge city to ransom. Most of the union's demands were met. Fare increase duly took place in the middle of 1966.

The Transport Workers' contract expired in 1967. Mr. Quill meantime had died. A new contract was negotiated without a strike (though not without threat of one), and matters proceeded peacefully.

A similar drama was repeated, with greater danger, in 1968. Then, an organization of municipal employees—the sanitation workers—struck when their demands were not met. Threat was made that the City of New York could drown in its own garbage unless their demands were satisfied, and this came perilously close to the fact. Mayor Lindsay appealed to Governor Nelson A. Rockefeller, asking him to call out the National Guard, presumably to dispose of the garbage. Governor Rockefeller, however, knew that the National Guard cannot be used for this purpose. It might have been used to guard nonunion trucks and workers in cleaning the streets and disposing of the garbage, but it at once became clear that the Teamsters Union local would strike if that occurred. He therefore endeavored to settle the strike himself, and eventually brought about compulsory arbitration within given

233

limits—unquestionably the only practical solution. The City of New York was outraged, first, by the garbage collectors' gambling with the health of the city, second, by Governor Rockefeller's failure to break the strike, though no one indicated how he could do that. Like the strike of the transit workers, the garbage strike was illegal, and its leader went to jail for violating an injunction against it.

In both cases, the people of the city paid the bill.

3. Overpassing Legitimacy

Change in the impact of labor's coercive power did not go unnoticed. Nominally, wage disputes and strikes are still settled by "bargaining" between employers and labor unions. Actually, a defenseless public, which must ultimately pay the bill, is beginning to demand that "statist" power be called in. Piecemeal efforts (many are still in a tentative stage) have been designed to deal with the effects of the new impact. To avoid strikes against railroads and consequent paralysis of the country, elaborate machinery for fact-finding and conciliation was set up by a federal law known as the Railway Mediation Act. In the State of New York, a local statute known as the Condon-Wadlin Act made it a criminal offense to call a strike against a municipality or any state or publicly owned agency of government. The trouble with both the Railway Mediation Act and the Condon-Wadlin Act was that neither provided for binding, final determination of the wage dispute.

Railway labor unions could go through all the prescribed routine—mediation, presidential fact-finding boards, bargaining sessions, and so forth—and still demand higher wages. Thereafter, nothing prevented them from striking. This, in fact, the principal railway labor unions threatened in 1964 and again in 1967. On the eve of these strikes President Lyndon Johnson interposed the power of the state. In each case, he proposed, and the Congress of the United States enacted, a special law requiring compulsory arbitration of the dispute. Labor unions disliked that. They complained, calling it legalized serfdom. They nevertheless acceded. Compulsory arbitration and the eventual findings of the arbitrators were accepted (though litigation on some aspects ensued).

In New York, unions simply paid no attention to the Condon-Wadlin Act and its penalties. Before the transit strike of January 1, 1966, an injunction was issued forbidding the union to call it. Before television cameras, Michael Quill publicly tore up the court order and announced his willingness to go to jail. He was promptly sentenced for contempt, and did go to jail—with considerable fanfare.

Labor-union history has commonly included an element of illegality; a union lawbreaker may be considered a hero. Especially prior to the Norris-La Guardia Act and the Wagner Labor Relations Act, workers assumed, not without reason, that law and courts were employers' instruments for oppression. The railway labor unions had not adopted this view of the compulsory arbitration forced on them by the Congress in 1964, but the Transport Workers' Union felt otherwise about the Condon-Wadlin Act. It made no difference to them whether their strike was legal or not. They made no bones about the fact that the transit-riding public—not the profits of a private enterprise—would have to pay their bill. They said they wanted it paid, and expected the public to pay it—which eventually is what happened.

Similar coercive impact was felt when the printers' union in New York struck and closed down the metropolitan newspapers in 1962–1963. There, the impact of union coercive power was only incidentally on the price at which newspapers were sold, though newspaper prices did go up to a uniform price of ten cents as a result. Unquestionably, the strike in classic fashion did inflict severe losses on the publishers of the papers. That fact, however, was overshadowed by other direct costs inflicted on the public arising from cessation of written news facilities. Theaters could no longer advertise their presentations, or have them effectively estimated by critics. Authors whose books were published during the strike did not obtain the usual reviews of their work; more than one excellent volume went unnoticed into oblivion as a result. Retail trade dropped by between seven and ten per cent because of lack of advertising.

The precise demands in the pressmen's strike are not without interest. They were not limited to demands for pay. A good many years ago, linotype machines had made much of the labor of hand typesetters unnecessary. The press labor unions had then insisted that the employers, though they might install linotype machines, must also continue to employ the printers who set type by the old hand method. It was clear and entirely understood that the type they set would never be used; it would immediately go back into the melting pots. But the hand typesetters would keep their jobs. It had been believed that this would maintain jobs for hand typesetters unable to learn new trades; they could keep their jobs and pay (though the work was useless) until in time they retired or died. There were substantial humanitarian arguments for this. However, the pressmen's union insisted that hand typesetters' jobs should not end when their holders died or retired. The employers, it was insisted, must take on new hand typesetters—although their labor was unnecessary, completely useless, and the fruits of it nil. (It would be interesting to know why any sane man would be willing to spend his life in that way; but there is no accounting for taste.) The union's position at this point began to raise moral as well as economic and humanitarian questions. Coercive power can be and has been used for humanitarian reasons to require continued employment of unwanted, even useless, labor. Justification may exist when workmen performing formerly useful jobs through no fault of their own find themselves displaced by machines. The subject changes when demand is made that new workmen be hired for now useless work. Coercive power is then applied merely to require cash payments to a named group of persons because the union wants them paid. The line between bargaining for economic position and gangsters' demands to have their friends paid off becomes nonexistent.

4. Is Power the Sole Guide?

The legitimacy of use of labor's coercive power at this point becomes relevant.

Labor unions came into existence to rescue the working population from outrageous conditions assigned to it by the economic order. Their early struggle was against these hideous and inhuman conditions, whose sheer horror was obvious to any impartial observer. The initial function of the organization and the coercive power they acquired was to assure living wages and acceptable conditions. Later it was expanded to capture for the workers a fair share of the growing productivity and profits that resulted as industrial society's techniques increased enterprise efficiency. Up to a point, any demand made on behalf of labor—however high—was quite as defensible as are the price demands made by employers who produce goods and services to swell their profits. There need be no great shock when moderately well-paid workers demand that their pay should lift them from lower-middle-class income to higher brackets. Manufacturers and sellers do not consider themselves unjustified when by handling their pricing power they rise from well-to-do to multimillionaires, or raise the value of their corporation's shares on the stock exchange. If the only rationale involved in this game is naked capacity to capture profits from the consuming public, workmen and their organizations perhaps have as good a right to enter the fray for themselves as do corporation managers on behalf of their stockholders.

Obviously, there is a great deal more to the situation than that. Business organizations, through price changes, and workmen, through a labor union, can make and collect demands whose payment will exploit the consuming public exactly as old-line employers exploited their labor. At some point use of either market power or labor power overpasses a "fair" price for labor done or goods sold; it can become mere extortion. That point is reached when payment is exacted, not because the labor done, the services

237

rendered, or the goods sold are reasonably worth the price, but when payment is mere tribute to power, like that levied by the medieval robber baron or the modern gangster. As the old "free market" passes into history, as the restraints and disciplines of competition become less effective, the economic power of both labor and employer can easily become the power of extortion, especially if the goods or services (whose price must ultimately pay the freight) are essential to great numbers of the public.

When coercive power can and does compel compliance with demand overreaching some reasonable economic limit, the function of justifying this power is left behind. We are then in a jungle. The limit of power is the only limit of its action. Medieval robber barons and Balkan brigands operated on this principle for many years. When might makes right, legitimacy has been left far behind. But what is the "reasonable economic limit"? It has never been defined, any more than the medieval Catholic church defined the limit of "just price." Extremes are easy enough to identify. Garbage workers could scarcely have demanded $1,000 a day. Conversely, when an employee is paid so little that he cannot live, he can fairly say that if society demands the service, society can make wages at least adequate to his need for subsistence, or go without the service. American law and custom do not limit an owner-proprietor or a big corporation in the prices he may charge or the profits he may seek, because even an imperfectly competitive market imposes a degree of discipline. Can it be said that a garbage collector is less useful than a shop owner or a corporate milk merchant? The problem is involved—and probably best left to pragmatic solution until customary standards are worked out.

Legality of the power to strike is a prima-facie test—but only a prima-facie test. The New York pressmen's strike had no taint of illegality. The legitimacy of some of their demands was nevertheless (to put it mildly) questionable. The Transport Workers' strike of 1966 was admittedly illegal. Legitimacy would turn on whether, under the conditions, the workers' demands ought to have been met, and on whether there were ways other than a wholesale and reckless sacrifice of the comfort and safety of millions of people by which a justifiable advance in the workers' conditions could be obtained. In the transit case, the probability is that there were other means. Moreover, the plain fact was that the interests sacrificed were entirely disproportionate to the interests of the thirty-four thousand workers involved. Equal—perhaps greater— interests were sacrificed in the case of the pressmen's strike, though they were less obvious. As a result of it and later strikes, three large newspapers, the New York *Herald Tribune,* the *Journal-American & Sun,* and the *World-Telegram,* were eventually forced out of business along with their editorial and reportorial staffs—for whom jobs were not readily forthcoming. For practical purposes, the New York *Times* became a monopoly in the field of high-level journalism, the *Daily News* attained like position in the more popular field, and the New York *Post* became the only New York City evening newspaper in circulation. All three thereby acquired a high degree of journalistic power in politics, in the presentation of drama and the arts, in molding public opinion on issues, and in the introduction of men to politics—a dangerous concentration indeed in a metropolitan area comprising some 15,000,000 people.

Labor's coercive power (for that matter, the coercive power of other economic organization) can, of course, be applied to achieve goals quite outside or apart from the conditions of the workers. This is particularly evident when political ends are sought. The United States has little experience—as a nation—with the "political" strike. But they are regular occurrences in Latin America and in Europe. One or another political party makes alliance with power holders in labor organizations. Their strike power is used to disrupt government until it adopts foreign or domestic policies desired for political reasons. Sometimes such strikes aim to require a change of political power from an existing government to a government composed of power holders satisfactory to the strikers. Communist parties specialize in this. Their theory is that the coercive power of labor should be used primarily to bring about the triumph of the Communist revolution. In justification, they advance the theory that such a government will be a government of the "workers," though the reality is that it would be a government of Communist power holders.

I have put the case against irresponsible labor power forcefully —as forcefully as the case has frequently been made against the oppressive power of ownership or of corporate management. Labor leaders' power has only recently reached its current height. Its present state raises difficult, perhaps dangerous, issues. One of them needs mention.

Is society as a whole, or is the employer, responsible for wage levels? If responsibility rests on the community, how far does it?

Where labor leaders find workers under their jurisdiction receiving less pay or working under worse conditions than any decent society should permit, they have, I believe, the right to call a strike even though its effects may inconvenience or upset the whole community. If the community wants a service, it ought to be required to pay a living wage. This was the situation when, in 1963, the hospital orderlies in New York formed a union and struck. Hospitals are not commercial enterprises; profits were not involved. The pay of the men was intolerably low, and everyone knew it. Labor power struck at the sick of the community because it had no other way to arrive at a decent result. On the other hand, an airline pilots' strike in the same year tied up much of the United States, though air pilots' pay averaged better than $17,500 a year. Basically, they wanted a larger share of the airlines' receipts than they were getting. Like businessmen who raise the price of the necessities of life to fatten their profit, to airlines and public alike they said, "Pay or go without." The hospital strike represented demand for pay and conditions dictated by decency and simple humanity. The airline strike turned on an unsolved question of whether pilots, through their power, should have (or could take) more of the potential profit pie from the public and air-transport companies than they had been getting.

In my judgment, the first represented a legitimate use of labor power. The second was essentially a business discussion as to who should get what from profitable airline operation. In the latter case, it would seem that power should not be used—and its use should not be allowed—when the results inflict substantial loss on the community. Other ways of adjudicating disputes over the pay to be allotted must be found. At a conference called by the

Department of Labor, I made a suggestion: a "reasonable" level of wages and conditions ought to be set. Where the pay and conditions of the workers are below that level, where the community ought not to tolerate this, the right to strike should be unlimited. But where existing wages and conditions are above that level, where the real question is how affluent ought the workers to be, and where a strike presses on the community rather than the employer, the case stands otherwise. For such a situation, an economic tribunal ought to be set up in which conflicting claims can be mediated and if need be adjudicated or arbitrated—the result to be binding. Such was the shotgun solution arrived at in 1964 and 1967 when the railroad workers threatened a national strike and the Congress passed a special law requiring compulsory arbitration. Such solutions will become increasingly familiar, until they are generalized into a system of law.

5. Appeal to the State

But if the state is called in to adjudicate a wage dispute and is required to determine rates of pay and conditions, and when it simultaneously deprives a labor union of its power to strike, some thorny questions emerge.

The state's power to adjudicate these disputes and to enforce its decisions unquestionably exists. Labor unions attained their present power largely because they appealed to the state to give them certain privileges. These they got by the Wagner Act of 1935 and by the Taft-Hartley Act of 1947. The state and its courts enforce on employers, private and public, the duty of bargaining with the chosen representatives of the workers—that is, with labor-union leaders. The state sets up and regulates election procedures by which a union is chosen as representative of the employees. Civil law sanctions and courts enforce the right of unions to collect their dues from workers by checkoff—that is, to require employers to deduct union dues from the employee's wages and pay them directly to the union treasury. Courts enforce labor contracts by which the employer agrees with the union not to employ persons unless they promptly join and pay initiation fees and dues to the union. Other provisions give the unions a large measure of power to determine who may and may not be employed. The unions may limit their numbers, select their members. The surprising result in some craft unions has been that preference to become a union member—and corresponding capacity to get a job in that particular craft—goes only to sons or relatives or friends of union members favorably looked on by union officers. In many cases, the effect has been to permit unions to enforce a nakedly dangerous exclusion of Negroes from employment opportunities. True, the Supreme Court has held that constitutional law forbids such discrimination when carried on by a labor union, but, as we have seen, illegality often does not decide what a union does.

Enforcement of the law, all the same, is not beyond the power of the state. Enforcement of administrative—that is, state—settlements of disputes between labor unions and employers is entirely feasible. Granted that even the state is in no position to imprison or even fine all or any substantial number of union members. But it can withdraw union privileges. Their cancellation— for instance, the checkoff or the right to bargain collectively— would cripple, if it did not break, a great many unions. Many laborers, left to themselves, would prefer not to be under union tutelage and power, though they like the pay and conditions unions have imposed.

But if the state can adjudicate what a laborer ought to have, should it not also adjudicate what profit the employer ought to have—or the price he should charge? How else can be answered the increasingly real question what price the consumer shall be required to pay? Ultimately, the public, directly affected as consumers or indirectly affected by the side results, finds the entire cost included in the price of the product or service. Employers, quite as much as labor unions, have therefore resisted compulsory adjudication. They prefer to deal with the labor unions, even at the risk of periodic strikes, rather than raise these questions: To what profit is your corporation entitled? What dividends ought you to pay? How much of your profits ought to be withheld as capital?

Professor J. Kenneth Galbraith, in a volume entitled *The New Industrial State,* reaches the conclusion that in the final analysis union power holders and corporate power holders are closer to each other in outlook than they are to the price- and freight-paying public. He believes the primary interest of both is to maintain their own power—which is true. He also believes that because price may be pushed to nonprofitable heights—that is, outstrip the capacity of the consuming public to pay—union leaders and corporation managers will eventually agree, with a minimum of fuss, though between them they may cause price inflation. This, I think, may be true when—but only when—paralysis of the enterprise does not bear too heavily on the peace, order, and welfare of the community. The transit strike in New York, relating to the pay of only thirty-four thousand workers, disoriented several million citizens, caused losses of irrecoverable millions of dollars, and also imposed an immeasurable amount of discomfort and personal suffering. For the able-bodied, walking several miles to and from work was time-wasting rather than hardship. For the sick who could not reach doctors or hospitals and the tiny shops for which the loss of two weeks' business was a crushing blow, the effects were disastrous. In the strike of the printers (and certain other unions) in 1965 and 1966, the effect was, first, merger, and then elimination of three metropolitan journals, resulting in a virtual press monopoly. Labor disputes have effects far beyond the range of mere quarrels over who shall pay or get what.

Three interests are here opposed: the vague, ill-defined, undefended, but almost violently real "public" interest; the wage earner's interest in what he shall get in cash, fringe benefits, and security of employment plus his union leaders' interest in maintaining their power; and (except in the case of nonprofit and publicly owned enterprises) the employing enterprise's interest in its market position and its year-end income statement. No one has yet undertaken to estimate or measure what "ought" to be the division among the three. Standards have never been worked out.

By the nature of the power structure, the "free market" ceases to act as arbitrator. The power positions, both of labor and of the employing enterprises, are represented, clear-cut, defined, and effective. The "public" can only act through the state if the state decides to become compulsive; and the state can only compel when some idea system of comparative compensation has been developed. Thus far it has not.

At a meeting of the International Political Science Association in Brussels in 1967, this question was debated in one of the sections. The Soviet delegation, headed by an able and interesting lady, insisted that these "conflicts" were an automatic result of the capitalist system. Under a Communist system, she asserted, conflicts had been resolved: the employer was "the people," the employees were "the people," the state was "the people." So their interests, Communist theory asserted, were the same. Minor conflicts, of course, might exist, but these could be readily solved by administrative procedure—that is to say, by the state, with the Communist party standing between as buffer and shock absorber, eventually counseling the state and the workers to accept some given solution. As discussion developed, it became plain that even in Communist systems, conflicts were much the same as in the United States. The difference lay in the virtually unlimited power of the Soviet state to set what it considered a "fair price" to the Soviet consumer, to dictate what it considered a "fair wage" to the Soviet worker, and to determine the "profit" of the enterprise as an item of state revenue or state planning. It did not need to give much consideration to the feelings of either workers or the "employers," who were, of course, commissar-executives. Its coercive powers and willingness to use them were unlimited. The result thus reflected arbitrary power. It was workable or not workable (frequently not workable) depending on whether the power holder could arrive, not at a just, but at a viable, solution. Such solutions were feasible chiefly because the Soviet state could—and would—compel their acceptance by force if need be. Noteworthy was the fact that, whatever the grievances, the Soviet state's paramount power would not admit any method of conflict solution involving a strike or interruption of the economic operation.

6. Control of Labor Power

Seen in perspective, the development of labor-union power and the placing of it in the hands of labor chieftains was a plain emergence of power to fill a vacuum.

Had the power of employers been directed, among other things, to reducing intolerable situations for workers, they, rather than workers' organizations, might have provided the institutional instruments for assuring rational and adequate order for laborers. They did not do so; they had no ideas corresponding to the plain needs. In any case, they considered wages and conditions of life as a market product, and labor as a market commodity. The result was more than inhuman; it was irrational. One has to remember how labor was treated, housed, and lived in the first two decades of this century to appreciate the fact. Thereupon men who united energy, ambition, and idealism moved in to fill the gap. The result was the power of organized labor as we know it in America today.

This power has about reached the stage that business and financial organization reached between 1920 and 1930. Labor leaders know as well as business leaders that they are part of an economic whole, and that the American state has already been called in to provide order and continuity, productivity and reasonable social conditions. Business leaders as early as 1920 appreciated that statist power must eventually bring the great economic machine into order. As always, power holders resisted change affecting their power—just as labor leaders resist legislation modifying their capacity to impose solutions today. But, as we noted, in ultimates the statist power prevails.

As in other phases of American economic organization, the philosophy is undeveloped. It has got as far as saying that the laborer is worthy of his hire, that his pay must not fall below a stated amount, that he is entitled to share the growing productivity of the country—and not much more. The next phase—determination of just comparison—is now coming up. Whether there should be dif-

245

ferentials between garment workers and airplane pilots, between truck drivers and schoolteachers, between banking officials and automobile salesmen now becomes important. That the compensation a man receives rests on his union leader's capacity to hold a community to ransom, exacting a price for his power instead of using reasoned evaluation, should be questioned. These and similar problems are at issue. To them, we have no real answers, and indeed only the most rudimentary dialogue. The debate has been opened; beyond that, little can be said. Unquestionably the next phase will be statist, because labor stoppage produces the most obvious kind of chaos. Institutions by which the state's determination can be made effective are in process of development. But the philosophy needs development, else the institutions cannot succeed.

V

Can Statist Economics Be Avoided?

1. Compulsions of Progress

Current political thinking considers organization of economic power in the world as divided between socialist (statist) and capitalist (nonsocialist) economies—some economies being "mixed." "Socialism," erroneously, is thought to mean state ownership and administration of property, particularly of productive property. "Capitalism," equally mistakenly, is thought to exist when private individuals or institutions predominantly own, operate, and sell production and its output and in which private individuals or institutions may, subject to limits, acquire and dispose of as much capital or wealth (stock or obligations) as they are able. Conflict between the two systems is assumed to be primarily political. The system adopted depends on the philosophy dominating the power institution constituting the state.

I do not so conceive the problem. States obviously can—as did the Soviet Union in 1917—decide to take over all property and own and operate all productive enterprise. They can permit individuals to acquire or hold only such minor fragments of wealth as the state chooses. Equally, states can elect—as does the United States—to leave production and commerce primarily in the hands of private capitalists or institutions, notably corporations, allowing individuals to have and hold such wealth as they are able to get, to employ or consume it as they choose, subject always to taxation. Historically, there has been political conflict between the two systems and their adherents in the past half-century.

The decade of the nineteen-sixties presents a radically different picture. The development of mass production and mass demand for goods, combined with the relentless onslaught of machines, of population, of the growth of cities, and of mass insistence on rising standards of living, suggests a far deeper and quite different conflict. It is only secondarily political. The real problem is whether either noncollectivized production, nondirected investment, and nonregulated consumption will be practicable much longer. It is beginning to be questionable how far undirected enjoyment of wealth, small or great, or its use for production (whether permitted in limited degree, as in the Soviet Union, or held as of right and without limit, as in the United States) will continue to be physically and economically possible. Or, to the extent it is possible at all, whether it can be kept available to more than a tiny fraction of the population.

In *The American Economic Republic,* I endeavored to point out the wide extent to which production in the United States had already become collectivized through the mechanism of the great corporations. These are nonstatist; nominal legal title to the railroads, factories, plants, computers, and so forth is held by them. Ownership—if the word now means anything—lies in their stockholders. Of these, there are more than 26,000,000 at present. In addition, stock ownership increasingly falls into the hands of other collectives, notably pension funds, mutual and institutional investors' funds. More than one-third of all personally owned wealth in the United States already is in the form of corporate obligations and stock ownership. Most of the rest of personally owned wealth consists chiefly of homes, automobiles, and household machinery.

Wealthy individuals may have two or three large homes, several automobiles, and a wide variety of gear for ease of living or enjoyment, but capable of no other use than consumption. The fragmented "ownership" of productive property—the millions of stockholdings in corporations—conveys no appreciable measure of decision-making power to the owners. Each takes what he can get by way of dividends from the directors. Or he can sell his stock, taking the market value from the stock market. He can consume, but not contribute in any way to the process of production.

"The consumer is king," as the advertising men say. But as consumer, his choices, though increasingly more numerous, are coming to be limited in actual result. More "things" are presented for his purchase in an American department store than were dreamed of in the greatest days of Egypt or Babylon. A stroll past the shop windows of Fifth Avenue offers a glittering panorama of possibility for anyone having the price. Only careful examination indicates that amid the increasing and brilliantly packaged panoply of purchasable things, there has been steady subtraction of things he once might have bought but can find now only in museums, antique shops, or occasional exotic markets. However wealthy the consumer, in America, and increasingly in Europe, a palace is becoming impossible to build, buy, or maintain. The late-nineteenth-century Newport villas of plutocrats exciting the envy and resentment of other Americans when they were built have become collectivized. Where they have survived at all, they are schools, museums, convents, public institutions, or, occasionally, hotels. Amid all the novelties coming in, something is going out.

Labor's changed place is beyond question one of the chief reasons. The price of labor is one factor. With a million dollars, I can still build a palace—not as fine as fifty years ago, because the skilled craftsmen who designed and executed the beautiful rooms are no longer alive. Tolerable imitation can be worked up if expense is no object, though the workmanship will be far worse. But palaces mean nothing without servants—and servants are hard to get or keep at any price. With wealth enough, I can perhaps offer the butler a salary better than that of an assistant vice-president of a bank, or pay maids better wages than they could receive as members of the staff of IBM. I cannot offer them social status or what is considered a "career"—the possibility of indefinite advancement. They cannot be released from their primary function—waiting on me. In America, men and women simply do not care—at any price—to spend their lives at that sort of thing. Increasingly, comfort, luxury if you like, is available only where it can be rendered by machine—but "do-it-yourself" luxury has not yet been devised.

The mass availability of affluent living—or what passed for it a generation ago—has itself become a limiting factor. I can buy a high-priced automobile. But if I choose to leave New York for New England or Long Island on the eve of a weekend, I must inch along bumper-to-bumper for a couple of hours to "enjoy" the car's facilities. That fact cuts down the luxury of the most elaborate car to the measure of the mass-made and mass-consumed vehicles before and behind. No payment frees me from this limitation. A privately owned plane at the moment offers me an alternative. By 1975, there will not be air space enough (even now, there is hardly enough) to accommodate private planes, just as in great urban centers there are not roads enough to afford full use of private automobiles.

The far countryside offers refuge. There are still open lands in America. The northern regions of Canada and the backlands of Central America and Brazil are still unoccupied. There is poverty there, and service is still available. Full use can be made of private planes and fast cars. But the price of obtaining luxury of this sort is now exile. Even this may not be possible indefinitely. In thirty years, the glorious open beaches of the Mediterranean, the West Indies, and parts of Brazil have become weekend resorts, chopped into tiny lots. That tide is just beginning.

This is no great social loss, one may say; civilization is not made to guarantee a sybarite's life for a few. Unhappily, the process that deprives me (cast for this chapter in the role of a luxury-loving multimillionaire) applies even greater pressure to the less affluent who seek the comfort of a "rising standard of living." My difficulty in finding exits from the city to my country place on Friday night is equaled by that of the workman with a cheap car taking the family for an outing. Finding a place to go (a wealthy man still can do this) already is more difficult, as well as more expensive, for him. Some few have already provided themselves with country camps. Those who have not are in difficult case. Annually, great numbers of people arrive in Florida to find every motel placarded with a "No Vacancy" sign; some are reduced to sleeping in their parked cars on the street.

Comfort in a nonluxurious sense already depends on machines. Some are dependable; some are not. Electric refrigerators commonly do function for long periods of time without trouble. But if comfort depends on a washing machine—or a clothes dryer or television set—any slight mechanical difficulty throws the operation out of order. Repair service is available, but often so delayed that the family routine has been inconvenienced, and someone has to resume the menial job of old-fashioned washing. At present the situation is endurable, and perhaps not too inconvenient, though the cost is steadily rising. Barring some change, we are only on the threshold of increased mass consumption made possible by machine-made mass production and growing distribution of wealth. Population increase may perhaps come to be moderate. Even so, there is a substantial foreseeable increase in personally received income, and this will be matched by increased production. The result will be congestion—constriction of the use that can be made of the purchased facilities. The pressure of a civilization based on production and wide distribution implacably and increasingly modifies the power to enjoy.

Somewhere an equation will be struck, but it will not be struck by politics. The Soviet Union is a huge country, sparsely populated, barely beginning to produce on the scale of Western Europe or the United States. It therefore has a golden gift: time and space to adapt production to wants. Conceivably, since the power structure is still formulating its real ends, the country may endeavor to dictate to its people what they shall want or, in any event, what they will get. It may, in short, purposefully control consumption and how its people shall live. The United States, in its current mania for living in great urban complexes, must meet the consumption-control problem long before it seriously worries the authorities in Moscow. Foreseeably, nevertheless, Moscow will have the same problem a generation or so hence. In America, conditions already begin to limit consumption: all kinds of machines are purchasable, but full use of them cannot be made. Space, time, maintenance, labor, supporting services, and a host of minor conditions crowd in.

The immediate remedy, obviously, is regulation and organization. Police rules can be set up to keep automobile traffic running. When more traffic runs, more police regulation will be necessary. In some smaller cities automobiles already are banished from central areas. Sooner or later, New York City, London, and Paris will reach the point at which public transportation only is allowed; the private automobile will be forbidden or its cost of storage and operation will be prohibitive. Private washing machines may become impossible; public facilities will replace them. Perhaps "packaging" (a present mania) will be cut to austerity solely to lessen the amount of litter and garbage to be disposed of.

Control of consumption by statist power necessarily involves control of life. Is this tyranny? Perhaps; yet as it comes it is likely to appear perfectly logical—the only practicable escape from unendurable congestion and confusion, if not chaos.

2. Protest without Purpose

Revolt against the entire economic system has been evident in some quarters in the past few years and deserves a word. Indictment is laid against West European and American society that

252

it is "materialist." Student groups in Germany, Britain, Canada, and the United States in varying phrases make a similar complaint. *Daedalus,* in its Winter, 1968, issue, reviewed a number of these. President Nathan M. Pusey, of Harvard, in his *Annual Report* for 1966–1967, reviewed the protest at Harvard in a passage worth quoting:

Their arguments start with the assumption, which they invariably call their "analysis," that Western society, and especially American society, is rotten through and through, and that this being so, all a sensible person can do is to wish for and to do whatever he can to hasten its demise. Moving on in their "analysis" they see our universities as having been taken over by the business and military establishments lock, stock and barrel. In their eyes these institutions have, as a consequence, forfeited their right to respect and what they call "legitimacy," and have therefore become fair game. They should be brought low by violence or by any effective means, the sooner the better. For, they say, our universities are now devoted to "the present and future oppression and domination of the people of the world—both in Vietnam and in our urban ghettoes." Obviously they live in a world of fantasy. But let me quote a little more:

"The social order we are rebelling against (that is, ours in the United States) is totalitarian, manipulative, repressive and anti-democratic." One of them asks, for example, "Who among us today would argue that America is not an imperialist power?" And they go on to say that "within this order of domination, to respect and operate within the realm of bourgeois civil liberties is to remain enslaved."

Such is the kind of belligerent nonsense with which many college faculties and deans are now confronted through some few students in many places who apparently have convinced themselves that, while making such statements, they are seeing the world whole and speaking truth. Safe within the sanctuary of an ordered society, dreaming of glory —Walter Mittys of the left (or are they left?)—they play at being revolutionaries and fancy themselves rising to positions of command atop the debris as the structures of society come crashing down.

These are not dreamers of a new society, still less of a new economics. Were the demanded revolution to occur, the economic problems would emerge within twenty-four hours—otherwise the revolutionized population would starve. This will not occur. Power will move in, probably in the form of a force dictatorship. The probability is that movements of this kind are not as independent as they seem, or, indeed, as most of their adherents believe. More often than not, a silent and undisclosed, well-organized group, careful not to expose itself in the early stages, encourages a chaotic revolution, intending to use the opportunity and take power to itself.

Human needs demand supply, and automatically produce some sort of economic organization for the purpose. "Materialism"— interest in having one's needs and wants supplied—is a normal, perhaps a necessary, ingredient. Enhancement of wants automatically follows—rises, indeed, to high levels when the capacity of a society to produce is established. Were the dream society to emerge tomorrow, it would require more, not less, economic power. It would also require more, and more precise, philosophical definition of the good life, and, as corollary, of the aggregate economic production and its distribution for the purpose of providing the material base for that life.

3. Mechanization and the State

Like tendencies are evident in production and distribution.

The whole art of distribution today is the trick of causing the customers to do as much of the work as possible. A tiny experiment in that field proved successful when a chain of New York restaurants (appropriately called "automats") eliminated service by requiring the customer to pick out food from coin lockers and carry it to his table. (No system was worked out for making him pick up and wash his own dishes, though some genius will perhaps invent one in time.) This was followed by "self-service" in shopping centers and even department stores. The secret of distribution was found to be organizing customers to form queues and wait in line.

These devices will presently seem rudimentary and unimaginative. The New York *Times* of May 9, 1967, carried the report of a meeting of the National Automation Conference of the American Bankers Association. It was not an essay in science fiction, but a sober meeting of businessmen. It forecast the end of bank checks, currency, and coins, probably beginning about 1975 and developing rapidly thereafter. In the words of the deputy director of the Association, Mr. Dale L. Reistad, it will be "full-blown," with a national system in operation, before the dawn of that "infamous prediction for an Orwellian world of 1984." Based on computers, there would be high-speed communications between a central computer center and terminals to serve bank customers —with the customer (that means you and me) as a "terminal." The president of the First National City Bank of New York, Mr. George S. Moore, challenged his colleagues to use the "greatest opportunity before them," saying: "If we rise to it, banks will be the heart and center of the money and business information flow of the world's economy. If we miss, we will see others do the job." Neither he nor Mr. Reistad observed that the system will require something very close to machine-made customers as well as a machine-made banking system. The business of banking, meanwhile, would be divided into two categories: machine operators, and a central core of men presiding over the standardization of operations. Since everyone must use money or some equivalent, this control mechanism would have impact on everyone.

Dropping to the level of production rather than distribution, we find a steady increase of mechanization. Some factories are almost completely automated; a few men plus a repair crew operate them from a central room. Chief resistance comes from organized labor, just as resistance to power looms came from British hand weavers in the 1850's when riots were organized to oppose the machines. The newspaper strikes in New York in the 1960's were a modern equivalent. The Chartists did not prevent the introduction of looms; nor can the printers prevent the automation of, or substitutes for, typesetting. Organized labor can delay somewhat the automation of great areas of manufacturing and transportation, but the machine, forced into monopoly or near-monopoly business, wins in the end.

The economic effects have not yet been squarely faced, but some are foreseeable. Mechanization lowers the cost of production. Immense amounts of capital are required to achieve it; these are already reflected by the steadily increasing annual requirements of American industry. The year 1967 was not a banner one, yet some $70 billion—nearly one-tenth of the gross national product —was spent for capital purposes, a substantial part of it for increasing mechanization. Small and even moderate-sized businesses do not have, and cannot readily get, capital in the amounts required; the giants can and do. They then come into the field with cheaper production costs ahead of their smaller competition. At this point, the small businesses (if they are not to go bankrupt) must sell out to or merge with some giant—if they are allowed to do so under the antitrust laws. Otherwise they disappear. In nooks, crannies, and margins, small and moderate-sized businesses will still be possible. But they will be increasingly insignificant in aggregate volume. If they are able to grow, they will be forced into the mechanized pattern. The growth of a few giants in each field and the elimination of most others seems inescapable.

Little of this is the result of human design, still less of human conspiracy. There was no conscious intent of automobile manufacturers in, say, 1910, at the beginning of the motorcar era, to remake the face of the United States into its present pattern. Machines develop economic forces of their own whose impact is perhaps beyond control of inventor, capitalist, or corporate manager.

But they are not beyond control of a political state. Government can, more or less arbitrarily, and with varying effectiveness, decide how much of this shall be allowed to happen. Through selective taxation or by direct regulation, enforced, if need be, by the police, it can inhibit or permit the process. When its people dislike the impact of mechanization-on-the-march, their only presently available recourse is to their government, seeking appropriate laws of limitation or prohibition. These can be effective, even when undesired. An American house is now built by techniques appropriate to 1910. Its cost is at least one-third more than would be the case were full mechanization allowed. Labor unions and building trades have exacted enactment by state authority of construction codes preventing building by modern methods. They have inhibited a measure of mechanization in housing. Law, not economics, accomplished that result. So construction methods remain about as they were two generations ago, and home buyers pay the bill. This is one facet of statist control of production, but it is typical. When and if mechanization reaches a point intolerable to sufficiently powerful groups, the state is bound to be called in.

4. The Merger of Private and Public Bureaucracies

As the situation is developing in the United States, two currents are likely to converge. Production of all kinds will increasingly be dominated by huge corporate organizations—as the motorcar industry is today dominated by three giant corporations, Ford, General Motors, and Chrysler. There are likely to be a few hundred (at most, a couple of thousand) such units. In each field of production a few units will struggle with each other to maintain or increase their share of the market—such is the requirement of American law. Enforced competition means, among other things, enforced mechanization, since each must match the other's machines by as good or better ones. Bigness is inevitable.

The other current—government—will be increasingly necessary.

It seems easy to assign responsibility for economic development to the heads of the great corporate units. Because I have had a good deal of opportunity to observe, my own conclusion is quite to the contrary. The outstanding fact is that while he has power in a limited field, the corporation head is almost impotent to control the underlying forces working on him. He can keep the organization running, but has limited power to guide its impact. He may steer his sled in one direction or another, but he cannot prevent it going downhill. He has more power now than he will have later; creation of future conditions is likely to be less and less in his hands. He is very much a Tolstoyan figure. If conscious choices are to be made, government will have to make an increasing share of them. Otherwise the combined forces of economics and galloping technique will determine the direction of affairs and create the conditions of the emerging social-economic complex.

"Socialist" control—that is, direction given and enforced by government—appears to be the single alternative. Ownership has little or nothing to do with it, and may not even be affected. Rather, the task will be to formulate an inventory of desires for those conditions life can afford—if consensus can be had—and devise social controls causing production and distribution to bring them about.

5. "Private Property"—a Packet of Permissions

Little mention has yet been made in this chapter of classic "private property." In fact, the property factor in future production is likely to become almost immaterial to the productive process itself. Even now, if the giant producers of the United States in communications, electronics, transport, oil, steel, and other basic industries were told tomorrow that all their stockholders had been expropriated, or all their stock canceled by law, the result would be an emotional shock more than anything else. Officers with stock options would be unhappy. Employees (if better informed than they now are) would wonder what was happening to their pension funds. One in every three or four would be fearful of his own modest investment in the shares of his corporation-employer or other companies. But the corporate officer would go to his office and behave about as usual. The employee would go to his job and expect his pay envelope on the accustomed date. Salesmen would go on peddling the product. Customers (after they had assured themselves that they would have continuing income) would go on buying, because they need the telephone, the electrical appliance, the motorcar.

Translation from a private collectivism to a state collectivism is the easiest trick in the world where (as is the case under the corporate system) the collectivism is already well organized for production. Lenin, in the semiprimitive Russian state, found much personally owned production and little collectively owned industry, and the take-over was difficult to work out. Hitler, virtually nationalizing plants in Germany, needed merely to coerce or arrange transfer of allegiance of the managers to his Nazi power apparatus. The state, taking over, might even decide to pay dividends to the previous stockholders, making them state pensioners instead of private *rentiers*. A really modern state take-over probably would not disturb stockholder, manager, or anyone else. It would merely prescribe methods of action as needed, levy taxes as desired, and work out measures for guiding production as wanted. This was done, in fact, when, between 1933 and 1938, the Federal Reserve Board acquired the power to determine the policies and in some measure the practices of privately owned banks.

The so-called "property owners" may, indeed, a generation from now be the real "socialists." Pension funds have grown from a negligible amount in 1947 to over $90 billion in 1968, nearly half of this being invested in the stock of corporations.[1] Early estimates that these funds would level off at that figure at the end of fifty years—say, by the turn of the century—proved grotesque understatement. Later, experts estimated that they would reach a maximum of $125 billion by 1980 or 1990. It is already clear that when that time comes the estimate will prove equally ridiculous. Current estimates are that by 1980 private pension funds alone will aggregate $222 billion. Pension funds are now paralleled by the so-called "mutual funds." These already have attained a size of nearly $40 billion, and apparently are destined to increase, though perhaps less certainly than the pension funds. Assuming that by 1980 the aggregate of mutual funds and pension funds plus institutional holdings of insurance companies will have reached $400 billion (the figure is arbitrary but perhaps not too far out of the way), these holdings would then approximate twenty per cent of the claims—stocks and bonds—upon existing corporations. If they chose to exert influence on the man-

1. See Dwayne Wrightsman, in *Quarterly Review of Economics and Business*, Vol. 7, No. 4, Winter, 1967.

agements of the corporations whose securities they owned (they vigorously disclaim any such intention), they would be able to make or break corporate managements at will.

Whether they choose this or not, they will find it increasingly impossible to refuse responsibility. In 1966, a contest for management arose in a relatively small corporation, M-G-M (Metro-Goldwyn-Mayer), whose business was moving pictures. Presently it became clear that a couple of mutual funds held the deciding blocks of stock. The maxim "When you dislike the management, sell the stock" proved wholly impractical—to sell would have slaughtered the stock value. So the rule was abandoned; the mutual funds determined which of the contending factions seemed most likely to choose a management that would make profits, and voted accordingly.

Pension trusts, mutual funds, and institutional holders of stock are not "owners." They are mere intermediaries, paid to buy stocks and securities and to distribute the income and profits from them to their own stockholders, pensioners, or insurance-policy holders on an agreed basis. As in Euclid's definition of a geometric "point," they have position only; but the position is steadily building up to a power position—the power to be used, in theory, only for the benefit of the beneficiaries of their funds. Meanwhile, for a growing portion of the population, investment possibilities are quickly shrinking. An individual having savings may put them in a savings bank or in a life-insurance company (which combines interest on his savings with protection against death or accident). He may buy bonds, though only the larger investors ordinarily do so. He may buy United States savings bonds, as many do. Or he may buy stock in corporations or mutual funds; increasingly, this is what most do. There is still a lively though diminishing field of investment in real estate, though real-estate investing has become a field for experts and wealthy individuals. A few can buy or build, say, a hot-dog stand. But practically, a large amount of individual savings is being herded either into the stock market or into the institutions just mentioned. "Private property" to these individuals and their families means a stock-market quotation and returns received by way of interest or dividends derived from huge corporate aggregates of which they can have little knowledge and over which they have no influence whatever. Meanwhile, mechanization, congestion, and mass are pushing these aggregates into the orbit and power system of the modern state.

The state, it is clear, cannot avoid the gradual expansion of its power function of economic control. There is, really, only one way by which it could do so. It could abandon the policy and enforcement of the antitrust laws, and await the then inevitable monopolization of industry. That process would take less than a decade. Economic power would then go squarely into the hands of corporate-monopoly managers; the state could relax and allow the new system of private government to try its luck. Probably the results would be disastrous unless the monopolies in the various fields of industry organized or combined in some fashion with their fellows, stating an ideology and setting up an institutional framework for an overt economic oligarchy or dictatorship. But were they to do that, they would at once be faced with the same problems now besetting the modern state. They would be forced to arrange distribution of income; otherwise there would be no markets. They would be compelled to make their production processes continuous; otherwise there would be distress. They would be forced to establish a working agreement with the overtly statist function of the creation of money and credit. And they would be held responsible for the resulting social-economic outcome, exactly as are modern governments. They would, quite simply, be forced to set up a socialist dictatorship of their own. Certainly they would find themselves held, formally or informally, to a dialogue with their vast field of responsibility and to political accountability more severely even than their political counterparts. And they would have no way of seeking a vote of confidence by submitting themselves to election.

Hence the theme of this chapter. The pace of mechanical development forces increased size and, with it, increased concentration of economic or business organization. "Pluralism"—that is, many centers of economic power instead of a few or one—can be enforced only by the laws and police of the modern state. But even a pluralist system requires the steadily increasing concern of the modern state with the conditions produced by the many enterprises, none of which can or are allowed to control the others. Standards of action, running all the way from depollution of air and streams to decent quantities and standards of taste in advertising, and possibly the limitation of the drive toward mechanization, are increasingly demanded. In time, the sacrosanct fields of the producers' price and the consumers' choice of product become state business also.

The problem is not whether some sort of socialism should or should not be chosen. Rather, it is whether some sort of socialism is avoidable by any means.

If it is not, we must seek solutions outside economics. We must accept the fact that economic power will be generated to an even greater degree. We must ask ourselves what we want that power to do, and refrain from doing. We must ask what individual action can and cannot be permitted, and what possibilities for individuals must not be limited or impaired, what values in life shall be kept available for realization, what protections must be developed against an "Orwellian 1984."

6. The Necessity for Consensus on a Value System

In the next phase, therefore, enhanced social control over economics is unavoidable.

It is almost immaterial whether this is accomplished, naïvely, by statist take-over of property or, with more sophistication, by statist dictation to property holders of what they may or may not do. Were the state to stand aside, the combined forces of growing population, growing congestion, growing mechanization, and growing mass affluence would compel power control into small groups of individuals brought to power by the existing producing organisms—specifically, by corporations and labor unions. These, to work efficiently in an orderly system, must communicate, develop

262

a theory of operation, and constitute an institution having overriding authority. That institution will need to own little or nothing. It will have to attain capacity to give orders. It will be a pure instrument of power.

Lest the reader consider that he is doomed to live under Orwellian tyranny, I suggest that the antidote is understanding of effective direction and consensus on the use of this power. What should it do? What values must it guard? What results should it seek to achieve? In other words, what philosophy or idea system should inspire, guide, and control it?

That decided, how should institutions be formed and handled to give effect to the ideological conceptions? What dialogue must these establish with the public, all members of which are affected by its decisions? What procedures must be developed so that power shall always be vested in individuals dedicated to seek the realization of the philosophical ideals? What methods can be established to assure order while at the same time preserving freedom of development and expression? (I am assuming that freedom of individual development is one of the values to be maintained.)

The problem will be the same whether the next phase is state socialist or merely capital-power socialist.

Debate on the values controlling economic power is inevitable in the coming American generation, and I think no less so in Communist countries. Americans have indulged the illusion that no control was needed—a hangover from the days when the "free market" would resolve all problems. Communists have cherished the notion that state ownership of property would resolve all human conflict, and the state and its power could then wither away. Neither theory has proved sound. The one led either to inhuman chaos or to monopoly. At the other, Zeus merely laughed; economic organization is essential if masses of men are to be fed, and organization begets power. On deeper analysis, the processes of economics are servants of human desire. What kind of life do people want, or can be persuaded to want, or be made to want? The composite of their wants, whether freely chosen or dictated by some philosopher-king, can then be measured. Economic organization and the power it engenders can then work toward providing the needed material base, and can make its products and services available to meet requirements.

Beyond that it cannot go—unless economic power holders are to become arbiters of minds and emotions no less than of production and exchange.

Combined with the resources of science and technique, economic organization can in the foreseeable future provide a material base satisfying any reasonable demands corresponding to any reasonable composite of wants developed by any national value system. Presently, it does meet the crude requirements of food and shelter, plus a measure of comfort, in the developed countries of Europe and North America. Essentially, nevertheless, the institutions constituting it, private and public, are like the dramatist Pirandello's famous six characters in search of an author. They, and the power they devolve on men, have outrun their primitive constitutive philosophy. They seek their next assignment and await political processes of dialogue and debate to tell them what it shall be.

3

Political Power in the
United States

Preface

The Power to Govern

Citizens of the United States belong to a country whose government has been one of the most stable in recent history. It has not been seriously challenged since the close of the War Between the States a century ago. Americans have taken power for granted—it is there, and prevents chaos. This condition may not continue.

The institutions of the United States, statist and private, allocate power; they choose and change the men who hold it. Their selections are rarely, if ever, questioned, thereby endowing power holders with legitimacy. These institutions adopt and embody working philosophies and idea systems, though little attempt has been made to embody them in comprehensive statement. New ideas and conceptions can enter these by processes of politics, legislation, court decision, administrative practice, or mere acceptance with general approval. In substantial, though somewhat disorderly, fashion, both governmental and private institutions recognize and organize a wide field of responsibility and are coming to understand that wider, unorganized fields also exist. Dialogue between power, privately or governmentally held, and action elements in fields of responsibility is continuous. The results have been satisfactory.

But currently there are disturbing phenomena. There is a Negro cry for "Black Power," accompanied by the assertion that no institutions evolved by white men (ninety per cent of the American population) can be valid for 18,000,000 or 20,000,000 American Negroes, largely concentrated in cities. Student organizations insist that academic institutions, especially universities, cannot be valid unless students (or some of them) acquire power to determine (by unstated criteria) what instruction shall be offered, what men shall give it, and how far they shall be upheld in challenging all authority but their own. Others insist that individuals may opt out of compliance with, or directly break, laws and duties or social obligations of which they do not approve. Artistic extremists in drama, painting, sculpture produce and compose works based on the principle that there are no laws, no rules, no norms. Writers join Europeans and happily proclaim the "death of God." Presently they will import from Paris the newer postexistentialist doctrine that man also is "dead," having become a fatalistically determined (not determinative) and therefore meaningless fragment in an undefined cosmic lump. Professor Marshall McLuhan's theories will no doubt be cited as supporting argument. Such challenges are, of course, as old as power itself. Their history too often has been written in bloody chronicles of revolt and repression. The late twentieth century offers the United States no immunity from problems that have beset Europe through the centuries, rising to revolutionary intensity in recent generations.

Unlike Europe, America has a system of high flexibility. It can accept and adapt new ideas, bringing them and new men with them into its institutional framework. It can act to redress grievances. It can create new and change old institutions within its pluralist system. What it cannot do is accommodate to mere destruction. Russian revolutionists following Mikhail Bakunin proclaimed that destruction was "creative." To anarchic thinking, any organization, any institution, any rules, any man or men enforcing those rules are enemies to be destroyed. In the resulting chaos, power in some expression invariably moves; the anarchists invariably lose. Some power centers, as did Lenin, feed the struggle merely to weaken existing institutions, having in mind and perhaps in organization new apparatus intended to devolve power on their adherents. This is brutal business, likely to test the tensile strength as well as the flexibility of the American system and the power of American governments to govern.

I am optimistic about the result. In historical perspective, the political institutions of the United States in the past generation have been changing with remarkable speed. Senior power as devolved upon the federal government up to now has eliminated chaos, has found, accepted, and changed power holders, has maintained itself through the massive demographic, technical, economic, and psychological changes and stresses of the twentieth century. Its very pluralism apparently has facilitated change— stress in any one institution does not necessarily mean stress in all. Whether the combined adaptability and tensile strength of its institutions will be sufficient to adapt to the growing pressures of the coming years is a question history only will answer. It can be said, I think, that the system has a better chance of coming through than most systems of the past.

The American government, like that of any country, is an institution, divided into subordinate and co-ordinated institutions. Institutions, as such, do not exercise power. They are instruments, partly to choose what men shall be placed in what power, partly to enable them to govern once they are in their positions. Institutions devolve power on men who will govern; but the men, not the institutions, make the decisions.

Institutions of government are undergirded by companion institutions whose function is essentially that of selecting or putting forward for selection men to occupy decision-making positions. These are political parties. In democratic countries, parties nominate, and some form of election decides between the nominees. In single-party governments, like those prevailing in Communist countries and in Mexico, selection is made by intraparty process, including self-advertising, struggle, intrigue. The party's selections automatically become political power holders without further effective choice. Naked dictatorships endeavor to dispense with party or other recognized selective apparatus. As a result, the end of most dictatorships is a chaotic period, commonly brought to an end by armed force.

The distinction between the institutions designed to govern and the institutions designed to select men who will govern is clear enough. Yet it has an implication often overlooked. The selective institutions find themselves also selectors, guardians, and expositors of the philosophy by which they consider government should be carried on and whose principles should guide the exercise of power. The philosophy, the idea systems, and the principles they put forward are the true cohesive force—perhaps the only collective force—in a power system. By their tenets, power holders and the results of their decisions are judged. The Communist party in the Soviet Union (as distinguished from the Soviet government) considers itself guardian of true Communist faith. In the United States, each political party has a philosophy and puts forward a program, called party platform, designed to apply its philosophy to the problems in hand. This program limits the decisions governmental power holders can make, or they encounter opposition and may not be selected when their terms of office are up.

Governmental institutions, on the other hand, have as their prime function the definition of power-holding positions and assignment of power to the men who occupy them. The first responsibility of any government is to staff these positions with the men who will exercise their assigned power.

Revolutions, overturning not merely the personnel, but also the institutions of predecessor governments, must at once create their own institutions. Starting from scratch, they locate power in a few men, construct governmental organizations and companion selective political apparatus by which power will devolve on and be vested in their successors.

The system prevailing in the United States is more complicated than most. Nominally, the Constitution split the power to govern into three co-ordinated functions: legislative, vested in the Congress; executive, vested in the president, and judicial, vested in "one supreme Court, and in such inferior Courts as the Congress may from time to time ordain and establish." The power paramount was in the Congress. The executive was expected to carry out its laws. The judicial power was intended to be independent of both, but primarily interpretative. The Bill of Rights was designed to prevent governmental power from being exercised at all in certain respects. But the play does not follow the constitutional script.

270

The paramount power of Congress rather rapidly was limited by two facts. Theoretically, the Congress "legislates." This is fiction. Actually, it passes on measures proposed to it chiefly by the president and executive departments, less often by party committees, public and private organizations, and individual representatives and senators. The overwhelming bulk of its work consists in examining, sifting, modifying, sometimes vetoing, a program of measures developed by the president, with the help of his departments or of task forces he sets up, and proposed in messages for congressional consideration. Lesser proposals are presented, usually at the instance of private organizations or localities, by a senator or representative. These go to committees of the Congress, whose proceedings are largely controlled by their chairmen. The committees commonly act through subcommittees, again largely controlled by chairmen. Decisions are taken by these men and their colleagues.

After processes of consideration, bills are reported out and brought to vote. At all stages—including that of a final vote—individual members of the Congress, in committee and in final action, vote aye or nay on their personal responsibility. Yet, as matter of fact, the work of proposing major legislation falls primarily on the executive, if only because, as a rule, he and the executive departments alone command the data and information on which legislation must be based. As a result, the Congress can modify or veto, rather than initiate. When it does initiate and enact, the legislation is not likely to be effective if the president and executive departments are unwilling or believe they are unable to carry it out effectively.

The president, in consequence, has long since ceased to be a mere "executive." He is the originator of most legislation; it is the means by which programs of the party that nominated and elected him must be carried out. He can create situations (notably in foreign affairs) requiring congressional action, which he usually secures. He is also the leading public exponent of a philosophy—that of the political party whose head he is. In ultimates, as when disorder threatens or the country is at war, he is held responsible, because as commander in chief of the armed forces he wields the instrument of force.

The judicial power—vested in the nine justices of the Supreme Court—has experienced a most spectacular change in its function. Theoretically, its business is deciding cases and controversies, applying the statutory and constitutional law of the land. Actually, its quite legitimate interpretation of the Constitution and the Bill of Rights has given it the supreme legislative power in great and growing areas. This was not done by usurpation. The Constitution, notably the Fourteenth Amendment, was deemed to require it to deal with a number of situations in which its fiat becomes law irrespective of the Congress or of executive rulings, or of the legislation (or lack of it) of the several states.

And yet the government of the United States is a unit. Its multitudinous institutions, in general, do work together. There is a general agreement—"consensus" was Walter Lippmann's word for it—on the results it must obtain. Emotional unity likewise exists. Anyone who has ever worked in the federal government does feel some kinship to everyone else similarly employed. The severe logic of the constitutional scheme has been mauled and molded by experience; the result is the federal government.

In the ensuing chapters, attempt has been made to capture realities rather than describe processes. To examine all the power positions in the United States government and their relation to each other would require an encyclopedia. Most of them, individually, have been described by scholars in detail, some of them many times. Yet the whole is greater than the sum of the parts, and is far more flexible in assigning and applying power than one might expect. Factual location of power shifts, sometimes rapidly, from one governmental agency to another. In 1969 the president and, next to him, the nine Supreme Court justices are far and away the major power holders. Changed conditions and changed men might alter that situation within a short time. Until Abraham Lincoln's assassination in 1865, the presidency was the effective repository of governmental power. Under his successor, Andrew Johnson, power almost at once shifted to the leading officers and personalities of the Congress.

Until relatively recently, governmental power did not extend to many, perhaps most, areas of American life. All religion, art, higher education, most forms of economic activity, race relations, and almost all instruments of cultural and social philosophy were left to private initiative and organization. That era ended in 1933; since then, governmental power, notably federal power, has steadily moved into one field after another—religion, art, the press, and mass media being outstanding exceptions. Political power now is clearly paramount. It has not been fully extended. Probably it will not be so. Nonstatist power-holding institutions are far too productive, too fruitful, too valuable, and too convenient in American national life. Americans, nevertheless, can no longer indulge the fiction that these institutions are forever sacrosanct.

In an era when thought, technique, and conditions all move (let us hope, forward) in a vast cataract, there probably is no alternative to statist—that is, political—power. Some Zeus must exist to whom appeal can be made when matters threaten to get out of hand. Apparently the United States (and, for that matter, the rest of the world) is fated to swift evolution. Whole populations must rapidly adjust to unprecedented ideas and situations. The corresponding evolution of a paramount power seems unavoidable.

I

The Federal Government

1. The Shifting Location of Political Power

In its dealing with power, the United States is congenitally pluralist. Inherently, it is afraid of concentrated power. Its system therefore seeks to divide power among a vast number of autonomous institutions: governmental, public but nonstatist (such as universities, foundations, churches, charitable institutions, newspapers), and private commercial institutions (notably, large corporations). Factually, the pluralism is less than appears.

Complete examination of power in America, as we have said, would require encyclopedic examination of these institutions. Sociologists and political scientists, in fact, are studying them, one by one. Each year produces a small library of volumes of this nature. Regrettably, neither sociology nor political science has yet worked out norms of description, though they may do so in future. My belief is that if all institutions are examined in the light of the five laws of power set out in Book 1, the detailed descriptions can eventually be combined to make a clearer picture.

This book is merely a series of essays covering certain focal institutions, chiefly governmental, by whose heads and through which power is exercised in the United States. Specialists in any one of them will readily find studies in greater depth. My hope here is only to add certain dimensions to the power structure where I have had occasion and opportunity to observe.

Any realistic sketch map of the major locations of power in the United States refuses to conform to most current thinking. At best, it could only indicate the situation at the time. The location of power and power holders is rarely static. The scene changes from generation to generation, often from year to year. During the Civil War, President Abraham Lincoln took and successfully maintained senior power throughout the Northern states; he probably would have held it in the reunified country after 1865. Shortly after his death, under the presidency of Andrew Johnson, power passed to the aggressive Northern leaders of the Congress. By the turn of the twentieth century, power had come to rest in a small group of nongovernmental plutocrats and a tiny financial oligarchy in New York, to whom political Washington was secondary. By 1914 and during World War I, some of it had been reconquered for the federal government by Woodrow Wilson. It was relinquished by President Warren Harding to the world of big business in 1920. It returned to President Franklin Roosevelt's government in 1933.

Subordinate power pyramids similarly rise or sink in importance both within and without the framework of government. After 1933, Roosevelt brought preponderant economic, as well as political, power into the hands of the president, conquering the barons of New York banking and finance. When World War II broke out, practically all this power moved into the hands of the executive branch of the federal government. Upon its close, part of the federal power over economic matters left Washington. It reverted to the business community, but, instead of returning to the financiers and bankers, most of it devolved on the operating heads of the great industrial corporations in Chicago, Pittsburgh, Detroit, Cleveland, and California—where some of it still remains. Later, centralization and technocratization of the American economy, expanding American social goals, and growing American military needs again relocated a substantial measure of this power in Washington. Any picture snapped in 1969 will certainly not correspond to the power facts of 1979. It would be changed overnight were the United States to experience a major war, a financial panic, a rapid fundamental technical revolution, or a substantial shift in ideology.

2. The Failure of Power System Clichés

For more than half a century attempts have been made to explain the organization of power in the United States by describing it as primarily a reflection of an underlying structure of "classes" or "interests." The theory came from Europe. At least since 1848 (the date of the *Communist Manifesto*), European states and their governments have been considered expressions of European class structures. Identify the dominant class, it was believed, and you at once identify power holders, their motives, and the ultimate direction of their application of power. Like attempts have been, and still are being, made to apply a similar analysis to the United States. I think they fail.

Solid historical reason perhaps existed for ascribing a class basis to European power holding. Classes in Europe were real; in some measure and in many areas, they are real today. Europe's institutions descend from the Roman Empire and the feudal system. Both were institutionally organized class systems as well as class structures. Slavery, in varying measure, existed everywhere; war captives commonly went to the slave markets of Rome, of

.provincial capitals, or to informal auction blocks immediately after victory. (The costs of Julius Caesar's wars in large measure were defrayed by the sale of his captives.) In the European feudal era, serfs, free landholders, knights, noblemen, and royalty had defined status and institutionally recognized power or servitude. The gulf between nobleman and commoner was fiercely maintained, and a millennium of that sort of thing sets up habits not readily discarded.

It was easy to suggest that the commercial and industrial revolution of the nineteenth century merely replaced preceding feudal landholding and royalist class structures by property and financial structures; that moguls, merchants, and millionaires replaced noblemen. I am not convinced this is correct. Nineteenth-century manufacturers, however rich and powerful, seem to me only partially to have replaced noblemen and landowners as power holders. True, industrialists and bankers, rather than soldiers and court favorites, became wealthy. Often they attained position as well as a great measure of influence in government. Yet the commercial institutions headed by businessmen did not vest political power in these men as a group. A new generation may make new analyses of European power development, and its studies may alter the thinking now current, but that lies outside our line of march. What is clear is that America cannot be described in these European terms.

The United States did have some experience with a recognized and accepted "class" system. For example, in early New England, Harvard rosters classified each student as "gentleman" or merely "Mr."—depending on his birth and station in life. Some of this had disappeared before the American Revolution. The Mayflower Compact of 1620 had none of it. In any case; New England Congregational Protestantism allowed little scope for that sort of thing. But a landowning class structure did exist in the slaveholding South, and its mark still subsists, though much of it was swept away in the Civil War and more was eroded by growing industrialization.

Historical luck helped to obliterate much of the American class heritage. Wave after wave of immigration, both before the revolution of 1776 and after, consisted of men and women who hoped or intended not to be bound in rigid status positions. Many, as in the German influx after the revolution of 1848, were purposely fleeing a class system against which they had revolted. Later and larger tides of immigrants quite simply sought a more prosperous and freer life than that offered in their native countries. Practically all had one hope in common: that their children could enjoy a higher status than they had, that their offspring would not be immobilized, as their forebears had been, in an enforced lower-class status. By the latter part of the nineteenth century, the bulk of Americans, in one way or another, had escaped from, when they had not rejected, the class system. Breaking the class system, in fact, was—and still is—a distinctive American achievement.

Strata certainly exist. There were—there are—higher- and lower-income brackets; families of great wealth, of middle-class standing, and of great poverty. There were—and are—all manner of degrees of life. Yet, Negroes aside, few were frozen into any stratum. The grandson of an Irish immigrant could, as did Joseph P. Kennedy, become a plutocrat. The grandson of a multimillionaire like Cornelius Vanderbilt could become dependent for his living on free-lance writing. Jews could throw off the impediments of historical discrimination. The result has been less a class system than a moving staircase. Aside from the brief era of plutocracy—say, 1885 to 1929—the top did not jell; even that plutocracy held together for only a generation.

The outstanding exception, of course, was, and in a measure still is, the Southern upper class emerging as a result of Negro slavery. That was real. It had been strong enough to attempt imperialist extension of the slave system in the years before the Civil War. It had sought conquest of Cuba in 1845. Its influence may have caused the Mexican War in 1848. It began a modified civil war in Kansas and Nebraska in 1854 even before outbreak of the great conflict between the states. It caused Southern secession. I am aware that some historians attempt to interpret the Civil War as a struggle of mercantile classes in the North against the economic life of plantations and cheap labor in the South. I do not think the theory has been proved. The antislavery movement in the North was not primarily resistance of Northern businessmen fearing Southern slave labor, any more than Abraham Lincoln was a bourgeois businessman defending himself against aristocratic landowners. The issue was moral. Samuel Eliot Morison's historical verdict, I think, is unassailable: "Abolition was an irresistible power in a world awakening to new concepts of humanity." [1] Economic determinism had little to do with it. Poets like John Greenleaf Whittier and James Russell Lowell and philosophers like Ralph Waldo Emerson and their allies, to quote Van Wyck Brooks, "made the American anti-slavery movement a part of the great world struggle of darkness and light."

A class system nevertheless did and does remain in much of the South. I suggest that it derives as much from the effects of plantation economy as from slavery. Plantation landowning vests power in owners and managers, with or without slavery—and does so without it in parts of South America today. Importation of Negroes obviously contributed a powerful and continuing element. The appearance in any country of any substantial population bloc visibly different in race intensifies tension and, usually, leads to an attempt by one or another race group to establish superiority. But race distinction does not automatically create a class in the economic sense. The State of Hawaii exhibits several race blocs living side by side with comparatively little class resentment.

3. The Failure of "Economic Determinism"

The endeavor to describe power in the United States as a reflection of economic interests also fails.

The attempt to find American power lodged in great financial and commercial institutions and their heads or owners is perennial. Charles A. and Mary R. Beard, in *America in Midpassage,*

1. *The Oxford History of the American People,* New York, Oxford University Press, 1965, p. 523.

developed a version of that theory. More recently, C. Wright Mills urged it in *The Power Elite,* though he added army and navy officers and the military in general to the bourgeoisie of finance and businessmen. Some justification exists for the body of doctrine heavily mixed with legend and myth contained in the literature of this analysis. At one time, indeed, it may have approximated truth. The latter half of the nineteenth century perhaps saw the deepest penetration of financial and mercantile figures into power positions, though the penetration did not last.

Even in origin, the theory did not go as far as contemporary critics claim. Classic writers like Adam Smith considered merely that capitalist operation would produce the best results in terms of production, prices, wages, and exchange. Therefore, argued Smith and his most brilliant successor, John Stuart Mill, the state should keep its hands off economics. This proposed a permissive relation—not that the state should give its producers and merchants anything they wanted, but, rather, that it keep out of their way. In essence, this meant that the merchants and manufacturers could establish subordinate organizations—factories, mill towns, and so forth—and within these they could set conditions. The nineteenth-century explosion in industrial life did in fact mean that the conditions of life in many countries were chiefly set by a considerable number of individuals or families who owned and operated mills, mines, banks, and commercial enterprises. Scrooge, of *Christmas Carol* fame, did determine the conditions of life for his clerk, Bob Cratchit. The spinning mills of Manchester, New Hampshire, and Lowell, Massachusetts, and, later, the mill and mining towns of Alabama and Pennsylvania pretty much settled what the employee-inhabitants could do and how they should live.

Yet there is a serious gap between this social fact and any theory of the turnover of ultimate governmental power to mill executives or bankers. In form, certainly, this was never done. Industrial enterprises did invade the business of government, especially in states and localities. The government of the State of Montana undoubtedly was dominated (and often selected) by Anaconda Copper Company to forward its interests in the Butte and Helena mining communities. Mr. Winston Churchill (American namesake of the great British statesman) gave a not unfair picture of the government of New Hampshire by the Boston & Maine Railroad in his novels *Coniston* and *Mr. Crewe's Career*. It was not overdrawn. Having spent part of my youth in New Hampshire at that time, I can bear witness. But the picture ceased to be valid about 1920 (if not earlier). The Beards and the Veblens saw American bourgeois capitalism at its apex half a century ago, and their observations carry forward an analysis no longer relevant. And even then there was a hole in the picture. Property and commercial institutions vested power in men for a limited purpose—that of making money. Power was an instrument to that end—and little else. Commonly, it was not a platform from which one attempted to climb to political pinnacles or seek to rule countries. The governmental function was thus highly dispersed and, indeed, its real possibilities were unappreciated and unrealized. One wonders what the possibilities might have been had a really great capitalist—say, a Morgan or a Rockefeller—indulged the ambition of a Louis Napoleon or a Benito Mussolini. Possibly lack of that kind of imagination on the part of these men saved the United States from violent political drama. In any event, it did not occur. Economic organization, and the power it developed, was conceived as a means to a specific end: the amassing of wealth by producing oil or copper, cotton goods or steel, automobiles or tin cans. To achieve this, the primary objectives of the magnates were three: to control prices, to control wages, to control and expand markets. Basically, this is true of their corporation successors today.

Within these limits, any one enterprise or group of enterprises can undoubtedly acquire wide economic power, provided it is not limited or challenged by other coexistent enterprises, or checked by the state. Other enterprises almost invariably did challenge in each area. The American state, chosen by the votes of most of the adult population, most of whom were not identified with a great enterprise, developed an increasing capacity to intervene. Professor Robert A. Nisbet, in *Community and Power*, quotes Marx as saying, "Political power, properly so called, is merely

282

the organized power of one class for oppressing another," and quite properly calls Marx's conclusion "naïve." Actually, it did not prove too difficult for the government of the United States to control even the greatest private economic organizations when circumstances required. Woodrow Wilson did so briefly when the United States entered World War I, though war controls were promptly abandoned at its end. Fifteen years after the close of that war, Franklin Roosevelt found it quite possible to assume still wider control as a result of the Depression of 1933. Lesser degrees of intervention, chiefly by enforcing competition through the antitrust laws, have regularly occurred. I am certain that the relative lack of intervention by the United States government has been due, not to "capitalist" or enterprise power, but to two quite different elements. The first was plain lack of adequate production—there was not enough of it to go around. The second was lack of imagination; few politicians realized what could be done by combining money, credit, and state initiative. Technical advance following World War I began to make clear that underproduction need not be inevitable; the fact now is taken for granted. The New Deal use of credit proved that credit and currency could be used to cause increase of production as well as to stimulate demand; such use is now a standard instrument of government policy.

The implications of these two facts are enormous. They are only barely realized even now. The use of money and credit was always within the reach, and after 1933 became a primary function, of the United States government. Their use is limited by productive capacity—or money and credit become worthless —but productivity is now capable of being indefinitely, though somewhat gradually, increased. Norms of human consumption have been and can be developed in all directions. The things, the services, the conditions of life wanted by people now can be had —due regard being maintained for the necessity of continuously increasing capital facilities to augment future production. The American economic problem becomes that of obtaining a reasonably clear picture of what a population does want or is likely to want in the foreseeable future. That attained, commercial enterprises—actually, a few hundred large corporations—become primarily order takers.

Rapidly, this is becoming the condition of modern economic life. For example, the United States today is in process of deciding whether it wants clean and beautiful cities and country-sides—a new "want" for our time. Setting up the productive capacity to provide them and scheduling the provision of money and credit for the purpose are a major part of economic administration. The dominant demand stems not from commerce, but from popular sentiment translated into government measures. Then any American corporation or enterpriser can bid for the job of supplying some part of the new construction and facilities or offer to supply the consumer goods used in connection with them. There is plenty of scope for economic power there—but it is subordinate, not dominant.

Oddly, analysts endeavoring to label the United States along lines of economic interest usually overlook the one class group disposing of disproportionate power. This is the rural farm group. Its members are diminishing. From having been perhaps sixty per cent of the United States population a century ago, it is less than nine per cent at present. Its agricultural product, though increasing, steadily drops in proportion to the growing national output of manufactures. Until a few years ago, nevertheless, the rural farmers found institutional organization in the politics of local communities. Through that system they did control the legislatures of a great number of states. Representatives in the legislature were traditionally elected from local districts and towns on a geographic basis. This meant that small districts—say, in northern Michigan—inhabited by farmers could, with very few votes, elect representatives to the Michigan Legislature each of whose votes would be equal to that of a representative from a Detroit district with ten times the population of the rural constituency. In aggregate, agricultural legislators controlled law-making in many states, to the detriment of urban areas. By 1960, the capacity of the rural group to lodge disproportionate legislative power in their representatives had become a mathematical and historic anomaly. It disappeared when the Supreme Court, in

Baker v. *Carr* (369 US 186 [1962]), ruled that, under the Fourteenth Amendment, state legislatures must be constituted on the basis of "one man—one vote," and thus happily dove into the thicket of forcing revision of most state constitutions.

The painstaking attempt to force the United States into a mold explaining lodgment of power along class or bourgeois or "capitalist" economic lines is unsound. The problem is deeper.

4. The Federal Government as Repository of Ultimate Power

The entire complex of organizations called the "United States" is subject to the ultimate power of the federal government, acting through the men who direct its various agencies.

Nominally, the federal government holds power by delegation from the fifty states of the Union. Historically, such a delegation did occur when the Constitution was adopted in 1787. The intent was to reserve, free of interference, a large measure of autonomous power to the governments of the several states. The present older generation has seen the virtual submergence of that idea, or, at all events, of its practical effect. For better or worse, the powers originally delegated to the federal government now extend in all directions as far as it cares to push them. States have and still do exercise a considerable measure of power. But they have it on sufferance. This is the only conclusion I can draw from the Supreme Court cases of the past twenty years.

Contrary to the contention of some impassioned pleaders for states' rights, the supremacy of federal over state law was not usurpation. Essentially, Washington did not reach out. Rather, the country moved in. Stagecoach transportation evolved into railroads, motor vehicles, jet airplanes. Commerce became interstate; it knew little and cared less about state lines. Money, banking, credit, and finance became, first, a quasi monopoly of New York and, by sheer necessity after 1933, a function of the Federal Re-

285

serve System and the United States Treasury. "Equal protection of the laws," between man and man, called for under the Fourteenth Amendment, implied and at length exacted uniform standards in all the states. Corporations, relied on for the country's service of supply, became national in size and scope. The current preoccupation for higher and uniform educational standards everywhere—and for upgrading where standards are low— is virtually forced by increased technical demand for more or less uniformly trained men and women and by social demand for country-wide equality of opportunity. A federally standardized and subsidized system of education is gradually emerging as the only practical means by which state and local needs can be met.

Dominance of national power is the only apparent tool by which these and other plainly essential objectives can be attained. This fact perhaps accounts for the comparatively quiet acceptance of increased dominance by the federal government.

The government of the United States at present holds the reins of ultimate power over practically all institutions, governmental and private. It needs only congressional legislation to authorize its use and is limited only by the Supreme Court's interpretation of the Bill of Rights—that is, the first ten—and the fourteenth and fifteenth amendments to the Constitution. These virtually make the Supreme Court into a variety of supralegislature.

Elections, not constitutional doctrine, are the real checks to American governmental power.

5. The Federal Government as Lawmaker

Another rein of power is potential federal monopoly of lawmaking.

It would be overstatement to assert that the federal government now has such a monopoly, and grossly untrue to say it claims one. In a country as large as the United States, where conditions differ as widely as they do between Reno, Nevada, and New York City, between Baton Rouge, Louisiana, and Seattle, Washington, between Traverse City, Michigan, and Los Angeles, California, an immense amount of local regulation should and must be left to localities. Diversity of conduct and of rules governing it is essential. All the same, the standards governing state and local rules are now those laid down by the Constitution of the United States as interpreted by the federal courts. These decrees command general assent. For practical purposes, a senior control is exercised by nine Supreme Court justices whose white temple to Justice stands hard by the Capitol in Washington. Beneath the constitutional rules, the extensive system of federal laws enacted by the Congress of the United States now reaches into every cranny of state life. Federal law can now be extended pretty much as far as the Supreme Court and the United States Congress desire.

How this federal superiority came about need not be discussed here. An adequate account would comprise a substantial part of American constitutional history. In part, it is the result of the Roosevelt revolution commonly known as the "New Deal." Conditions decreed the extension of federal power; President Franklin Roosevelt needed it to carry out his plan for social-economic reconstruction of the country. He met an obstacle in the devotion of the Supreme Court of the time to an older concept—the theory that the federal government had only limited, delegated powers— and to a crumbling conception of inviolate "property." To overcome it, Roosevelt in 1935 proposed a reorganization of the Supreme Court itself. It never occurred, chiefly because it became unnecessary. A great chief justice of the Supreme Court, Harlan F. Stone, whose reputation will grow as time passes and the malice of his great enemy, Justice Felix Frankfurter, recedes to oblivion, undertook the reinterpretation of the Constitution of the United States. Chief Justice Stone advanced the authority of the United States government when expressed by the Congress in federal legislation. He brought a majority of the Supreme Court to his view. The task proved bitter and caused his untimely death; but, next only to President Franklin Roosevelt, he was the architect of the present structure of American governmental power. He set its limits: neither the legislative nor the executive power, federal or state, could infringe the freedoms of speech, religion, the press, the right to vote and participate in political action, or the other rights guaranteed by the Bill of Rights. As a result of his judicial statesmanship, since the end of World War II the popularly elected federal government has become master in the American house.

6. The Monopoly of Force

A monopoly of force is held by the president and the executive branch.

This monopoly is not complete. State governments still have National Guard units and state police. Municipalities and towns have local police. But these cannot be effectively used contrary to the laws of the United States. When they are, court orders can and do inhibit their action—and mandates of the federal courts thus far have been obeyed. The president can place state National Guardsmen under federal orders. As federal funds increasingly finance state activities, Washington's range of action and corresponding influence over state-government operations grow. The Congress can make federal grants to states conditional on their carrying out federal policies or maintaining federal standards. No one has quite cared or dared to say so, but in fact federal policy and federal law are supreme. If they do not cover the entire area of state and local control, it is because the federal government does not choose to do so. The most spectacular recent state-organized attempt at independent action was that of Governor Orville Faubus, of Arkansas. In 1958, he attempted to resist carrying out a federal-court order directing desegregation of the Little Rock high school. President Dwight D. Eisenhower immediately sent a contingent of American troops to protect Negro children entering it. The revolt (if such it was) crumbled.

Opposition, almost reaching the stage of revolt, does occur from time to time without benefit of official state-government sanction.

Such a condition exists today in the State of Mississippi and parts of other Deep South states. The Supreme Court of the United States in *Brown* v. *Board of Education of Topeka* imposed non-discrimination between whites and Negroes and desegregation of whites and Negroes in public schools, requiring "equal protection of the laws" under the Fourteenth Amendment. It carried the principle into other fields. The Civil Rights Act of 1965 provided federal protection of the rights of Negroes to vote and required equal treatment in restaurants, hotels, and businesses offering public accommodation. Opposition to these changes in community habits developed at once; it presently became organized through local institutions like the Ku Klux Klan and informal vigilante groups. Particularly in Mississippi, intimidation, beatings, mob action, and organized murder were used to prevent Negroes from asserting their right to vote or to a position equal to whites. Southern lawyers, because of intimidation or sympathy, refused to represent Negroes. A condition of smoldering rebellion still exists, and the federal authorities are endeavoring to meet it by the combined efforts of persuasion, political action, pressure, and court orders. It cannot be said that federal standards of conduct and even federal force have gone unchallenged. It can be said, with certainty, that the outcome is not in doubt: federal rules will eventually prevail—though the conflict is grievous.

Like resistance to federal standards sprang up when, just after World War I, the Congress of the United States enacted "Prohibition" (the Volstead Act) and the country adopted the Eighteenth (Prohibition) Amendment to the Constitution. That resistance was successful. The objectors convinced the United States that it was both impractical and wrong, and in 1933 the Prohibition Amendment was repealed.

These, nevertheless, are exceptions that prove the rule. For practical purposes, federal law reigns to the extent the federal government chooses to make it. Lawyers do not put it that way, and federal officers, elected or appointed, do not push power to ultimates. Yet it is the immanent fact. This is the background of the American power structure.

The greatest result of the American system is its square imposition on the federal government of the responsibility for maintaining order and preventing chaos. For practical purposes, the burden rests, first, on the president and his executive departments, and, second, on the Congress and, in some circumstances, on the Supreme Court of the United States.

Such is the fact though not the theory. Nominally, preservation of order is the function of state governments. In most local situations—for instance, race riots in Chicago or Los Angeles—the state governor, his police, and, if need be, his militia hold both federal and institutional responsibility. Unhappily, disorder may not observe state lines. A strike tying up the national railway system or the Pacific or Atlantic ports transcends state lines. Even a local disorder may result from resistance to federal law or to a Supreme Court decree. In any case, if the situation gets out of hand, the federal government rapidly becomes involved. The power of the president and of his government is expected to maintain public order. The expectation is trebled if danger exists as a result of war.

On December 7, 1941, the Japanese bombed the American bases in Hawaii. The top government officials immediately went to work at the White House; their first preoccupation was with military affairs. Meanwhile, great parts of the country felt unsafe. Many local officials instantaneously looked to Washington for guidance. I was part of a small informal liaison committee working with the Department of Justice, with the head of the FBI, and with the Coast Guard (which in peacetime works under the Treasury Department). Because few others were readily available, many of the inquiries came to me. My executive assistant, Fletcher Warren, went back and forth to the Justice Department; my associate, Frederick Lyons, vibrated between the State Department and the Treasury. For a spectacular twelve hours, everyone from the Mayor of New York, a police chief in Chicago, the Governor of Arizona, and the Attorney General of California—and hosts of officials in between—telephoned for instructions. We gave them. The Governor of Arizona, for instance, pointed out that two or three thousand Japanese were working on or near the lines of the transcontinental railroads passing through his state, and asked what he should do. Having watched the Nisei, American-born Japanese, I told him we thought there would be little trouble, but suggested he watch them and, if help were needed, call for the dispatch of American troop contingents stationed in the region. I also arranged to have appropriate orders sent them, and for the FBI to close in on a large number of possible sources of sabotage. Similar decisions were made through that day and the following night.

The authority of an assistant secretary of state in these matters was precisely nil. The Department of Justice had a little more leeway but not much. Port authorities were in the same situation. But this was not a case for legalisms. Everyone, it seemed, expected the federal government to take charge. When they could get no higher than the State Department liaison committee, that had to be the federal voice until matters could be formalized— as, of course, they were twenty-four hours later. It occurred to me to wonder, momentarily, whether I should have replied truthfully that I had no right to say anything unless authorized by the Secretary of State or the President. In practical effect, this would have been equivalent to saying, "Do anything you please." This was not a solution. So we filled the momentary vacuum, and later put affairs in authorized channels as rapidly as we could.

Fortunately, dramatic circumstances like this rarely happen. Yet they occur just often enough to prove the point. The action of the Governor of Arkansas in submitting to more or less organized white mobs and, in defiance of a court order, keeping children out of school has been cited. (President Eisenhower's action in response is one of the few cases in history where troops have guarded children's right of entry to their school. There are plenty of instances where troops have been used to *prevent* them from entering, though not in the United States.) The President was right in intervening, though there may conceivably have been other ways of doing so.

The conclusion is self-evident. Any gap in public order must be immediately faced. If the local community or the state does not act, the federal government is expected to step in. Congressional action may be required. On two occasions a nationwide railroad strike has caused the president to recommend and the Congress to take emergency action virtually amounting to compulsory arbitration. When chaos impends in default of solution, Washington is expected to act. As the economic and social machine we call the United States increasingly becomes a concentrated, centralized, interdependent machine, this unwritten constitutional responsibility of the federal government increases in intensity and can be instantaneously invoked.

7. The Search for Philosophical Order

Americans, knowingly or not, are searching deeply—because it is almost nakedly philosophical—for the content of life itself, for a conception of the "good life" in the same sense that Socrates, Plato, and Aristotle sought it in the centuries before Christ. They seek to know (or, rather, to feel, since it is an act of faith) that there is a cosmic order, enduring if not eternal. They seek to convince themselves that they, as individuals, have relation to such an order and that their works and deeds have significance, however microscopic. They seek a value system to guide their efforts. They hope to find avenues toward greater as well as lesser personal satisfactions: serenity, happiness, beauty, joy. They are beginning to discover that these cannot be sought as ends in themselves, or derived from material satisfaction. They result from some harmony between their efforts and a value system convincing to them.

This evolution, this change, and the disturbance it creates are in no way surprising. In this context, economic conditions necessarily become means to an end, not ends in themselves. In two generations, most of the American population has been lifted from a condition of endemic want and privation to a condition of comparative comfort. The America of my childhood looked much like underdeveloped nations—such as Brazil or Argentina—in 1967. Most of its people then literally struggled against fear and too frequently experienced want, hunger, even lack of shelter. By 1968, eighty-five per cent of Americans were well enough off to choose, within limits, what amenities of life they would seek. Their problem became not whether they could live, but how they wished to live. Prosperity and the wider diffusion of income removed most of them from the brute struggle for survival, and offered them modest but increasingly greater resources with which to determine the esthetic content of their lives.

The fact demanded that they find a philosophy. Answer to that problem did not, and does not, lie presently at hand.

Prior to the independence of the United States, every civilization assumed the existence of state religion or state philosophy as a matter of course. An established church, allied to or part of the political state, was an accepted part of social structure. Most American colonies before independence had one. These offered answers (or at least working hypotheses) for the philosophical question and set up at least tentative value criteria. Even if rejected, they provided a base for new thinking. But the philosophers of the French Revolution, from Voltaire on, had convinced intellectual America even before 1787 that established religions were instruments of oppression and regression, that union of the power of religious institutions with the power of statist political institutions was intolerable. Religion or its philosophical equivalent was indeed considered essential—but the state must have nothing to do with it. Hence the clause in the First Amendment to the Constitution "Congress shall make no law respecting an establishment of religion"—a mighty emancipation, which left the philosophical problem to each individual and to disestablished ̇churches or intellectual movements to which they might turn and with which, if they chose, they could affiliate.

Movements in the nineteenth and twentieth centuries went farther. They assaulted the validity of any religion, and, later, the existence of any cosmic order and the value of any philosophical system, whether or not allied to the state. Older faiths, doctrines, symbols, dogmas, and parables came less and less to guide individuals in their choice of values. Great numbers of people cling to them, but mid-twentieth-century America is in a mood to question even as, emotionally, it seeks their equivalent. Young men and women especially ask not only what philosophy they can have, but, indeed, whether there is any philosophical system, any order, any obligation at all. Inevitably, this mood brings in question Aristotle's basic propositions: that every state is a species of association, that all associations are instituted for the purpose of obtaining some good, and that political association is the most sovereign and inclusive. Power is organized by it and through it.

But, if it be true that a philosophy (or, if you will, an idea system) is essential to any association and its organization, decline or absence of a philosophical system necessarily erodes the organization of power, endangering order. This is the fundamental problem in America today.

The current mood of Americans will pass. Even now it conceals a vast, silent, nonestablished but still regnant value system holding together the large population of the United States. It was not by accident that the most acclaimed phrase of the late President John F. Kennedy was "Ask not what your country can do for you, but what you can do for your country"—and it was the young generation that cheered. There is basic acceptance of, and, indeed, desire for, an order imposing obligations and deeply satisfying those who fulfill them. Were this not true, we should have to expect the breakdown of order, a vacuum that would be promptly filled by some form of more or less extreme dictatorial power, whether of the left or of the right.

I do not expect this to occur. Still less, I think, will the next phase be determined primarily on economic grounds. American capacity to produce, though still insufficient, is great enough and growing enough so that (war aside) human life and its content need not be wholly defined by the supply of available goods and services. These can be provided and distributed. The problem will be what value system shall control their apportionment. How much should go to individuals for the satisfaction of their needs? How much to cities and states for the satisfaction of wants that can only be collectively met? How much for scientific research? How much for beauty and the arts? How much for the education of youth as economically productive agents? How much for the education of youth to enable them to search for and realize their esthetic and spiritual values?

These are today's and tomorrow's problems. They are enigmas of power. For better or worse, the government of the United States is the power apparatus through which philosophical consensus must be given reality. Against that background, it must be observed.

II

The American Chief of State—Reality
and Romance

The executive Power shall be vested in a President of the United States of America. . . .

The President shall be Commander in Chief of the Army and Navy of the United States . . . he may require the Opinion, in writing, of the principal Officer in each of the executive Departments, upon any Subject relating to the Duties of their respective Offices. . . .

He shall have Power, by and with the Advice and Consent of the Senate, to make Treaties. . . .

He shall from time to time give to the Congress Information of the State of the Union, and recommend to their Consideration such Measures as he shall judge necessary and expedient. . . . he shall . . . take Care that the Laws be faithfully executed, and shall Commission all Officers of the United States. . . . (The Constitution, Article II)

No person shall be elected to the office of the President more than twice, and no person who has held the office of President, or acted as President, for more than two years of a term to which some other person was elected President shall be elected to the office of the President more than once. . . . (Article XXII)

The Constitution's intent was to vest power paramount in Congress, with co-ordinate judicial power in the Supreme Court and a president to see that the laws be faithfully executed. But it made the president chief of state. That state was fated to become a superpower in military and in economic strength.

Military problems and, at the time of the Civil War, threatened chaos demanded exercise of power; successive presidents used it. Economic crises and, in the breakdown of 1933, existing chaos demanded redress, and the president perforce was expected to provide it. "Necessary and expedient" measures required research, knowledge, expertise, and judgment; these the president was expected to find and supply.

Through the election process the entire United States was made his field of responsibility. It came to demand of its governmental institutions that they allocate to him power corresponding to the responsibilities it expected him to assume.

Successive presidents responded to the demands made on their office. Economic breakdown in 1933 forced the chief of state to become senior economic arbiter. World War II and ensuing American victory lodged vast international power in the commander in chief; the presidency was the only instrument by which that power could be wielded. Circumstances, rather than the Constitution, forced power on the chief of state.

The party institutions of the United States nominate and the political institution of elections chooses the president of the United States, allocating to him the greatest single quantum of sheer power in the current world outside the Soviet Union. Safeguards exist. American democratic institutions choose and change the holder of the office. They deny him power beyond a limited span of years. The White House staff and office group is the only part of government necessarily reflecting his individual desires. His Cabinet and Supreme Court appointments are subject to Senate ratification, but they are usually, though not always, approved. In other respects, the congeries of national institutions making up the government of the United States are existing organizations capable of being changed only by the Congress, somewhat, though not necessarily, responsive to his influence. Yet the entity of the nation, and by consequence his field of responsibility, comprehends the over 200,000,000 of its population, and these he must satisfy. To this must be added those parts of the world's population lying abroad but consciously affected by the actual or potential use of American national power.

To the American nation, he must explain what he is doing

with his power both at home and abroad, and why he does it. He explains in double sense: as a man, justifying himself as occupant of the White House, and as president, outlining and arguing for the policies he lays down, the measures he is administering, the measures he wishes the nation to adopt.

It is sometimes said, wrongly, that he responds to and follows the wishes of the American people. More accurately, the president makes opinion; he does not follow it. If he studies opinion and popularity polls (and he usually does), it is not to find out what he ought to do. Rather, he does so to discover how good a politician he is, whether he is reaching the American people, how far he has gathered support for his policies. As a man, he will presently be seeking re-election or (if his administration is approaching its end) election of a successor sharing his outlook and carrying forward his policies. As president, he must be evolving new measures and administering and developing policies already adopted, and estimating their results. The duality of the function is not always obvious but always there.

Excellent studies of the presidency—as an institution—have repeatedly appeared in American literature. Woodrow Wilson included such a study in *Congressional Government* (1885), and updated it twenty-three years later in his *Constitutional Government in the United States,* then observing of the president, "His office is anything he has the sagacity and the force to make it." Louis Brownlow, an authority on public administration, analyzed the White House as a working institution in 1949 in *The President and the Presidency.* Harold Laski published a brilliant if misleading essay on the subject, *The American Presidency,* in 1940—though that work may have been influenced by Laski's desire to obtain an important foothold in the household of President Franklin Roosevelt. A recent volume is that of Professor Louis W. Koenig, *The Chief Executive,* published in 1964, and revised in 1968. These and a number of other books were important and authoritative for their time—but will have to be rewritten in each generation. Of particular interest here is Professor Koenig's observation that a president has many publics: the national electorate and also a host of lesser but perhaps more informed and efficient pressure groups. Beyond the American scene, the president needs to be concerned with a series of publics abroad. In times of great crisis, their feelings may come close to being, as Woodrow Wilson said, the "opinion of mankind." Both the man as a man and the president as a national spokesman emerge in the continuous dialogue between presidential power and its expanding field of national and international responsibility.

The president is almost invariably a romantic and legendary figure as well as an institutional officeholder and a man.

Romance and legend attach in some measure to any power holder at any level. This is my observation, though I hesitate to state it as a law of power. Heads of government departments, executives of corporations, bureau and section chiefs, university deans, even professors in their classrooms and heads of families usually find themselves carrying on a romantic as well as an actual existence. The romance and legend attaching to each may be true or false, justified or bitterly unjust, good or bad. It may make the subject a hero or a villain. Illusion, hope, perhaps malice, ascribe to him qualities, motives, capacity for good or evil action beyond his human ability or his official scope of operation. The White House occupant encounters this romantic polarization in unlimited intensity. Most human beings harbor an intense desire to believe in the existence of a personal power holder able to give help, redress wrongs, offer inspiration, rebuild their worlds. Not a few desire a scapegoat for their own shortcomings. The president of the United States automatically becomes a focus of the hopes, wishes, and ideals—or of the condemnation—of many millions of Americans, and on occasion of millions outside the United States. The resulting pressure can scarcely be realized by any who have not lived close to it.

During the presidency of Franklin Roosevelt, thousands of personal letters arrived daily at the White House. It was his practice from time to time to read batches of a hundred or so of these letters. Many asked for jobs; these he put aside as merely showing self-interest. Others gave poignant and often passionate pictures of men and women reaching toward the president as though asking for the intercession of an archangel or patron saint. To me, President Roosevelt commented that no mortal being could live up to these hopes—and he might occasionally give expression, encouragement, or direction to them—but he ought to consider it part of his job to do so. Living with an unreal picture of himself seems to be an inescapable condition of any power holder. The father of a family of children, the head of a ghetto settlement house, the executive officer of a company trying to see his employees through a bad time have all felt the same combination of stimulation and frustration. Each is asked to be more than himself—and he knows that he can never wholly fulfill the naïve hopes. In the case of the presidency, the gap between the man and the myth is extreme. The dimensions of the man are left behind in the hoped-for qualities of the power holder as expectations overpass the limit of possibility.

The results of this psychology register themselves in political history; they become a political force. They endow a president with an aura—often extending to his children as well as himself. One product sometimes approximates the effect of blood royal in medieval monarchy, even when the president is held in low political esteem. It is not accident that sons of presidents have automatic entry into American political life, and that many enjoy surprising success. The Federalist President John Adams was far from popular. He was booted out of office in 1800 by the popular Democratic revolution of Thomas Jefferson, whose followers hated, and were hated by, Adams with almost modern bitterness. Yet in 1825 his son, John Quincy Adams, became the sixth president of the United States. In 1840, William Henry Harrison, a frontier governor and general, was elected president. Though he died after a month in office, his grandson, Benjamin Harrison, was elected in 1888. William Howard Taft occupied the presidency for a single term and was resoundingly defeated in 1912 by Woodrow Wilson. His son, Robert Taft, became senator from Ohio and was a formidable candidate for the Republican nomination for the presidency on two occasions during the Roosevelt era. John F. Kennedy was elected president in 1960 by one of the narrowest majorities in history. At the time of his death in

1963, one brother, Edward, had become senator from Massachusetts and another, Robert, soon became senator from New York. At the assassination of Robert during his run for the presidential nomination of his party in 1968, his mantle inevitably dropped to his surviving brother's shoulders. American political institutions give no basis for claim to power based on blood or heredity. American romance does.

The phenomenon is not limited to the United States. More than American sentimentality is at work. To have held the senior national power position apparently sets up psychological forces, even though not embodied in institutions or sanctioned by the accepted philosophy. The first dictator in the history of Brazil was Getúlio Vargas. Forced to retire from his dictatorship, he later ran for and was elected, in 1934, president of Brazil. Still later, his young associate João Goulart, claiming, perhaps not without reason, to be his spiritual heir, developed sufficient support to be elected vice president of Brazil, and succeeded to the top office when President Quadros resigned in 1961. Thoroughly detested dictators have been eliminated amid general rejoicing. Yet not infrequently, after a bit they or members of their entourage have proved able to win a majority of votes in ensuing elections. The roots of this phenomenon run deep.

Medieval legendry recognized (I doubt that it created) these currents of human sentiment. All manner of historical magic has been invoked. An aspirant to a lost throne is the descendant of forty kings, or the descendant of Charlemagne. Royal power was bestowed by the grace of God; somehow it ought, therefore, to extend to offspring. Factually, the family power basis may have been far from romantic. The fortune was founded perhaps by a freebooter captain, as was the case with the Sforzas and the Viscontis of Milan. It may have resulted from shrewd operations by a wool merchant later become banker and able to hire mercenaries, the case of the Medicis in Florence. It may have been achieved through a bastard's military genius, as happened to a Duke of Normandy who later made himself king of England. The operative fact was that they attained thrones or other titles of national rule. This set up a psychological process leading to the

301

myth that God—or history—had marked them for power. Quite aside from its nature, power holding seems to engender some sort of myth as a resulting and operative political force.

In the case of the American presidency, it is strong. So strong, indeed, that it reacts on the power holder himself. He understands its reality—and unreality—better than anyone else. No one can know with certainty whether medieval kings really believed they were God's anointed, though historical record (and Shakespeare) suggests many of them did. An American president commonly does not—usually he takes pains not to—take the political romance too seriously. But he knows—he would be a fool to ignore—that it creates an aura of popular expectation. He is bound to attempt to fulfill some fraction of it. More, he will, if he can, use it as a political instrument to help effectuate his policies. President Roosevelt once commented that if the president were as big as he was expected to be, he would have to be fifty feet tall, but the illusion could sometimes be made useful.

The assigned institutional task of a president, leaving the man aside, is closer to romance than to human reality. American statutes increasingly delegate to the president vast areas of decision-making. The Congress knows as well as anyone else that there are not hours enough in the day for any president even to catalogue the problems. They expect him to subdelegate the power to executive departments. Equally, they expect him to take responsibility for the results.

Louis Koenig considers the president to be a party chief, a legislative leader, an administrative chief, a chief diplomat, a commander in chief, and a political engineer charged with seeking a greater measure of social justice. He is ordinarily regarded "with suspicion and even with disapproval by the progressives or liberals whose reform convictions are more advanced than his" —usually because he seeks what he can get and does not crusade for the impossible better. Administrators and advisers more often are chosen for their capacity to get results than for their eloquence as crusaders. Against an obbligato of romantic expectation, the president works amid a drumbeat of political advocacy (from his supporters) and opposition (from his enemies). Both demand decisions or results they want—and both are "irresponsible" in the sense that the president, not they, must meet the reaction of press, politicians, congressmen, and, eventually, voters. Unlike them, he has to take the risk nationally, for the country, and politically, for himself. He must estimate the limits of possible action, as well as appraise its desirability. Satisfying everyone is impossible

Though the president's romantic image usually brings him passionate support, it also carries an explosive cargo of danger. To some, he may be a benignant father image, but to others, a personal embodiment of all evils in American civilization. The illusion that he is all-powerful makes it easy to hold him the cause of all manner of social injustice, administrative incompetence, moral slackness, spiritual emptiness. Most Americans encounter frustration in some aspect of their lives; some make it a major part of their emotional reverie. These find little difficulty in attributing their unhappiness to others, and the president is always visible. There is even a certain emotional logic in ascribing troubles to a powerful and spectacular public officer.

President Herbert Hoover, in the campaign of 1932, was held personally accountable for the economic disasters that befell the United States after 1929. The only basis for that was his misplaced faith in the then accepted and classic doctrine of *laissez faire* and the virtues of free convertibility of currency into gold. The growing wave of unemployment, the crescendo of bank failures, the spreading misery were, unjustly, considered the work of his administration. President Roosevelt's New Deal alleviated matters considerably, but it excited and presently disappointed hopes as well. Groups whose economic power had been lost to Washington wanted it back. Vortexes of bitterness appeared. After a time, "Roosevelt haters" became familiar in cartoons and literature. Conservative groups were presently joined by the more extreme "liberals," who reviled Roosevelt for not having gone farther in social change. In Roosevelt's case, these did not become serious political dangers, but they were a constant source of unhappiness.

Similar phenomena emerged in the closing days of President

303

Lyndon Johnson's second administration. Frustrated liberals were perhaps the chief focus. Their indictment was laid on three counts. First, Johnson should have been able to avoid escalating the Vietnam war; second, solution of the racial and urban crises should have been given major attention and funding; third, American civilization was crassly and sordidly materialist, little more than a mechanism for profitable manufacture and sale of goods and services, many of them unnecessary. The three allegations have a germ of truth; the error was in placing the responsibility wholly on President Johnson's shoulders. The United States was not all-powerful in 1964; the President of the United States had the terrible responsibility of so handling its national power that an extremely precarious world balance should not be overset. That was the danger when the Vietnam war began. It grew as the war grew, and with it grew the feeling that priority for the Vietnam crisis superseded priority for the "war on poverty" at home. American materialism and the racial and urban crises were the products of the value system of 200,000,000 Americans; unless the president were a superlative saint, he could scarcely change it overnight.

A president can, it is true, take on the mantle of a lay priest and seek to change accepted American values. Some presidents, notably Theodore Roosevelt and Woodrow Wilson, have done so. Franklin Roosevelt occasionally did, though he actively resisted the temptation; he disliked the Wilsonian role of moral preceptor. Some of us around him occasionally urged him to take the pulpit. On rare occasions, he acceded. But, I think, he considered political office a bad platform for ethical instruction; in any case, he did not fancy himself in the role. Uniting the functions of Pontifex Maximus with those of Rex-Dux (as Bertrand de Jouvenel says, "King-Missionary") is dangerous business. It can warp the power holder's view of himself and cause him to lead the country along perilous paths. And yet there are moments in the life of a president when the role of moral leader is inescapable.

Perhaps because this possibility exists, Americans emotionally involved with presidential power frequently find themselves picturing the president as saint or devil, rather than chief executive.

American constitutional law and tradition in the interest of free speech permit virtually unbridled freedom of written, verbal, and pictorial attack. Scurrility and mendacious malice can make the president a romantic image of evil, just as adulation can set him up as an improbable messiah. Either image unquestionably has psychological effects—sometimes profound on many individuals. As Marshall McLuhan would say, "The message becomes the man." In extremes, they can endanger a president's life. Both William McKinley and John F. Kennedy were assassinated by psychotics who, according to such fragmentary evidence as we have, built images of evil from such materials. A third endeavored to assassinate President-elect Franklin D. Roosevelt (his misfired bullet killed Mayor A. J. Cermak of Chicago instead). Sometimes substantial numbers are affected. Their combined illusions merge into a kind of irrational emotional wave—for or against the man in the White House. Political opponents and, more recently, propagandists and psychological warriors serving other governments stir the pot. The scurrilous picture of President Kennedy and, after his death, of President Johnson regularly created by Fidel Castro's Radio Havana and repeated by left-wing agitators in the United States may serve as illustration.

Shrugging aside false images—whether saintly or satanic—is not the least difficult task of an American chief executive. It is hard enough to live up to the realities. Further complicated by the unlimited demands of romance, whether for or against him, the assignment reaches Homeric dimensions. So a president regularly finds himself wryly deflating adoration and turning aside invective. Franklin Roosevelt, as did Abraham Lincoln, met both by inducing laughter. Unhappily, all presidents do not have elephant hides or the God-given gift of humor.

My impression is that America is naïve in this game of romance. Older countries cynically assume that both public praise and public abuse are invariably planned political moves. They have had longer experience. In the sixteenth century, Philip II of Spain used abusive propaganda against his opponents, intentionally causing the deaths of William of Orange and both Henry III and Henry IV of France. He encouraged attacks by unbalanced fanatics to assassinate all three power holders as enemies of the Christian faith—meaning, of course, of Spanish imperial designs. Induced passion is part of European and Near Eastern political weaponry. This, perhaps, was why many Europeans assumed (as some still do) that the murder of President John F. Kennedy in 1963 must have been the fulfillment of a political plot, rather than the act of a half-crazed man. Color, to be sure, was lent by the almost immediate shooting of Lee Oswald by Jack Ruby; killing the assassin who alone knows the facts is a standard maneuver to prevent his plot from being disclosed.

Even with the possible overflow of Arab hatred of Israel and its American friends in the assassination of Senator Robert F. Kennedy, the European interpretation may be dismissed. What cannot be dismissed is American propensity to attach romance to power, entailing peril to the president. While in office, he is the pinpoint target of an uninterrupted and relentless spotlight. He is perpetually surrounded by a horde of reporters, cameramen, correspondents, and gatherers of unconsidered trifles. His every word and act, even his sleep and rest, are recorded and relayed by press, photograph, and now by television screen to all corners of the United States and much of the rest of the earth, flashed into endless homes. The transmitted image focuses uncounted millions of individual attitudes, too often predetermined by favorable or hostile romantic stereotypes previously built up. Continuous overexposure tends to direct personal emotions and thinking, for the president or against him, as the case may be. Television, particularly, exacerbates this process; it is a new medium, whose results are still unknown and are unforeseeable. We know a little about mobs and mob psychology; these have developed occasionally when masses of men are gathered together and their emotional state generates (or is caused to bring about) common action. Mobs have been studied and, to some extent, understood. No one has yet analyzed the kind of continuing low-key mob psychology television can induce. Still less understood is the technique of using this instrument for predetermined ends, though it undoubtedly can be and is so manipulated. Obviously, the president is a permanent target of the television process. In consequence, the perils of the presidency have been vastly enhanced.

Danger to the personality of the president, by the same token, has been increased. He is always at the center of a stage, the object of an audience, and he can escape from neither. Compelled to play a central role, he must also preserve his inherent integrity, must never allow his judgment of reality and the decisions he makes to be warped by the desire or political need for theatrical success. He knows he is a constitutional president, not a theatrical performer. He knows that, great though his power may be, it is limited. He knows the Congress need not obey his will, that the Supreme Court, and not he, is the ultimate interpreter and in substantial measure maker of the laws of the United States. Little of that appears in the printed press; far less on television. The millions of men and women within the field of his responsibility imperfectly apprehend these limitations and tend to attribute to him his apparent, rather than his actual, power.

Some presidents become unhappy. President Harry Truman on one occasion said to me that the White House was the finest jail in the United States. Others have envied one attribute of the British throne: because the ceremonial and theatrical functions of the king are traditionally distinguished from the personality of the man, a British king at times can discreetly step off the stage. An American president rarely enjoys that measure of relief.

Worse practice has developed in recent years. It has become fashionable for intimates, confidants, associates, secretaries, and house servants of the president to put down their experiences and, at the next available opportunity, sell them, often for large prices, to book publishers, magazines, and other mass media. Through the president, they have had contact with history; their records are historical material, often of human interest. But they also have substantial cash value. It used to be well-kept, unwritten law that these intimate memories were not publishable until a decent interval had elapsed. The tradition apparently has changed. As a result, a president cannot even trust his household staff, let alone his intellectual and political advisers. The new theory claims that the demands of history and current politics outweigh the older interest of a president's privacy. I have never been able to accept it. A president should, to function soundly, have the absolute right to develop his thought and explore his ideas with his intimates with a frankness possible only when he does not fear that his evolving thoughts, explorations, and chance remarks, easily capable of being taken out of context, will reach the public print. The result of the modern doctrine is that the president must even *think* alone. His burdens, often enormous, cannot now safely be shared with anyone. It is not a safe atmosphere for decision-making and the procedures leading to it.

From this cauldron is distilled the reality of presidential power. The basic element is the fact that the president is head of most (though not all) of the institutions of government—an excellent ingredient, but by itself not enough. To it is added the president's position as central and dramatic figure in the widespread mass-communication apparatus grinding forth its daily grist of news, information, adulation, attack, and response. This gives him stellar position in conducting the dialogue with his field of responsibility—again, a powerful element but insufficient in itself. It is meaningless, or even worse, unless the president in his own manner conveys the impression that he understands the problems and expresses the apt application to them of the philosophy inspiring and holding together American institutions. Finally, he must carry conviction that he has the essential capacity to cope with situations. Transmitting this conviction requires a human quality beyond that of using the right words on the right occasions; he must communicate certainty that he means what he says. He must not play a part; he must be himself. The performance must raise and maintain confidence that the president can meet any assault of chaos in any contingency. He can do that only if he believes in American institutions and in himself.

In this aspect, human and personal elements involved in power holding become crucial, and the problem of power no longer yields to academic analysis. Confidence in ability to maintain order, to use institutions, to apply a philosophy may be shaken when institutions are clearly not working, or when adequacy of the philosophy grounding them is questioned. Such was the case

308

in 1933. Economic institutions had failed; confidence in individual initiative had been shattered. New conceptions of economic life had to be introduced and new institutions invented. The then president, Franklin Roosevelt, achieved unprecedented power because the country assumed he would see it through the deep waters and accepted him personally as determined and able to change concepts, overhaul institutions, and direct thought, as well as take action.

Somewhat similar conditions, perhaps more fundamental in their implications, began to appear in 1968. The event remains in the hand of history. A president's armory of power elements—constitutional and extraconstitutional—is well stocked. The moral, emotional, intellectual, and instinctive make-up of the man determines his capacity to fuse them into the power of the United States. In ultimate analysis, not the attainments, but the quality of the man determines the issue. Heroes have not been made obsolete by the American historical process.

III

Political Officers and Bureaucrats

In the executive departments—as also in the Congress—two classes of officials are sharply distinguished. One comprises those men held to political responsibility for their words, records, and acts; the other, the bureaucratic civil servants.

In a tidy system, the politically responsible officers would be distinctly defined—as are cabinet ministers in Great Britain. In Washington, political responsibility may turn as much on the publicly accepted position of the man as upon the institutional means by which he reached his office. As a rule, offices filled by presidential appointment and with terms of office that end with his administration (or, earlier, at his displeasure) are considered political. Despite that, men who hold higher administrative position not subject to the president's pleasure, and therefore not deprived of office when he leaves, may attain political responsibility because they have become identified as power holders, have made and executed policy, are known to the press and the electorate as having done so, and thus engage in the dialogue of power with its field of responsibility.

The chairman of the Federal Reserve Board, appointed by the president, is not subject to his pleasure; his term of office is not coterminous with the presidency. The institutional arrangement is specifically designed to remove him from the political arena. Yet a strong and capable head of that piece of economic machinery can become a political officer, as William McChesney Martin had done by 1967. Legally, Federal Reserve Board members are not responsible to the president, but to Congress. Only a major political disturbance could cause them to be legislated out of office. Mr. Martin, after more than twenty years in office, first as member and later as chairman, has rendered unmatched service in the handling of the monetary and credit affairs of the United States. In doing so, he had worked, usually in co-operation with, though occasionally in opposition to, the president and the secretary of the Treasury. First the banking community and later the public credited him with having the power to handle this key function of government. He enjoyed and wholly deserved the growing confidence of the American public. That fact made him more than a mere nonpolitical civil servant. Economic conditions throughout the United States were in part his doing. Justifiably, he shared acclaim for the brilliant results of the American economy from 1960 to 1966. The increasing difficulty encountered in late 1966 through 1967 was, justly, not attributed to him, but, rather, to failure of the Congress to accept his views on fiscal as well as on monetary policy. Insensibly, he had become recognized as that power holder in the federal system whose use of power could cause its success or failure. Because of this, by Washington standards, he became a political figure of the first order.

The same process can elevate a career diplomat, a State Department officer, or a bureau chief in other departments from the ranks of the permanent civil service to political as well as professional position. An ambassador or the chief of a powerful division in an executive department in theory (aside from advising) only executes the policies of the president or the head of his department. If, nevertheless, he gradually assumes or long occupies a position in which his authority is unchallenged, and the fact becomes publicly known, he is recognized as a power holder making policy, taking action, and guiding events. Then he enters the public dialogue and is judged by results: favorable opinion will give him permanent historical position; unfavorable verdict probably will compel his retirement. The power of men can overreach their technical legislative position; no one knows it better than they. It is one thing to discuss matters with a man, asking that he refer to a superior for orders. It is another affair when he has, formally or informally, power to decide the matter. A nominal subordinate whose knowledge is greater than his political chief's and whose word is ordinarily unchallenged has authority beyond the terms of his theoretical mandate because of his personal attributes, his sustained record, and public knowledge of the functions he actually discharges. Many in subordinate office seek to avoid power; some seek to have the power but avoid public knowledge of it; some, by force of personality, by idealist motivation, by personal capacity, or from ambition, assume as much power as they can, intending to hold and extend it.

Politically responsible officers holding their positions by formal appointment or by informal attainment are commonly subject to a single check: the confidence of the president of the United States. Whether institutionally invested or informally conceded, power at political level invariably is involved with the president's regard and position. Their failures, their successes are also his. He, after all, has allowed them to attain power, if he has not actually placed it in their hands.

Presidents differ in their attitude toward these officers. Some, like Dwight D. Eisenhower, frankly delegate power, allowing the men to make the records they can, and limiting themselves to throwing out those who attract too much opposition. Others, like Franklin D. Roosevelt, associate themselves with these men, counseling them often, changing them rarely, removing them from the line of fire when circumstances indicate. President Eisenhower's administration was judged by its political officers—notably his secretary of State, John Foster Dulles, and his secretary of the Treasury, George Humphrey. The successful administrations of President Roosevelt and President Kennedy were generally considered the result of their personal handling of, and their work with, the men they brought into office.

Not unnaturally, the politically responsible men are those who chiefly dominate Washington at any given moment, whether they are in the executive departments, in the independent establishments, or in the Congress. Taken together, they constitute and carry on the administration of the president. His capacity to make them work together, to compose their quarrels, to restrain or satisfy their ambitions, and to release their talents in fulfillment of his policies is crucial. Yet in his absence, or weakness, or decline of power, they must keep the machine going until the next phase.

The vital distinction between political officers and civil servants, it seems to me, depends on whether they enter or are absent from the dialogue of responsibility. Functionaries, mere transmitters of power decisions, ordinarily do not, indeed are not expected to, carry on any part of the dialogue process. Newsmen do not ask them questions, or, when they do, are snooping for information, using the answers merely to help interrogate or pass judgment on the real power holder in the affair. The civil servant plays a silent part. But if, by chance, or circumstances, or capacity, the civil servant does form policy or make decisions, he is promptly drawn into the dialogue, whether he chooses to be or not. Automatically, this involves the credit and reputation of the ruling administration and draws the attention of the head of his department, perhaps of the president. He becomes an asset or liability to them. Then he, like his superiors, enters politics—rising, surviving, or falling as the endless debate goes on.

Bureaucrats in Washington, as in most capitals, constitute the great numerical majority of public officers. These are men having statutory positions in the various institutions or departments of government who expect to make office holding their lifework. To reduce it to lowest terms, all institutions are staffed by men organized through bureaucratic hierarchies into captains of tens, captains of hundreds, and captains of thousands. Their duties and powers are assigned by the formal organization or occasionally by informal custom. Below the level of politically responsible officers, these staffs tend to be permanent. Highly organized bureaucracies commonly demand and secure protection by law of tenure of bureaucratic position and their partial insulation from the perils inherent in political change or the personal ambitions or prejudices of power holders. The civil-service laws of the United States and of most of the states were enacted for that purpose.

The existence of a separate bureaucracy in and of itself checks the power of politically responsible chiefs—not excluding the president. When the position of each officeholder in it is protected by law, the capacity of the organization to prevent action by the chiefs can be considerable. Protected statutory position means quite simply that the president or the cabinet officer or other politically responsible officer cannot hire and fire at will, cannot recruit a whole new staff, can only gradually fill positions with men responsive to his own conceptions and desires. The bureaucracies making up the government of the United States nominally are there to carry out the policies of the president and his appointees. Actually, they can be and frequently are an independent force. They cannot initiate policy, and therefore cannot act independently; but collectively they have power to retard or occasionally block execution of policies made above. They usually control the information and intragovernmental channels of communication on which power holders act and by which their decisions are transmitted. What the bureaucracy in any division of government thinks of its chief and his policies and what chiefs think of their bureaucrats can, especially in sensitive fields, change the timing and often the direction of affairs.

The scope of power assigned any individual bureaucrat depends on that assigned to the precise niche or office he occupies in the hierarchy. It may be extended if, to his technical position, he adds the personal influence accorded his known capacity, knowledge, and wisdom, or augments it by a measure of independent political following or support he has succeeded in attaining. Loosely, the entire group is called the "bureaucrats" or the "bureaucracy." The term, if applied generally, is inexact. Actually, each institution achieves its own hierarchy. Bureaucratic Washington (like bureaucratic Paris, London, and Moscow) is a collection of many separate institutional bureaucracies, made to work in a degree of harmony partly by the top governmental power holders and partly by a comprehension of "constitutional morality." Within that framework, each separate bureaucracy attains more or less unity; each struggles, first, to protect its own existence, then to realize the philosophy or idea system on which the section, division, bureau, or department is based. It struggles to aggrandize its own importance and power; each subchief in it does the same for his own office (and incidentally for himself).

Each bureaucracy carries on two functions: the upward passing of information and advice to the decision-maker who guides its action; and the downward transmission and application of power decisions to the interests and individuals subject to its jurisdiction. Within the framework provided and maintained by the institution of the government as a whole and of each department, subordinate bureaucratic units and their chiefs ceaselessly maneuver both to make their applications of power felt and to increase the scope of their operations. It is a mistake to think of bureaucracies as static. They are in constant competitive though restrained motion.

Top- and second-echelon power holders change regularly in a democracy, and frequently though irregularly in oligarchies and dictatorships. Government nevertheless must go on. In periods of change of government, power drops to the next echelon below— that is, to the bureaucrats. Continuity of government is one of the great functions of bureaucracies.

Bureaucracy in twentieth-century Washington is less highly developed than that in twentieth-century France. There, through centuries of development, it has attained the stability, continuity, and organization of power that make it the recognized "second government"—the appliers of power and administrators of func-

315

tion that continue irrespective of shifts in the cabinet or changes of presidents or even of revolutions. When, under the third and fourth French republics, premiers and cabinets changed on an average of every three or four months, top power holders obviously could not themselves direct—let alone carry on—most functions of government. They stayed in office too briefly even to gain understanding of the departments they nominally headed. Permanent undersecretaries or directors and their bureaucratic staffs, whose tenure of office did not change with each shift in ministry, comprehended and recognized the fact that they, as well as the discharge of their functions, would continue in any event. It made only transient difference, and often in great sectors no difference at all, when governments fell before an onslaught in the Chamber of Deputies. In any case, the power holders could work only on the basis of the information, reports, and recommendations the bureaucratic units collected and forwarded to them. Decrees of apparently all-powerful ministers of state had little reality except as the bureaucracy transmitted and enforced them. Consequently, in France, whether under the third, fourth, or fifth republics, and even today under the presidency and virtual dictatorship of General De Gaulle, the great bulk of governmental power was and is continuously maintained and exercised by the "second government." Spectacular national or political changes occurred, but the system remained much the same. Affairs and curriculums in government-controlled schools and universities went on as always. Taxes were collected as usual. The system of courts of civil justice and administration of the police and criminal law did not vary. The same men, the same ideas, the same dossiers and permanent records, the same administrative rulings and practices continued to prevail. Unless major revolution dissolves and rebuilds the institutional structures, the bureaucracies continue to govern.

In substantial measure, this is also true of Washington. Laws are highly developed for the protection in office of civil servants. In America, as in France, there is often a high degree of popular complaint when they are changed. In the Department of State, the Foreign Service is protected by the Rogers Act, giving permanent rank, status, and tenure to diplomatic officers until retirement age (except for major misconduct). The civil-service laws maintain other departments and agencies in similar manner.

For these men, changes in administration are not too important —unless, of course, the individual bureaucrat has close connections with, or has excited the violent antagonism of, the incoming president or his chief power-holding delegates. They consider, not wholly without reason, that they know more about the precise business of handling foreign problems or fiscal policy, operating the Internal Revenue Bureau or dealing with social security, or running the postal system or the Library of Congress than anyone else. Incoming political officeholders can only work—at least in their early period of office holding—through the machinery the bureaucracies have set up and administer. Each cabinet secretary is almost, though not quite, helpless in the hands of his inherited bureaucrats if he antagonizes them. If they seriously disagree with policies he puts forward, they do not even need to enter into public controversy. They need merely drag their feet or silently oppose by delaying, requiring further study, seeking interpretations, raising practical objections, and leaking information to opposition senators, congressmen, and press commentators. Though a bureaucracy that wants to get something done can only occasionally arrange to do it, if it desires to block action, it can hinder realization of almost any project.

It would be a mistake to regard as disloyal this view of bureaucracy as being semi-independent. Almost invariably the chief of a bureau, division, or section is entirely sincere in thinking that he best serves the United States in the attitude he takes toward declared policy. Not infrequently he is right: he knows that some decision, however well intentioned, will make trouble, perhaps has failed before. Usually he really believes that he is "protecting" the president or his department head, and with him the United States, from a blunder. In any case, most men dislike having their habits disturbed, and bureaucrats perhaps more than others. So they expedite the machinery if they are in favor, and retard it if they are not, awaiting the inevitable time when the

317

top power holders either leave office or come around to their point of view.

When matters are running smoothly, perhaps little damage is done. In mid-twentieth century, however, bureaucracy, normally a stabilizing element, may become dangerous. Change in conditions in the past generation has been extraordinarily rapid; all circumstances suggest acceleration of change in the next. Speed of adaptation, foreseeing and meeting new conditions, may outweigh the interest of smooth-running, continuous stability, only gradually changing as the logic of circumstances becomes obvious. At the time of the New Deal in 1933, economic convulsion forced bureaucrats (outside the Department of State) to be hospitable to rapid innovation. But convulsions are rare, and the education of bureaucrats normally has to proceed by other means.

Charisma, either of a president or of a cabinet officer, at this point becomes important. The capacity to make it clear to a great department and to all the subordinate bureaucracies in it that something must happen and the ability to convey a sense of urgency along with confidence that top power holders know where they are going and are sound in their judgments make the difference. The first task of any power holder, anywhere, at any level, is to conquer the apathy and annex the allegiance of the bureaucrats manning the institutions he heads. There is always a certain lag. All bureaucracies, initially, are inherited from previous regimes. Few are newly organized. Their heads are those who worked under previous power organizations. If asked to change their ideas and practices, they must be both emotionally and intellectually convinced that the new policies and the administrative innovations are necessary.

Difficulty, as I have observed it, generally develops along two fronts. The first and greatest is that bureaucrats carry on only limited dialogue. They are responsible upward to their next-echelon supporters and downward to the men under their orders and to that portion of the public served or regulated by their bureau, and, not infrequently, laterally to congressional committees. But they themselves are not, except in rare instances, the subject of widespread comment. They do not present themselves to an electorate or regularly submit themselves to public account-ability in any orderly fashion. Protected in their tenure of office, they are not obliged to maintain contact with outsiders. The judg-ment on them, affecting their careers, is commonly the judgment of their peers—that is, their bureaucratic associates—and su-periors who "rate" their performances for civil-service records. Information on their discharge of function is rarely a matter of general knowledge, though their decisions occasionally attract the attention, favorable or unfavorable, of the press. They can easily become enfolded in the mono-ideology which is the philosophy of their bureau and may or may not be affected by the pounding dialogue constantly maintained between the public and the politi-cally responsible officers.

Probably this was true in the days of the Pharaohs; probably it will be true as long as government exists. It becomes accentuated when governments and the associated bureaucracies constituting them become vast. Small offices can be scrutinized more easily than large. When he was secretary of State, Cordell Hull resisted every expansion of the State Department bureaucracy, whose personnel then was about three thousand. At the close of the Truman administration, it had expanded to between twelve thou-sand and fifteen thousand, and has grown considerably since that time. A great deal was known about the operations of the State Department in Secretary Hull's time—and he chose to keep it that way. In later years, ferreting out any operation in it became a major task of journalism, investigation, or research. A great por-tion of the constituting bureaucracies of the government of the United States does not have the benefit of continuous dialogue, for the excellent reason that its decisions and operations are too difficult to follow.

Bureaucrats nevertheless are a part of and subject to the re-peated continuous conversation of Washington. They go out to dinner, talk to their friends, read the newspapers, and in the field of their own interests are extremely well informed. They are discussed at other dinner parties, in other groups and circles. Some results are surprising. A young lieutenant assigned to Washington in 1918 got a room in a humble house behind the Capitol. The owner of the house was a chief clerk in the then War Department. From time to time, he would talk to his young tenant about affairs. Especially, he told him what his next orders were going to be weeks in advance of his receiving them. Because they were unimportant, he did not add that with a few words he could probably have secured their change—but he did, slyly, suggest that if they looked unpleasant something might be done about them. Multiply this situation by thousands, and one begins to perceive the actual, as contrasted with the formal, workings of government.

In a bureaucracy, as elsewhere, power opposes disorder, is individually held and institutionally applied, has an organizing and guiding idea system, carries on a dialogue with a field of responsibility. As the functions of government grow, bureaucracies are bound to increase; they, indeed, are the running gear of power application. Their limitations are largely due to the limited dialogue they maintain. Intradepartmental personnel discuss, criticize, process, pass judgments, but the sector of the public affected rarely knows anything but rulings or results emerging from a distant, faceless organization. Washington has yet to invent an adequate dialogue with the bureaucratic machine.

IV

Congress and the Men Who Exercise
Its Power

The Congress of the United States is the institution in which, nominally, all legislative powers are vested. Actually, it is only in part capable of legislating. Laws more often than not are drafted in the executive departments, are recommended by the president, and are modified (or occasionally vetoed) by the Congress. Major exceptions occur from time to time, as when an exceptionally able legislator works up a projected law, secures its passage and the assent of the president. Senator Paul Douglas did this when he evolved the Employment Act of 1946—part of the fundamental law of the United States. Senator Robert Taft achieved the Taft-Hartley Act, revising the National Labor Relations Act pioneered by Senator Robert Wagner. As a rule, nevertheless, the president and his men propose and recommend the measures finding their way to the statute books; the Congress may modify, amend, or revise these laws before passage. Its greatest present power is that of granting or denying the money needed to give reality to laws that would otherwise remain so much paper.

So it is not exact to say that "the Congress" exercises the power it nominally holds. Its houses (one hundred senators and four hundred and thirty-five representatives) are abstractions. As groups, both are clearly too large to act. They therefore allocate power to and through congressional committees and, beneath them, to subcommittees, each of which elects a seniority-determined chairman. A recent study of the Congress, Douglass Cater's *Power in Washington,* quotes with approval an earlier student, George B. Galloway, who described these chairmen as "masters of their committees." Though locally elected and nominally responsible only to their districts, these men in key positions divide the powers of Congress among them. Cater considers them as holding "baronial" position, almost immune from outside control. As to each: "When it suits his views or his ambitions, he can be a powerful ally for a President. Or, if it suits, he can defy the President and challenge him with persistent rear-guard actions. With any canniness, he can hold areas of the Executive in a form of thralldom." [1] In the Congress, as elsewhere, power is personal.

Under vigorous leadership, some committees are able to dominate areas of the executive power—as the Joint Congressional Committee on Atomic Energy was able to dominate the Atomic Energy Commission set up in 1946, and as the Military Affairs Committee exerts steady influence in the Department of Defense. For practical purposes, most men holding power in Congress exercise it by permitting or withholding appropriations or legislation. Included in that power is the capacity to favor or penalize districts, areas, and commercial interests, and occasionally to forward or destroy individual careers or commercial interests.

1. *Power in Washington,* New York, Random House, 1964, p. 160.

Criticism of the system has been continuous—and rarely effective. Members of Congress (especially when they are not in baronial positions) often complain, and with reason. Yet it is not easy to see how the immense business of Congress could be transacted were it not for the fact that it does sublet its powers to these committees and subcommittees and through these to their chairmen. Without such delegation, chaos might be the result.

In the closing session of Congress in 1932, when the Hoover government lost control and the system virtually broke down, such a chaotic situation almost did exist. Only the demonic energy of men like Fiorello La Guardia got anything done at all. If there is anything worse than arbitrarily distributed power within Congress, it is disorganization making it impossible for the Congress to act. Yet, of necessity, through organization, power promptly becomes individual, as any who have dealt with the Congress come rapidly to understand. At any given moment, the personal power of a strategically placed member of Congress may control the national policy of the United States.

Illustration was perhaps never more dramatic than in late 1967. Then, for some months, circumstances located dominant power in the hands of Wilbur D. Mills, of Kensett, Arkansas, chairman of the Ways and Means Committee of the House of Representatives. The Constitution lodges the power to initiate appropriation bills in the House of Representatives; the House places jurisdiction over such bills in the Ways and Means Committee; by seniority, Mr. Mills was chairman of that committee. The fiscal affairs of the United States badly needed attention; successive administrations had spent more money than they took in by taxation. In moderate amounts, this fact produces little danger in a country annually increasing its production, as does the United States. But in 1967 the costs of the Vietnam war added to those of the government's social programs and its foreign-aid expenditures vigorously increased its cash outgo.

Simultaneously, crisis developed abroad. The United States had been supporting the British pound sterling, which found itself in still greater crisis. The hostile government of General De Gaulle in France undertook to exacerbate the trouble. In combination, these circumstances began to cause inflation of prices in the United States and endangered the value of the dollar abroad.

One obvious necessity was to reduce the governmental deficit. Anticipating the problem, the Johnson administration proposed that Congress enact an increase in taxes, especially income taxes, and the bill duly arrived in the Ways and Means Committee. By the month of November, the crisis had become acute. The British government was forced to devalue the pound sterling. European gold speculators, supported by General De Gaulle, at once undertook to compel devaluation of the American dollar—on the ground that American inflation was certain. Experts in both the United States Treasury and the Federal Reserve System demanded prompt action on the tax bill.

At this point, Mr. Mills took charge. The bill could not get out of committee until he assented. He believed no tax increase should be voted unless the Johnson administration was prepared to cut its spending. Because the expenses of the Vietnam war could not be cut without endangering military operations, this meant cutting down on the government's social and antipoverty programs, and on a variety of other expenditures, chiefly for urban renewal and scientific and technical development. With the general social policy of these expenditures, Mr. Mills disagreed.

On November 30, 1967, Mr. Mills simply suspended hearings on the tax bill, putting it over until 1968, and until cuts in federal expenditures satisfactory to him and his committee should be presented. The immediate effect was to increase pressure for credit, raising interest rates throughout the United States and making the dollar vulnerable to foreign attack. No comment is here offered on the merits of the controversy; the point is that power devolved, not on the Congress, but on its delegate, the Chairman of the Ways and Means Committee, who did not hesitate to use it, and eventually had his way.

In such situations, power holders deal with each other as individuals, as Mills was then dealing with President Johnson. Personalities mix with policy. Mr. Mills's local field of responsibility was a conservative congressional district in Arkansas, far removed from and not sensitive to the intricacies of national monetary policy and foreign exchange. President Johnson's responsibility was to the entire United States. For the moment, Mr. Mills held national power. He conducted his dialogue through the medium of the press and other mass media and his decision controlled the immediate event.[2]

The surprising fact is that the system works. For there is a controlling philosophy in the Congress—Douglass Cater calls it "Constitutional morality." It leads men in power to assume a dialogue with their field of responsibility (note that the immediate field is not their congressional or senatorial districts, but the area of executive government in which they act in Washington). Effectively, they are responsible to their colleague power holders, whose collective opinion of them eventually can make or break their careers.

I disagree with David Riesman's belief, elaborated in *The Lonely Crowd*, that power in Congress resists analysis. It is not accidental, or even mercurial. The congressional system puts power in men because it must. It does so by the least defensible system, that of seniority. Yet its philosophy exercises immeasurable control over them. Such a system would be disastrous in Latin America or on the European continent. It nearly became so in 1868 when Benjamin Wade (president of the Senate) and Thaddeus Stevens (chairman of the Ways and Means Committee in the House of Representatives) sought and nearly achieved the overthrow of President Andrew Johnson after first attempting to take over control of the executive departments. In the United States, ballasted, guided, assisted, and sometimes opposed by the huge reservoir of power in the executive branch, the system transacts an astonishing amount of business, great and small. In the main, it responds to its field of national responsibility with intelligence and fidelity. When crisis impends, the machine can turn over with remarkable speed. During the Bank Holiday (March, 1933) and for some time thereafter, legislation could be got in a few days on White House request. After Pearl Harbor, in 1941, a like situation prevailed. Petty and great congressional

2. The account here given is in part taken from *U.S. News & World Report*, November 11, 1967.

barons abandoned intramural squabbles, sank their differences, and followed the President.

Absent crisis, each area of legislation—and of the money-granting power which is Congress's greatest prerogative—is chopped into segments. Within each segment, a subcommittee or a full committee directed by its always dominant chairman holds almost absolute sway. Their philosophy (Cater's "Constitutional morality") fortunately includes one imperative. The business of government must get done, and they do it. But within that conception there is endless possibility to grant or withhold favors, geographical or personal, and to exact conditions for their action. One cannot but agree with Cater's conclusion: to those frightened by the prospect of vesting power in leadership, "The answer has to be made that power has to be vested somewhere."

As always, the problem is whether to concentrate power at the center—that is, in the presiding officers and central steering committees—or to fragment it among specialized committees, which in turn means placing it in the hands of individual committee officers. "Corporate wisdom" in bodies the size of the Senate and the House may be an ideal, but it is also in substantial measure a fact. The ideal attains reality chiefly because the American governmental philosophy is strong, and the men holding power abide by it.

In government there is one cardinal, unforgivable, irreparable offense: failure to govern. When that occurs, the motives, hopes, ideals, and characteristics of the men responsible for the failure cease to be of interest—except to later historians or the Recording Angel. Their political careers are usually ended.

V

The Mass Media

One of the greatest locations of power—government officeholders aside—lies in the Washington offices of the mass media—the television and radio offices, bureaus of the great newspapers, press services, news syndicates, syndicated columnists, and weekly magazines of wide circulation. Rarely are they corrupt. Their decisions are limited to some extent by the policies and prejudices of the newspapers, publishing companies, and broadcasting corporations employing them; but their own judgments in the main are controlling. Taken together, these media transmit news and views, facts and interpretation of them, throughout the whole field of responsibility of the United States government. Their comment, editorial views, and news of reaction from outside return the response of the field to the capital. Incidentally, they keep the men in various branches of the government informed of activities in other branches. The daily grist in outflow and inflow constitutes a great part of the endless dialogue.

Promoting themselves slightly, the individuals directing, working for, or having standing with the press and mass media like to describe and think of themselves as the "Fourth Estate." By that they mean—if anything—that the aggregate effect of the individual decisions they make as to the news they transmit, the personalities, description, and publicity they accord men, their approval or disapproval of actions, and the "slants" they give to news is to influence governmental power holders and thereby events at all levels.

There is much truth in this estimate. It cannot quite be accepted fully. Mass media are not institutionalized except for elementary purposes of protecting their freedom to write and transmit and of expanding their access to information. These are the chief functions of the press associations. On the other hand, no process exists by which their respective views, comments, opinions, slants, assignments, and denials of publicity are determined. In these matters, power lies in the hands of each bureau chief—not of the "press" or "television" or the "mass media."

Even when consensus of mass-media opinion somehow emerges, it is not necessarily determinative. In 1936, President Franklin D. Roosevelt was running for re-election, and perhaps three-fourths of the press opposed him. (Radio comment was then relatively less important, and television nonexistent.) Roosevelt's own statement of his case, accompanied by the statements of his responsible political officers, was steadily reported, attaining a high degree of publicity. Editorial writers and columnists in the main took a hostile line. Roosevelt was nevertheless re-elected by a great popular majority, as well as by an overwhelming majority in the Electoral College. The "power of the press" is certainly qualified.

More determinative is its power at lower levels. Freshmen in

Congress, newly appointed subcabinet officers, subadministrators in the departments are often likely to succeed or fail depending on the amount and kind of publicity they achieve. Their problem —especially true for congressmen—is to get themselves noticed, or they are little regarded either in Washington, in their district, or in their home communities. They must devise some means of attracting attention, of identifying and distinguishing themselves in some fashion. Chance or destiny may do it for them if, in some crisis of affairs, their vote or their position becomes important. Otherwise they must identify themselves with some movement, make themselves representative of some cause, or become recognized as expert in some important field, in order to be worth a half-column in the daily newspapers or a couple of minutes in a television newscast. The decision of the bureau chiefs, perhaps acting on the judgment of subordinate reporters, accords or denies publicity. A career may be made by a favorable burst, destroyed by an unfavorable report, or wither on the vine if it goes unnoticed. No one knows this better than the Washington press-bureau chiefs. Though they rarely admit it, they are prime instruments of political selection.

The "right to know" is the slogan of the Fourth Estate. Its philosophy is that every decision made and the causes and motives leading to it ought to be within the knowledge of the American public. In practice, the principle is often extended beyond reason. It is claimed that the public has a right to know what power holders are thinking about long before decisions are, or perhaps need to be, made. The greatest achievement of a journalist is to report, in advance, what will happen a week later. Second only to that is to report, with some drama, conflicts real or supposed between powerful men. Yet it is often important that decisions not be reported until they have been made, lest stock-market speculators, unscrupulous politicians, or foreign opponents take advantage of the situation. Personal discussions, which may amount to nothing more than a difference of opinion on the merits of alternate decisions still needing study, can be whipped to promote personal suspicions or to incite sterile or paralyzing controversy. Mere speculation as to possible decisions (including many that no decision-maker has thought of) can be causative—can assist or block appointments, can influence government action and administrative measures. It can let loose lobbyists or inside propagandists, or set up tensions within departments. The "right to know" has never been defined. Gossip journalists endeavor to penetrate the White House clothes line; columnists plant informants in the offices of bureaus and congressional committees, and work up newsworthy quarrels.

Out of the welter of justified and unjustified "knowledge," a rude justice perhaps emerges. Sooner or later the public does arrive at a judgment of a man. It may not come soon enough to do him any good. John F. Kennedy's book *Profiles in Courage* describes a number of situations where a man was broken, yet later received that coldest reward, vindication by history.

There being no institutional control and no possibility of it, a system rightly committed to freedom of the press requires a philosophy of journalism committing the men in that crucial profession to principles of impartial justice, tinged (let us hope) with a measure of compassion for power holders. G. K. Chesterton, in his famous novel *The Man Who Was Thursday*, raises the question whether power holders are in company and identified with the men they govern, or whether governing is a lonely business in which the power holder stands solitary against the crowd. I should put it a little differently. The power holder may be and often is in the forefront of a company which supports him; or he may be solitary, standing for his opinion, defending his actions against a hostile throng. But of one fact there is no question: applauded or condemned, he finds power holding a lonely business. When he makes an important decision, neither plaudits nor abuse determines his own opinion of his action and himself. But this is not the business of journalists. They are not primarily concerned with, still less interested in, saying whether his decision entitles him to go to Heaven or to Hell. They are reporting and commenting on him as an integer, a decider, a switch steering the current of events this way or that. Their judgments, designed to influence their readers or hearers, are likely to be based on their agreement or disagreement with the importance of the problem and the results of the decision-making process; or, perhaps, on whether their reporting will attract wide attention.

Substantial power is thus located in the offices of the various organizations of the press and mass media in Washington. Though not determinative, it is nonetheless great. Power holders in the Fourth Estate, as in other fields, need (and rarely receive) scrutiny and analysis of themselves, of the institutions putting them there, of the philosophy on which they operate, and of their relations with their field of responsibility. In effect, they are informal officers of government.

VI

The Capital and Its Court

The political capital of the United States is a vast lens. It picks up innumerable small and great currents of opinion, interest, and pressures, generating heat and light in the process. These are, in fact, threads of dialogue between federal power holders and elements in their fields of responsibility. The lens selects and focuses these into specific policies and legislative and executive action. Surprisingly, the result is a vast unity, from which is derived the power of the government of the United States.

Formal framework is provided by the Constitution and the enacted laws, within which function the Congress, the courts, the presidency, the departments, the bureaucracies, organizing and transmitting the executive power. Informally, but no less potently, an unending process of contacts, conversations, exchanges of view, cajoleries, pressures, conflicts, sometimes corruption continually takes place. The dialogue of federal power with those affected by it includes all these elements and many more besides. Probably the process does not differ fundamentally from that always prevailing in great capital cities, as, for example, in the Paris of Louis XIV or the London of Queen Victoria. The result gives both direction and style to national action.

In February, 1913, I was invited to stay in Washington for a few days as guest of Winthrop Murray Crane, then junior senator from Massachusetts. The Republican administration headed by President William Howard Taft had been defeated in the election of 1912. Some weeks remained before his successor, Woodrow Wilson, was to be inaugurated; the period was an interregnum. I was asked to come at nine o'clock to the office of the chairman of the Senate Rules Committee, over which Senator Crane presided. Among other powers, that committee (and Mr. Crane as its head) could decide what bills should come up for vote. Since the Republican majority was to be displaced on the ensuing March 4, his power was about to expire. The Senator had been at work for a couple of hours. He at once suggested that we go "downtown." On the way, he laconically explained a few facts of life. The government was in Washington, but the gathering power center lay with President-elect Wilson. The hordes of men seeking appointment, favors, or action waited outside his headquarters rather than in the anterooms of the White House or the Capitol. A citizen, Louis Brandeis, who held no office, at this moment could accomplish more than Crane, although (as he did not add) he had been the Warwick of the Republican party and for a decade the most powerful man in the United States Senate. But the government had to go on, and the chief business of the Taft administration at the moment was arranging the orderly transmission of power to its incoming successful rivals. We drove to the White House and were, without announcement, admitted to an office that thirty

years later was to become familiar to me. President Taft gave me
a courteous greeting, then, after saying, "You will excuse us for
going on working," motioned me to a seat at a little side table.
Crane sat down in an obviously accustomed chair on the opposite
side of the President's desk, and they tackled a pile of papers in a
clearly habitual routine. Occasionally, by way of courtesy, one
of the two tossed me a question, listened for a brief answer, and
plowed steadily ahead. Lunchtime came; a hot meal was served
to me at my side table; sandwiches sufficed for the principals.
About half past two, after the pile of papers had been demolished,
we had a few moments of kindly conversation. At its apex, governmental power finally lodges in a tired man on one side of a
desk with his most trusted friend (if he is fortunate enough to
have one) on the other.

In 1918, a brief tour of duty at the War College in Washington
gave me, a twenty-three-year-old second lieutenant, my first real
experience of the capital process. A great lady, Mrs. Florence
Keep, invited the neophyte to one of her then famous small dinner
parties. (A "lady," according to the aphorism of the late Dr.
Harold Wolff, is a woman who transmits the best values of the
past generation to the more perceptive members of the next. The
most unforgettable favor position can grant a young man is to
take him seriously.) After coffee, conversation became general,
with a cabinet officer, an ambassador, a couple of high officials, a
famous journalist participating. As they made their adieus at
the traditional moment of ten-fifty, Mrs. Keep told me to linger a
few moments and asked me about my impressions and myself. She
then made two observations whose truth I came to appreciate.
"Washington," she said, "is a city where no one is missed—and
no one forgotten. Men here are important while they have power
and negligible when they lose it—unless they are men in their
own right." Also, and more incisively, she remarked, "Washington is a city of repeated conversations"—a kindly hint that one
had best watch one's tongue. On talk and its repetition are
based estimates of the caliber of men as well as leakage of information. She tried to explain, in a few words, the accommodation
of the loyalty expected of a subordinate to his chief with the

parallel loyalty he ought to have to his own intellectual integrity, and the difference between the obligations of politically responsible officers like the recently departed cabinet secretary and those of subordinates (and I certainly was one), whose political views were of scant importance but whose fidelity in handling information and affairs was crucial. The former had both right and duty to express themselves publicly; the latter, to state their views to their chiefs and otherwise keep quiet. Civil servants—like army officers—should not resign; their business was to keep the government running. Political officers, on the other hand, must always decide whether the views they held and public positions they took assisted or obstructed the government they were appointed to serve. They could stay in power or, for adequate reason, leave it when conscience dictated.

No appreciation of Washington—or perhaps of any great capital—is valid without including the continuous flow of private conversations and contacts enveloping the men who exert power. They talk to each other formally, in cabinet meetings, in interdepartmental committees, in staff meetings. They meet outside—and with outsiders from the ends of the earth—at dinner parties and at clubs. Informal organizations exist, like the famous "Cooperative Forum" maintained as a public service by the late Mrs. Alice Estes. There, members of Congress and the executive departments, powerful bureaucrats, colleagues, and opponents, army officers, newspapermen, and commentators come together. One of them explains what he is doing and why; the others cross-question him on his presentation. (These discussions are off the record; remarkably, the restriction is invariably observed.) Less formally, columnists and correspondents develop friendships—up to a point— with men in office, the former to obtain background information, the latter to ascertain public opinion and reaction, often with the incidental hope of favorable or at least understanding publicity. Reporters and columnists cultivate contacts with committee clerks, secretaries, and lesser-echelon officials, not omitting those who have grievances against their chiefs and may be prepared to "leak" confidential information to be used against them. Civil-service and Foreign Service career men cultivate relations with influential members of Congress and senators, partly to secure favorable action on departmental requests for legislation and appropriation of funds, partly to secure for themselves powerful protectors on the floor of the House or Senate. Legislators acquire in the process valuable knowledge of the policies, internal workings, intrigues, or perhaps scandals, in the branches of the executive.

Almost all important economic organizations and interests have resident representatives at the Washington court, sometimes independently ensconced in impressive headquarters buildings, sometimes modestly accoutered in small offices. Some are former high officers, often members of District of Columbia law firms retained to represent trade associations, powerful companies, labor unions. Some are Washington agents for cities, local government units, strong social-progress associations. Essential to the business of all of these is cultivating contacts with power holders whose decisions affect their clients or causes. The list of lobbyists runs an entire gamut—from charlatans who peddle influence they do not have, to established industry representatives on whom congressional committees and administrative bureaus rely for accurate information. With these must be associated a category of specialized journalists, correspondents, editors of trade periodicals, whose knowledge of affairs in their fields is likely to be more up-to-date than that of the government services.

Tactfully or flamboyantly, capably or sloppily, overtly or covertly, wisely or deceptively, responsibly or corruptly, these insert their knowledge, their criticism, their special pleading, their attempts to reward their friends or make trouble for their enemies, serving their special-interest clients, sometimes for high pay, sometimes from pure idealism. They are part of the dialogue of power with those affected by it. Like groups have probably existed about every power holder in history.

The information, views, prejudices, understandings, knowledge, praise, slander, and malice daily conveyed through these endless conversations and interchanges are difficult to measure. A volume of contemporary history could be distilled from the content transmitted in a single Washington week. Disconnected, the items reflect all manner of human emotion—admiration, antagonism, hatred, idealism, treachery, vanity. Aggregated, they are the dialogue of national power. Amazingly, they constitute the form—the *Gestalt*—of a national capital. They do so because at all times they are unified by a single theme: the national power. Each is a tiny strand continually revolving around that power and wound into an enormous cable that transmits impressions, views, and interpretations of the power process as well as pressures on it. Against this, power holders in all positions must make their decisions. It is, in fact, essential to them. Lacking it, they could not estimate the interests, public and private, seeking to be forwarded, reconciled, or protected, or the extent of problems, present or prospective, they will have to meet. Without it, they could not comprehend the results of the actions they take and the realities limiting or extending their capacity for effective action.

4

Judicial Political Power:
The Supreme Court of the
United States

Preface [1]

Statist power in the United States is, as we have noted, nominally divided into three parts: the executive, the legislative, the judicial. They are theoretically co-ordinated, with the legislative the supposed paramount institution. But the actual play does not follow the script. As often as not, the president of the United States and his executive departments are the true initiators of legislation, and

1. Most of the material contained in Book 4 was originally presented as the Carpentier Lectures at Columbia University in March, 1967, and subsequently published as *The Three Faces of Power,* New York, Harcourt, Brace & World, 1967.

hence the true lawgivers and lawmakers. From time to time, the executive is checked or deflected by the power of a congressional officer, usually the chairman of an important committee, who acquired his mandate by seniority.

The most surprising evolution has placed the nine members of the Supreme Court in a power position senior to both the executive and the legislative branches, though the area in which their supremacy is complete remains smaller and is far less clearly determined. The unique position of the Supreme Court entitles us to an examination of how that overpowering position has been reached. Briefly, a revolution has taken place and is in progress. The unique fact is that the revolutionary committee is the Supreme Court of the United States.

The first of the three following chapters relates to the acquisition and exercise by the Supreme Court of senior legislative power in the United States, particularly in the field of education and local government.

The second relates to a like power claimed by the Court over economic organization—large corporations—under the federal antitrust and other laws.

The third chapter suggests a possible method of extricating the Court, in some measure, from the position of danger as well as honor it has acquired.

Use of the word "revolution" implies no criticism of the Court.[2] I think it could not have acted otherwise than as it did. Far from arrogating to itself powers it did not have, the Court had its latent constitutional powers, granted it by the Fourteenth Amendment, activated by the pace of technical and social change. When this history is written, it will probably be found that the Supreme Court's action saved the country from a far more dangerous and disorderly change.

2. Former Associate Justice Abe Fortas of the Supreme Court: "It is fascinating, although disconcerting to some, that the first and fundamental breakthrough in various categories of *revolutionary progress* has been made by the courts—and specifically the Supreme Court of the United States." James Madison Lecture at the New York University Law School, March 29, 1967, reported on the editorial page of the *New York Law Journal*, Wednesday, April 5, 1967. (Italics added.)

Yet the situation does impose on the federal government problems of power which must be solved if the Supreme Court is not to endanger or lose its mandate through tides of political action. Revolutionary progress does fuse judicial and legislative power, and possibly a degree of executive power as well. A common sequel is liquidation of that power as increasing sectors of opposition or fear become active. In the case of the Supreme Court, some are evident now. Thirty-four states by legislative act have called for a constitutional convention, the motive being to end the power of the Supreme Court used in *Baker* v. *Carr,* as well to nullify the result of that case. Since the Congress, required to call the constitutional convention, will probably resist, a first-class constitutional crisis could easily ensue, with the Supreme Court as its focus.

No apology is needed, accordingly, for raising or discussing the problem. As noted in the text, I am in accord with what the Court did. I would merely like to ease the transition that must inevitably ensue.

I

The Supreme Court as Holder of Legislative Power

1. Supreme Court Power and the Economic Revolution

Ultimate legislative power in the United States has come to rest in the Supreme Court of the United States. This broad statement of an unrecognized fact is not made in opposition. Given the social and economic revolution of the United States, I do not see that the Supreme Court could well have avoided the legislative position in which it now finds itself; and I am in accord with the results it has achieved. But the situation does require additional development making it possible for ultimate development providing for two inevitable problems. One of these is an institutional base for the gathering of data on which the legislative decrees of the federal courts may be soundly based. The second is provision for dealing with the political problems inevitably resulting from the use of legislative power.

We must consider the surprising position of the Supreme Court against the background of the five laws of power developed in Book 1. The first four are clearly applicable—indeed, they are responsible for the remarkable acceptance of Supreme Court decrees throughout the vast area of the country. At the beginning of America's independent history, the power of the Supreme Court entered and organized a situation capable of falling into chaos. The power of the Court was personal, coming to rest in nine fully identified men. Judicial power was vested in defined institutions: the Supreme Court itself and inferior courts with jurisdiction over the entire country and over any territory administered by it. The philosophy or idea system expressed by these institutions was that of British common law, supplemented and augmented as American legal thinking evolved.

The fifth law—that of dialogue between power and its subjects—is not comprehended, so far as I can determine, in most theories of judicial action.

Courts were designed to decide cases or controversies under the law. Before decision, a "dialogue" takes place—the argument of the cause by trained attorneys and advocates. Were court decisions limited to "controversies," and were all parties to them before the court, this arrangement would be adequate.

But where decisions of the courts assume the dimensions of legislation, the traditional trial of facts and argument on the law scarcely scratches the surface. In any event, it does not correspond to the scope or impact of the power's use. As the Supreme Court moved into a legislative position, its field of responsibility widened; no longer were litigants and disputants the parties principally affected, but, rather, the entire community. The field of responsibility widened precisely because the decisions began to affect thousands of individual lives. With that field, no formal institution of dialogue existed. Federal judges are not elective. No political campaign requires them to lay out their views in advance, or submit their actions to discussion and review. The dialogue must therefore be informal, carried on through the press, mass media, and discussion in local assemblies or forums.

Further, the dialogue involves other branches of government. As will presently appear, the Supreme Court sits in judgment on the governments and legislatures of states and of the Congress of the United States, acting to correct their sins of commission and omission under the mandates of the Bill of Rights and particularly of the Fourteenth Amendment. But the other branches of the federal government and of the states are continuously in organized dialogue through political campaigns as well as in unorganized dialogue through the press. The Supreme Court, having no normal avenue for entry into this dialogue, nevertheless finds itself the subject of vast and unorganized debate.

Endeavor is here made to consider the present position of the Supreme Court in the light of this situation.

The process by which a measure of legislative power devolved on the Supreme Court is interesting. It is the product of a mandate contained in the Fourteenth Amendment, multiplied by the forced intrusion of laws into fields of activity originally supposed to lie outside statist action.

Article I, Section 1, of the Constitution provides that

All legislative Powers herein granted shall be vested in a Congress of the United States, which shall consist of a Senate and House of Representatives.

Article III, Section 2, provides that

The judicial Power shall extend to all Cases, in Law and Equity, arising under this Constitution, the Laws of the United States, and Treaties made, or which shall be made, under their Authority. . . .

Prima facie, this is no grant of legislative power to the Supreme Court. The Constitutional Convention accepted the doctrine of "separation of powers," the theory being that only by separating the legislative, the judicial, and the executive powers could a country preserve "a government of laws and not of men."

Thereafter, at the close of the Civil War, the Fourteenth Amendment was adopted, providing, among other things, that

No State shall make or enforce any law which shall abridge the privileges or immunities of citizens of the United States; nor shall any State deprive any person of life, liberty, or property, without due process of law; *nor deny to any person within its jurisdiction the equal protection of the laws.* [Italics added.]

At the time of adoption, protection of life, liberty, and property bulked very large in general thinking. "Equal protection of the laws" was a quite separate subject, potentially of far larger import, and took off from a desire that no institution like slavery should be permitted.[1]

The ensuing century saw a revolution in national habits, institutions, and social standards whose proportion we have yet to apprehend. Included in it was transition from an agricultural to an industrial society; the concentration of industry, transport, and, to some extent, finance in the hands of a few hundred corporations; the concomitant concentration of power over wages, conditions of labor, and, in large measure, access to employment in the hands of powerful labor unions. Following the catastrophe of 1933, the federal government assumed responsibility for the economic condition of the country and presently codified that responsibility in the Employment Act of 1946. Since this act is less well known than it should be, I quote the key provision:

The Congress declares that it is the continuing policy and responsibility of the Federal Government to use all practicable means consistent with its needs and obligations and other essential considerations of national policy, with the assistance and cooperation of industry, agriculture, labor, and State and local governments, to coordinate and utilize all its plans, functions, and resources for the purpose of creating and maintaining, in a manner calculated to foster and promote free competitive enterprise and the general welfare, conditions under which there will be afforded useful employment opportunities, including self-employment, for those able, willing, and seeking to work, and to promote maximum employment, production, and purchasing power. [15 USCA §1021]

1. *Vide* Samuel Eliot Morison, *The Oxford History of the American People,* pp. 771–772. "The Supreme Court in 1873 declined to intervene between the state of Louisiana and the New Orleans butchers, who alleged that state regulations were confiscatory. The Court explained that Amendment XIV had been adopted to protect the freed slaves, not to make the federal judiciary 'a perpetual censor upon all legislation of the states . . . with authority to nullify such as it did not approve.' But this was before the judges began reading Herbert Spencer."

Heightened responsibility and ensuing state and federal action brought a vast body of state and federal legislation into existence.

Thereafter (it was not wholly, but chiefly, a development since the close of World War II), the social-economic operations of this complex organism we call the United States made enormous progress.[2] The average of personally received income moved from $1,491 per capita in 1950 to an estimated $2,900 in 1967.[3] The country learned that education was an essential part of this process. Studies summarized in *Sources of Economic Growth* (Committee for Economic Development, 1962) indicate that between twenty per cent and twenty-five per cent of the increase in the gross national product—and, of course, in personally received income—could be ascribed to expenditure for education. Presently, a heightened social conscience led to the campaign to eliminate poverty—a campaign that obviously will not abate, though methods of attack may change.[4] Attempt to give more or less equal access to the benefits of medical knowledge and medical care is the precise object of the recent statute providing for medical aid.[5]

Other extensions of government responsibility are appearing over the horizon. The proposition that every American family is

2. See J. W. Kendricks in *The United States National Bureau of Economics Review*, Princeton, New Jersey, Princeton University Press, 1961.

There is no single statement of the extent of technical change—probably to make one would require an encyclopedia. An illuminating essay is found in *The Changing American Economy*, edited by John R. Coleman, New York, Basic Books, 1967, "Automation in Perspective," by Lloyd Ulman, pp. 182–197. More technical—and of one extreme development—is the number of *Scientific American* for September, 1966, devoted to computers and their use, in, among other things, technology, organization, and education. Anyone older than forty-five need only look at the world around him—and remember his school days.

3. *U.S. Book of Facts*, p. 334.

4. Surprisingly, the war on poverty is supported not only from the side of the "poor," but also by the great corporations. The *Wall Street Journal* of April 19, 1967 (p. 1) chronicles the appearance of executives of the following corporations in support of the "war on poverty": General Electric, Hotel Company of America, Radio Corporation of America, U.S. Industries, Inc., Xerox Corporation, International Business Machines Corporation, Montgomery Ward Co., and a number of others.

5. "Medicare," Public Law 89–97, The Social Security Amendments of 1965 (USCA Title 42).

unconditionally entitled to an income of subsistence level has already been substantially supported. The immediate proposal— a "negative income tax," supplying that income—may not be the solution eventually adopted,[6] but something like it has already appeared as the relief operations in the states slowly move away from the field of charity toward the field of economic right.

To revert to the Fourteenth Amendment, the field of the laws whose "equal protection" must not be denied to "any person" within the jurisdiction of "any State" has been vastly increased —and is still being increased. At some point, the question was bound to arise, "What is 'equal protection' under the new conditions and concepts?"—as, of course, it had arisen under the more limited conceptions and provisions of laws existing at the time of its adoption.

When it did arise, the revolution began.

The first stage was square determination that the "equal protection of the laws" clause did not merely inhibit action by the states; it also required them to *create* a situation giving "equal protection." State "inaction" (as Justice Arthur Goldberg later observed) within the meaning of the Fourteenth Amendment was itself responsible state action. If a system existed that did not provide equal protection, then primarily the state or, if not the state, some other authority was obligated to create it.

The second stage of the revolution came when, faced with state "inaction," the federal courts assumed the task of filling the vacuum, remedying the failure. In plain English, this meant undertaking by decree to enact the rules that state legislation has failed to provide. This second phase was the really revolutionary development—and, incidentally, set up the Supreme Court as a revolutionary committee.

6. It is by no means beyond possibility that in a couple of decades conception of "equal protection of the laws" may require enactment of a guaranteed income to everyone at some level. Presumably by that time everyone not enjoying an income will have some right to relief, or perhaps will be on a Social Security allowance. Might not the Supreme Court rule, first, that government (presumably federal) had already entered the field of guaranteeing most individuals against destitution and, second, therefore rule that failure to provide such protection for all denied equal protection?

As noted earlier, this statement is not made in criticism. I do not see that the Supreme Court could have done otherwise. By assuming the function, it is clear to me, the Court safeguarded the United States from an otherwise chaotic and dangerous situation which might have led to catastrophe.

2. Education and Equal Protection

Historically, the moment was reached when the Supreme Court was presented with the case of *Brown* v. *Board of Education of Topeka* (347 US 483 [1954]). Chief Justice Earl Warren and a majority of the Court then decided that segregation of white from Negro children in state-maintained public schools denied Negroes "equal protection of the laws." At this point, predictably and I think unavoidably, the reserve legislative power of the Supreme Court became overt. The Supreme Court's lawmaking power in constitutional fields was implicit since adoption of the Fourteenth Amendment. Unquestionably it had been exercised before 1954. Legal historians may be left to discuss its slow emergence into general consciousness. Politically, it can hardly be doubted that the *Brown* case pushed judicial legislation into public awareness. The school-segregation cases brought the subject over the crest of the hill, and there it certainly remains.

In my view, no other result was possible. The Constitution contemplated a Court chiefly occupied with the specific solution of cases and controversies. In constitutional matters, its original and primary power was to say "No"—that is, to strike down statutes and administrative or judicial actions violating the Bill of Rights or taken outside the power granted to legislatures or executive officials, or trespassing on the division of powers between the federal and state governments. Seven of the ten Bill of Rights amendments are cast in the negative: "Congress shall make no law respecting an establishment of religion"; "the right of the people to keep and bear Arms shall not be infringed," and so forth. In most

351

of these cases, naysaying is very nearly sufficient. Capacity to strike down the offending rule or action covers most cases. Positive requirements were set up chiefly in respect of procedure: "the accused shall enjoy the right to a speedy and public trial"; "the right of trial by jury shall be preserved," and the like. These relate specifically to judicial procedure, clearly under the control of the courts.

But consider the Fourteenth Amendment: "No State shall . . . deny to any person within its jurisdiction the equal protection of the laws." The double negative effects a highly positive command. "Equal protection of the laws" often cannot be created by the mere striking down of an offending provision. An implacable dialectic emerges. Here is a scheme of laws. The Court must decide whether it denies equal protection. Power to say "No" in some situations inevitably implies power to say "Yes" in others. Even with the conceded equity power giving the Court capacity to decree a remedy, a question comes up in each case. Unless prepared to draw a decree itself, the Court may, and in practice must, remand the case to the lower court with instructions to draw a decree creating a situation in which the aggrieved party will have equal protection. A mere negative decree is likely to create a fragment of unfilled chaos. If the federal courts do not prescribe positive action, the Court's decision is likely to be *brutum fulmen*.

The narrow issue before the Supreme Court in *Brown* v. *Topeka* was whether it or the lower federal courts should undertake to remedy the wrongs complained of by decree. Any such decree would be legislative in character, with sweeping results. The Court might have evaded in some fashion both decision- and decree-making, as Justice Felix Frankfurter on various occasions urged that it do.[7] His forecast of the thickets and difficulties into which the Court would be plunged was unquestionably accurate. Nevertheless, I think he was wrong. To have abstained from dealing with the issues presented would have produced a chaotic rather than an orderly revolution. Especially in race-discrimination cases, abstention would have thrown the issue straight to the

7. First, in *Railroad Commission* v. *Pullman Company*, 312 US 496 (1941). For the history of abstention, see *Harvard Law Review*, Vol. 80, No. 3, January, 1967, pp. 604 ff.

streets in a number of localities—and only an omniscient deity can tell what then would have happened. When Chief Justice Warren grasped the nettle in *Brown* v. *Topeka* and thereafter, he was entitled, not to a call for his impeachment, as some extremists did, but to the public thanks of the United States. The Chief Justice was revolutionary. But he was right.

Latent in his decision was whether the Fourteenth Amendment set up an *affirmative* requirement to provide "equal protection" and, if so, whether its mandate required action by the Supreme Court. Impliedly, at least, the Court determined the former— the Fourteenth Amendment required the states to set up an "equal protection" system, and that requirement could be enforced by the courts. The Court did not explicitly so decide, until the problem was forthrightly dealt with in *Bell* v. *Maryland* (378 US 226, 309–310 [1964]). In *Bell*, Justice Goldberg (joined by Chief Justice Warren) quoted correspondence of Justice Joseph P. Bradley, who had decided the civil-rights cases in 1876, as saying that "denying [equal protection] includes inaction as well as action, and denying the equal protection of the laws includes the omission to protect, as well as the omission to pass laws for protection," and Justice Goldberg added, "These views are fully consonant with this Court's recognition that state conduct which might be described as 'inaction' can nevertheless constitute responsible 'state action' within the meaning of the Fourteenth Amendment."

It is difficult to believe that the Chief Justice in *Brown* v. *Topeka* did not recognize the course of probability. The Supreme Court, under the Fourteenth Amendment, would be called on not only to strike down discriminatory laws, but also to *create* non-discriminatory conditions—and that involved the probability of judicial legislation on an extremely wide front.

Probably no one was more aware of the implications than was Chief Justice Warren himself. The Court unanimously determined several propositions: first, that "where the State has undertaken to provide [public education], it is a right which must be made available to all on equal terms"; [8] second, that, in the light of modern knowledge, segregation had a tendency to retard the edu-

8. *Brown* v. *Topeka*, at p. 493.

cational and mental development of Negro children and deprive them of some of the benefits they would receive in a rationally integrated school system,[9] and, third, that the doctrine of "separate but equal facilities" had no place in public education, because it deprived Negro children of "equal protection of the laws." [10]

The Chief Justice at least impliedly accepted the fact that the Court's ruling was legislative in character. Because of the wide applicability of this decision, and because of the great variety of local conditions, framing the orders presented problems of considerable complexity.[11] The Court therefore restored the case to the docket for argument on the formulation of decrees—and directed that the Attorney General of the United States and the attorneys general of those states requiring or permitting segregation be invited to appear as *amici curiae*. In other words, the Court determined the principles of the legislation, and called a hearing to determine its exact terms. Mere injunction prohibiting race segregation without more would have accomplished nothing.

3. The Widening of the Court's Legislative Power

Though the school-segregation cases were and perhaps still are the most spectacular exercise of legislative power, they are only one sector of a great and growing number of such cases. Description of all of them would require a volume; a few illustrations will suggest part of their scope.

9. Note ought to be made of a point involved in the Supreme Court ruling. Clearly, Negro children are entitled to education equal to that provided for whites. Whether a "racially" integrated school system necessarily affords that is a matter of educational judgment. Quite possibly a generation hence educators may consider that children up to, say, the age of ten receive better education if in a group of children wholly familiar to them than in a group with mixed or diverse backgrounds and habits. A point of educational dogma was accepted by the Court; behavioral science may later shift the conclusion.

10. *Brown* v. *Topeka*, at p. 494.

11. *Ibid.*, at p. 495.

The Tennessee Legislature in 1901 provided that the General Assembly should be composed of thirty-three senators and ninety-nine representatives, to be apportioned among the various counties. Some of these elected one representative, others elected two, three, six, or eight representatives. The least populous counties were grouped into blocs, and two, three, and four counties jointly elected one representative. A somewhat similar scheme determined election of senators.

No change in apportionment was made between 1901 and 1960, by which time the population of Tennessee had increased from 2,000,000 to 3,500,000, and the population eligible to vote from 487,000 to 2,100,000. As might be expected, the county growth was not uniform, so that "37% of the voters of Tennessee elect 20 of the 33 Senators while 40% of the voters elect 63 of the 99 members of the House." [12] Justice Tom Clark later observed that "the apportionment picture in Tennessee is a topsy-turvical of gigantic proportions. . . . Tennessee's apportionment is a crazy quilt without rational basis." [13]

In *Baker* v. *Carr*, a group of voters brought action in the federal court asking relief from denial of "equal protection of the laws" because they were virtually deprived of opportunity to cast a meaningful vote. The lower court dismissed the complaint, and appeal was taken. The plaintiffs not only asked that the Tennessee apportionment be ruled unconstitutional; they also asked an injunction preventing further elections from being held under it and "unless and until the General Assembly enacts a valid reapportionment, the District Court should either decree a reapportionment by mathematical application of the Tennessee constitutional formulae to the most recent Federal Census figures, or direct the appellees to conduct legislative elections, primary and general, at large." [14]

The Court decided that disparity of representation was indeed a denial of "equal protection of the laws," and that decision of the cause ought not to be avoided by describing it as a "political

12. *Baker* v. *Carr*, at p. 707.
13. *Ibid.*
14. *Ibid.*, p. 673.

question" to be left to some other branch of government. Graceful bow was made to the doctrine of "separation of powers," but the Court found no difficulty in crossing that Rubicon. A state exercising power wholly within the domain of state interest is insulated from federal judiciary review. But where state power is an instrument for circumventing a federally protected right, the federal courts may move in (*Gomillion* v. *Lightfoot*, 364 US 339).

So the Supreme Court, against the warning of Justice Frankfurter,[15] moved in. It declared the principle of "one man–one vote," deciding that irrational and discriminatory apportionment of voting power denied "equal protection of the laws"—and that the Tennessee Legislature was badly elected.

But then what? The majority of the Court merely remanded the cause to the lower, three-judge, court for appropriate action without attempting to formulate remedy. Justice Clark disliked this, believing that appropriate remedy should be formulated by the Supreme Court itself. In a concurring opinion, he suggested a formula. Justice John Marshall Harlan did likewise, though his formula was different. Justice Frankfurter prophesied doom and gloom, partly because he thought the Supreme Court had no business in this area, and partly because it gave no guidance to the lower court on how to enforce the new requirement. He considered that the lower courts of the country had been catapulted into a "mathematical quagmire . . . without so much as adumbrating the basis for a legal calculus as a means of extrication." [16]

In effect [continued Justice Frankfurter], today's decision empowers the courts of the country to devise what should constitute the proper composition of the legislatures of the fifty States. If State courts should

---

15. "A hypothetical claim resting on abstract assumptions is now for the first time made the basis for affording illusory relief for a particular evil even though it foreshadows deeper and more pervasive difficulties in consequence. The claim is hypothetical and the assumptions are abstract because the Court does not vouchsafe the lower courts—state and federal—guidelines for formulating specific, definite, wholly unprecedented remedies for the inevitable litigations that today's umbrageous disposition is bound to stimulate in connection with politically motivated reapportionments in so many States" (*ibid.*, at p. 715).

16. *Ibid.*

for one reason or another find themselves unable to discharge this task, the duty of doing so is put on the federal courts or on this Court, if State views do not satisfy this Court's notion of what is proper districting.[17]

Frankfurter wanted to abstain from the whole affair, acknowledging that "there is not under our Constitution a judicial remedy for every political mischief, for every undesirable exercise of legislative power."[18] The Court's judgment in remanding the case to the district court for "further proceedings consistent with this opinion" meant, in practice, either persuading the state legislature to reapportion or decreeing reapportionment itself.

Justice Frankfurter's premonitions were not wholly unjustified, though the problems he foresaw have not yet proved insoluble. A string of cases demanding reapportionment was immediately brought, and all manner of problems were raised thereby.[19] Solutions have generally been reached. The legislative decrees of the

17. *Ibid.*, at p. 716.

18. *Ibid.*

19. In *Reynolds* v. *Sims*, 377 US 533 (1964), the apportionment of legislators in Alabama was challenged on the ground that the urban counties were unrepresented. A three-judge federal court (United States District Court for the Middle District of Alabama) ordered a temporary reapportionment. On direct appeal, the Supreme Court of the United States affirmed, Clark concurring. Justice Potter Stewart supported his concurrence because the three-judge decree afforded "the State of Alabama full opportunity, consistent with the requirements of the Federal Constitution, to devise its own system of legislative apportionment" (at p. 543). Justice Harlan, dissenting, said—accurately as it proved: "The consequence of today's decision is that in all but the handful of States which may already satisfy the new requirements the local District Court or, it may be, the state courts, are given blanket authority and the constitutional duty to supervise apportionment of the State Legislatures. It is difficult to imagine a more intolerable and inappropriate interference by the judiciary with the independent legislatures of the States" (at p. 558).

Since the Supreme Court decision in *Reynolds* v. *Sims* requiring that elections to state legislatures assure the rights of all citizens "to cast an effective and adequately weighted vote" (at p. 581), the principle has been carried into county government. There were recently pending in *the courts of New York alone*, cases affecting the following counties: Albany, Broome, Chemung, Clinton, Dutchess, Erie, Genesee, Herkimer, Monroe, Oneida, Onondaga, Rockland (in the federal as well as the New York Supreme Court), St. Lawrence, Saratoga, Schenectady, Seneca, Steuben, Suffolk (before a federal court), Sullivan, Ulster, Washington, Westchester (litigation in the federal as well as in the state courts).

federal courts in general have worked out, though at times the results have been surprising.

One example was the situation in New York.

A group of citizens residing in the most populous counties of New York brought suit challenging the apportionment for electing state assemblymen and state senators. A three-judge federal district court dismissed the case on the ground that the apportionment did not violate the United States Constitution. The Supreme Court of the United States, by six to three, reversed this decision; it said that the "equal protection" clause requires representation in both houses of the state legislature to be apportioned substantially on an equal-population base—as they were not in New York. Again the case was remanded to the court below for further proceedings, though the dissenters in the Court thought the majority wrong and suggested alternative affirmative plans.

The New York Legislature thereupon adopted four alternative plans and submitted them to the federal district court for approval. Three were thrown out at once; the district court thought that the fourth satisfied constitutional requirements. Meanwhile, in simultaneous litigation in the New York state courts, the New York Court of Appeals, applying the state constitution, considered the plans proposed by the state legislature and held all four of them bad.[20] The fourth—the plan approved by the federal district

20. See *WMCA* v. *Lomenzo, Secretary of State of the State of New York*, 377 US 633 (1964). Five of New York's most populous counties challenged the apportionment of the legislature in New York. A three-judge court dismissed the complaint (208 F. Supp. 368). On appeal, the Supreme Court of the United States reversed. During the litigation, a similar challenge was made in the New York courts. The Supreme Court of the United States reversed the district court and recommended further proceedings consistent with the Court's view expressed in *Reynolds* v. *Sims* and in its opinion in this case.

This time Justices Stewart and Clark joined with Harlan in dissenting—they had concurred in the earlier cases, though for other reasons. Justice Stewart said: "I am convinced these decisions mark a long step backward into that unhappy era when a majority of the members of this Court were thought by many to have convinced themselves and each other that the demands of the Constitution were to be measured not by what it says, but by their own notions of wise political theory" (p. 584), and denied states the right of experimentation.

court—required election of more state assemblymen than the constitution of the State of New York allowed! Appeal was taken from the district court decision, but, in *Travia* v. *Lomenzo*,[21] the Supreme Court by memorandum dismissed the appeal. Justice Harlan, dissenting, plaintively observed that the Supreme Court ignored the fact that the New York Court of Appeals held that *Plan A* (the plan approved by the federal district court) violated the state constitution—as it plainly did—but he got nowhere. So *Plan A* became effective in the State of New York, and a legislature of the State of New York was elected under an apportionment scheme decreed by the federal court with an assembly containing more members than the state constitution allowed![22] For practical purposes, the federal district court supervised by the Supreme Court of the United States briefly became the legislative, perhaps even constitution-making, authority of New York. Other similar cases have been in litigation elsewhere in the United States.

The impact and the political importance of the holding in *Baker* v. *Carr* (the one man–one vote decision) and subsequent cases are very nearly unlimited. Effectively, they call for transfer of control of legislatures in many states from the sparsely inhabited, overrepresented agricultural counties to the previously underrepresented large cities and urban regions. Theretofore, relatively small numbers of farmers and voters in small towns were final arbiters of legislation. Hereafter, the elected representatives of the urbanized masses will become the arbiters instead. Change in point of

---

21. 381 US 431 (1965).

22. *Travia* v. *Lomenzo*. In *Scott* v. *Germano*, 381 US 407 (1965), the United States District Court for the Northern District of Illinois declared the Illinois Senate invalidly apportioned and directed that if a valid plan were not submitted, the Court would require all parties to show cause why the next Illinois Legislature should not be elected at large. On appeal, the Court vacated the district court's order because the Supreme Court of Illinois had also held the apportionment invalid. The Supreme Court said that the United States District Court should have "stayed its hand," and directed the district court to fix "a reasonable time within which the appropriate agencies of the State of Illinois, including its Supreme Court, may validly redistrict the Illinois State Senate" in time for the elections of 1966 (p. 409).

view as well as in economic interest must inevitably take place—indeed, has done so already.

Revolutions have been fought for less fundamental changes in power structure.

4. Other Fields of Revolution

The two illustrations given in some detail are merely the more dramatic of a series of lesser changes stemming from the same root. They are here mentioned rather than described.

In the field of industrial organization, court-made revolution is becoming as evident as in the fields of education and state government. Long ago, the Sherman Antitrust Act was given quasi-constitutional standing by the Supreme Court of the United States.[23] In due time, it was implemented by the Clayton Act,[24] which in turn was amended to permit governmental intervention preventing mergers whose effect was to "substantially lessen competition." [25] But any contract by which supplies are bought or sold from or to a particular party over a period of time lessens competition. Whether the lessening is "substantial" is a matter of opinion.[26] Finally the Supreme Court moved into the picture

23. *Appalachian Coals Company* v. *United States*, 288 US 344 (1932), at pp. 359–360. "As a charter of freedom, the Act has a generality and adaptability comparable to that found to be desirable in constitutional provisions," wrote Chief Justice Charles Evans Hughes. The statement has often been repeated; see *U.S.* v. *E. I. Du Pont de Nemours & Company*, 361 US 381 (1956), at p. 386. Whether Chief Justice Hughes intended to go as far as his successors may be questioned—but there is no doubt of the result.

24. Act of October 15, 1914. Chap. 323, 15 USCA §§12, 13, 14–21, 22–27.

25. 15 USCA §18 as amended by Act of December 29, 1950, to prohibit the acquisition of the whole or any part of the assets of another corporation, when the effect of the acquisition may substantially lessen competition or tend to create a monopoly.

26. Later, in *Federal Trade Commission* v. *Procter & Gamble Company*, the Supreme Court was to rule that the merger of the two noncompetitive companies, creating large market power, might substantially limit competition if

and asserted its opinion by deciding *Brown Shoe Company* v. *United States.*[27] It there held that in certain "relevant markets" competition was lessened by three per cent; therefore a merger could be prohibited. As one looks into the subject further, the growth of a number of companion ideas can be discovered. Mere size may in itself constitute a limitation of competition. So, perhaps, may expansion of a corporation into a number of unrelated fields. There is under consideration in the Department of Justice an attack on a corporation on the ground that the massiveness of its advertising, in and of itself, may diminish or preclude effective competition—as indeed it may.

It has long been established by law that when a corporation is found to have violated the Sherman Antitrust Act or the Clayton Act, the federal courts may prescribe a remedy—prohibiting practice, ordering divestiture of properties, or dissolving the defendant corporation. In practice, the Court then prescribes the extent and outline of the company's organization. If, through the gate of determining what is "competition," the Court undertakes to determine the limits of size, of ownership of diverse operations, of advertising, it will move yet more deeply into regulation of the organization and conduct of American business. The blanket of "interstate commerce" now covers most of that field. The mental constructs of the Supreme Court—its conception of "competition," of advertising, of the dangers of size, of the dangers of lessening competition where size is not the major consideration—of necessity could become the senior controls over American business.

In another field, the First Amendment to the Constitution, prohibiting Congress from making any law "abridging the freedom of speech, or of the press," taken together with the Fourteenth Amendment, has already led to a rewriting of much of the law of libel and slander. Justice William O. Douglas maintains, and the Supreme Court has held, that an individual in public life, and

---

the merged companies decided to compete in other fields, and insisted that prediction rather than proof must necessarily enter into the decision. This goes pretty far.

27. 370 US 294 (1962).

particularly an officeholder, is entitled to no protection whatever. If one's life lies in the public domain, he argues, comment or characterization of it must be free. As a result, however malicious, mendacious, or outrageous a slander may be, a person in public life has no redress at law. A widely advertised play, *MacBird*, may be cited as illustration. (Its innuendo sought to suggest that President Lyndon Johnson—MacBird—had connived at the assassination of President John F. Kennedy!) Regrettably, other redress, such as access to mass or other media assuring scope of answer equal to the scope of attack, has not yet been worked out —though it is not difficult to imagine that just such countervailing right might be developed in future judicial decisions.

Two years ago, in *Schneider* v. *Rusk*,[28] the Court had before it a federal statute providing that a naturalized citizen lost nationality if he resided continuously for three years in the foreign state of which he was formerly a national. A majority of the Court held the statute bad as a discrimination against naturalized citizens under the Fourteenth Amendment—although similar clauses and naturalization treaties had contained similar provisions for nearly a century.

5. The Essential Problem

Concern here lies not with the merits of the decisions reached by the courts, though in general I agree with them. Greater concern lies elsewhere.

This revolution, like others, had as its first effect a tremendous concentration of power—in this case, in the hands of the Supreme Court of the United States. That was the result of erecting the Fourteenth Amendment into a command that states shall create conditions satisfying the requirements of "equal protection." Standards of "equal protection" change with time and conditions,

28. 377 US 163 (1965).

as Chief Justice John Marshall long ago foresaw they would.[29] In the past half-century, conditions and concepts have changed, perhaps more rapidly than in any similar period in recorded history. The Supreme Court considers—and the American public accepts its view—that it has the power and the duty to determine when these changes impose new or different obligations on the states. If a case is brought before it, the new conditions can be assessed, new obligations imposed by judicial command, and new implementation required by the federal courts—unless state action makes this unnecessary. The discussions of the Court in *Bell* v. *Maryland* were essentially debates in a revolutionary assembly. The only odd circumstance is to find them taking place in a court.

The dialectic imposed by the present interpretation of the Fourteenth Amendment inexorably pushes the Court into the causative and essentially legislative position it now holds. Given the degree of change, the manner and method of this judicial revolution were perhaps the least costly and most effective possible under the circumstances. Revolutions have been going forward all over the world, many of them at the cost of endless bloodshed, disorder, and human misery. Without its judicial revolution, the United States might have encountered like periods of chaos.

Yet every revolution is eventually faced with the problem of relocating power and providing it with sustaining institutions. That has been true at least since the days of Oliver Cromwell. This problem, it seems to me, the Supreme Court and the federal political and legal systems must presently solve. Thinking along that line had best be done before the problem becomes acute, and no apology is needed for raising the question now.

Specifically, an institutional solution must be devised that will, first, indicate the areas in which the system of laws prevailing has failed to give "equal protection," and where action is needed. Second, orderly mechanism must be provided for having the problems thus developed placed before the appropriate political bodies for action. Third, the Supreme Court itself should be persuaded to require that political action through the Congress and the legis-

29. *McCulloch* v. *Maryland*, 4 Wheaton 316, 407 (1819).

latures should be sought before the Court's decree-making and judicial legislative power be invoked. Judicial legislation should be availed of as an ultimate and emergency power rather than as standard operating procedure. We shall explore possibilities of doing this, in the hope that, since the Court quite justifiably assumed the powers of a limited revolutionary committee, these powers may be redevolved in orderly fashion on the institutions devised to deal with them.

It appears, on reverting to the five laws of power, that the Supreme Court asserted its power to prevent a potentially chaotic situation; that it found a fairly well-defined idea system or philosophy embodied in the Constitution and the history of American democracy; and that it utilized the system of federal courts as an institutional framework giving effect to its decrees. So far, so good.

II

Revolution in Economic Organization

Revolution, as we have seen, is already well under way in the fields of education and local government. Less evidently but no less surely it is taking place in the field of economic organization, now intensified by mechanics and cybernetics. Here the process has been slower and less obvious, but that is because our chief means of economic organization—the corporation—for some decades has already been a revolutionary instrument of the first order. That its development should force change in power relationships as well as legal concepts is hardly remarkable.

1. The Background

Agriculture aside, most of the business of the United States, where it is not carried on by the government, is carried on by corporations—to be specific, about 1,200,000 of them, big and small. But four-fifths or more of the total activity is carried on by about thirty-five hundred corporations in all, whose stock is listed respectively on the New York Stock Exchange, the American Stock Exchange, or the over-the-counter markets. Even this is not a fair index. Eight hundred corporations probably account for between seventy and seventy-five per cent of all American business activity; two hundred and fifty corporations account for perhaps two-thirds of it. These figures do not take into account the fact that great numbers of smaller concerns are in effect, though not technically, controlled by their large associates. Thousands of gasoline stations and automobile dealers in the United States are nominally independent; practically, most of their decisions are predetermined by supply arrangements, franchise contracts, or agency agreements with the large corporations whose oil or cars or gadgets they sell. Far and away the major part of the American supply-and-exchange system is constituted of a few hundred (at most) clusters of corporate enterprises, each of whose major decisions is determined by a central giant.

Simultaneously—and, oddly enough, exactly contrary to a famous prediction by Karl Marx—these aggregations have not proved machines for accumulating personal wealth. They have, it is true, accumulated productive assets, tangible and intangible, to a degree staggering imagination.[1] But they split the personal-wealth factor from the productive factor. (That is the real rationale of corporate stock.) But corporate stock has been increasingly distributed rather than accumulated. Directly, there are

1. American Telephone & Telegraph Company was estimated to have approximately $30 billion of liquid and tangible assets. General Motors' assets were said to be in the vicinity of $20 billion; Standard Oil of New Jersey, about $11½ billion—to name only a few. And 1,119 companies had total assets of $269.4 billion (*News Front*, August, 1966, p. 49).

26,000,000 owners of stock in the United States in 1969. The number has since increased. Indirectly, through pension funds and other financial institutions, some 30,000,000 or 40,000,000 more Americans have a beneficial interest in the market value assigned by share quotations to the accumulated corporate assets —and a still more direct interest in the income generated and partly distributed by them. The erstwhile village blacksmith would today be an employee of, say, Cyclops Steel, and would own a few shares of stock in the concern or have an interest in its pension fund.

Meantime, the United States has come to rely on the corporate organization for supply of most of its goods and a substantial part of its services, including the most essential of both—to say nothing of the fact that a substantial amount of employment is expected to be maintained by this system.[2]

The result—this one without intervention of the courts—was to bring about a minor revolution in itself. The classic ownership relation between men and producing assets has been dissolved. Instead, men hold jobs—protected by labor unions and the National Labor Relations Board—and they own, directly or indirectly, pieces of paper carrying expectation of dividends, with salability provided by stock markets whose operations are federally regulated under the Securities Act and a widening jurisdiction of the federal courts under Rule 10-b-5 of the Securities and Exchange Commission prohibiting fraudulent practices in security exchanges. (That rule, it may be noted, was made not by a legislature, but by an administrative commission, and it is more often cited than the statute itself.) [3]

Because all this was happening (and the statistics are stag-

2. The effect of corporate policies on employment goes far beyond direct employment in plants or offices. The recession of 1956 was in part due to the fact that the three principal automobile manufacturers, General Motors, Ford, and Chrysler, sold 8,000,000 cars in the previous year. *The National City Bank Economic Review* estimated the "normal" market for cars at the time at 6,000,-000. The following year the motorcar companies sold only 4,000,000 cars, and, naturally, purchased far less from their suppliers of raw materials, glass, et cetera. The effect on employment was severe.

3. William L. Cary, *Politics and the Regulatory Agencies*, New York, McGraw-Hill, 1965.

gering) none need be surprised that the underlying institution—
the corporation—is at length coming in for revolutionary judicial
overhaul. Examination of this movement is our present task. Perhaps we may also be able to peer into the future.

2. What Is a Corporation?

First among the problems raised is that of the real nature of the
corporation. What is a corporation, anyhow? I do not wish to raise
here the historic, hoary, and romantic problem of the mystic
"corporate entity," though that subject has intrigued authors for
more than a century, with roots going back to the days of *Sutton's
Case*,[4] if not before. Rather, I want to examine a more modern
question: Is a corporation a "person" within the purview of the
Fifth and Fourteenth Amendments? If not, what are the consequences?

Until a few years ago, the question would have been laughed
at. In 1889, Justice Stephen J. Field, in *Minneapolis Railway
Company* v. *Beckwith*,[5] formally held that "Corporations can invoke the benefits of provisions of the Constitution and laws which
guarantee to persons the enjoyment of property, or afford to
them the means for its protection." That was that for nearly
three-fourths of a century.

Fifty years later, a routine case came along—*Connecticut General Life Insurance Company* v. *Johnson*.[6] The State of California
had undertaken to tax reinsurance contracts, made in Connecticut,
designed to indemnify other insurance companies for losses on
policies written in California. This was attacked as being in violation of the Fourteenth Amendment. Chief Justice Harlan Stone,
writing for the majority of the Court, held the California tax bad

4. *Sutton's Case*, 10 CO. 1 (1612). See, for one of many discussions of it, 21
Harvard Law Review, p. 305 (1908).
5. 129 US 26 (1889).
6. 303 US 77 (1938).

under the Fourteenth Amendment. Dissenting, Justice Hugo Black drove at the basic doctrine. He said the language and history of the amendment did "not support the theory that it was passed for the benefit of corporations," [7] and that the amendment applied only to natural, not artificial, persons.[8] Glumly, he noted that of the cases before the Supreme Court to which the Fourteenth Amendment was applied during the first fifty years after its adoption, more than fifty per cent asked that its benefits be extended to *corporations*—and only one-half of one per cent invoked it in protection of the Negro race, for whose protection this amendment was primarily designed.

Justice Black's was a single voice crying unnoticed in the wilderness. A few years later, however, Justice Douglas joined him (see *Wheeling Steel Company* v. *Glander*),[9] and in 1964, in *Bell* v. *Maryland*, he returned to the charge. There, the owner of a restaurant invoking police protection against Negro sit-ins was a corporation. The Attorney General of Maryland, arguing in support of their conviction, somewhat incautiously suggested that the restaurant owner was a "person" having the right to choose the parties with whom it would deal—a right analogous to that of opening or closing the door of one's home. This was Justice Douglas' opportunity, and he drove at the whole conception of analogizing corporate personality and individual personality. To his concurring opinion he attached a series of appendices, four of which were designed to show that most restaurants were operated by corporation chains, and that corporations were not "individuals" either in fact or in law. Giving them the status of individuals,

7. *Ibid.*, pp. 86, 87.
8. See Clarence Cyril Walton and R. S. F. Eells, *The Business System*, New York, Macmillan, 1967, p. 1679, quoting from Woodrow Wilson, "The Lawyer and the Community" (Report of the 33d Annual Meeting of The American Bar Association, 1910, pp. 426–431). Wilson said: "I regard the corporation as indispensable to modern business enterprise. I am not jealous of its size or might, if you will but abandon at the right points the fatuous, antiquated, and quite unnecessary fiction which treats it as a legal person; if you will but cease to deal with it by means of your law as if it were a single individual not only, but also—what every child may perceive it is not—a responsible individual."
9. 337 US 562 (1949).

guaranteeing them rights of privacy in the use of their business property, would in effect give them power through intracorporate regulation to determine practices in race relations. Not only was any property devoted to business not "private" in the individual property sense, but also, if in corporate hands, it was not "personal" property at all. He renewed his head-on stricture of the ancient doctrine of *Minneapolis Railway Company* v. *Beckwith* and powerfully reaffirmed his position and Justice Black's that corporations were *not* "persons" entitled to the protection of the Fourteenth Amendment.

It so happens that as matter of history, of sociology, and even of verbal interpretation, the Black-Douglas argument is unanswerable. The Fourteenth Amendment was designed to protect natural persons; no other interpretation can be given the language. Sociologically, a corporation, especially a large corporation, is anything but a natural person. Legally, the fiction of its personality has already been punctured. A corporation, for example, does not have the privilege of self-incrimination guaranteed by the Fifth Amendment.[10] Attempt to give it the quality of a natural person is patent nonsense.

Despite that, mere removal of the corporation from Fourteenth Amendment protection does not answer all the range of questions. The corporation may not be itself a person. But it certainly is a composite of natural persons. These may be few—as in a close corporation—or may run into millions—as in the case of the American Telephone & Telegraph Company (actually, 3,142,100, according to its 1968 report). If we disregard the fictional personality of a corporation and withdraw from it the protections of the fifth and fourteenth amendments, we are still obliged to consider the individuals comprised in the composite. They do have rights. It is scarcely arguable that by yielding part of their property to a corporation through the stockholding device, they have *pro tanto* surrendered it out of all constitutional protection. Were that to happen, some 26,000,000 personal stockholders[11] and

10. *United States* v. *White*, 322 US 694, 698 (1944).

11. Of the personally owned property held by citizens of the United States, between one-fourth and one-third consists of corporation securities, chiefly

30,000,000 to 40,000,000 holders of pension rights would find themselves outside the constitutional system.

We have to look, therefore, beyond the immediate effect of the Black-Douglas doctrine—the more so because I believe that doctrine will eventually prevail. Possibly the corporation as a Fourteenth Amendment "person" will vanish. But behind it will appear aggregates of natural persons, each one of whom does have a relationship to the corporation, as employee or as holder of a property interest in it. As to their interests, they are entitled not to be deprived of "property" without due process of law. They are even entitled not to be denied "equal protection of the laws" or the protections guaranteed by the Bill of Rights.

"Personality" of the corporation was a fiction, and for Fourteenth Amendment purposes perhaps can be dispensed with. Yet the fact remains that a corporation is a composite of natural persons; these do have property interests entrusted by them to corporate managements. Justice Douglas was right in asserting that their individual "personality" did not carry over into the corporation. Ordinarily, the corporation could not set itself up as representing them in assertion of their individual or combined rights of privacy. On the other hand, a corporation, though not a "person" under the Fourteenth Amendment, not only can, but should and must, defend their combined property interests. Savings of individuals, directly represented by their stockholdings or indirectly represented through some $80 billion of pension trust funds held for their benefit, do mean a great deal to them, and are entitled to be represented and defended by the composite organism.

If the Black-Douglas doctrine prevails—as in logic it eventually should—I think that a rule suggests itself. The corporation would have standing to represent and defend the aggregate of individual rights held by or entrusted to the corporation. These ordinarily would be the property rights of shareholders; perhaps also the

stocks. The census of stockholders in 1965 showed 19,963,000 individual shareowners; the number has subsequently increased. In 1968 the Stock Exchange estimated it at 24,000,000. See *New York Stock Exchange 1965 Census of Shareholders–Share Ownership U.S.A.*

contract or other rights created through bargains reached collectively with employees; possibly even rights under agency and other arrangements reached in agreement with, let us say, salesmen and dealers.

The corporation, as such, would not be entitled to any of the constitutional rights that inhere in individual persons: the right to privacy or the like. Yet it would seem that a corporation should be protected and should be allowed to maintain (as corporations successfully have) actions to defend such rights in representation of individuals within or as part of its operations.[12] For example, a corporate newspaper or broadcasting company should be protected as the defender of the right to freedom of speech of the composite of its reporters and editorial writers who had exercised that right through the corporate medium. An incorporated school or university should have like right to defend the freedom of speech of the composite of its faculty, students, and research workers or any of them.

It is entirely arguable that while a corporation can have no religion, if it is organized by men to carry forward religious purposes, their personal freedom of religion must be respected under the First Amendment and may be protected through appropriate protection of the corporation's activities. There seems no reason to "abridge" freedom of speech because it is exercised through the corporate form.

The problem in each case would be to determine whether there is a personal right entitled to defense and whether the right can properly be defended or asserted on behalf of the individuals by the composite we call a corporation.

So I do not see that the demise of the rule of *Minneapolis Rail-*

12. In older conceptions, the corporation was considered a "trust" or fiduciary for its shareholders. The conception is still valid. It would seem that the corporation had not only the right, but also the duty, to defend the interests of the individuals for whose property it was responsible—irrespective of whether it had "personality" or not. The difficulty would lie in distinguishing between the interests of its shareholders and the interest of the corporation as a whole. Probably on analysis it would appear that where the interest of the corporation validly could be invaded or constricted through police power, regulation, and the like, the individuals as individuals would not be protected either.

way Company v. *Beckwith* and of the doctrine that corporations are "persons" within the meaning of the Bill of Rights would be any great disaster. Rather, it might clarify the situation.

3. Corporate Regulations as "Laws" under the Fourteenth Amendment

More immediate is another Black-Douglas contention; namely, that because of the size and scope of corporate operations, corporations can and do make rules having the effect of legislation.[13]

This is an indisputable sociological fact. It was the subject of judicial scrutiny in *Plessy* v. *Ferguson*,[14] giving rise to the now discarded requirement of "separate but equal" accommodation for Negroes, first on public carriers. Internal rules and regulations made by corporate managements (like those involved in *Plessy* v. *Ferguson*) or running their businesses can and do vitally

13. Justice Douglas—quite rightly—in *Bell* v. *Maryland* added a few appendices to his concurring opinion, as we said. Because argument had been made that the restaurant owner had a right to choose his own customers and associates, one of these memoranda pointed out that the owner was not a person, but a corporation; that, indeed, most owners of property offering facilities to the public were corporations; that a corporation was not a "natural person" whose "personal right" was infringed when forced to open its lunch counter to people of all races, and he attached a list of corporate business establishments involved in Negro "sit-in" cases before the Supreme Court in the 1962 and 1963 terms. Of twenty cases involved, two were partnerships or private proprietorships; the others were chiefly chain operations with thousands of stockholders. Justice Douglas said further, "Affirmance would make corporate management the arbiter of one of the deepest conflicts in our society: corporate management could then enlist the aid of state police, state prosecutors, and state courts to force apartheid on the community they served" (*Bell* v. *Maryland,* at p. 880). As Douglas saw it, if the Court did not legislate, corporate managements could and would use their commercial organizations as institutions, and their notions of the probable greatest profit as their philosophy.
14. 163 US 537 (1897). The Court had under examination the claim that a Negro was denied "equal protection of the laws" because he was not allowed to ride in a railway carriage reserved for whites. Corporate regulations as well as state laws offered to Negroes "Jim Crow" accommodations.

affect the lives of their employees, their agents, their suppliers, their customers, and the public. Employees are, of course, protected—if they so choose—by the countervailing power arising from rights of organization and collective bargaining guaranteed under the Taft-Hartley Act and the rulings of the National Labor Relations Board, though that should not and does not exclude protection of them as individuals under the Fourteenth Amendment should corporate rules, resting on economic power, impair their rights. The other categories, notably suppliers and customers, are not as a rule protected by any organization giving them "countervailing power." Danger that intracorporate rules governing the operations of the business might deprive Negroes of equal protection was the focus of Justice Douglas' discussion in *Bell* v. *Maryland*—but he barely scratched one surface of a huge area.

Take, for example, the case of consumer-credit terms in the automobile-finance business. It is statistically provable that great numbers of American citizens can have and hold jobs only if they have automobiles taking them to and from work. It is also a statistical fact that about ninety per cent of all automobiles are bought on credit. It is also true that the great bulk of automobile-finance credit is handled by a few large corporations under more or less standard terms and guidelines dictated by them. Admittedly, credit-worthiness is a somewhat delicate matter, difficult of reduction to absolute terms. Under these circumstances, a finance-company regulation denying credit to one category of applicants or discriminating against others can, quite simply, deny applicants access to their jobs and their living as well as to easier lives.

Unlike the situation in *Bell* v. *Maryland* and *Shelley* v. *Kraemer*,[15] the corporation does not have to call in local police or courts to enforce its regulations; the customer simply does not get the service. No pretense can be made that governmental

15. 334 US 1 (1948). An action to prevent a Negro from taking title to a house because of a covenant prohibiting its sale to Negroes was struck down by the Supreme Court on the ground that the state courts violated the Fourteenth Amendment by enforcing such a covenant.

mechanism of any kind was called in to prevent him getting it. Is it open to serious doubt that the judicial revolution already requiring elimination of discrimination against Negroes will eventually reach discriminatory practice in other fields?

At risk of being accused of a flight of fancy, I suggest a further possibility. Increasingly, information on men is being accumulated for credit purposes—and for employment purposes. Under corporation-made "programs," it is increasingly stored in machines called "computers." Insertion of an item into these machines may affect or wreck a career, low or high, or a journey at home or abroad. The computer can erect walls, unbreakable though invisible. It may block a man in any number of directions—from obtaining a license to drive a motorcar to getting a credit card or a job.

It is to be presumed that an individual wrong caused by combined corporate and computer machinery will be dealt with by actions for damages under normal rules of tort liability. Should this happen, "equal protection of the laws" will be provided by normal processes.[16] Active development of law in this field has been, and still is, the best protection against unfair extension of the power of judicial legislation granted the federal courts. We cannot, however, ignore the possibility that state law may not adequately deal with the field. In that case, we must contemplate a still-greater extension of the Supreme Court's power—consonant with its duty of providing "equal protection."

The capacity of computer operations to impinge on human life has yet to be fully imagined, still less realized. But it already exists.[17] Take a single situation, presently in rapid development.

16. Even so, remedy through tort action is not a reason for denying habeas corpus. For example, a person may be imprisoned in a private hospital. He may have a fully adequate remedy by action for false imprisonment. This is not, however, reason for denying habeas corpus. A money judgment is not adequate reparation for loss of liberty.

17. In 1939, the Temporary National Economic Committee (TNEC), constituted by Congress, investigated concentration of economic power. Part 10 of its hearings related to intercompany agreements between life insurance companies (pp. 643–648). It developed that the Association of Life Insurance Medical Directors maintained what is known as the Medical Information Bureau (M.I.B.), in which was collected all the information derived from medi-

Intercommunication of machines by machines with machines—
that is, between computer systems—is already in operation. Let
us suppose that the computer systems presently used by the great
New York banks are made to intercommunicate with the computer systems presently being used in other financial or consumer-
credit corporations (many of them owned by these same banks).
Add to the credit data they store, the budget of computer information regarding a man's record for, let us say, safe automobile
driving, previous satisfactory employment, and the like. In fear
of overstating, I do not add the possibility of intercommunication
between these and the machines presently scrutinizing federal income-tax returns or classifying FBI records, though that possibility
cannot be altogether ruled out. Then let us suppose a simple case.
A man traveling on an airline credit card is abroad or away from
home. The computer complex picks up a piece of information—it
may be false—that on one occasion he issued a check that

---

cal examination of individuals seeking life insurance. In 1939 it had records
of approximately 6,700,000 people (p. 4637). It is computerized today. The
number has immensely increased.

In 1966 a Task Force under the chairmanship of Dr. Carl Kaysen completed
a report (available through the Bureau of the Budget), *The Report of the
Task Force on the Storage of and Access to Government Statistics.* It proposed
a National Data Center, though its thrust was statistical. Yet, in Kaysen's
words, "for the data center to achieve its intended purpose, the material in it
must identify individual respondents in some way, by Social Security number
for individuals, or an analogous code number now used within the Census for
business enterprises called the Alpha number. These numbers need in turn
to be keyed to a list of respondents which identifies them by name and address within the data center itself," or "within the actual data collecting
agencies." (See Carl Kaysen, "Data Banks and Dossiers," *The Public Interest,*
No. 7, Spring, 1967, pp. 52–56.)

The Bureau of Internal Revenue maintains a computer data bank designed
to cover virtually all income-tax returns. Kaysen himself believes (p. 58)
that the Congress might specifically prohibit the inclusion in the proposed
data bank of dossier information—that is, information in which the specific
identity of the individual is essential for its purposes rather than a file of data
for statistical purposes.

Of course, nothing prevents the accumulation of private dossier material—
as, for instance, the Medical Information Bureau information and the files
maintained by great bureaus. Separate public agencies maintain dossier files
for police purposes. I feel that the proliferation and increase of these data
banks can no longer be prevented.

bounced, or he failed to pay an installment contract on time. It grinds out the conclusion that his airline credit card should no longer be honored, and, also by computer, transmits this ruling to every airline office in the country. He is duly denied credit for a ticket home; he is unlikely to be able to obtain money at any bank. He is left hanging. He, of course, is totally unaware of the internal operation of the machine. All he knows is that the credit operation on which his voyage has been constructed has shut down on him.

The computer-transmitted facts may be true but so long lived down that they should have become irrelevant. Or they may be false, inserted by error or malice or by a slip in the machine. Even after getting out of his travel predicament, he has no ready way of discovering what the difficulty is, of demanding some sort of hearing thereon, or any readily practicable way of clearing the record.

Is it too farfetched to suggest that the time may come when a writ of habeas corpus will be granted against the possessor or operator of a computer? I do not think so. Imprisoned within the computer is an extension of the man—his record and reputation, his ability to get a job or secure credit. If the machine is favorable, he is enfranchised in this organized world; if it is unfavorable, he may be barred from great segments of it. Prison limits, even at common law, were not necessarily fixed by stone walls or iron bars.

But there are corporate developments proceeding rapidly where men are left unprotected by current legal evolution. A spectacular one is the growing scope of private pension trust funds designed to provide retirement pensions and other benefits for workers. Most corporations have such funds, either by their own wish or because such funds are required as "fringe benefits" connected with their wage arrangements with labor unions. The subject was pioneered at the Columbia Law School by Dr. Paul Harbrecht in his book *Pension Funds and Economic Power*.[18]

Now pension trust agreements, while beneficial, can also be tremendously oppressive. They can, for example, provide that

18. New York, Twentieth Century Fund, 1959.

377

the worker who leaves or changes his job sacrifices a large part of the payments made into the fund as part of his compensation. They can make it difficult if not impossible for an older man to get a job—because the payments required under the pension trust arrangement become greater as he grows older. Conversely, they can increase the sacrifice of accumulated pension rights if an older man leaves his job to take another one. A pension trust can thus tie a man to a job by economic pressure, or prevent a man from getting a job by like pressure. The subject is being discussed at both state and federal levels. It is, I think, possible that legislation may cover the field—but there is no guarantee of that. At the pace at which these pension trusts are increasing, in coverage, amount, and impact, we could easily be faced with a situation in which whole classes of individuals, through no fault or consent of their own, are severely constricted. As the system becomes general—a present possibility—"equal protection of the laws" against some of the results could well become an active question. The constitutional problem could be avoided by legislation setting up a clearinghouse and permitting interchange of accumulated pension rights, and by permitting newcomers into the pension funds to accept lower benefits than those granted to beneficiaries who have contributed over a long period of time. This is what I hope will happen. But if it does not, how long will the exclusion or immobilization of some workers be accepted as merely a regrettable though irremediable consequence of corporate economic arrangements?

The point need not be labored. Life in a modern, industrialized, intricately organized world is a reality. This is the world of great corporations and, now, of computer action. Neither probability nor practicality suggests return to the older, simpler organization in which multitudes of individual relationships were the doors through which men moved. Then, closing of any one door did not materially limit freedom. Today, it is otherwise. Men move within the frameworks of great organizations and their increasing mechanization. The rules of their mechanization are far more compulsive, binding, and privative than were governmental dangers to freedom premising the Constitution's Bill of Rights.

They are carried out by artificial persons whose capacity to make them was erected and granted by the several states in their respective corporation acts. Already, as in *Bell* v. *Maryland,* the Supreme Court has reached the point of saying that where the local state police or courts are called in to enforce them (*Shelley* v. *Kraemer*), there is state action, controlled by constitutional protection. But in the case of a credit regulation, intervention of the police or the courts is not needed; the corporate rule is self-enforcing. Are we to assume in such case that the positive duty of states to maintain a system giving "equal protection of the laws" has not been infringed? The state of the present judicial revolution suggests an emerging doctrine. Rules, regulations, and practices, machine-made or otherwise, by which corporations carry on their business are, in and of themselves, subject to judicial scrutiny and, if need be, change by judicial decree under the current standards of the Fourteenth Amendment.

In an appropriate case, the Supreme Court should declare that corporate action denying "equal protection of the laws" is in essence state action, because the effectiveness of an action is derived from state power to grant the corporate form privileges or (at least) from the state's failure to control the corporation by appropriate law—that is, inaction constituting responsible state action within the meaning of the Fourteenth Amendment. If anything is clear, it is that a state does have power to determine what a corporation of its creation shall and shall not do. It may, by statute, lay down requirements for corporate action. It can set up administrative tribunals to which any individual aggrieved may apply for summary remedy, as New York has done in the employment field. Such remedies could be made applicable to corporate action ground out by computer machines as well as by corporate officers or employees.

Far from worrying about this constitutional development, I welcome it. Corporate power has served the United States well. In substantial measure, the material prosperity of the country is due to it. Like any other power, it can be abused. A major bulwark against that abuse is the body of rules and doctrines emerging from the judicial revolution we have been examining.

As a corporation lawyer, I believe these fascinating, frightening, and fantastic institutions will be strengthened rather than weakened by the application of constitutional limitations—and requirements of action—to them.

A final point is in the nature of a glance down the vista.

Business increasingly is becoming interrelated with government processes. In many states of the Union, it is illegal to drive an uninsured car. The right to drive, under proper licensing or regulation, is clear enough. The right to get insurance, so far as I am aware, does not as yet have legal sanction. It has been assumed that insurance companies would provide coverage. Yet, so far as I am aware, they are entitled to choose what risks they will insure and what risks they will deny. Already, and perhaps on sound actuarial grounds, they charge discriminatory rates for teen-age drivers and for adults whose families include teen-agers. They could—as some of them are beginning to do—refuse the business altogether, or accept only selected categories of individuals whose probability of being involved in accidents they consider low. The growing number of cars on the road, the losses suffered in the casualty insurance business and appellate court acceptance of irresponsible verdicts for losses contribute to making the business increasingly unattractive. In effect, the result is more and more to make private companies final arbiters of whether men can drive cars. This was tolerable enough a generation ago, when driving was a privilege and a luxury. It becomes dangerous when driving is, virtually, a necessary adjunct of life for most citizens.

The illustration given is only one of a number of similar interrelations. In many situations, the right of an individual to enjoy quite ordinary attributes of life is made dependent on the willingness of a private business to attend to his needs and provide (for a price) the necessary evidence that the work was done.

Project this situation a few years. By the turn of the century, the population of the United States will be well over a quarter of a billion. The density in certain areas may become very great. Large demonstration by words is not needed to show that "equal protection of the laws" must mean equal access to certain kinds of services. That in turn means that many substantially private businesses will find themselves in a position to permit or deny at will the usual accessories of life or living. Access to the service of a chain store may be needed to keep the family fed, to the local garage to have the brakes inspected on the essential car; and so on through the list.

But by now the character of business is changed. It is more than merely rendering private goods and services for a price by a willing seller to a customer who wants to buy. The services may not be "state services" in the ordinary sense; but they are projected to cardinal importance as the state increasingly recognizes, uses, and requires that these services shall have been rendered in some cases and, in others, that they shall not be denied on request.

4. "Abstention" from Use of Judicial Power—an Illusion

The problems of the field of economic organization—like those of the field of local government—are immense and growing. Other similar problems are certain to emerge. Conceivably, the federal courts could avoid them by exercising their ancient power of "federal question abstention" on a number of hallowed grounds. Abstention ordinarily is invoked on the ground that the problem raised is essentially political, or to avoid unnecessary constitutional adjudication, or to allow state courts to determine issues where the state law appears unclear. In view of the many massive legal questions now presented and of the unforeseeable impact of decisions, one can sympathize with those who feel that the Supreme Court should be astute enough not to decide many of the issues presented and to be presented.

All of us are aware of the late Justice Frankfurter's solution reached in *Railroad Commission* v. *Pullman Company*—that of the Court's stepping out of the legislative power position so far as possible and in other matters leaving the problem of providing "equal protection of the laws," except in matters of judicial procedure, to the mechanisms of the state government.[19] Avoidance of tough questions is indeed part of established judicial procedure, but it is increasingly in disfavor, as pointed out in an elaborate note-article published in the *Harvard Law Review* for January, 1967.[20] In my judgment, avoidance is not now possible. A corollary to the first law of power (that it always replaces chaos) is the implacable rule that power cast aside without provision for its further exercise almost invariably destroys the abdicating power holder—as Shakespeare's King Lear found out when he improvidently abandoned his power, and was promptly crushed.[21] Conceivably, the Supreme Court might have avoided assuming the power position in the first place—but cannot renounce it now. It has entered, created, and accepted a field of responsibility. Elements in that field might wreck the Court were it now to desert the function it has assumed. Picket lines directed against municipal governments, schools, or businesses would then be turned on the Supreme Court itself.

Obviously, the first duty of the Court is to resolve the specific case before it. The second—in this context a more important task —is to lay down a rule of general application to like cases. This involves the legislative function. Sometimes, to be sure, simple determination of the case will include the secondary effect. In the sit-in cases (*Bell* v. *Maryland*), two concurring members—who, in fact, wanted the widest legislative effect possible—believed the Court should have dismissed the proceedings for criminal trespass, with the result, in Justice Douglas' language: "Were we today to hold that segregated restaurants, whose racial policies were enforced by a State, violated the Equal Protection Clause, all restaurants would be on an equal footing and the reasons given in this and most of the companion cases for refusing service to Negroes would evaporate."[22] But simple determination that a school is segregated and should not be, or that this legislature is

19. 312 US 496, 498, 500.
20. Vol. 80, No. 3, pp. 604 ff.
21. *Vide* Book 1, Chapter II, Part 5 *supra*.
22. *Bell* v. *Maryland*, p. 246.

badly apportioned, does not desegregate the school or reapportion the legislature.

More often, the reason given for the disposition of the case has more legislative effect than the *ratio decidendi*. Certainly this was true in the reapportionment cases (as, for example, in *Reynolds* v. *Sims*). In the school-segregation cases, the problem has been, and now is, to give effect to the principles enunciated in *Brown* v. *Topeka*. In a recent case, a district court judge, required to draw a decree for the desegregation of schools in a number of consolidated cases, sought outside guidance. He discovered that the Department of Health, Education, and Welfare had issued a document containing "guidelines" for desegregation, and he adopted this document as part of his decree, directing that by September 1, 1967, these guidelines should be made effective by the school authorities involved.[23]

Bluntly, litigation in these fields has reached the point where, in many cases, the Supreme Court lays down the principle but sends the case itself back to a district or a state court with instructions to draw an appropriate decree—that is, to draft a decree law. In doing that, the federal courts at any level need settled procedures and expect help. Legislative bodies, of course, have such help. Their procedure commonly includes committee hearings on the legislation they intend to pass where interests may

23. *United States* v. *Jefferson County Board of Education*, 372 F. 2d 836 (1966). See the New York *Times*, March 11, 1967.

A three-judge court handed down an order on December 29, 1966, directing desegregation of nine school districts in Louisiana and Alabama. On appeal to the United States Court of Appeals for the Fifth Circuit, twelve judges were present; the head of the Department of Justice civil-rights division argued for a general ruling; the National Association for the Advancement of Colored People was represented, as were attorneys for various Southern cities.

The three-judge decision under appeal had indicated that the burden of integrating schools should be shifted to the executive branch of the government—therefore, they had used guidelines suggested by the Department of Health, Education, and Welfare.

The fact was that the Court of Appeals for the Fifth Circuit was conducting a legislative hearing. Fundamentally, they were deciding whether they should adopt as legislation the guidelines of the Department of Health, Education, and Welfare as applicable law covering a large area of the United States with the possibility that the precedent might become applicable all over the United States.

be balanced, and they may have the benefit of expert reports from executive departments having most to do with the enforcement and results of the legislation. Not infrequently, legislative committees have expert staffs of their own. Court procedure has no similar assistance.

This fact outlines the problem. The "equal protection" clause under present doctrine requires the courts not only to strike down action affirmatively denying such protection, but also to remedy the lack of action that *should have been taken* to give such protection. Abstention—avoidance of the problem—seems no longer practicable. Some addition to American legal institutions seems needed. Given the staggering rate of change in economic and technical development, and its ever greater impact on individual life, we must expect more, rather than fewer, problems like those examined here to emerge within the next few years.

Let us turn then to the possibility of adding some institution that will afford the federal courts better facility than perhaps they now have to meet the obligations imposed on them by the revolutionary era. It might, by channeling some of these problems toward the Congress and state legislatures, relieve the Supreme Court of some of the dangerous burdens placed on it by fate and the federal Constitution.

III

The Redistribution of Judicial Power

1. Power and Its Dialogue

An invariable result of revolution is a sudden concentration of power. This is as true of revolutions mandated by a constitutional provision such as the Fourteenth Amendment and conducted by courts as of more violent forms. To achieve their objective, there must be capacity to state the goal, develop the philosophy, set up the legislation, and draw the appropriate decrees. This is the position in which the Supreme Court today finds itself—a position, let me repeat, entirely legitimate in our constitutional system.

Yet it poses a second question with which every revolution has had to cope. Concentration of power must eventually be devolved on supporting institutions. Where revolutions are not constitutional, and institutional development is not indicated in advance, the results may be explosive, not to say disorderly. The French revolutionary authority had its Thermidor liquidating Robespierre and leading later to its 18th Brumaire and the beginning of the Napoleonic system. A familiar solution has been a dictatorship which promptly sets to work organizing the institutions that will maintain its regime after the immediate power holders are gone. A somewhat similar process has been going on in the Soviet Union since the death of Stalin. Some rearrangement seems to me essential if the Supreme Court is to survive.[1]

Happily, the United States has a very well-developed philosophy, vigorous institutions, and can devise orderly solutions. It needs no Thermidors.

I attempt here to suggest one method of approach, not because it is necessarily the right or only one, but to stimulate thinking along this line.

The necessity of tackling the problem now rather than later should be self-evident. Two observations may help to guide one's thinking.

First, the revolutionary process (in this case mandated by the current interpretation of the Constitution) arises essentially from lack of adequate legislation.

The restaurant sit-in case (*Bell* v. *Maryland*) here used as a case study would never have been brought, and the decision need never have been made, had the State of Maryland passed the anti-discrimination laws which in fact it later did adopt. Perhaps the decision would have been unnecessary had the Congress of the

1. Signs are not wanting that crisis is developing in the situation of the Supreme Court. As noted in the preface to this Book, thirty-four states have adopted the call for a constitutional convention, designed to amend the federal Constitution. Its primary intent is to propose a measure, sponsored by Senator Everett M. Dirksen, of Illinois, aimed at overruling *Baker* v. *Carr*, the "one man–one vote" ruling. The suggestion is that the federal Constitution be so amended as to permit representation for localities, irrespective of population. The Congress will have to call such a constitutional convention, and it is evident that there will be congressional opposition. Obviously, the result of a constitutional convention might enter areas other than those proposed by Senator Dirksen.

United States already adopted the Civil Rights Act of 1965—which was actually passed a year and a half after *Bell* v. *Maryland*. Had the Congress—or the several states—adopted legislation governing discrimination in housing, the courts probably would not have had to deal with the problem they now must solve by a succession of decrees. If regulation arising from economic power—such as that of large corporations or great aggregates of competitors—safeguarded civil rights, judges would not have to study the principles and contrive the remedies they must unquestionably design if the vacuum is left unfilled. Chief Justice Warren and Justice Goldberg were entirely right, in *Bell* v. *Maryland*, in recommending that course to the Maryland courts, because, during the pendency of the litigation, Maryland had in fact legislated. In effect, the Maryland legislation took the place—as it should—of the *ad hoc* decree the federal courts would otherwise have had to make. Our first conclusion must be that where the vacuum has been or is in the course of being filled by regular legislative process, following the recognized political philosophy and methods of the United States, courts should take judicial notice of that fact and give fullest opportunity for its realization.

Second, where courts legislate, there is failure of the essential continuing and orderly dialogue between power and the field of its responsibility.

When a president, or a congress, or a governor, or a legislature acts, the ground must be prepared politically, and opportunity given for all interests to be heard and considered, both before and after the power holders act. In American procedure, this dialogue is more or less orderly. Hearings in committee normally precede legislation; all interested parties desiring to do so have the opportunity to speak their piece. The factual situations and probable results can be estimated in advance. Interest can be balanced and dealt with accordingly. After action has been taken, public critique and comment, through the press, through local committees, through interested citizens, follow as matter of course. If the power holder has acted badly, or if the legislation is unsatisfactory, the individuals and institutions involved are politically responsible—the individuals can change their position or they can be defeated at the next election; the institutions can be modified or changed.

Little of this dialogue obtains, however, with respect to court action. True, the press can comment or criticize. In more orderly debate, law schools and law professors can criticize. This fills part of the gap. Yet essentially there is no appeal when the courts have acted; there is no compulsion on courts to take account either of the press or of the law reviews; much of the comment may never reach the judges. And Supreme Court justices are not elected; they hold office for life. Factually, the halls and publications of the law schools are the only institutions there are for reviewing Supreme Court decisions, other than agitation, or, at worst, mobs on the streets.

Any solution sought must therefore be double in character. It should provide a channel for assuring the legislation necessary to fulfill the revolutionary mandate of the Fourteenth Amendment (and probably also of the first ten amendments). And it should provide a forum in which orderly dialogue can take place between power, on one hand, and those affected by its use, on the other.

2. Institutionalizing Judicial Legislation

There is, I suggest, a method of doing this, though no model for equivalent action has yet been pounded out. Seeking an analogue, the most useful one I can find is that of the Council of Economic Advisers set up by the Employment Act of 1946.[2] The analogue is far from close, but in fundamentals it is useful. There, the United States was faced with the problem of economic power, great parts of which had come into the hands of the federal government. Particularly, it came to appear that the combination of monetary power (located in the Federal Reserve Board) and fiscal policy applied through the federal budget, together with certain other cognate federal powers, went far in determining the

2. 15 USCA §1021, §1025.

level of employment and prosperity of the United States. In 1946, no recognized standards had been set down for the use of that power—and only the most disorderly dialogue existed for determination or revision of its use.

In these circumstances, through the patient genius of Senator Paul Douglas, of Illinois, an institution was worked out which has now become classic in American economic administration. The Council of Economic Advisers was created, along with a join congressional committee and the requirement of an Economic Report. Its effect was to place responsibility for action where it belonged—in that case, not on courts, but on the executive branch, to propose, and on the Congress, where necessary, to legislate. Simultaneously, it set up an orderly dialogue by requiring an economic report from the president, its referral to a joint committee of the House and Senate, and hearings thereon. Like all institutions, the Council of Economic Advisers took time to establish itself in the public conscience and confidence. It has done so. Debates on measures to assure adequate functioning of the American economic system proceed in regular course. Properly, problems were transferred from mere protest against unsatisfactory conditions on the street to a forum where desired results could be stated and measures proposed. Orderly critique of measures previously taken could be had and their modification or change could proceed in accordance with the regularly constituted political institutions in a democracy.

Briefly, I seek something of the sort in the constitutional situation with which we are now faced, though, as noted, the solution must be somewhat different in application.

Let us suppose that the president be directed to transmit to the Congress a report—it might be called "The Report on Realization of Constitutional Rights." (May I add the hope that it will not be in January of each year; the twin reports on the "State of the Union" and on the American economy already required in that month are enough to sink any president for the previous two months.) It should set forth a review of the areas in which effective realization of constitutional rights and, particularly, "equal protection of the laws" appear to be defective and should recommend a program for remedying the defects as the president may deem necessary or desirable.

There might be created, in the executive office of the president, a "Council of Constitutional Advisers," composed of three or five members, appointed by the president with the advice and consent of the Senate. Each of these should be a person who, as a result of training, experience, and attainment, is exceptionally qualified to analyze and interpret constitutional developments, to appraise programs and activities of the federal government and of the states, and to formulate and recommend policies to promote the effective realization of constitutional rights.

If the experience of the Council of Economic Advisers is any guide, the members of the Constitutional Council would be professors of law, men with judicial experience, men with legislative experience, and men with social awareness.

The duties of the Council should be:

1. to assist and advise the president in the preparation of his report on constitutional rights;

2. to gather timely and authoritative information concerning current constitutional developments in perspective, to analyze and interpret such information in the light of a policy of active realization of constitutional rights, to determine whether developments or trends are interfering or likely to interfere with such realization, to compile and subscribe to the presidential studies relating thereto;

3. to appraise the various programs of the federal government for the purpose of determining the extent to which such programs are contributing—and the extent to which they are not contributing—to the achievement of such realiaztion and to make recommendations to the president with respect thereto;

4. to make and furnish such studies, reports, and recommendations with respect to federal constitutional policy and legislation as the president may request and, on request, to make similar studies and recommendations for the governors or state legislatures as these may request;

5. to make and furnish such studies, reports, and recommendations with respect to constitutional rights as the Supreme Court

may request, and, upon its request, to act as master for the purpose of determining and making recommendations as to decrees.

There might be established, by like legislation, a joint congressional committee, to be composed of, say, eight members of the Senate and eight members of the House of Representatives, the majority party to be represented by five members and the minority by three.

This committee should make continuing study of matters relating to constitutional rights, should hold hearings on the report of the president with respect to each of the main recommendations made by the president in that report, and should have power to employ attorneys and other experts to assist it.

The right of the joint congressional committee to hold hearings should not prejudice the right of the Council of Constitutional Advisers to hold hearings on any constitutional question on its own behalf, reporting to the president, to the joint congressional committee, and to the Supreme Court where requested. Such reports might contain recommendations for legislation to be submitted to the Congress, and in appropriate cases to the governments of the several states.

The double-barreled impact of such legislation will not go unnoticed. It is, first, a mandate to the president, with the Constitutional Council as expert adviser, to review the situation annually, and, where legislation is necessary, to propose it. In other words, it is a mechanism by which legislation can be proposed before, and not after, the Supreme Court is forced to assume the responsibility. The institution would also be adapted to gather the kind of data and material on which legislation can be founded, to work out the conflicts in the Congress instead of in the courts, to be ahead instead of behind the kind of situation with which the Supreme Court has been forced to deal for the last decade through judicial legislation.

Its second effect is to set up a forum, which under this suggestion can be either the Council of Constitutional Advisers or the joint congressional committee, wherein dialogue can take place between power and those affected by it. To balance or canalize the work of protest committees, and press denunciations, and indeed to provide publicity for situations needing remedy, a forum would thus be provided. Absence of such a forum is one major difficulty in the current situation. Those prejudiced by state inaction or by oppressive state action or by oppressive action by economic concentrates would know where next to go. It is entirely true, as Justice Frankfurter remarked, that many wrongs arising from a political or economic system cannot readily be remedied by judicial action—political action is really required. But, in the absence of any readily available place in which it may be sought, the only alternatives are the courts and the streets—and, in some cases, only the latter.

Access to the courts is itself time-consuming and can be immensely expensive. As of April, 1967, two committees, one operating under the auspices of the American Bar Association, the other established, I am told, at the insistence of President Johnson, are presently functioning in the field. Neither has official standing; neither is adequately financed; both are wrestling with the failure of constitutional rights in certain parts of the United States with totally inadequate resources. There is also a section of the Department of Justice having to do with civil rights, though it, like the unofficial committees, deals only with a single though important field—that of race discrimination. Analysis nevertheless suggests that the problems are to become far wider than those of discrimination against Negroes, important as these are.

3. Channeling Legislative Problems toward Legislatures: Education of Local Government

Not least of the attributes here suggested for the Constitutional Council is that of acting as master, referee, or research assistant to the Supreme Court of the United States. That Court (I cannot, of course, speak for it), better than anyone else, must know the staggering burdens increasingly imposed on it.

Let us take a recent case in the District Court of the District of Columbia—*Julius Hobson et al. v. Carl F. Hansen, Superintendent of Education in the District of Columbia* (Civil Action 8266). It stems from *Brown* v. *Topeka*. Because an overwhelming majority of the children in the District of Columbia schools are Negroes, the schools are *de facto* segregated. No amount of nonsensical devices—such as busing white children from one part of the District of Columbia to an otherwise wholly Negro school in another—can really remedy racial separation. So plaintiffs in the litigation (it has accumulated thousands of pages of testimony) advocate a decree forcibly incorporating into the District of Columbia educational system the school administrations of a series of surrounding towns—these, of course, lie in the states of Maryland and Virginia. One of the judges of the District of Columbia court, Judge J. Skelly Wright, sitting in the *Hobson* case, in a lecture given at the New York University Law School[3] adverted to the problem placed before him. He indicated the enormous depth of the essential legislative problem presented. No state-created political lines, he observed, can protect the state against "the constitutional command of equal protection for its citizens or relieve the state from the obligation of providing educational opportunities for its Negro slum children equal to those provided for its white children in the affluent suburbs. . . . When the Supreme Court decided the first reapportionment case, *Baker* v. *Carr,* just as when it decided *Brown*, it left to the district courts the task of fashioning the remedy."[4] If this involves dealing with the fact that white families flee to suburbs, leaving Negro and poor children within the boundaries of the city, still the courts must deal with it. "Obviously, court orders running to local officials will not reach the suburbs. Nevertheless, when political lines, rather than school district lines, shield the inequality, as shown in the reapportionment cases, courts are not helpless to act. The political thicket, having been pierced to protect the vote, can likewise be pierced to protect the education of children."[5]

Reaching across state and local lines compels regional arrange-

3. *New York University Law Review,* Vol. 40, No. 2, April, 1965, pp. 285 ff.
4. *Ibid.,* p. 306.
5. *Ibid.,* p. 305.

ments other than relocating school districts. Local and state and county financing, educational standards, school administration, and local relations to the school system are all affected. To carry out a decree of the kind suggested by Judge Wright would involve the Court's intrusion into all these affairs, and effective orders would be far-reaching indeed.

Courts are organized and staffed and judges are trained to resolve cases and controversies, and decree remedies in individual cases. But where in doing that they are expected to enunciate rules applying to multitudinous situations at the same time—that is, to legislate—the problem of collecting data and arriving at a solution certainly goes beyond their ordinary function. It is unfair as well as unwise to expect from courts legislation reorganizing county and state governments, rearranging school districts, directing school superintendents how their schools should be administered, determining whether the education given is sufficiently uniform to constitute "equal protection of the laws."

The situation may be still worse when some other problems arise. A small labor union, controlling an essential service—for example, New York City transit or garbage collection or, perhaps, one day, electric light and power—has a right to strike. At some point, exercise of that right will deprive great areas of the community of the capacity to exercise liberty—may even, indeed, take from them their lives. That happened during the transport workers' strike in New York in January, 1966. Now a union under the Taft-Hartley Act has privileges and responsibilities placed on it by federal law, and from these rights and privileges its power is chiefly derived. Already it has been held, in *Brotherhood of Locomotive Engineers et al., Petitioners* v. *Louisville & Nashville Railroad Company,*[6] that the limits of the Fourteenth Amendment apply to some of a union's action: it may not lawfully exclude from membership, and therefore from a job, a man who is a Negro. But its use of its power may also deprive members of the public of rights they have to life and liberty. Drawing the limitations which ought to circumscribe action by labor unions will

6. 370 US 908 (1962).

be a legislative task of first importance—and courts ought not to be asked to do it.

Yet, as we have seen, the "equal protection" clause is held to be a built-in mandate to require action—as well as merely to strike down offending action. The case being stated, the courts must act or else resort to judicial abstention—hiding behind one or another device to avoid exercise of federal jurisdiction. But abstention from deciding federal—in these cases, constitutional—questions is itself a maze of judicial doctrine; see, for example, *Turner* v. *City of Memphis*.[7] There the lower federal courts abstained from deciding constitutional questions, and were duly overruled. Since the retirement of Justice Frankfurter, abstention has become unfashionable. In any case, while abstention may get the federal courts out of difficulty, the fundamental problem remains unsolved. This is why it is not perhaps an impertinence to set up an institution to which such questions may be referred for expert opinion, not on the facts of the case, but on the effects of any decision.

This is what a Constitutional Council of the kind suggested could do. If legislation were proposed or in progress, that fact could be suggested to the courts. Abstention to get away from a problem is one thing. Abstention to permit orderly resolution of the problem (other than of individual rights in the situation) is quite different and perhaps justifiable. If in a case the Supreme Court has to make a decree, it would have the equivalent of a committee report, presumably rendered after research of the relevant material. If, on the other hand, the Council reported that the matter was in ordinary legislative process, there would seem to be honorable reason for the courts, possibly retaining jurisdiction, to stand aside and leave the remedy to the Congress, or perhaps to the state in question, as the case might be. Specifically, it would provide a method for recommending questions essentially legislative in character to the institutions presently in existence to deal with them, backed by the political processes of the United States, in light of an appropriate dialogue carried on before the Constitutional Council or the joint congressional committee.

7. 369 US 350 (1962).

I have not overlooked one ultimate in this situation. No matter what arrangements are set up, the case may arise in which, political processes having denied action necessary to create "equal protection of the laws," the Supreme Court must move in. From this possibility there is under the present system no escape. If by political processes, including majority votes, even taken under the "one man–one vote" rule, the majority oppresses a minority— as when a duly elected Congress passes a bill of attainder, or refuses to wrestle with a problem of civil rights—the Supreme Court not only may, but must, act. At long last, its honorable judgment must control the limitations on its action.

This the American system and the American public accepts— has accepted, indeed, by giving the Supreme Court of the United States authority almost unknown in judicial history. That authority obviously cannot be stretched beyond the limits of its continued public acceptance. The Supreme Court, I suggest, might welcome an institution such as the Constitutional Council, permitting it to use its final and reserved authority only where conditions required it to do so. Exercise of such authority necessarily puts the Supreme Court in politics—and subjects it to a political result.

The object of the suggestion here made is to precipitate political questions, so far as possible, before, rather than after, the Supreme Court enters the arena.

4. Channeling Problems of Economic Organization toward Administrative Authorities

Parallel suggestion is offered to deal with the functions of the Supreme Court in problems of economic organization.

Legal basis for the Court's operations in this field differs from its authority in the field of civil rights and the organization of government. Prima facie, there is no constitutional warrant for judicial legislation in this area. The Sherman Antitrust Act had to be elevated to quasi-constitutional status. Yet, how the United States chooses to organize its economic affairs is the business of the Congress of the United States so far as interstate commerce is affected, and in other respects is the business of the several states. There may be—there is—legitimate reason for curbing undue or dangerous concentration of economic power. There may be—there is—solid reason for assuring that great corporate aggregations shall not use "market power" to the detriment of the public, or perhaps shall not be allowed to acquire "market power" in significant degree. But the existence of economic concentration and the acquisition of market power are not, in and of themselves, denials of "equal protection of the laws." Undue competition indeed may create more hazards than market stability. The elected representatives of the American public may so decide if they choose, and it will not be for the Supreme Court to say them "nay." Nothing in the Constitution and its amendments delegates the power of legislation in this field to the Supreme Court.

Unless, of course, under the system as it emerges the power does deprive citizens of equal protection. Such situations can arise. But it is one thing for the Court to decree a remedy when such a situation has arisen. It is quite another for it, fearing future abuse, to decree whether and where economic power shall be located. That is a political question for the voters when they elect the Congress and legislatures. If they choose to maintain or continue methods of economic organization carrying the hazard of oppression, they have a right to do so, whatever the Court may think. In any case, the political debate should revolve around the essential question, not around the power of the Supreme Court. Corporations and congressional action on antitrust laws should be the focuses of discussion, not the views or power of the Supreme Court.

Danger to the Court is obvious in the current state of affairs. Until recently, the Court had rested its ever-widening action in the field of economic organization on the two antitrust laws—the Sherman Act and the Clayton Act. It stated in the *Brown Shoe Company* case that the people of the United States had placed their faith in the continuance of a system of free competition, even though it might be more costly than some other. This was sound; the Employment Act of 1946 declared the policy of the United States to be that of fostering maximum employment, maximum production, and maximum purchasing power under a system of free competition. There was demonstrable, if small, lessening of competition in *Brown Shoe Company*. But in *Federal Trade Commission* v. *Procter & Gamble,* a proceeding was brought by the Federal Trade Commission to prevent acquisition by Procter & Gamble of Clorox Company, a concern engaged in an entirely separate field—that of manufacturing liquid bleaches. There was no competition between the two companies. The Court reversed a district court decision sanctioning the merger on the ground that Procter & Gamble was already powerful—if not dominant—in its own field, as was Clorox in another, and that acquisition of Clorox plus Procter's capacity to use its resources and advertising power could give Procter market capacity in the future to prevent other concerns from competing. Lessening competition was not present. Undue market power capable of forestalling potential competition *in future* became the test.[8]

8. In *Federal Trade Commission* v. *Procter & Gamble Company* (decided by the Supreme Court April 11, 1967, October Term, 1966, No. 342), the Court considered that § 7 of the Clayton Act "can deal only with probabilities, not with certainties," and thus justified a decree enjoining merger because the firm "may substantially reduce the competitive structure of the industry by raising entry barriers and by dissuading the smaller firms from aggressively competing"—and also because Procter & Gamble, though it never had competed with Clorox, would not do so after acquiring it.

Clorox had 48.8% of the premerger liquid-bleach market. Procter was not in that market—but the Federal Trade Commission found that its purchase of Clorox eliminated it as a potential competitor. The advertising budget of Procter was ten times that of Clorox; entry into the liquid-bleach market was found to require large expenses for advertising, but Procter had resources for the purpose. The advertising capacity of Procter combined with the share of the liquid-bleach market already held by Clorox, the Federal Trade Commission thought, entailed "the reasonable probability of a substantial increase in barriers to entry and of enhancement of pricing power in the liquid bleach industry." Procter was accordingly ordered to divest itself of its holdings in Clorox.

This is a long projection into the "field of possibility"—valid as justification for precautionary legislation but somewhat speculative when it comes to a judicial decree.

An interesting comment both on *Brown Shoe Company* and on *Procter &*

Again I agree with the result as desirable legislation. But this further entry of the Court into the field of economic organization strikes me as a dubious elevation of the Court's functions. It is constitutionally mandated to become a revolutionary committee in the field of "equal protection." When called on to do so, the Court must take the political chances involved in assumption of that function. But *Federal Trade Commission* v. *Procter & Gamble,* without the mandate of the Fourteenth Amendment, pushes the Clayton Act into new, unlegislated ground. The Supreme Court legislated against market power because it *might* prevent future competition. Let us assume—I myself believe—that some such legislation is needed. Let us further assume that some delegation of power to a tribunal other than the Congress will be essential when such legislation is passed. The Federal Trade Commission exists for such purpose. But it is not clear that the Supreme Court, even with a Federal Trade Commission opinion as a base, using its own conceptions of desirable economic organization, can enter the field itself and undertake the job.

The Congress of the United States exists. Through the years it has been at least as good, if not better, a synthesis of the desires of the United States.

Contrast the issue raised by *Federal Trade Commission* v. *Procter & Gamble* with the issue which would be raised if, let us say, one or more great corporations undertook to interfere directly with the liberties, privileges, and persons of individuals. Let us suppose that a corporation undertakes to collect a data bank of information on individuals it considered to be undesirable, violating the right of privacy, either because these individuals were obnoxious to it or because they held doctrines the corporation's

---

Gamble is found in Andrew Shonfield's *Modern Capitalism* (London, Oxford University Press, 1966, p. 327): "It is hard to imagine a British judge being called upon to decide not the question of ascertainable fact about the existence or not of monopolistic conditions in a given market, but whether a particular merger between two firms *was likely at some future date* to create conditions in an industry which would weaken the competitive process in it." And again (p. 328): "In the traditional British system there is no place for the use of the courts to further some evolving purpose of public administration. In America there is."

executives disliked. (Some corporations have done this.) Obviously, the economic power of the corporation is here used directly to assault an individual or group of them. In such case, a square constitutional question would be raised: Did the corporation in question conspire to violate the individual's rights or deprive him of equal protection of the laws? If existing legislation were insufficient, the Court, on the ground given in *Bell* v. *Maryland* might utilize its reserve revolutionary power under the Fourteenth Amendment and decree a remedy.

Questions of economic organization differ markedly from those raised in the school-segregation cases or the "one man–one vote" cases. They present the problem, not of violation of right, but of danger. This is a matter for precautionary legislation rather than for remedying a denial of equal protection. Normally, problems of economic power do not call for a Council of Constitutional Advisers. Rather, they call for examination of existing laws governing economic organization itself.

My suggestion in this field would be that the Federal Trade Commision be given an additional function. It should be directed to report on such questions to the Congress. When advocated by President Woodrow Wilson and first established by the Congress in 1914, the commission was expected to defend against monopoly. The "New Freedom" under whose aegis it was constituted aimed at just this result. Fear of undue economic concentration was one of the battle cries of the campaign of 1912. The thinking of the Supreme Court of the United States rather markedly approximates the political attitudes of that time.

The Federal Trade Commission could be directed by the Congress to carry on a steady review of the problems of economic concentration and organization in the rapidly changing context of American development. It can, and should, review the problems of concentration of economic power, of market power, of the mechanical centralization of power, and of the impacts on competition and business and individual capacity to enter or leave markets. It can and should be charged with proposing legislation. It should work in conjunction with the Council of Economic Advisers, whose measures are supposed to maintain a system of free competition.[9]

Wherever the federal courts are asked to deal with the economic organization of an industry, or with extensions of market power and cognate questions, they should refer the problem to the Federal Trade Commission for a report. In these cases, reference might be made directly by federal district courts, where antitrust proceedings are begun. After a finding of illegality, the device of using the Federal Trade Commission as a master to propose a decree could be availed of. Where the Federal Trade Commission foresees danger not dealt with by existing legislation, it should report to the Congress and the president, asking for legislation.

There is not, I suggest, danger that the United States will be misgoverned by a revolutionary committee known as the "Supreme Court." The danger lies deeper.

It inheres in the nature of that "revolutionary progress" pinpointed by Justice Abe Fortas and quoted on page 342. "Revolutionary" is an overworked word, meaning drastic change of some sort. Nevertheless, revolution of any kind implies change in the functioning of existing institutions if not in the institutions themselves. More specifically, it involves change in the power structure. Such change is going forward rapidly, and the Supreme Court has, as Justice Fortas observed, been the active agent of such change. Change is justified because impelled by a combination of material, mechanical, and economic growth moving at breakneck speed, plus an enhanced social awareness of the impact of

9. Under the Employment Act of 1946, the Council of Economic Advisers, in theory, has two objectives: to maintain conditions offering useful employment for all seeking to work, and to maintain conditions promoting maximum employment, production, and purchasing power—but these conditions are to be created "in a manner calculated to foster and promote free competitive enterprise."

As economic development proceeds, it may appear (or may be true now) that "free competitive enterprise" may be inconsistent with either or both of the other objectives. This fact has not yet been taken into account by politicians, and few economists (J. K. Galbraith excepted) have been willing to deal with it.

this on individual life. The result of Court-made break-throughs has been salutary.

The danger is that they constitute the Supreme Court a variety of benevolent dictator.[10]

Acquiescent acceptance of any benevolent dictatorship in time deadens the public to its responsibility for apprehending needs and dangers and demanding that their elected executives and legislators take appropriate measures. As John Stuart Mill observed, it compromises the future. Nonacceptance, on the other hand, piles up political pressures focused against the institution itself. Judicial legislation is not a substitute for political and legislative institutional processes. The will of the most enlightened Court is not the same as the will of the elected representatives of the people, and may cease to be the will of the people itself. Acceptance of its mandates based on respect for the Court is not the same as acceptance of active laws commanding popular assent after political debate.

Awareness of the dangers and needs requires continuing statement of them and confronting them as problems to be dealt with by legislation.

10. Resignation of Justice Fortas and criticism of Justice Douglas in the spring of 1969 crystallized political attack. Nominally caused by their outside activities, both were really occasioned by extension of the Court's activities in "sensitive areas of social policy." As Machiavelli observes, "Hatred is gained as much by good works as by evil."

5

International Power

I

World Power against Chaos

1. The Rise of the Modern Conception of World Power

In international affairs, power follows the laws applicable to power in other contexts. Invariably, it emerges to replace continued chaos. Though decisions are made by individuals, power is exercised through and depends on institutions. These reflect a system of ideas or philosophy; they are confronted and interact with a field of responsibility. The force of these laws is less apparent on the world scene than in regional, national, and lesser situations. Yet, perhaps for the first time in history, they now are applicable to an entire planet. Slowly, they are organizing the world.

Readers fresh from newspaper, television, or radio news may feel surprise at this statement. Power has not prevented chaos in much of the globe. Individuals undoubtedly do exercise power, but no one or combination of them appears capable of settling problems. World-wide and regional institutions, notably the United Nations, the Organization of American States, the North Atlantic Treaty Organization (NATO), are in being, but in outline rather than as effective instruments. No agreement exists on an idea system capable of guiding international affairs or supporting international institutions. An amorphous field of responsibility loosely called "world opinion" perhaps does exist. But dialogue with it is confused and disorderly, and its capacity to influence events appears to be minimal. Surprise and doubt are wholly understandable.

Deeper analysis may resolve some doubts.

Twentieth-century development has, for the first time in history, required world power consciously to act in and upon an undivided world theater. Only following World War I did radio, and, later, television, come to blanket most, if not all, the earth. True, this coverage is still arbitrary, inadequate, incomplete, often corrupt. Most of the world, nevertheless, now lives in the presence and with consciousness of events and developments in all other parts. A generation ago few knew—and therefore few cared— what went on in regions other than their own. Ignorance being complete, few concerned themselves with events in most of Asia, Africa, and South America or even with conditions in great parts of Europe and North America. Contrast that condition with any morning's grist of printed and electronic news—demonstrations of Chinese students against the Soviet Embassy in Peking, a youth tossing paint at President Johnson's car in Manila; the Brazilian President's closing of Congress because it failed to expel elected deputies opposed to the government; a press conference with General de Gaulle on his European policy; the failure of a Communist conference in Moscow to issue a communiqué—to skim the surface of no more than one day's reportage.

At outbreak of World War I, only a handful in the United States, a minority in Europe, and almost none in Asia knew of the growing power struggle in the Balkans that touched off the assassination of the Austrian Crown Prince at Sarajevo in 1914 and precipitated the conflict of the Great Powers of Europe. No substantial accounts of Japanese ambition to seize China were general in the Western press before World War II. After its close, Chinese developments, culminating in the Communist revolutions of 1949, were of interest chiefly to a handful of experts. The Paris Peace Conference of 1918–1919, following World War I, almost wrote off Russia. That empire had been defeated; it was in the throes of civil war; a halfhearted and unsuccessful attempt was made to stop its revolution. Thereafter the conference left it to stew in its own juice. But in the 1960's the Maoist convulsion in China engaged the attention of the entire world.

International power today is recognizably, though perilously, applicable to the entire planet. No longer is it limited, as in the past, merely to existing empires or spheres of influence or chiefly evident through the workings of "balance of power," though these are still operative. In the space of twenty years (1919 to 1939), thanks chiefly to the swiftness of communication and air transport, and, since 1950, to the universal threat of intercontinental rockets, the entire globe has become an undivided theater of international affairs.

The implications are probably graver than yet realized. Until recently, chaos, even war, could be limited or "contained" within isolated countries or geographic regions. In the later twentieth century, few make that assumption. Brush-fire wars anywhere can escalate into roaring world-wide disaster. Almost nostalgically one thinks of the Franco-Prussian War of 1870, in that happy Victorian century when one nation could make war on its neighbor while surrounding countries remained ceremoniously neutral. In 1914, the United States watched the unexpected outbreak of World War I with the strong conviction that it was not responsible for it and with the ill-founded conclusion that it was not and ought not to be involved. National power holders did not then consider themselves responsible in whole or in part for chaotic situations outside their bailiwick.

In part, this resulted from the fact that, in modern times, few emperors, kings, presidents, or politicians in any country, however powerful, really considered that any one of them, or his country, could become master of the world. In earlier and more romantic periods, ambitious men had dreamed of, and even attempted, just such mastery. The Roman Empire had conquered the Mediterranean basin, parts of continental Europe, and much of Asia Minor. In the seventh century, Mohammed and his successors claimed the world, and in the space of a century and a half actually did convert the Mediterranean basin, most of the Near East, and substantial parts of Europe into an Islamic empire. In the thirteenth century, Genghis Khan and his immediate successors asserted that God had given them the earth, and the armies of his son, Ogadai, and his grandson, Kublai, came perilously close to realizing the claim in the Eurasian land mass.

By the eighteenth century, dreams of this kind had foundered. Discovery and geography had vastly expanded the earth's known surface. Multiplying nation-states steadily increased resistance to world empire. As world power seemed increasingly impossible, world responsibility appeared beyond the province of any power holder. World power could not be opposed as antidote to world chaos. In any case, the world was not an entity, but a congeries of more or less disparate countries and, beyond them, of regions frequently unknown. In my own school days the entire central portion of "darkest Africa" was represented on maps by a black blotch whose obscure content was meagerly illuminated by the candlelight of Stanley's description of his expedition to rescue Livingstone.

The twentieth century changed this condition with remarkable rapidity. Steamships, geographic expeditions, colonization, telegraph, and, later, wireless, air transport, and television brought torrents of information, exact and inexact, first from some, then from most, parts of the earth to most other parts. As the century moved into its final third, the girdle of awareness moved toward completion. Each country, and each power holder in it, became conscious of motion in all or at least most other regions. The strange and fateful fact emerged that any nation anywhere might be affected by events anywhere else. Worse yet, world chaos could be produced from almost any point on the globe by technicians with strange inventions. In this system of world-wide consciousness, few nations are loved, no nation ignored.

Thereupon, necessarily, the conception that international power might eventually be interposed to prevent or replace chaos made progress. An almost pathetic belief emerged in the personal power of great national leaders. "Summit conferences," composed of a few men, each assumed to hold power over a great country or complex of countries and therefore to be able to affect events, were—perhaps still are—expected to convene, decide, take action, order affairs. Such capacity, in fact, almost did exist when, during World War II, Franklin Roosevelt, Winston Churchill, and Joseph Stalin met at Tehran in 1943 and at Yalta in 1945. They apparently did have power to guide events, though, as it proved, this power was limited and in many respects illusory. Particularly at Yalta, one of their precise reasons for meeting was to avoid chaos at the end of the war. I can testify that this certainly was in President Roosevelt's mind, and I think in Churchill's also. Stalin's objectives can only be guessed at until Soviet archives disgorge their historical secrets. The certainty is that most of the world then looked to a few national leaders, wielding international power, to create a condition of hoped-for world order.

At Yalta there was no institution or set of institutions by which world power could be allocated or on which world order could be based. Such an institution—the United Nations—nevertheless already had been designed. Factually, the instruments of power held by these men meeting at Yalta were their empires and their armies in the field backed by the organizations of their respective countries. They expected victory and planned that, as military organizations were disbanded, the projected Security Council of the United Nations and to some extent its General Assembly, proposed at Dumbarton Oaks, would pick up order-keeping where the World War II armies and supporting supply organizations left off. Agreement on this had been reached. A few weeks later the United Nations did come into existence as planned. It was designed to carry out the task unfulfilled by the aborted and incomplete League of Nations imposed by Woodrow Wilson at the close of World War I through the Versailles Peace Treaty.

The United Nations may—I believe it will—become the nucleus

409

from which effective institutional organization of world power will emerge. Few would claim it has yet attained that status. But it has a better chance than the old League had. At Versailles in 1919 such an institution was thought of as little more than a creditable utopian monomania of President Wilson and a few European statesmen. Its possibilities and intentions were skeptically regarded in Europe. The American public repudiated it in 1920. Lenin hooted at it. But in 1945 an institution of world power was regarded as a plain necessity. In the late twentieth century, tropism toward institutional organization on a world-wide basis is so evident that few statesmen fail to pay it at least lip service, and the first responsibility of each is considered to be a contribution toward the development of world order.

2. The Philosophical Lacuna

Are the preconditions for a system of world order present?

The third law of power—that power, and its institutions, depend on a philosophy or idea system—here obtrudes.

Bluntly, there is no present consensus on an accepted philosophy of international relations. Beginnings unquestionably have been made, but how widely or deeply they go is not known.

When, in 1945, Stalin, like Mao Tse-tung in 1966, talked about world organization, his real philosophy probably was messianic. History, through Marxian Communism, had willed that he and his successors be rulers of the earth, just as the current convulsion in China seems, among other things, an assertion that Mao Tse-tung and his ideas must triumph throughout the world. Churchill's conception was different. He, romantic but realist, thought world organization could be only a concert of powers—actually, of empires. These he knew and understood. Imperial organizations, working together, had been the chief creators of the Victorian peace. World organization might give them better means for understanding each other, co-ordinating their will. Roosevelt, who admired Churchill as a great captain, but described him to me as essentially a man of the nineteenth century, had a conception that differed from, and in a measure contradicted, the other two. He thought of a community of nations acting under and restrained by a system of law interpreted by a world court. This was an expansion of the federalist process by which the United States had been constructed in 1787.

Until consensus emerges on a philosophy capable of sustaining world institutions adequate to serve as a basis for their power, an institutional organization of world power like the United Nations must fight for its life—as it is now doing.

But this international organization has a minimal, and growing, philosophical base. The science or technique of necessary world-wide facilities is gradually developing its own imperatives. There must be world law governing air channels if radio and television communication is to exist at all. There must be world regulation of civilian aviation if any airplane leaving any airport anywhere is to know how to land anywhere else. Foreseeably, the technique of international money and its imperatives will be a precondition of world commerce and will compel institutional expression, whether through the International Monetary Fund or in some other manner. The technique of disease prevention dictates universal rules for world health. Scientific imperatives in a number of universally wanted services are thus dictating a gradually increasing nucleus of self-imposed world law.

Failure thus far to achieve a workable world idea system ought not, I suggest, to induce undue pessimism. A world whose races, nations, and elements face each other for the first time understandably finds difficulty in reaching a common divisor of ideas, let alone common consensus on their application. But such a common divisor does appear to be in slow making. If anything, without underestimating the difficulties, we have a right to be gratified at the progress already made.

Necessary, too, will be a dialogue between the world-organization leadership and its field of responsibility. In rudimentary form, this has become a fact of life in international as well as national and local power. Any field of responsibility is an aggre-

411

gate of the content of responsibilities in larger and lesser power systems plus the aggregate of individual opinions. A field as wide as the earth contains an infinity of power structures and opinions, endlessly shifting, disputing, receiving information fair and false, making judgments, and forming prejudices well- and ill-based alike.

The phenomenon of world-wide communication is recent. Its operation is incomplete and arbitrary, its technique badly developed. The impact of its newer media is not yet understood. A single, distorted television picture may ruin or unmake the work of the ablest and most high-minded statesmen, diplomats, analysts, correspondents, or reporters. The crucial fact is that such communication does increasingly exist. For the first time, raw materials are present from which a field of responsibility for international power can be made to function and with which dialogue may be had.

3. Elements of International Power

Nations on the international scene depend on and work through the power held by their leaders and executives. Great nations— "superpowers," as they are sometimes called—have primacy when their power holders are able to mobilize and use their large resources and inherent capacity, and still more when they can recruit adherents in other countries. Lesser powers, like Gaullist France and Congress India, seek and sometimes attain a position enabling them to balance or play off the superpowers against each other. Small countries, like the Netherlands and New Zealand, seek safety in alliances and common policy with neighbors.

Presently, international power is derived from a combination of elements giving each nation-state, acting through its leaders, a degree of ability to enforce its will or influence events outside its borders.

The ultimate instrument is obviously the capacity to use force.

Force still is the *"ultima ratio regum"*—the final argument of sovereigns. A second element—a bad second, in fact—is economic power. The capacity of a nation-state to give, sell, or withhold, to buy or refuse to buy products to or from another state can be and is used to influence action. Connected with this is the capacity to give or withhold, to accept or refuse movements of capital in, to, or from its neighbors.

Organized propaganda is a third, long-range, instrument. It consists primarily in the delivery of words, by radio, television, newsprint, books, magazines, or talk carried on by agents. It can become effective only when it energizes action in a foreign country, when it stirs up political approval of or opposition to policies and power holders the sending country likes or dislikes. With increased effectiveness, it can perhaps induce strikes, demonstrations, riots, or disturbances. In extremes, it can induce armed revolt. Almost every substantial power in the world uses propaganda to some extent, if only to induce support for its policies. When allied with forms of local organization in the target country, results may be great. For example, in the years prior to the outbreak of World War II, Soviet propaganda in France was, naturally, allied to the French Communist party, and this combination dominated the action of much of French organized labor. At one time it actually controlled the output of airplanes for the French army, and Paris sent an unofficial mission to Moscow to ask that France be permitted to increase its production of this essential armament.

Propaganda can, and often does, use any local current of dissension capable of being used to the advantage of the sending country. In June, 1967, the Negro race problem was causing widespread disturbance in American cities, including New York. Suddenly, a bitter element of anti-Semitism appeared in the "Black Power" and "anti-Whitey" outpourings of Marxist-oriented Negro extremists. This occurred precisely at the moment when both Soviet and Chinese propaganda was strongly supporting the United Arab build-up designed to destroy Israel. Projecting Negro racism against American sentiment for supporting Israel was a wholly natural move in Soviet-Chinese psychological warfare; as

413

was also propulsion of that current against American policy in carrying on the Vietnam war.

Propaganda can run the entire range from offering legitimate popular presentation of a country's point of view to stimulating outright subversion or undermining the receiving country's system of order. In the hands of skillful operators, the propaganda instrument may have substantial effect. This is usually accomplished over a long period of time, though it may, depending on conditions, cause immediate results.

Moral and cultural standing, achievement, or strength can also become an instrument of international power. Admiration for and desire to simulate the culture, technical capacity, or social achievement of another nation can induce imitation and action by other countries. It can influence their policies and thereby affect events.

A dimension limits or extends the national capacity to use instruments of international power. This is the degree of will, at any given time, of a nation-state to apply them, accompanied by knowledge on the part of others whether it will do so. It is not enough for a nation-state to have inherent power potential. It must also be so organized internally and so disposed psychologically and politically that its power holders can apply its power through one or all of its various instruments. Other nations must be prepared to believe that it can, and also that it will, use them in certain eventualities. Experts call this the element of "credibility." The most powerful nation in the world may be paralyzed by internal disunion. It may be inhibited from using power by moral or legal considerations. A relatively weak nation may attain a measure of power because the men leading it are able to use its lesser capacity of force, economics, or propaganda while its more powerful neighbors are not prepared to act. Both Mussolini and Hitler demonstrated that proposition between 1930 and 1939, as did General de Gaulle when he precipitated the gold crisis against Britain and the United States in 1967–1968.

Chaos is more apparent than order in the foregoing summary. Chaos, indeed, never has been too far beneath the surface of international fact since recorded history began.

Why? The answer may lie in two facts. Unpredictability (except in shortest run) in the course of international development is the first. Absence of international consensus on an idea system or philosophy is the second. Perhaps the second is caused by the first; at all events, they come together.

Bertrand de Jouvenel, in *Futuribles: Studies in Conjecture,* put forward the proposition that the result of decisions in foreign affairs is invariably unforeseeable. As illustration, he examined the decision of the Japanese government to attack the United States fleet at Pearl Harbor on December 7, 1941. Japanese military experts calculated the short-term results correctly: that the U.S. Pacific Fleet would be put out of action; that, thereafter, Japanese force could take control of the entire South Pacific, its archipelagoes, islands, littoral, and resources. Incorrectly, they concluded that Japan's position and empire in that part of the world would thereafter be established on a solid military and economic base. The immediate prediction proved sound. But the longer-range result was the defeat of Japan and reorganization of its social structure. Beyond the immediate and nearby intermediate effect, the prediction failed completely.

Slightly more optimistic is the view of Saul Friedlander, also writing in *Futuribles: Studies in Conjecture.* He thinks that, under certain conditions, forecasting international relations is possible, in respect of both short- and long-term relations between states, though with a severe limitation. "In a crisis situation between antagonists who have nuclear weapons at their command, analytical forecasting appears to us to lose its relevance. It is impossible to predict the moment and the exact circumstances in which one of the antagonists will decide to use his nuclear weapons. In our view the development of the situation which would cause these arms to be used is equally unamenable to prediction, and the concept of a limited nuclear war is a fiction." [1] Uncertainties enough existed before the nuclear age, but with its advent "there opens a period of complete uncertainty as to the probable future of humanity." He derives a limited optimism from the fact that

1. Geneva, Librairie Droz S.A., 1965, Vol. II, p. 111.

the new situation conditions the very existence of humanity in human decisions, and consequently in the creation in the future of a truly universal culture.

In practical fact, prediction in international affairs beyond the most immediate future issues is rarely possible at all. Even in the short term, prediction of results can be applied to only a few, extremely limited, categories of decision. Allowing fullest scope to Saul Friedlander's theories of prediction, it is impossible to be sure that, except for the briefest period, they can, or will, be used as a power holder's guide to decisions. At longer range, prediction of results is almost literally out of the question. Friedlander consequently advises power holders to fall back on "intuition," as more useful than analysis—but only when antagonist power holders have had time and opportunity to "apprehend" each other. Even then, the antagonists' culture backgrounds must not be so widely different as to preclude apprehension by each of the other. There is scant comfort in that. One conclusion only is possible. If none can foretell the long-range results of a power decision, it is impossible to lay down objective guides for international power holders.

Lack of foreseeable results would be dangerous enough even if some accepted philosophy or idea system existed in the international field. It is more so when no such system exists. Does anyone really know whether the result of decisions in foreign affairs is "good" or "bad," or even "desirable" or "undesirable"?

Lacking any criteria of what is "good" or "bad" in foreign affairs, power holders are forced to seek their own guides. They may save their souls by acting morally according to their culture and their time. But power is not granted men for the purpose of saving their souls. Thus, they may act in accordance with law, conforming to international standards and procedures as interpreted by jurists, but if the result is catastrophic, they are held accountable for the ensuing pain, suffering, and destruction of their fellow creatures. If they guide action by moral standards prevailing in their own country, they must take into account the fact that their neighbors or rivals (or some of them) may indulge no similar scruples, or even that the effect of their morality may be devastation to their neighbors. There is now no international forum or institution to which they can appeal for an impartial and effective declaration of rights and duties. Where such institutions do exist, their decisions are apt to be empty words.

Power in international affairs thus has few valid guides for its exercise. An individual power holder faced with a decision (it always comes down to an individual) at long last is governed, first, by his capacity—that is, what he can do—and, second, by calculation of supposedly predictable immediate results. Beyond those limits he can be guided only subjectively.

The individual exerting power has before him a range of things he can do. Probably he can, or thinks he can, predict the short-term effect of any decision within his capacity. In longer, historic range, he can at best have only a vague guess. In large measure he usually is guided by his own philosophy and conscience. But the premises of conscience are many, and far from obvious. Especially in international matters, honest men have differed on them since the world began. He may consider controlling events for the maintenance of the strength and well-being of his people and his state. Where these are not directly menaced, he may consider he has a duty to assist the well-being of other states, or perhaps the peace or order of the world. President Truman did this one Sunday in June, 1950, when he instinctively decided to oppose American force to the Soviet-backed North Korean invasion of South Korea. So did President Kennedy when in 1961 he committed American military advisers "to assist in defending South Viet Nam." Some sort of decision is usually unavoidable. Decision not to act can be, and often is, as vitally causative or destructive as action itself—as British and French power holders discovered at the time of the Munich crisis in 1938.

It is possible, nevertheless, to suggest some premises every power holder is likely to invoke in making international decisions.

Where his own state is threatened, he will defend it if he has the capacity. Lacking the force to do so, he may submit to external threat and seek to save what he can by diplomacy. President Eduard Beneš, of Czechoslovakia, submitted to Hitler in 1938 when the British government advised him that none would aid in his defense, that armed resistance was therefore hopeless, but that his state might remain in existence if he surrendered. The decision proved a fatal mistake—but the calculation was clear. Beneš could not defeat Hitler; he was convinced the European powers would not help him; he believed a bad agreement better than military seizure, and that this bitter treaty would save Czechoslovakia. Had he possessed adequate military force, he unquestionably would have fought. Hindsight suggests that had he done so, help might have arrived, though none can prove this. Preservation of his state will always be the first consideration of a power holder.

When chaos or anarchy develops close to his borders, the power holder is likely to act, if he can, to restore order, calculating that if he does not fill the power vacuum, someone else will.

When disorder threatens or breaks out in any part of the world far removed, and the power holder has the capacity to act, he will consider whether he, alone or in agreement with others, can control events in that area. Twentieth-century world-wide rocket systems have generated for every nation an unavoidable interest in world peace everywhere. Were explosion to occur in central Asia, an American president on the other side of the globe would probably seek unified action, if he could get it, to reduce the danger. He would not act alone; he has not the capacity. But peace there, though the area is not in the American power sphere, is an American interest; war anywhere is dangerous. Explosion in the Caribbean, where he might calculably control events and where danger to the United States is great, would lead him to act in any event. In South Korea and Vietnam, the two instances on the Asian coast, both President Truman and President Kennedy moved to give military assistance because they considered these situations, like other threats to world peace, might escalate into a threat to the United States.

Where the power holder considers he cannot control or influence events, at least within a predictable short term, he will stand aside and abide the course of affairs. Lacking effective institutions of world power, he can do little else.

4. Consensus or Chaos

What we have then is a collection of unco-ordinated institutions—states and groups of states—each with its own philosophy, vesting power in its respective chiefs. Each of these, as head of his state, holds a measure of power, microscopic or massive, in international matters. At any given moment the condition of international affairs, its trend toward order or toward chaos, is the product of the aggregated effects of the decisions of these men. The current of time and history is always in motion; each morning's news reflects yesterday's decisions and conditions tomorrow's situation.

Consensus grows that some organization of world power is needed to prevent chaos. A semblance of it has been located in the secretary-general of the United Nations and its Security Council. This institution does exist, bringing together power holders whose aggregated power could add up to control of world affairs. Unhappily, their power is not aggregated. The institution is paralyzed unless its chief power-holding members are in agreement and, being agreed, are prepared to make necessary decisions and take practical measures. Disagreement has existed (except in a few cases) from the very beginning.

Disagreement, and, with it, paralysis of the only existing institution of world power, will be endemic so long as there is no common philosophy or value or idea system guiding decisions of the constituent power holders. At present, there are competing idea systems, variously motivated, guiding the individual states and their power holders. They are diverse and not reassuring.

A few elementary value conceptions commanding world-wide acceptance are, I believe, nevertheless emerging.

Though there is no consensus prescribing "peace," there is agreement that the use of nuclear force, even in war, simply cannot be permitted. No formal agreement so provides, and Communist China even claims dissent. But all power holders—including Mao Tse-tung—know that rocket systems are in being capable of delivering nuclear destruction and knocking out national institutions at any point on the earth's surface. If any rocket is fired, no state, strong or weak, can be certain of its continued institutional existence. This is balance of power or, if you choose, balance of terror. Thus far, over a period of twenty-four years, it has inhibited nuclear war, has guided power holders having nuclear-rocket capacity in their decision not to use it. Rudimentary though this value may seem, it probably will inhibit war between major power holders (since nuclear conflict might then be inevitable), and thus holds in check the probability of ultimate chaos.

There is a continuous groping for a limited idea system on which at least minimal institutions of international order (such as the Security Council) may in future be effectively based.

There is a world-wide field of responsibility, visible though rudimentary. Dialogue with it, enormously inadequate and unsatisfactory, does go on, and on a world-wide scale. It does have effect on the decision-making of individual power holders. Elements of the raw material from which institutions of world power, vesting decisions in power holders, can be constructed are therefore beginning to be apparent.

Aside from this tiny but vital center, international power remains divided, very unevenly, among more than one hundred and thirty nations, variously grouped. Each endlessly maneuvers within the limit of its capacity, guided by its individual national philosophy. Yet consensus grows that some sort of order is imperative. Impelled by fear and hope, the search for a unifying idea system and the construction of corresponding power institutions continues. Conscious opinion in most nations is coming to realize that, however quarrelsome, the world is one.

We must examine present realities, philosophical and institutional, and soberly consider whether they can lead to international order.

II

The Personal Element in International Power

1. Presidential Decision

Since World War I, American power to act abroad has been lodged in the person of its president. Capacity to involve or detach the vast United States, its people, its emotions, its resources rests in the hands and mind of the occupant of the White House. It is not wholly uncontrolled—the Congress of the United States has residual power—but the ultimate options rest with the White House, and the president's decisions are rarely reversed. His power, for better or worse, has been used in two world wars and two lesser wars in this century. Less fatefully, it has been used in minor situations involving the use of or threat to use force. Continuously, since 1939, elements of American power have been present in many parts of the earth and in great areas of world affairs. In all cases, decisions have been personal—the president alone could say "do" or "do not."

2. The Unforseeable Consequence

Take, for example, one of the most questionable power decisions ever made by an American president, James K. Polk, who became president on March 4, 1845. He had a strong desire, based on highly inadequate information, to secure California—then Mexican territory—for the United States. He sent John Slidell to Mexico with instructions to attempt its purchase. Learning of President José Herrera's refusal to receive Slidell, he ordered General Zachary Taylor to cross the Rio Grande, causing Mexican forces to recross the river in retaliation and skirmish with a troop of United States dragoons. Two weeks later, he asked for a declaration of war. Samuel Eliot Morison, greatest of living American historians, concludes on quite adequate evidence that Polk "baited" Mexico into war over the Texas boundary question to get California after concluding that Mexico would not sell. Two years later, by the Treaty of Guadalupe Hidalgo, the United States acquired Utah, Nevada, upper California, Arizona, New Mexico, and parts of Colorado and Wyoming—roughly, almost the southwestern fourth of the United States.

Power was never more obviously personal than in President Polk's use of it in the Mexican affair. His aim was aggressive, acquisitive, expansionist, imperialist. The reader can imagine the editorials, demonstrations, teach-ins, outpourings of wrath had a comparable decision been taken in the year 1969. There was, in fact, plenty of outraged disapproval even in 1848.

Consider the results presently apparent. The acquired territory is integrated into the United States. Its present wealth and the prosperity of most of its population (now numbered in tens of millions) is undeniable. Politically, it has realized itself. One of its constituent states, California, exerts enormous, perhaps disproportionate, influence in the national government. Consider also the history and development of Mexico from 1848 to the present. Would the result have been better had President Polk withheld his grasping hand or followed the advice of the legislature of Massachusetts, which declared the Mexican War to be essentially a war to sustain slavery and "unconstitutional, insupportable by honest men"? Can one say the pragmatic result of a morally unjustified personal power decision, taken by a proslavery president, was "bad"? No one can prove the alternative historical "might-have-been." No one can know whether the territory would have remained in Mexican hands (other powers besides the United States were prowling for conquests in North America at the time), or what would have happened, either to the region or to Mexico, had it remained Mexican.

Objectively, time and history seem to have vindicated Polk's decision—for the well-being of the United States. If the well-being of his state was the controlling consideration, he acted wisely. Subjectively—according to moral standards applied to individuals—Polk's use of power was and still seems indefensible. If objective, pragmatic prediction is impossible, can there be any standard of decision save current ideas of morality, ethics, legality, and so forth?

Woodrow Wilson decided to bring the United States into World War I in the closing days of March, 1917. The precise act was determining the content of a message to be delivered to the newly elected Congress; specifically, whether he would ask for a declaration that the imperial German government "was embarked on war against the government and people of the United States" and that the United States formally take up the status of belligerent. Given the political indications, there was little reason to doubt that the Congress would declare war if the President so asked; equally, that without presidential request, the United States (in the short term at least) would not become an active participant in the European struggle. Political forces pushed in both directions. The East and most intellectuals (like those of Harvard University, as I, a student there through 1916, can testify) had reached an emotional state of war not long after Germany invaded Belgium in 1914. Great masses of voters in the Midwest and a number of vocal race groups were either pacifist or actively antiwar, though their sentiment had been revolted by unrestricted submarine warfare, by the Zimmerman telegram revealing German attempts to induce Mexico to move against the United States, and by bungling German propaganda. Wilson could have moved either into or away from World War I.

Events could have vetoed his decision either way. A German break-through forcing Allied surrender a few days after April 6, 1917 (the date when Congress did declare war) might have made the declaration itself almost meaningless. Though the United States in 1917 was not adequately armed to play an immediate part (only one American division had arrived by July 4, 1917; almost no Americans saw front-line action until the following year), it was predictable that the Allied lines would hold at least long enough to permit arrival of substantial American force—though in the event it proved a close thing. Refusal to enter the war could have been vetoed by the imperial German government. It could have declared war on the United States—though this was highly improbable. More likely, it might (and probably would) have attacked more American ships, blown up more American munitions plants, as it did that at Black Tom, in New Jersey, or committed some other outrage, forcing a state of war on the country. Even then, the people and the country, which had succeeded in avoiding war when the *Lusitania* was sunk in 1915, might have been led to accept a good many affronts in 1917 without going over the brink, though they might have given the President a rough time during the remainder of his term. Politically and historically, the decision lay with Woodrow Wilson alone.

In long retrospect, the issue seems less clear than in 1917. Essentially, the stake was whether the next stage of Europe's history would be dominated by Hohenzollern Germany, and everything (good and bad alike) it represented, or by France, and everything it represented under Marshal Ferdinand Foch, Georges Clemenceau, and other politicians, influenced and diluted by the Britain of David Lloyd George, Sir Edward Grey, and Herbert Asquith. Reviewing the situation a half-century later indicates there may have been somewhat less difference than people thought at the time. A Europe dominated by the Prussian army might well have been preferable to a Europe dominated by Hitler and his Nazi troops. The Hohenzollern Empire, along with its militarism, maintained some of the finest universities and had made effective some of the best social legislation of the period. Britain and France were behind in social legislation, city planning, and technical organization. But they had proudly cherished the priceless gift of intellectual and spiritual freedom, evidenced by their art, their music, their literature, their men; and they had maintained peace. It is as interesting as it is futile to speculate on the possible current of affairs had America stayed out, had Germany been victorious (as probably it would have been), had the Austrian Empire been held together, and had this postwar European structure dealt with a defeated Russia and its Communist revolution.

There is no way of knowing whether much speculation of this kind entered into Wilson's decision-making. Events had settled for him (and clearly for a great many Americans not involved in the decision) the feeling that German social, military, and governmental processes were bad. Its soldiers had violated international law by attacking Belgium. They were believed to have behaved atrociously in territories they occupied. Their government was a carry-over of eighteenth-century monarchy ineffectively modified by a carefully controlled democratic façade. Worst of all, it was considered—probably accurately, though some historians dispute the verdict—to have intentionally unleashed the war by encouraging Austria's attack on Serbia and by mobilizing to meet contingencies. Thereafter, and during the war, Germany had followed the severe military logic of attacking neutral supply ships and unarmed merchantmen, like the *Lusitania*, irrespective of the effect on neutral life. Its internal war propaganda preached hatred (especially against England). Many announced German values went counter to the expressed values of most Americans.

On the subjective side, Wilson's emotional, intellectual, and philosophical content (so far as they can be reconstructed) went against the Germans. An ambitious man, yearning to do something of importance in the service of the world, he had steadily endeavored to become a peacemaker, to bring about a new era in Europe. In January, 1917, he had outlined his conception of an idealist peace. His diplomatic efforts failed because neither side was willing to accept peace without victory; Germany, especially, demanded harsh terms. He believed in democracy both for its own sake and because he considered no government controlled by its people would go to war as Austria and Germany had done in 1914. He thought that with victory a league capable of enforcing peace could prevent repetition of the slaughter fest then in progress. Included in his thinking was probably a Presbyterian view of God and His cleansing righteous wrath, of which the force of the United States might be an instrument.

Wilson decided. He wrote his own speeches with his heart's blood, and probably never more so than in his war message to the Congress in April, 1917. In it he said that "right is more precious than peace, and we shall fight . . . for a universal domination of right by such concert of free peoples as shall bring peace and safety to all nations and make the world itself at last free." A Woodrow Wilson who could contribute to accomplishing this would be a man to whom the American people justifiably had entrusted power.

History is unpredictable, and nonhistoric unfulfilled possibilities are unknowable. The first frequently does, and the latter unquestionably could, give dusty answers. Wilson's war message at once became and was the action of the people of the United States. Samuel Eliot Morison records in his *Oxford History of the American People* that the war was perhaps "the most popular" ever fought in American history. Victory brought the assembly of the Paris Peace Conference, attended by most of the world. Conspicuously absent was revolutionary and war-torn Russia, whose power holders claimed to be the hope of the human race but squalled at all other countries more viciously even than did Marat, Danton, and Robespierre in 1793 at the time of the French Revolutionary Terror. By the Versailles Peace Treaty, the "concert of free peoples" did reach institutional form as the League of Nations. Unhappily, it appeared more a league of victors embodying the ideas of Clemenceau than an organization to assure the "universal dominion of right." To the defeated Germans, the treaty was a cruelty and an insult. To the war-wracked people of Belgium, Britain, and France, it offered insufficient reparation for terrible sacrifice. To China, concessions made by it to Japan seemed an outrage.

In the event, the Treaty of Versailles neither destroyed an enemy nor made a friend. To many Americans, the League of Nations, and especially Article 10 of its Covenant, appeared to require continuous entanglement in a hateful and dangerous European situation pregnant with future wars. In the ensuing debate, Wilson's physical strength (like Franklin Roosevelt's in a later instance) broke, in September, 1919. The United States Senate declined to ratify the treaty. The country moved implacably toward isolation and "normalcy." Venom remained in Europe, presently to produce full-blown and spreading gangrene, a new war, and a new chapter in history.

These, historically, were some of the unforeseeable results of Wilson's decision. They might have been worse. Decision to stay out and allow a German victory might have had ghastlier results. Yet, fifteen years after the German surrender great blocs of intellectual opinion, not alone in America, considered the game's results not worth the bloody candle. Other forces, some came to think, would have perhaps modified, if not conquered, the might of Hohenzollern Germany. As it turned out, the venom spawned in defeat came to cause agony perhaps greater than that which might have occurred had the Central Powers won. After the fact, might-have-beens can appear attractive in contrast with the bulletins and unhappinesses of day-to-day reality.

The power holder can never know. He must decide according to the best that is in him and abide the event. Wilson did so. He is entitled to sleep with heroes.

3. The Decision to Control Events or Abide Them

As a minor diplomat at the Paris Peace Conference in 1919, spectator and, from time to time, special missioner between wars, assistant secretary of State during World War II, and in government service as the Cold War was at its height in 1961, I have observed a substantial sector of twentieth-century American foreign affairs. Included has been opportunity to observe the workings of power. Some instances are recorded here. In substantial measure, they are the basis for one of the propositions set out in this book: power, ultimately, is personal. In each of the recorded cases, the power holder could have made a different decision from the one he made.

Woodrow Wilson could have decided not to take the United States into World War I, but determined otherwise. Franklin Roosevelt in 1941 could have decided not to take the country into World War II and, in fact, struggled against that step. Japan dictated the contrary decision by attacking Pearl Harbor. Harry Truman could have decided not to involve the United States in the Korean War in 1950; actually, he almost instantaneously sent troops when the Soviet Union organized the North Korean invasion of South Korea in that year. John F. Kennedy's involvement with Cuba in 1961–1962 was a personal decision: he could have stood aside, though Khrushchev's adventurous move into the Western Hemisphere left little alternative. Lyndon Johnson could have decided to stay away from the Dominican Republic on April 28, 1965; but he felt impelled to block what he considered would be a seizure of that country by Cuban-Soviet force. I will not attempt an estimate of American decisions involving the United States in Vietnam; all the evidence is not in, and the precise moment when decision to act or not to act was required is still an open question. My belief is that the crucial die was cast by President Kennedy before President Johnson took office, and that President Kennedy had to make the real choice.

A cautionary word is in order. Decision to use—or not to

use—international power can be made by a power holder, but it can be vetoed or reversed by events. Decision to use power in international affairs springs from an attempt to control events. Decision not to use it necessarily means abiding the current of events—at least for the time being. That current may later create situations forcing action, or negating the action taken, leaving the power holder little further alternative. Machiavelli said, in the chapter in *The Prince* on "Fortune in the Affairs of Men," "I think it may be true that fortune is the ruler of half our actions, but that she allows the other half or thereabouts to be governed by us." After half a century of observing events and power, my own estimate is about the same.

Decision-making, particularly at crucial moments, comprises two elements. One is an estimate of possibilities synthesized from the body of facts, information, and analysis provided the power holder by his assistants. By the nature of things, this information is invariably incomplete. Probably no research, however extended, would turn up all the relevant or perhaps even all the important data on which safe forecasts can be based. In any case, there rarely is time for research. A well-staffed government with good field men and rapid communication techniques can present a fairly reliable picture of the current position of affairs. Certainly it can provide a president with a better picture than that available to outsiders. From this data, a measure of calculation of the risks to be run and results to be obtained under alternative courses of action can be made. Crucial decisions usually cast shadows ahead at least a short distance. Even so, the calculations will include a large factor of inference, estimate, or guesswork. A president must stew over the problem for a time—short or long, depending on the speed of events—and act on the information he has.

The second element is the sum of subjective, emotional, philosophical, almost instinctive thinking. These processes go on inside the president's head. History cannot record them. After the fact, it can at best merely find indications of how his mind worked. In large measure, probably, the workings are subconscious. They bring to focus impressions inherited and accumulated, value judgments drawn from lifetime experience, habits, preoccupations, even prejudices. This process—or collection of simultaneous processes—is what Saul Friedlander may have meant by "intuition." Combining them, the president decides and gives orders.

4. The Illusion of Personal Decision

Two instances of presidential power holders making crucial decisions have been sketched and passing note made of a few others. In each case, the individual involved endeavored to guess the probable results of a specific action or nonaction. In retrospect, it is clear that only the most immediate results could be forecast, and even those involved substantial risk of error.

James K. Polk, rightly, considered he could win a war with Mexico and annex some of its territory. He stopped there. His prediction was justified; the present boundaries of the United States are the result. Unpredictable history had to take charge after the Treaty of Guadalupe Hidalgo; Polk was content to have it so. If, as some historians think, he expected expansion of slave-state power, he was wrong. Woodrow Wilson considered that American force might be determinative in the outcome of World War I and thereby establish powerful American influence (his own) in drawing the ensuing peace. He was right on the first count and partly right on the second; after which, political history in the United States firmly vetoed his peacemaking effort. Franklin D. Roosevelt stood aside from World War II at least partly because he was sure he could not predict events. In international affairs, short-range prediction alone is possible. The long-range historical results of any decision are unknowable.

In part, the very unpredictability of history motivates the endless quest for a system of world power and world order. To be afloat on a current of affairs whose direction and impact are beyond knowledge is essentially chaotic. Men strive to create situations they can understand, and in which to some extent at least they are masters, rather than servants, of blind destiny. Dominant world empire, apparently, is now impossible. There remain, so far as I know, only two final escapes from this chaos. One is to create world order. The other is to take refuge in some kind of transcendental faith. The latter is not in our province except as it occasionally influences men. If one really believes that the will of God, or Allah, or Communist-personified "History" determines all things, struggle for world order is unnecessary. God, Allah, or History will order your inescapable destiny. Choice or decision-making then becomes secondary.

But while many men profess such faith, few really surrender themselves to it. In ultimates, few are willing to believe that God will defend the right without their active help; few consider that fate will produce better results than calculated decisions and action. Certainly, at any given moment, it will not produce the best result for them. Men threatened with destruction, whatever their faith, do not ordinarily assume that divine or other outside factors will save their lives. They resist, they dicker, or they flee.

Today, Russian missiles are trained on several hundred European cities. Each carries a warhead capable of destroying the entire city and its life. Undoubtedly, every American city is covered by similar rockets. Undoubtedly also, every Soviet city is under constant coverage by the United States. There must be other target cities throughout the world. Enough of the civilization of the human race is menaced to threaten almost complete downfall of the modern age and extermination of a large part of the population of those countries presently having the chief measure of world power. Every national power holder knows this. Strangely, this very fact introduces a degree of international order, however unsatisfactory. Possessors of world-wide nuclear-rocket systems are few in number, and they are known. Equipoise of force for the moment exhibits itself, buying time to create a more reliable regime of order. No power holder able to discharge these missiles can predict the consequence of their use more than a few hours ahead. He can destroy; but countermissiles at once will be launched. This is not a formula for action; it is the best reason possible, I think, for their nonuse. It is why the least immediate of my own fears is nuclear-rocket war. Forms of action not involving the only predictable consequence of rocketry will always be preferable—except to madmen.

Less drastic power decisions, nevertheless, may set off a train of events escalating finally to holocaust. No statesman can tell. For this reason, if for no other, dreams of world order, flaccidly indulged in the past, today become visions shrieking for realization. No power holder can make any substantial move in international affairs, offensive or defensive, without the consciousness of its danger. Where power holders are so weak that what they do seems to matter only locally, they can take major local decisions involving use of their modest power. These are the men who apparently can and do act—the little power holders, the Nassers, Ho Chi Minhs, Fidel Castros, and African dictators of this world. But then, larger power holders are likely to enter the operation. Force operations going forward today in Vietnam and in the Red Sea area appear less deliberate than accidental; less the result of major power holders' direct decision than unforeseen consequences of power decisions taken long ago, frequently by minor characters but no less dangerous on that account.

Hence there is today's quite sincere quest for world order by most national power holders, whatever their motivation. This is new in the history of the last three centuries. Louis XIV, Napoleon I and Napoleon III, Kaiser William II, and Adolf Hitler wanted no supranational world order; it would merely have limited their power. Like them, most power holders probably still want to aggrandize their power if they can. As the situation has developed, nuclear rocketry cannot be used for that purpose. As long as it is loose in the world, national power is more protected—and may be better aggrandized—within a system of world order than without, quite aside from more idealist considerations. Most power holders know this. Though history is unforeseeable, the effects of nuclear catastrophe are not. Like Zeus, will they, nill they, national power holders must seek continued confinement at least of the modern monsters of Cronus.

This was not so in 1870 when Bismarck was at work, or 1914

when German field marshals toasted *Der Tag*. It was not so in 1936 when Mussolini pushed his fleets through the Mediterranean and his armies into Ethiopia and Spain. It was not true in 1939 when Hitler ordered his divisions across the Polish border. It was not true in 1941 when the Japanese war lords bombed Pearl Harbor. Already a strange control imposes itself on power holders—unreliable, imponderable, but real. Their problem is whether this control can be reduced to a system of predictability within which they can safely maneuver.

National power is personally wielded. It is nonetheless beginning, in major aspects, to be limited—a limitation on personal power holders as well as on the nation-state institutions they head.

III

Philosophies
of International Power

There cannot be institutions of world government without world consensus on their underlying philosophy. Though there are reasons justifying hope that such philosophy and institutions will emerge—indeed, are dimly visible on the horizon even now—it would be cruelly unrealistic to overestimate the institutions now existing, still more so to suggest that an idea system commands general assent on which world government could be based.

The institutions actually possessing international power, commanding the use of some or all of its instruments, are the individual states. A few of these are grouped. In all of them power holders in different degree can exercise fragments of such power. The variation is huge. Chiefs of tiny African or Caribbean states can and do exert a minimum of power beyond their own borders. Leaders of superpowers, notably the Soviet Union and the United States, given the will to do so, have a degree of capacity to exert power almost anywhere on the globe—perhaps even in outer space if they are willing to assume an intolerable burden of risk.

For itself, each state, great or small, does, in fact, have a framework of ideas guiding or at least influencing its power holders in international action. No state consistently follows the idea system it professes, just as no man consistently lives up to the tenets of his own code. Power holders in all states, nevertheless, within their capacity, do tend to act along the lines of the philosophies they profess. It must be added that philosophies are rarely static; they also evolve with the national history or may be changed by revolution.

Paper formulations, designed to carry a freight of ideas to which most of the world's nations have agreed, do exist. We must look at the realities behind these documents; unhappily, they create the illusion rather than produce evidence of consensus.

A number of operative idea systems in fact guide and influence the decisions of most states and their power holders. Observing affairs, I find four accounting for most power decisions in the international community. They are: nationalism, messianism, racism, and order under a rule of law.

1. The Illusion of Consensus: The Covenant of the League of Nations and the Charter of the United Nations

International agreements—purporting to embody a world-wide philosophy of international order—are now in theoretical effect. Attainment of these is an achievement in itself. Regrettably, these paper systems cover up differences, rather than give evidence of or command general assent. As yet they are unreliable in guiding action.

Extended wars generate waves of popular yearning for peace. World War I certainly did so. Capitalizing on this sentiment, President Woodrow Wilson induced the not-too-receptive Paris Peace Conference to adopt the Covenant of the League of Nations.[1]

1. Because the Covenant of the League of Nations did present a paper formula purporting to be a philosophy of international relations, the more important sections agreed on are worth reprinting here:

"The High Contracting Parties,

In order to promote international cooperation and to achieve international peace and security

by the acceptance of obligations not to resort to war,

by the prescription of open, just and honourable relations between nations,

by the firm establishment of the understandings of international law as the actual rule of conduct among Governments,

and by the maintenance of justice and a scrupulous respect for all treaty obligations in the dealings of organized peoples with one another,

Agree to this Covenant of the League of Nations. . . .

Article 8

REDUCTION OF ARMAMENTS

1. The Members of the League recognize that the maintenance of peace requires the reduction of national armaments to the lowest point consistent with national safety and the enforcement by common action of international obligations.

2. The Council, taking account of the geographical situation and circumstances of each State, shall formulate plans for such reduction for the consideration and action of the several Governments.

3. Such plans shall be subject to reconsideration and revision at least every ten years.

4. After these plans shall have been adopted by the several Governments, the limits of armaments therein fixed shall not be exceeded without the concurrence of the Council.

5. The Members of the League agree that the manufacture by private enterprise of munitions and implements of war is open to grave objections. The Council shall advise how the evil effects attendant upon such manufacture can be prevented, due regard being had to the necessities of those Members of the League which are not able to manufacture the munitions and implements of war necessary for their safety.

6. The Members of the League undertake to interchange full and frank information as to the scale of their armaments, their military, naval and air programmes, and the condition of such of their industries as are adaptable to war-like purposes. . . .

Article 10

ACTION IN CASE OF WAR OR THREAT OF WAR

The Members of the League undertake to respect and preserve as against external aggression the territorial integrity and existing political independence of all Members of the League. In case of any such aggression or in case of any threat or danger of such aggression the Council shall advise upon the means by which this obligation shall be fulfilled. . . .

Article 12
DISPUTES TO BE SUBMITTED FOR SETTLEMENT

1. The Members of the League agree that if there should arise between them any dispute likely to lead to a rupture, they will submit the matter either to arbitration *or judicial settlement* or to inquiry by the Council, and they agree in no case to resort to war until three months after the award by the arbitrators *or the judicial decision* or the report by the Council.

2. In any case under this Article the award of the arbitrators *or the judicial decision* shall be made within a reasonable time, and the report of the Council shall be made within six months after the submission of the dispute.

Article 13
ARBITRATION OR JUDICIAL SETTLEMENT

1. The Members of the League agree that whenever any dispute shall arise between them which they recognize to be suitable for submission to arbitration *or judicial settlement*, and which can not be satisfactorily settled by diplomacy, they will submit the whole subject-matter to arbitration *or judicial settlement*.

2. Disputes as to the interpretation of a treaty, as to any question of international law, as to the existence of any fact which, if established, would constitute a breach of any international obligation, or as to the extent and nature of the reparation to be made for any such breach, are declared to be among those which are generally suitable for submission to arbitration *or judicial settlement*.

3. *For the consideration of any such dispute, the court to which the case is referred shall be the Permanent Court of International Justice, established in accordance with Article 14, or any tribunal agreed on by the parties to the dispute or stipulated in any convention existing between them.*

4. The Members of the League agree that they will carry out in full good faith any award *or decision* that may be rendered, and that they will not resort to war against a Member of the League which complies therewith. In the event of any failure to carry out such an award *or decision*, the Council shall propose what steps should be taken to give effect thereto. . . .

Article 20

1. The Members of the League severally agree that this Covenant is accepted as abrogating all obligations or understandings *inter se* which are inconsistent with the terms thereof, and solemnly undertake that they will not hereafter enter into any engagements inconsistent with the terms thereof.

2. In case any Member of the League shall, before becoming a Member of the League, have undertaken any obligations inconsistent with the terms of this Covenant, it shall be the duty of such Member to take immediate steps to procure its release from such obligations.

Article 21

Nothing in this Covenant shall be deemed to affect the validity of international engagements, such as treaties of arbitration or regional understandings like the Monroe doctrine, for securing the maintenance of peace.

Article 22

1. To those colonies and territories which as a consequence of the late war have ceased to be under the sovereignty of the States which formerly governed them and which are inhabited by peoples not yet able to stand by themselves under the strenuous conditions of the modern world, there should

By 1920, most nations—the United States was a notable exception, and the Soviet Union was not invited until late—had ratified it. Its philosophy, scattered throughout the document, was not unlike that contained in the current Charter of the United Nations. It was designed "to promote international cooperation and to achieve international peace and security" by acceptance of the obligation not to resort to war, and "by the prescription of open, just and honourable relations between nations, by the firm establishment of the understandings of international law as the actual rule of conduct among Governments, and by the maintenance of justice and a scrupulous respect for all treaty obligations in the dealings of organized peoples with one another."

Though it was signed with majestic fanfare in the Hall of Mirrors at the Château of Versailles, no real consensus for the League Covenant existed. The French delegation was guided by Georges Clemenceau and Marshal Foch. So far as I could judge as a staff aide to the U.S. delegation, they represented the views of the French people. They conceived the League of Nations as a permanent alliance of victors whose primary task was to keep Germany in military and economic subjection. Probably they did not wish another war, but they certainly did not accept any idea system that barred resort to war.

An undertaking contained in the famous Article 10 of the League Covenant—"the Members of the League undertake to respect and preserve as against external aggression the territorial integrity and existing political independence of all Members of the League"—meant something different to almost every signatory. Each thought it implied some claim to assistance from others in case its territory or empire was attacked—actually, a rather indefinite form of defensive military alliance. Few accepted any duty to act when they were not directly involved. The United States felt that the obligation might prove real. Fearing involvement in new wars, the Senate refused to ratify the treaty. The Soviet Union, headed by Lenin since 1917, scoffed at the

---

be applied the principle that the well-being and development of such peoples form a sacred trust of civilisation and that securities for the performance of this trust should be embodied in this Covenant."

whole notion. Lenin considered the entire Versailles arrangement merely a method of sharing booty among a few marauding nations—as witness his preface, dated July 6, 1920, to a second publication of his essay on imperialism, "the highest form of capitalism," first published in 1916. The Peace of Versailles, he thought, "added another hundred or hundred and fifty million people to the population of the oppressed nations"—for the benefit of the governments dominant at Paris. Defeated Germany, for its part, proved quite capable thirteen years later of developing a warlike Nazi movement and regime. Far from feeling an obligation not to resort to war, Nazi philosophy affirmed the right of Nordic nations (specifically, Germany) to attain rule by force. The Japanese government cautiously said little but, even as the Versailles Treaty was signed, was at work conquering Manchuria and seizing parts of China.

(I myself thought—and later wrote, with the injustice of angry and disillusioned youth—that the whole business was a cynical sham. With a number of other young men, I resigned from the American delegation in protest against the Versailles Treaty. The gesture had all the gallantry of a mosquito attacking a battleship —and about the same result.)

Faced with the rise of Fascist Italy, which happily engaged in a colonial war against Ethiopia in 1935, with Hitler's discarding of the German disarmament clauses in the Treaty of Versailles in the same year, with overt Italian and German support of General Franco in the civil war in Spain, and with Japan's massive but undeclared war against China in 1937, the League of Nations proved impotent. There was no evidence of any generally accepted idea system or philosophy guiding action in international relations and corresponding to the spirit of the Covenant of the League. When, on September 1, 1939, German armies pushed into Poland, the League of Nations gave up with scarcely an audible whimper.

If any accepted philosophy did exist at that time, it was that of Machiavellian nationalism. Its content is simple. Each state must protect and forward its territory, its economic welfare advantages, and its military strength; this is the highest morality for princes and power holders. Not, it will be noticed, that each state must merely defend itself; rather, each must aggrandize or at least strengthen itself where it can. In pursuit of those goals, success justifies measures; the attained end justifies the means.

Nationalism, I am sure, was the true philosophy of the powers represented at Paris in 1919. It was not changed by President Wilson's appeal for a world ruled by law in which aggression was forbidden. Though the national units were far larger than Renaissance city-states, the ideas governing affairs were about the same as those ruling when Machiavelli wrote *The Prince* in 1517.

As World War II was closing in 1945, another conference was held, at San Francisco. It agreed to a "Charter of the United Nations." Its philosophical formulations were more concise than those of the old League. Their statement is contained in the preamble and the first two articles of the Charter.[2] Was there consensus on the principles (and their implications) set out in the Charter any more than there was consensus on those agreed on twenty-six years earlier at Versailles? If there was, has it carried over to 1969? The answer to the first question is partial: there was a higher content of consensus in 1944 than at Versailles in 1919. The second answer must be a qualified "No."

At least three systems of thinking were rife and rampant in 1945. One was continued Machiavellian nationalism. The second

2. "We the peoples of the United Nations determined to save succeeding generations from the scourge of war, which twice in our lifetime has brought untold sorrow to mankind, and to reaffirm faith in fundamental human rights, in the dignity and worth of the human person, in the equal rights of men and women and of nations large and small, and to establish conditions under which justice and respect for the obligations arising from treaties and other sources of international law can be maintained, and to promote social progress and better standards of life in larger freedom, and for these ends to practice tolerance and live together in peace with one another as good neighbours, and to unite our strength to maintain international peace and security, and to ensure, by the acceptance of principles and the institution of methods, that armed force shall not be used, save in the common interest, and to employ international machinery for the promotion of the economic and social advancement of all peoples, have resolved to combine our efforts to accomplish these aims. Accordingly our respective Governments, through representatives assembled in the city of San Francisco, who have exhibited their full powers found to be in good and due form, have agreed to the present Charter of the

United Nations and do hereby establish an international organization to be known as the United Nations.

CHAPTER I. PURPOSES AND PRINCIPLES

Article 1

The Purposes of the United Nations are:

1. To maintain international peace and security, and to that end: to take effective collective measures for the prevention and removal of threats to the peace, and for the suppression of acts of aggression or other breaches of the peace, and to bring about by peaceful means, and in conformity with the principles of justice and international law, adjustment or settlement of international disputes or situations which might lead to a breach of the peace;

2. To develop friendly relations among nations based on respect for the principle of equal rights and self-determination of peoples, and to take other appropriate measures to strengthen universal peace;

3. To achieve international co-operation in solving international problems of an economic, social, cultural, or humanitarian character, and in promoting and encouraging respect for human rights and for fundamental freedoms for all without distinction as to race, sex, language, or religion; and

4. To be a centre for harmonizing the actions of nations in the attainment of these common ends.

Article 2

The Organization and its Members, in pursuit of the Purposes stated in Article 1, shall act in accordance with the following Principles.

1. The Organization is based on the principle of the sovereign equality of all its Members.

2. All Members, in order to ensure to all of them the rights and benefits resulting from membership, shall fulfill in good faith the obligations assumed by them in accordance with the present Charter.

3. All Members shall settle their international disputes by peaceful means in such a manner that international peace and security, and justice, are not endangered.

4. All Members shall refrain in their international relations from the threat or use of force against the territorial integrity or political independence of any state, or in any other manner inconsistent with the Purposes of the United Nations.

5. All Members shall give the United Nations every assistance in any action it takes in accordance with the present Charter, and shall refrain from giving assistance to any state against which the United Nations is taking preventive or enforcement action.

6. The Organization shall ensure that states which are not Members of the United Nations act in accordance with these Principles so far as may be necessary for the maintenance of international peace and security.

7. Nothing contained in the present Charter shall authorize the United Nations to intervene in matters which are essentially within the domestic jurisdiction of any state or shall require the Members to submit such matters to settlement under the present Charter; but this principle shall not prejudice the application of enforcement measures under Chapter VII."

was Marxist-Leninist messianism. The third was that of the United States, but it was idealist hope rather than accepted doctrine. The United States—more accurately, Secretary of State Cordell Hull and most of his associates—indulged as dominant belief the idea that a rule of law should, could, and would govern international relations. The United Nations and the World Court should become the institutions bringing this to pass. This position commanded appreciable support; British public opinion and most British statesmen agreed, as did a large number of smaller nations.

Yet, in 1945, Russian messianism was, perhaps, the most active force. At the time the Charter of the United Nations was being worked out, Stalin was a bold, effective, and highly unsentimental statesman. He had achieved dictatorial power in the Soviet Union. As German defeat became increasingly probable (actually, in the fall of 1944), he had gradually withdrawn from co-operation with his Western allies. His armies in Poland and the other East European countries were displacing the old regimes there, though, especially in Poland, these regimes had fought the Nazis to the limit of their capacity. He was openly putting into power "friendly"—that is, client—Communist governments subservient to Moscow. (At that time, to be "Communist" meant not only devotion to Marxist-Leninist doctrines, but also acceptance of Stalin as their sole authentic interpreter.) For practical purposes, the new client governments virtually became part of the Stalinist empire.

This messianic process differs from old-fashioned imperialism in one way only. Its doctrine is unlimited and universal. It assumes that Communist social organization is the only valid and acceptable way of organizing social systems, that all other systems are inherently evil, and therefore enemies. It assumes that the triumph of Communism in the entire world is ineluctable; this is willed by History. Imperialism may—in fact, always does— have limits. Messianism has none, except perhaps the planet on which we live. Factually, from 1945 until 1966 (when China, become Communist in 1950, broke away from Russian leadership), Soviet foreign policy contemplated extending Leninist Communism everywhere: by force where Russian armies dominated, by paramilitary operations where they did not, by missionary work and fomenting internal revolutions where other means were not available.

A competing schismatic messianism—Chinese Communism— emerged later, becoming impressive only about 1964, though probably latent long before. In that year, Nikita Khrushchev was ousted as Soviet premier and Communist party chief. Before that, he had attacked and effectively damaged the huge image and myth of Stalin, thereby breaking up Communist unity on Stalin's interpretation of Communist doctrine and permitting Chinese Communists to assert their own interpretation of Marxism-Leninism as the true faith. This, Mao Tse-tung presently did, incidentally offering Peking as fountainhead of Communist philosophy. Underlying the Chinese claim is a powerful current of racism, rooted in the conviction that Chinese civilization and culture are superior to all others. Given the inherent power potential of the 700,000,000-strong Chinese state, it was perhaps natural for Chinese leaders to proclaim themselves not only custodians of orthodoxy, but also inheritors of its world mission. Today, Soviet and Chinese versions of messianism compete with each other. Being messianic, each opposes all non-Communist nations and all heretical Communist countries.

British policy, in general, supported the American dream of a world ruled by law. It was, however, quite naturally and prudently equivocal. Empire had been the greatest British experience. Despite all criticisms of it, British imperial policy in the twentieth century had perhaps accomplished as much for the general good of men and women in the world as any other instrument. Its existence and warring power had been the key and crucial element in preventing Nazi victory and a vast extension of Hitlerian racist tyranny. A practical people, Britons were prepared to work for a regime of world law under the United Nations, but they were not prepared to bet their na. onal safety and survival on its speedy arrival. A like emotion unquestionably governed most American power holders. As a State Department officer in this period, I felt the same ambivalence. Just as the League of Nations had proved impotent in the past, the United Nations might prove impotent in the future. Like many men in the government at the time, I fervently wanted the United Nations to succeed. I certainly was not prepared to make American safety and survival wholly dependent on its success. French policy was less developed. The thoughts of French statesmen, notably of General de Gaulle, defeated in World War II, were naturally centered on restoring France at least to its old position—a primarily nationalist position.

Yet, all things considered, the Charter of the United Nations did represent a striking advance over the acceptance grudgingly vouchsafed the League of Nations Covenant in 1919. It was not, like the League Covenant, an almost cynical concealment of the real sentiments of its most powerful signatories and the real feelings of their countries. I think the men at San Francisco, Stalin excepted, and the peoples they represented preponderantly did accept, and intended to steer their nations toward, a world organization dedicated to bringing about world order under a rule of law.

What of today?

Machiavellian nationalism was not dead in 1945 and is lively now. Messianic nations do not renounce it; they merely co-opt it as an aid to their larger ideas. Non-Communist nations, including the United States, essentially do not forsake it. American policy still sticks to formal hope that a world ruled by law may emerge; but, until it does, nationalist policy must serve as defense until better days arrive. Governments like that of General de Gaulle in France quite openly maneuver to aggrandize themselves, and make no bones about it.

War has been formally renounced by the United Nations members. But one huge nation—China—is not a member and does not pretend renunciation. Among the United Nations members, the Soviet Union frankly maintains its right—perhaps even its duty —to maintain and support "wars of liberation," by which is meant wars to impose Communism on non-Communist countries where expedient. True, these wars are not declared. The fiction is maintained that they are "internal revolutions." In them, troops are commonly camouflaged as "volunteers" and put into uniforms of civil-war insurgents. Renunciation of war has at least this much force: it is considered advantageous not to be an overt war maker. This is about the extent of the change. Emergent countries, members of the United Nations, chiefly in Africa and the eastern Mediterranean, engage in highly nationalist border wars among themselves, knowing not or caring little whether the Charter of the United Nations applies.

On two occasions—in Korea in 1950 and in Vietnam in 1961— "wars of liberation" were begun and resistance was organized. In Korea, the United Nations formally accepted the burden of defense, though the United States first acted and carried most of the burden. In Vietnam, the United Nations did not act, so that American troops aligned with South Vietnamese forces and with contingents from Australia, the Philippine Republic, Thailand, and South Korea have borne the brunt. Allegedly, the opponents are South Vietnamese Communist insurgents. Actually, a large proportion are organized North Vietnamese troops, armed and munitioned by Communist China and by the Soviet Union—both of whom insist that any outside (American) assistance to or defense of South Vietnam is "imperialist aggression." That same insistence was made when in 1967 the United Arab Republic mobilized armies (equipped by the Soviet Union) against Israel and it was thought outside powers might give Israel aid.

Surveying the scene twenty-four years after the San Francisco Conference and the formation of the United Nations at the close of World War II, a casual observer might well be discouraged. The paper formulations are far from reality.

2. Machiavellian Nationalism

Nationalism is at present the standard operating practice of every state to the extent of its capacity. Each state tries to forward its own interest. Great states, especially superpowers, endeavor to handle their international affairs in such fashion that their power, prestige, and capacity to influence events will be maintained, if not increased.

When a country enters a co-operative group, like the European

Common Market, or when it allows its policy to be dominated by a neighboring empire, as do the Central European countries when dealing with the Soviet Union, its purpose is to forward its own interest by working with the other nation-states involved, either because it believes the co-operation advantageous or because it cannot do otherwise. In such situations, each state endeavors, often unsuccessfully, to make sure that in case of necessity it can act independently.

The logical end of nationalism—if the game is, or could be, played to perfection—is either world empire or a concert of empires. The first has never been successfully established, though there have been in the world's history a few almost successful attempts. The second, a concert of empires, has been successfully achieved for short periods of history, notably in the late nineteenth century. Such a system of world power, with, historically, a high content of resulting peace, did obtain at the close of the Victorian era; it continued until 1914. For better or worse, groping toward a similar system is going forward at present. As in the case of the Victorian concert of powers, it is a product of enlightened nationalism. Basic to it is the existence of a small number of superpowers whose nationalist policy has given them a measure of control over great parts of the earth's surface.

"The desire to acquire possessions is a very natural and ordinary thing, and when those men do it who can do so successfully, they are always praised and not blamed, but when they cannot and yet want to do so at all costs, they make a mistake deserving of great blame," says Machiavelli in *The Prince*. This was—and perhaps still is—the essence of nationalism. Yet it cannot be condemned out of hand. The great Western European countries— France, Germany, Italy, Spain—were constructed from their medieval elements by Machiavellian nationalism, and who is to say their peoples have been the worse off for it? One hardly envies the fate of the peoples of the pre-existing, perpetually quarreling feudal principalities and sovereignties. These were mauled, conquered, or dynastically combined into a few large states. From time to time, someone proposes to undo the work of consolidation. During the Versailles Peace Conference in 1919,

Paris was placarded with posters—put up by adherents of Georges Clemenceau and parties of the French right—shrieking, "Undo the work of Bismarck," accompanied by a map showing Germany broken up into the constituent kingdoms, grand duchies, and principalities that existed before it had been made an empire in 1871. The purpose was to make France dominant in Europe; but the proposed atomization of Germany did not promise a stable Europe. In 1942, Hitler, at the time conqueror of France, proposed its dismemberment, with Brittany and Normandy to be set up as autonomous Nordic provinces—as, indeed, they once had been. Few in Europe or elsewhere were attracted by this scheme. Germans and Frenchmen were better off as citizens of the larger countries. Germans and Frenchmen alike considered peace more probable if the two countries were maintained. The emergence and unification of both countries had been the result of nationalism. The Machiavellian devices and measures bringing these two and their contemporary European states into being supplied the main narrative of European history.

The United States owes its present extent, organization, and position primarily to nationalist ambition and action. From the day when the new country made peace with Great Britain in 1783, its politicians and statesmen took every opportunity to expand its borders. In 1803, President Jefferson maneuvered the Louisiana Purchase. President Monroe "acquired" Florida in 1819. By 1840, the country's "manifest destiny" to sweep across the American continent to the Pacific Ocean was dominant political dogma. Such opposition as existed stemmed less from objection to expansion than from fear lest all or part of the territories the United States so acquired would adopt slavery as an institution and become "slave states." In American politics, as elsewhere in the world, taking over territory wherever possible was standard policy. Imperial Russia picked up territory in Europe, Asia, and North America, aggregating about one-sixth of the land area of the world. Smaller states pursued the policy no less avidly where they could. In 1919, even before the Treaty of Versailles was signed, the newly liberated states of Central Europe were fighting each other for pieces of territory. In the interwar period, Rumania seized a great part of historic Hungary; Poland, part of historic Lithuania. Today, new African states seek to strengthen their position as against each other by force, fomented revolutions, or other measures within their capabilities.

Where the struggle is not for territory, it is carried on in the field of economics, and, more constructively, in the field of culture. Even altruistic moves—while entirely sincere—will, it is hoped, bring to the country giving or receiving gifts or loans greater trade and commerce and the advantage of contacts with cultures other than their own. More often than not, there is an underlying expectation that the country exporting its aid, economics, education, or ideas will be better able to influence events in the receiving countries. Communist nations, exporting doctrine, literature, propaganda, and organizers, insist that their motive is to "liberate" the recipient countries. The success of this "liberation" seems to be measured by the degree of capacity of Moscow or Peking to guide the policies of the "liberated" areas.

All this is nationalist. It cannot be dismissed as basically "immoral." Nationalism is as nationalism does. British nationalism in the seventeenth, eighteenth, and nineteenth centuries set up India as a subject empire; the independent India of today would not otherwise have come into existence.

"Modern imperialism is the natural development of the Great Power system which arose, with the foreign office method of policy, out of the Machiavellian monarchies after the break-up of Christendom." [3] It is quite true that nineteenth- and twentieth-century imperialism is a direct outgrowth of nationalism. Whether it is as megalomaniac as Wells also insists is less clear. Unquestionably, it was so before 1914. Yet even as the clash of empires brought on World War I, men in all the empires dreamed of using them as instruments of world order. The notion implied balance of power, accompanied by self-restraint on the part of all the major imperial units. A concert of empires was a more probable means of arriving at stable peace than the creation of a world empire like that dreamed of by Mongolian conquerors, medieval Catholic popes, and Holy Roman emperors. "Balance of power"

3. H. G. Wells, *The Outline of History*, New York, Macmillan, 1920, p. 1024.

implied acceptance of limits to extension of the nationalist principle, at least so far as territorial ambitions were concerned. No system of world order was likely to emerge if the only objective of empire was to conquer more territory, necessarily at expense of others. Enlightened nationalism could conceive that the national interests of the central country in an empire would be best forwarded by stopping, rather than by expanding—as the Emperor Trajan had once decided in the greatest days of the Roman Empire. Discussion of that, however, is academic. The imperial systems began to break down in 1914. By the end of World War II in 1945, all but the Soviet Union were in process of dissolution.

As World War II drew toward its close, statesmen everywhere were faced with two massive facts. First, world peace, based either on balance of power or on the concert of empires, had failed—failed so decisively that the empires themselves no longer existed. Second, each nation was now forced to rely on itself and its own powers for its survival, defense, and production. Each must therefore depend on itself to safeguard or forward its own national interest. Without more, this situation would have been prelude to chaos. Necessarily, power immediately began to fill the obvious lacuna. Specifically, a group of nations in mid-Europe were promptly captured by the power holders of the Soviet Union. Another group gravitated toward the United States, and the power holders in Washington. "Polarization" around these two focuses became the temporary substitute for the concert of empires prevailing before 1914.

Polarization into two groups did not, of course, provide an idea system in place of the vanishing philosophy of nationalist imperialism. Within each of the polar systems were many nations. Each remained as nationalist as before. They merely adapted their nationalism to prevailing conditions. Under the Soviet system, captive Poland, Hungary, and Yugoslavia dreamed of strengthening themselves to the point of being able to throw off control by Soviet proconsuls. Nations grouped around the power of the United States made the best of it, but many resented their position and waited for better times. The overt nationalism of

Gaullist France, for one example, was entirely predictable. Unless the two polar systems found a unifying philosophy and crystallized into political empires, those blocs were bound to break up, as, in fact, they are breaking up now. Nationalism is thus left as the prime operating principle in international power.

3. Messianism

Messianism is extant. Messianic systems do not modify the nationalism of states professing them; they merely add a wider dimension to it.

Men and nations have from time to time concluded that some single faith is destined to prevail throughout the world and that institutions professing and applying that faith are fated to become universally regnant. It then becomes the duty of such institutions and their power holders to extend the true faith by all means in their power, not excluding military conquest. Complete success would result in a world empire or organization following principles embodied in this faith and governing the world.

Two ideas are embraced in this conception: doctrine and the creation of an institutional power structure embodying it. The latter aspect chiefly concerns us here. Fusion of the two is not essential. Christ could and did say that the kingdom of God was separate from the rule of Caesar. St. Augustine, in the fifth century, considered the "City of God" as existing separately from the institutions of kingdoms and empires. Faith might well rule the actions of men without having to express itself as a structure of power. Unhappily, it is singularly easy for priests to consider that they ought also to be kings, and for kings to consider themselves high priests. Messianism, as it has appeared in world history, exhibits the work of doctrinal institutions headed by power holders more often than the deeper achievements of faith forwarded by philosophers, priests, or saints. Messianic power holders consider that they, their associates, and their successors are predestined to govern earthly affairs. Saints sometimes know better.

Messianic philosophy certainly fused with dreams of earthly world power in the early history of the Catholic church. "The idea of a world state, the universal kingdom of righteousness of which every living soul should be a citizen," H. G. Wells said in his *Outline of History*,[4] came into the world with Christ. Later, the papacy asserted a tentative claim to world dominion, tying up, in A.D. 325, with the autocratic power of the Roman Emperor Constantine the Great. St. Augustine's "City of God" did not directly contemplate making the world an organized heavenly kingdom, but its theory could readily be given political application. Roman popes claimed, and for brief periods occasionally established, political overlordship of pagan kings as they were converted to Christianity. "The history of Europe from the fifth century onward to the fifteenth is very largely the history of the failure of this great idea of a divine world government to realize itself in practice."[5] In fact, such international organization as did exist in the medieval Western world was based on Christian messianism, given earthly effect by the universal Catholic church. From time to time, monarchies aspired to world rulership in the light of this institution. Charlemagne, crowned emperor of all Western Europe in A.D. 800 by Pope Leo III represents a high-water mark in the movement. Whatever ideas Charlemagne may have had as to the real location of power, there is little question about those of Leo III. He planned and intended an unlimited imperial extension of Catholic power, devolved by the church upon the pope.

Today it is unclear whether the dream of Christian messianism and world government based on it has expired or whether it merely has adopted a more intelligent approach to extending its political as well as spiritual power. The Council of Rome, in the years 1964 to 1966, was a brilliant initiative toward ending divisions in the Christian world. It reduced the barriers dividing

4. Pp. 797–798.
5. *Ibid.*, p. 526.

Protestantism from Roman Catholicism, and Roman from Greek Catholicism. It even emphasized toleration of non-Christian faiths. Pope John XXIII labored for the adoption of doctrines that would make for world peace. His successor, Pope Paul VI, continued the work. Both pontiffs disclaimed intent to increase the temporal power of the church. It seems clear that faith, rather than political institutions—spiritual, rather than temporal, power—was the instrument they chiefly had in mind. Christian spiritual messianism nevertheless cannot be wholly dismissed as a possible idea system on which temporal world organization may ultimately be based, though it would have to join with other religions to achieve world-wide consensus. Currently, it appears to be tending toward strengthening the tenuous institutions of world organization, such as the United Nations, now in existence rather than toward taking them over or replacing them.

Other messianisms have repeatedly appeared in history. Stoic philosophy, best represented and expounded in the second century A.D. by a crippled Phrygian slave, Epictetus, claimed universality, but disclaimed any power apparatus. Its virtual adoption by Marcus Aurelius, greatest of the Antonine emperors of Rome, mightily increased the influence of Stoic ideas but engendered no Stoic political structure. In A.D. 622, a fifty-two-year-old Arab fled from Mecca to Medina and there founded the religion and presently the empire of Islam. He proclaimed himself the Prophet of God, divinely inspired to bring the world under a universal religion, and many came to accept his claim. But he also was a temporal ruler, and intended to be. His prime minister and disciple, Abu Bekr, proposed to subject the whole world to Allah, with his Prophet as vice-regent on earth, using Arab arms for the purpose. Their success was remarkable. By A.D. 730, a loose Mohammedan Empire controlled territory bounded on the east by India, on the west by the Atlantic coast of Spain, Portugal, and Morocco, on the north by Turkestan (presently part of the Soviet Union) and the Black Sea, and on the south by the Sahara Desert. It penetrated deep into France and threatened to engulf Byzantium and the Balkans. The push faltered because in 732 it was defeated in Europe by Charles Martel, Charlemagne's grandfather, on the battlefield of Tours in central France, and because local Islamic chieftains presently broke away from the central power structure.

Possibly as reaction, the Catholic papacy presently renewed its bid. Defense against Islamic incursions was certainly one of the motives leading Pope Urban II to organize the First Crusade in 1096. In the next century, mobilized by the church, one crusade followed another. They were used to conquer territory for feudal captains and abused by the empires, kings, and noblemen who took part in them. The spiritual functions of Christian messianism meanwhile steadily lost out to the individuals administering the power mechanisms; Euopean kings and nobles, not spiritual priests, led the armies. One result was a direct struggle between the Pope—at the time, Gregory IX—and the German Emperor, Frederick II. The men of the papal organization thought less about establishing the kingdom of God in men's hearts; "they wanted to see the power of the church, which was their own power, dominating men." [6] The kings and emperors may have been philosophical about control of the hearts and souls of men, but they had no doubt that power ought to rest in themselves.

Christian messianism, as a power structure, slowly crumpled, though it made a huge recovery and renewed power push when, in the sixteenth century, the Hapsburg power was, nominally at least, at its height. By 1580, its ablest exponent, Philip II of Spain, had succeeded in dominating all of newly discovered America, and he almost made himself master of the few parts of Europe not under his and his fellow Hapsburgs' rule. This, the last great effort of Christian messianism, finally failed as the Protestant Reformation both divided the Christian faith and split the temporal European power apparatus in the sixteenth and seventeenth centuries, giving rise to a series of religious wars. Its demise was complete when, after a generation of confused conflict, the devastating Thirty Years' War (1618–1648) made permanent the division between Catholic and Protestant states. During that period, Machiavellian nationalism took over.

6. *Ibid.,* p. 655.

Meanwhile, a modified Mohammedan messianism had taken a new lease on life. Its power institutions moved from Arabia to Turkey; its conquest of Constantinople in 1453 carried Mohammedan power deep into Europe. An Ottoman sultan bought the title of "caliph," and his son, Suleiman the Magnificent, pushed the Mohammedan frontier to the gates of Vienna.

One cannot say that messianism has not played a great part in world history. Nor can it be accounted dead today. In new form, the Marxian-Leninist faith and the Communist power structures based on it have been outstanding in the twentieth century. They rule more than one-fourth of the world's territory and nearly a third of its population. They have had all the elements of a world messianic push. First was their universal faith. Marx was sure that all forms of social organization other than Communism were certain to destroy themselves. "Revolutions are locomotives of history," he said. Lenin remarked in 1920 that "World imperialism must fall when the revolutionary onslaught of the exploited and oppressed workers in each country . . . will unite with the revolutionary onslaught of hundreds of millions of people who up to now have stood outside of history and have been regarded merely as the object of history." [7]

After completing conquest of the vast Russian Empire in 1920, messianic Communism considered the Soviet state an instrument for enlarging its rule. From it Communist leaders expanded the power of the Soviet Union through direct conquest, through client states, through alliances. "Through the conflict comes power,/ Each will lift high his face./And thus will come to flower/At last, the human race," went the anthem. Under Stalin, Communist messianists everywhere took it seriously.

Communist messianism and the system it created are breaking up. Eventually, the leaders of the fragments may accept a stabilized situation in which Communist faith is not regnant in the world, or a Communist empire master of the world. We do not yet know. Preliminary indications sufficiently suggest the probability. From 1917 on, the Communist faith was virtually fused

7. *Lenin Reader,* ed. by Stefan T. Possony, Chicago, Henry Regnery Co., 1966, p. 308.

with the institutions and power apparatus of the states it dominated. This, really, was the work of Lenin. His writing and
speeches were primarily directed toward the strategy and tactics
of extending Communism as a method of social organization.
Chief in his thinking was the use of power—as might be expected
from a man to whom class war was an article of faith. (Any war,
including class war, is an exercise in power.) The Soviet state was
a chief proprietor of instruments of power, propaganda, money,
arms, extraterritorial organization.

But it is not easy to avoid fusing revolutionary power exercised through a state (in this case the Soviet Union) with the less
universal attitudes and interests of that state. Communism was
established outside the Soviet Union first in the East European
nations conquered by Russia. Later it triumphed in China. Attempt was made to set up all these countries as Communist
brothers, yet to maintain ultimate control over decisions in the
hands of Moscow's power holders. The formula was that the
Soviet Union was "elder brother" of other Communist countries,
and its decisions were accordingly entitled to respect. The associated Communist states presently began to feel that the decisions of the Moscow rulers were dictated more by desire to aggrandize the Soviet Union than to spread the true Communist
faith. Yugoslavia broke away in 1948, claiming the right to take
"its own road to socialism." In 1956, Hungary revolted altogether, though the revolt was broken by Russian troops. In that
same year, Poland came to the brink of open mutiny. A "Titoist"
named Wladyslaw Gomulka—follower of the Yugoslav line—
came out of prison and negotiated a degree of doctrinal freedom
for the Polish Communist party and a faint measure of freedom
for Poland from Moscow control. (It is not clear how far the
Polish government will be able to maintain these freedoms, but
it is certain its people wish them expanded.)

Greater defections occurred in 1966. Under the rule of Mao
Tse-tung, China had jibbed against accepting Moscow as "elder
brother," and had begun to quarrel not only about doctrine but
also about territory. For some years, Chinese politicians had insisted that much of Soviet-held Siberia was really Chinese ter-

455

ritory seized by Czarist imperial robbers in the nineteenth century. These claims were presently extended to include Turkestan. Mao Tse-tung's followers did not accept the Soviet condemnation of Stalin or Khrushchev's nominal renunciation of war as a means of extending Communism to capitalist countries. "Peaceful co-existence" became anathema in Peking. Endeavors to patch up the quarrel failed when, in 1966, Communist China refused to send a delegation to an international party congress in Moscow and openly denounced its Russian coreligionist. The ensuing two years intensified the disintegration. In 1968, Czechoslovakia liberalized its institutions and practices, whereupon Soviet forces with contingents from other East European Communist states invaded the country and forced return to a harder Communist line. Controversy between the Soviet Union and Communist China has reached the point of armed border conflict. Some Marxist-Leninist countries, like Cuba and Rumania, openly maneuver between the two great empires, seeking to maintain their own freedom of action.

Communist messianism, like Mohammedan and Christian messianism in their time, thus appears to have lost its universality. At least four separate strands are today apparent: "national" Communism, exhibited by Marshal Tito in Yugoslavia; Chinese nationalist Communism, propounded by Mao Tse-tung in Peking; a somewhat equivocal, mildly independent, middle-of-the-road Communism, proposed by the present government of Rumania, and an evolving Communism possibly based on a measure of "peaceful co-existence," urged by Leonid Brezhnev, Aleksei Kosygin, and the government in Moscow. Fundamentally, nationalist considerations underlie the differences between these countries, though each claims to be forwarding the only true Communist faith.

The breakup of messianic Communism appears to parallel the failure of earlier messianic movements dedicated to setting up a world power structure. Power institutions—in this case, nations—develop a dynamism of their own. Each seeks to forward the interest of the nation rather than the universal interest of the true faith. Medieval Christian messianism broke up because of the opposed interests of nation-states included in it, even more than because of Protestant-Catholic doctrinal disputes. The Mohammedan Empire suffered like fate as its component units first split, then opposed each other. The second Christian messianic push, in the sixteenth century, foundered for the same reason. No one need be surprised to find the story repeating itself in the Communist empires of our own time.

As we have seen in these pages, the men leading an organization —the power holders—are always in tension with the men of their professed faith—priests, theorists, intellectuals, apostles of reform. In any given decision, they will sacrifice their theoretical faith to the practical interest of their organization. International messianism, erecting a power structure, invariably degenerates into exaggerated nationalism; the client or component states revolt against it, or it engages in war and is destroyed on the field of battle. Had Hitler been successful in his attempt to create a vast Nazi empire based on the ideology of race, with the German state as the chief power apparatus, the result probably would have been its disintegration within a few decades.

4. Racism

Extant in the twentieth century have been movements toward world rule based on the superiority of one race. Strangely, the theory has had some pragmatic success. This seems odd. By its very nature, racism is not universal; it places one assumed ethnic group in superiority over all others. Automatically, it would seem to force these others into opposition—as in fact it does.

Nazi doctrine asserted that Nordics were the "superior" race. There are, of course, a number of more or less identifiable "Nordic" peoples—German, Scandinavian, Dutch, Anglo-Saxon, to name a few. In the Nazi scheme, German Nordics were, of course, to be at the top of the pile—though Nazi philosophy nominally accepted all Nordics as being in the "master race" group. Allegedly, superior capacity, industry, intellectual capabilities were asserted as giving them the right to establish rule over the rest of the earth.

Theory went further. It assigned to other races lesser functions. They might be high-class laborers, low-class laborers, servants. A famous speech by Walther Darré, one of Hitler's ministers at the time of his conquest of Czechoslovakia, illustrated the point in ghastly detail. Germans in that area were to have commanding positions. Slavic Czechs and Slovaks were to be laborers. They were, therefore, to be kept uneducated, and consequently under Nordic direction—in other words, a variety of serf. On another occasion, Hitler and Mussolini discussed the partition of Brazil between them (somewhat illogically—most Italians are not Nordic). The Portuguese and mixed-race Brazilians were to be assigned the function of high-class servants.

A world power structure was then envisaged; its center to be, as one might expect, Nazi Germany. German colonies or groups in various parts of the world were to take over local rulership. This fantastic nonsense had a measure of success. At the height of his power—1941—Hitler's Germans actually did control most of Europe west of the effective boundaries of the Soviet Union. In Latin America, German groups were endeavoring to establish themselves in power in Argentina, were organizing to attempt domination of Uruguay, were making some progress in Chile, and were asserting themselves elsewhere. The scheme fell to pieces when the German navy was defeated on the seas, Hitler's armies were routed in Europe, and Nazi power was smashed in 1945. But if Hitler's arms had been successful in Europe, and if his submarines had proved able to break British and American naval power, the world might have seen a racist system dominant over much of its surface.

Roots of this surprising philosophy can be discovered in the political fact that white supremacy actually existed in the nineteenth and early twentieth centuries. Factually, world control did rest in the hands of thirteen or fourteen great empires. Of these, all but two—the Japanese and Chinese—were ruled by white men. There was, however, a vast lacuna. No idea system or theory asserted any right of whites to be and remain in this position of dominance. Their rulership had happened; it had not been designed. Military success plus technical competence, not a doctrine or an idea system, brought the condition into being. Colonialism in Asia and Africa had indeed resulted from it. The "white man's burden" (propounded by Kipling in 1898 to induce the United States to annex the Philippine archipelago at the close of the Spanish-American War) was as near as they came to a philosophy. Even Kipling did not assert that the white man's duty to civilize other races was an eternal mandate. Yet it is easy to see why a factual white supremacy could be translated by power holders in an aggressive white nation—in this case Nazi Germany—into a philosophy of world rule.

Another current of racism may be incubating. The Chinese may become its foremost protagonist. With some reason, the Chinese have regarded their civilization as the finest and greatest, as well as the oldest, in the world. It has survived for several millennia. It is artistic, intellectual, spiritual, and can be highly technical. From time to time, Chinese military achievements have been outstanding. With its culture transmitted in some part by the great Mongolian conquests of the thirteenth century (Genghis Khan) and the fourteenth (Tamerlane), its thrust and impact have been undeniable. Chinese colonies in many parts of the world have steadfastly maintained their racial integrity and their fidelity to central Chinese conceptions. An attempt to convert the national administration of continental China, with a population of perhaps over 700 millions (probably to attain a billion within a few decades), into a world empire based on Chinese superiority is by no means inconceivable.

Negro racism is a newer manifestation. Its ambitions are more explicitly stated by some of its protagonists. In part, it is a defensive reaction. The people of Negro Africa and Negro colonies elsewhere in the world were, factually, second-class citizens in the nineteenth- and early-twentieth-century world. A Negro traveling anywhere, in or out of Africa, found other Negroes only in subordinate or servile positions. Everywhere the white man was dominant, if not positively master. Legally, Negroes held equal status in the United States, but they were actually dealt with as inferior. Not unnaturally, Negroes, especially those having access to education, fought against this condition. Considering that their only real remedy was "Black Power," by 1966 some of them opposed this conception to "White Power" in situations little and big. The emergence of a great number of Negro states as the German, British, and French African empires were liquidated offered the possibility of organization. Standard doctrine among these states calls for the elimination of neighboring "white supremacy" states like Rhodesia, the Union of South Africa, and the Portuguese African colonies—where the Negro population is in the vast majority. In some countries with more evenly distributed populations—for instance, the new state of Guyana (formerly British Guiana), on the eastern shoulder of South America—the Negroes act more or less together, as a political group—in Guyana opposing an East Indian–Asian group of comparable size.

I do not consider Negro racism a doctrine likely to claim status as a world philosophy on which a wide power system can be based. More likely it will limit itself to "self-determination"— the right of Negroes to dominance when they are in a majority. It is too early to tell. But when one considers the savage results of white supremacy—the many millions of Negroes enslaved or massacred during the seventeenth, eighteenth, and nineteenth centuries—one cannot rule out the possibility that Negro racism may claim dominance and the loyalty to its principle of power holders in substantial parts of the world.

5. The Co-operative Grouping of States

Diverting from review of attempts to set up power organizations based on general philosophies, one must note the emergence of institutions that are neither states nor empires, but something in between, must be noted. These may be called group "organizations" or "communities" [8] designed to achieve a specific end or ends common to all the participants. The European Common Market is an outstanding example.

All composite international organizations with which I am familiar revolve around a specific "function" or group of functions—that is, they are expected to encourage and forward some particular activity or related activities whose functioning the members agree is to their advantage. The six nations in the European Common Market are all agreed that a high level of commercial activity is a "good thing" and, further, that absence of trade barriers is useful, if not essential, in achieving a high level of such activity. In addition, they consider certain economic operations as best performed under common control; for example, production and distribution of coal and steel resources within the European Common Market. Manifestly, it is easier to find a common philosophical base for limited functions, such as trade, than for larger ones, such as common government. The North Atlantic Treaty Organization (NATO), though now breaking up, constituted, when it was established in 1949, a group whose single function was that of common military defense. Other similar groups exist to carry on limited economic activities; the International Monetary Fund is one. Still others are readily imaginable; for example, a "petroleum community" of oil-producing and oil-consuming states, or a "technological community" for exchange of scientific and technical data.

In all such communities, power is required, at least to forward the limited ends of the organization. Institutions are accordingly set up to delegate a fragment of the national power of the constitutive states to the community, to vest its exercise in certain individuals, and to provide for its regular devolution. The philosophical base (as well as the institutional form) is almost invariably outlined in the constitutive agreement. The North Atlantic Treaty Organization declares the desire of its members to

8. The unhandy words "organization" and "communities" are needed because those are what many of those groups call themselves in their constitutive treaties or charters.

live in peace with all peoples and all governments, and "to safeguard the freedom, common heritage and civilization of their
peoples, founded on the principles of democracy, individual
liberty, and the rule of law." The forerunner of the European
Common Market (the Benelux Convention) declared the desire
of its members "to create the most favourable conditions for the
eventual establishment of an economic union and for the restoration of economic activity." The Council of Europe, a more ambitious attempt at grouping, declared that "the pursuit of peace
based upon justice and international co-operation is vital for
the preservation of human society and civilization," and affirmed
"their devotion to the spiritual and moral values which are the
common heritage of their peoples and the true source of individual freedom, political liberty and the rule of law."

Regrettably, it must be noted that the more general the affirmation of philosophy, the weaker, usually, has been the institution
created.

Organizations to carry out specialized economic functions—
such as the International Monetary Fund and the European Common Market—have been remarkably successful. The Council of
Europe remains only an outline of an institution that may, in
time, achieve capacity for common action, establishing common
policies and action with regard to "economic, social, cultural,
scientific, legal and administrative matters and in the maintenance and further realization of human rights and fundamental
freedoms," but it remains chiefly an impotent, though useful,
discussion club.

Power in these "communities" is as much a fact of life as anywhere else. If strong enough, any member can decide to secede.
By threat, it may coerce its weaker associates into action it desires. All the same, these groupings have had a considerable
measure of success in subjecting the power of any one of its members to those decisions on which most of the members agree;
progress here has been substantial, though limited. In 1967, five
of the six members of the European Common Market would have
liked to admit Great Britain to its membership and privileges but
were unable to persuade and could not coerce Gaullist France

into agreeing. (There is some reason for belief that in time they will be successful in doing so, though the event is uncertain.) What can be said, realistically, is that operations of groups of states to achieve important though limited functional ends has proved more successful in the twentieth century than ever before. They have created areas of order and progress in fields and functions previously left to, and impeded by, purely nationalist struggles.

My conviction is that these instruments will grow in significance and scope. As the world shrinks, geographically, technically, and economically, some of them will expand, attaining within their fields institutional capacity to set up world order and world co-operation advantageous to all concerned. New communities will be formed with new functional objectives. In each such group, the member states have ceded to it a fragment of their nationalist power, and in many of them are finding it more advantageous to live with the pooled power than with the results of mere nationalist scramble for advantage. It could be that community groups of states offer a substitute for the naked power empires prevailing before World War II.

6. Order under a Rule of Law

Finally, we must coolly appraise the possibility of building a full-scale world-wide system of law equipped with adequate power institutions capable of guiding and governing national power holders and under whose rules order can be maintained and disputes adjusted. Were such an idea system generally accepted, it would be possible to build institutions and endow their administrators with power adequate to maintain peace and establish standards of social conduct for most of, if not all, the earth.

The dream is old, vital, and essential. During the eleven years of his secretaryship of State, the late Cordell Hull urged it in season and out. More recently, two eminent and brilliant Americans, Mr. Grenville Clark and Professor Louis Sohn, have argued elaborately and learnedly, first, that such a system is possible; second, that parts of it are already emerging; third, that with patient work it could become sufficiently accepted to serve as a basis for an institution or institutions of international power, possibly the United Nations. The conception is valid and logical. The problem is whether it has relation to reality. True, such a system was envisaged in a document drawn up for the United Nations; it is desperately called "The Revised General Act for the Pacific Settlement of International Disputes" (Resolution, General Assembly, 268 (III) A-p. 87). The International Court of Justice, brought into existence by Chapter XIV of the United Nations Charter contemplated such a world-wide legal system applying to international relations, to be interpreted and applied by it. And then came the lacuna.

Unless rules of law are enforcible and enforced, they are idle preachments. Nowhere in the United Nations Charter was adequate provision made for enforcement. The Security Council was to arrange for that. Its action can be blocked. It has wide authority, but its use is subject to "veto" by any one of the Council's five principal members. Actual enforcement—police action to keep peace or to require fulfillment of any decision by the International Court—must command the assent of all the Security Council's permanent members. And, in addition, these must provide the money and the force required. The Security Council may be bypassed by action taken by the United Nations Assembly under the famous "Uniting for Peace" resolution. But when this has been tried, nations that disagree or do not wish to contribute money or troops for enforcement simply have not done so. Enforcement in each case is a matter of negotiation between governments—and when that occurs we are back to the Machiavellian game again.

Worse yet, there is no present machinery for assuring immediate or preventive action. While the Security Council or the Assembly is debating a question, a small but determined force operation may create an irreversible situation. One nation may, for example, seize a weak country or close an essential trade route. Solemn pronouncement either in New York at the United

Nations Building or at the Peace Palace in The Hague (where the World Court sits) may have no effect whatever on the ground. If delayed, the pronouncements may be wholly useless. In any case, the "General act for the pacific settlement of international disputes" got no farther than referral to the members of the United Nations. Americans have to recall that the United States government has never accepted compulsory jurisdiction by the World Court; it reserves the right to accept jurisdiction in cases of its own choosing.

International law is still based, and continues to expand, chiefly on the principle of national sovereignty and the legal equality of nations. Professor Wolfgang Friedmann, after carefully canvassing the situation, comes sadly to the conclusion that the "only serious justification for any hope that the deeply divided and antagonistic nations and power blocs of the world may merge their powers and purposes into a universal organization equipped with more than a debating function, lies in the overwhelming threat of contemporary technological and scientific developments to the security, and indeed to the survival, of mankind." [9] Meanwhile, the sheer terror of nuclear warfare may induce the contending blocs to remain at arm's length and develop limited understandings, sufficient to permit live-and-let-live co-existence. This is a far cry from developing principles and institutions constituting a rule of law in the world.

Proponents of a universal system of law rarely face one of its cardinal realities. Power is an essential element. Power needs its institutions. Institutions need their idea systems. But idea systems are valid only when they are applied by institutions and— lacking almost unanimous acceptance—can be made effective only by power.

Nevertheless, though a universal system of law and power institutions making it effective seem far away, there are glimmers of light through the cloudy sky. One is the fact that institutions having power based on accepted law in fact are extending themselves over geographic regions that a few years ago were dan-

9. *Law in a Changing Society*, Berkeley, Calif., University of California Press, 1959, p. 479.

gerous cockpits of nationalistic government rivalries. The Common Market area of Western Europe appears to be one such. The American hemisphere is growing to be another. The systems of these two areas have been effective for only two decades. They appear, however, to be gaining strength. There have not been threats of war in Western Europe since the Berlin blockade of 1947. Interruptions of order in Latin America, notably in Cuba and in the Dominican Republic, did not arise from disputes between members of the Organization of American States. They arose out of the intrusion of an overseas imperial system—the Soviet Union—which sought to enter the hemisphere. Wars in both these regions had occurred with regularity until the close of World War II.

Prediction that there will be no more wars in these two areas may be overoptimistic. Yet, at present, none are in sight, and there is no basis for assuming they will emerge. Meanwhile, within its own sphere of influence, the Soviet Union and the nations associated with it in the Warsaw Pact for their mutual aid and defense have (except for the Soviet Union's bloody entrance into Hungary in 1956 and Czechoslovakia in 1968) been at peace. After the violent and bloody record in Balkan and Eastern European history before 1945, this is itself an achievement.

Here, therefore, are three regional areas slowly developing principles and rules, embodied in regional institutions, apparently able to mobilize power sufficient to maintain order. True, the element of power is contributed, in each of these cases, by the superpower in the region: in Latin America, by the United States; in Eastern Europe, by the Soviet Union; in Western Europe, originally by France, though at present Germany may be an equal contributing partner. But it is also true that the senior power holder in each region is supported by enough regional associates so that the result is co-operation.

After traveling through Italy, an American historian, Dean C. Mildred Thompson, of Vassar College, once made an observation. Most of that country had been chopped into tiny areas, each dominated by a fortified castle. These castles are now dead or in ruins. Their tiny fiefs have been aggregated into larger states.

Men simply could not live, Miss Thompson noted, under a system of tiny baronies, so the baronies disappeared into the larger, order-giving units. Italian unity is only a century old, and history moves more rapidly in the twentieth century than it did in the nineteenth, infinitely more rapidly than in the seventeenth or eighteenth. In another half-century the regional groups of today are likely to become as unviable as were the tiny Italian duchies and German principalities existing in 1848. Another fifty years is likely to see even great regional organizations pushed into larger order-maintaining institutions. Ultimately, the world community already outlined by communication seems certain to emerge.

Not now. Not yet. The forces bringing this about seem, to me, ineluctable. But it would be cruel and unreal to suggest that their work is on the verge of completion.

7. The Eternal Problem

Within the presently existing diverse and often conflicting idea systems, international affairs must be carried on. In the absence of any world government, and with only the shadowy outlines of effective world law, each conflict between states must be dealt with empirically. That means getting the best result possible, given the realities of the case, as each state calculates its national interest and seeks to establish it.

There is a general feeling that peace is usually preferable to war; this operates as a guiding principle in most cases, though by no means all. Unhappily, in every given situation there is only one certain prescription for peace. It is, quite simply, prompt surrender or nonresistance to the demands of the state prepared to use its force or go to war. Quite properly, there is also a general feeling (backed by considerable experience) that surrender as a peace-keeping means is more likely to lead to chaos than to order. Some conception of elementary justice—or at least of elementary tolerability—is essential, or else the temporary order resulting from mere nonresistance will not last long.

I vividly remember a visit to me by the late Jan Masaryk (then ambassador) just as Czechoslovakia was being torn to pieces at Munich in 1938. Concealing a pounding emotion beneath his usual brave mantle of ironic humor, he posed an unanswerable question. "Look here, Adolf," he said, "if the sacrifice and slaughter of my country were the way, and the only practical way, of assuring peace in the world, I would be terribly unhappy. Intellectually, all the same, I could bring myself to accept the hideous injustice. But do you really think dismemberment and probably the death of Czechoslovakia will get you peace?" It did not. Jan Masaryk's dramatic death in Prague ten years later at the hands of Stalin's agents was not the least of the losses flowing from that ghastly surrender to Hitler.

Surrender avoids immediate armed conflict, and that is all. It compromises and clouds the future, often leading to tomorrow's war. Values must prevail besides the naked principle that might has made its own right, and that force should not be resisted lest the result be war. Consensus, consequently, on a world philosophy that includes at least minimal viable standards of human rights and international justice must be present. Otherwise we are back at the old practice of nationalism, leading to empire, which, when inspired by messianism, may have unlimited and fearful impact.

IV

Is Empire Avoidable?

Preface

Empire is the classic institutional expression of national power extended to control other countries. The word has many meanings. All connote capacity by a strong power to dictate decisions to weaker nations. It may be limited to negatives: capacity to prohibit the weaker from certain uses of its territory by force. It may go further, allowing the stronger to set standards or norms for the institutions and government of the weaker. It may go to the length of determining who may be power holders in the lesser country. In ultimate expression, empire has meant direct government of the weaker by a stronger nation.

Twentieth-century debate has accepted its weakest definition—that is, it considers "empire" as capacity by one power to dictate decision in any field to some other country or countries. This definition is vulgarization of a Leninist formula; it accounts for the familiar description of the United States, and indeed all strong non-Communist powers, as "imperialist." Obviously, it applies with equal force to Communist empires as well.

"Empire" and "imperialism" are currently condemned by the words and perhaps thinking of most contemporary politicians, commentators, and intellectuals, Communist and non-Communist alike. Leaving aside a value judgment, I raise a more acute question. Absent an effective world government, which certainly does not now exist, is empire avoidable?

I am unhappy at some of the conclusions reached in this chapter. That does not release me, as a student, from obligation to state them. In international analysis, blinking reality is inexcusable.

1. The Mirage of Mastery

Americans in Europe during the summer of 1967 found themselves in a strange atmosphere. They were dealt with, somewhat dubiously, as citizens of a country considered to be a purposeful master of the world—a picture of the United States unrecognizable to its inhabitants.

This was one aftermath of the Middle East crisis of June, 1967. The Arab states had then brought to a head their quarrel with the resented State of Israel. The American Sixth Fleet maintained its more or less permanent station in the eastern Mediterranean, and an American warship was dispatched through the Suez Canal to the entrance of the Gulf of Aqaba, at whose head lies Israel's Red Sea port, then under Egyptian blockade. The Soviet Union had contributed a billion dollars' worth of arms to the Arab forces; its commitment was unclear, but its diplomacy supported the Arab cause. Included in its propaganda strategy was the projection of Israel as an armed outpost of United States force and agent of that country's imperial designs. A Soviet flotilla (outgunned, it is true, by the American) steamed through the Bosporus and Dardanelles, and deployed off the Egyptian coast. The Secretary-General of the United Nations, Mr. U Thant, received and hastily complied with a peremptory Egyptian demand that he withdraw the token United Nations peace-keeping force from the Gaza Strip. It was immediately replaced by an Egyptian army. Gamal Abdel Nasser proclaimed his purpose to wipe Israel off the Near Eastern map. Israeli columns moved against and defeated the Egyptians at once, while its air force destroyed the Egyptian warplanes before they got off the ground.

Dramatic as it was, the Arab-Israeli war was overshadowed by belief that a far greater crisis was brewing. If the Soviet Union followed its hand, if it used its ships or landed forces to assist the Arabs, would the United States respond by entering the war on the Israeli side? Mastery of the region came close to carrying with it domination of half the world. The two superpowers were in direct confrontation.

The American President, Lyndon B. Johnson, and the Soviet Prime Minister, Chairman A. N. Kosygin, promptly communicated by the "hot-line" Moscow-Washington telephone. The result was an understanding that neither would enter the hostilities. The Six-Day War produced a decision for Israel and its uninterrupted advance to the banks of Suez. Neither of the world's two superpowers moved.

To many Europeans (Monsieur Raymond Aron dissenting), this was culminating proof of American mastery, of that country's tenure of a variety of world empire believable to few Americans. The European reasoning was simple. In 1962, the Soviet Union had attempted to move in Cuba; it had been compelled to withdraw its missiles when confronted with American force by President John F. Kennedy. Working with China, the Soviet Union had attempted to take over South Vietnam. In 1963, President Kennedy, followed in turn and more forcefully by President Johnson, interposed American force, preventing the operation's success. American naval force plus U.S. military potential and diplomacy in 1967 prevented the Soviet Union from throwing its weight into the Arab-Israeli war and establishing primacy in the European-Asian-African land bridge. On a world scale, therefore, Washington was credited with having inhibited expansion of the Communist empires in three crucial and widely separated areas—Southeast Asia, the Caribbean, and the eastern Mediterranean. Paris newspapers were asking whether American world supremacy was myth or reality, more than one commentator concluding that it was real.

The historical correctness of the foregoing account is certainly open to question. I do not underwrite it. Ascription of the results (for good or evil) entirely to American determination and force is likely to prove both inaccurate and unjust to the power holders in the Communist empires, notably the Soviet Union. Good sense, fear, desire to avoid war, instinct for an orderly world certainly exist in Moscow, and possibly even in disturbed Peking, as well as in Washington. Yet in these matters other men's conclusions and illusions are themselves operative facts. A good part of the intellectual world in most countries did believe that the results, especially in the eastern Mediterranean crisis of 1967, were imposed by American power. An image was being constructed of a United States policing the world and, through power, dictating the decisions of even its greatest rivals. Mirage-like, the figure of a world-dominant America seemed to materialize. It excited a predictable combination of fear, respect, suspicion, admiration, envy, apprehension, dislike. It also evoked a measure of grudging thankfulness that power was there, could guide events, and, everything considered, could perhaps keep chaos at bay. True or false, the impression spread that the United States had become a functioning world empire.

2. What Is Empire?

"Empire" may be variously defined. As used in mid-twentieth-century discussion, it means in its most attenuated sense capacity by one country to compel major policy decisions of weaker nations. Such power may be extended to choose the power holders, dictate the forms of government and institutions, or, in ultimates, directly govern other nations or areas. Prime requisites are that the imperial nation has the will and, when necessary, the capacity to threaten or deliver coercive military force outside its borders. Granted the will and the capacity, mere existence of such force usually will be sufficient to impose an imperial will. An important but far weaker instrument is economic power—capacity to give to or withhold from others needed products or capital, or to open or close markets or trade routes to them. Though economic power can substantially affect decisions and attitudes in another country, by itself it is rarely adequate; most decision-making power remains within the capacity of the other country involved, if it feels strongly on the subject. The economic condition of an imperial country is of importance principally because it can give capacity to maintain force and support its delivery and use in one form or another.

There have been times when force could be organized and employed against another by a country having relatively small economic resources. Some of the greatest world empires were built when force could be cheaply delivered by relatively small and economically weak countries. The naval empires—typical from the sixteenth to the nineteenth centuries—are illustrations. Queen Elizabeth's England was far from impressive in population or in economic strength. But sailing ships were not expensive, the number of men needed to run them was small, and target areas often lay along coasts. A few capable and determined naval captains, commanding ships with a moderate degree of firepower and carrying handfuls of tough fighting men, were all that were needed to dominate great and weakly organized areas of the period. In that world, even small seafaring nations could compete for empire. Vandal fleets and Scandinavian raiders proved that in the early centuries of the Christian era. After them, Venice, Portugal, and the Netherlands, as well as Spain, France, and England, set up empires governing much of the earth's surface. Until about 1890, when battleships became intricate and increasingly expensive machines, sea power was within the grasp of the people of any maritime country with a coastline.

Land armies, to the contrary, are an expensive and ponderous means of force delivery. In earlier eras they could sometimes be developed on a relatively economical base; the Tartar and Mongol forces of Genghis Khan and, later, Tamerlane were not especially numerous, but, cavalry-borne, they were fast-moving and able to live off the countries they invaded. Up to a point they were able to substitute rapidity of movement for numbers. Even so, to hold their conquests required continuous recruiting, supply, and maintenance of growing numbers. This may explain why these empires were relatively transient.

Long-range delivery of modern force, on the other hand, is extremely expensive. Air-borne soldiers must be reinforced with surface-transported supplies or troops. Even more, air and airborne forces require an enormous manufacturing and logistic base to put and keep planes in the air. The same is true of modern navies. Rocket missile systems—the current method of force—are very costly indeed; they require huge expenditures—or, to put it differently, huge diversion of national product—to make, mount, and guide them. But they have a major defect: they do not deliver men in large numbers. The winner (if there could be one) of a rocket battle could do little but contemplate the destruction it had accomplished.

There is another method of delivering force at long range, sometimes described by the misleading name of "ideological warfare." It consists of capacity to induce men in other countries, by securing their fanatic loyalty to an idea system, to use force at the direction of the imperial country; to kill and risk death in obedience to orders given from outside. Such men develop terrorism into guerrilla force. The method has been used in Southeast Asia and Latin America. Establishing apparatus for force delivery in this manner takes time, requires high organization, depends on communication (technologically provided by radio), on supply of arms and money, and on the tensile strength of the idea system. But the process does not impose undue economic burdens on the applying country. The method perhaps reached maximum effectiveness about 1965; defenses to it may well render it unimpressive in another few years. In the sixteenth century, Catholic Counter-Reformation propaganda, directed and fostered by the Spain of Philip II, used this tactic; it proved formidable until the religious wars came to an end. After the Peace of Westphalia, in 1648, and acceptance of the principle of peaceful coexistence of princes' religions, its use faded out. My surmise is that the effectiveness of ideological "liberation" tactics from 1945 to 1965 will not be paralleled from 1965 to 1985.

Large countries with high technological development can develop and deliver force, however expensive, because they alone have large enough population and economic strength to recruit, organize, transport, and deploy munitions and land armies, supporting them with naval, air, and missile power. The United States was uniquely successful in doing this on an intercontinental scale in World War II. Such delivery and ensuing land occupation in fact is the only really effective method of force use for any period of time. Unlike warships, warplanes, and rockets, armies can occupy substantial areas. Their occupations can last for substantial, sometimes long, periods. Twentieth-century civilization, nevertheless, has conspired to raise immensely the cost of such power application, and thereby to cut down the number of possible aspirants for empire. Ability to evolve, maintain, and apply it on a large scale is limited to a few countries whose population and economic resources are great, and whose ability to organize is outstanding.

For practical purposes, capacity for widespread empire is presently limited to two great powers—the Soviet Union and the United States—though several potential aspirants are capable of developing it in a few decades or less: a unified Western Europe, continental China, Japan, a unified India, and Brazil. Lesser countries may (unless superior powers interfere) attain a measure of empire in their immediate vicinity.

Potentiality for empire, of course, is far from being empire itself.

There must be not only the capacity to develop power, but also the will to expend the treasure and blood of the country to apply it. This presents questions. Why empire at all? Why has it been so persistent a phenomenon in world history? For persistent it is. Never at any time in world history—on the smaller geography of antiquity or the planetary scale of the twentieth century—has it not been present.

I suggest that something more than mere wrongheadedness is the cause.

3. The Logic of Empire

A. DEFENSE

The primal reason for empire is fear of a rival empire capable of being a vital threat.

Temptation must be avoided to go into the endless drama of history. One may note, casually, that one reason for Rome's wars against Carthage was black fear on the Tiber lest Carthage take weakly held adjacent territory and endanger Rome itself. In the first Carthaginian war, for example, one of the Samnite states in the region of Naples proposed to maintain its "neutrality"—another way of saying that it might be conquered by or choose to become an ally of Rome's principal military competitor. (Pompeii, known to every American tourist, was a part of that state. Roman concern lest it fall into hostile hands was not wholly unreasonable.) Before World War I, governments in St. Petersburg, Vienna, Paris, and Berlin never ceased cogitating what might happen to their peoples if the weak areas between and adjoining them were occupied by their rivals. Between the two world wars, an aggressive Fascist Italy, pushing into the Balkans and expanding in the Mediterranean, demonstrated that concern was justified. Presently, Mussolini's policy was imitated, then surpassed, by the still more aggressive Nazi state Hitler set up in Germany. Properly fearing for the safety of his own country,

Stalin tried to buy off Hitler by ceding him half of Poland, Stalin occupying the other half for the Soviet Union. Simultaneously, he annexed the three independent bordering Baltic states of Latvia, Lithuania, and Estonia. A cardinal reason for seeking empire is to deny to possible enemies control of regions capable of becoming a military threat.

The United States experienced the emotion when in 1959 the Soviet Union via Cuba unexpectedly made its appearance in the Caribbean Sea. This is an area from which the United States can be threatened. So long as no country in the Caribbean is or is likely to become ally or tool of a hostile expansionist empire, there is scant reason for the United States to control its decisions. But when, by the end of 1960, it was clear that Cuba had come into the Moscow orbit, the reaction was, first, the ill-fated Bay of Pigs adventure and, a year and a half later, direct force confrontation with Moscow in the missile crisis. When it was thought in 1965 that the Moscow-Cuba combination might expand into the Dominican Republic (as it avowedly hoped to do), the United States occupied that country; then, having dispelled the threat, withdrew. Illustrations could be multiplied. It is enough to say that the first and least avoidable reason for empire arises when one strong power believes another strong power proposes to take control of an area vital to its safety.

Weak or chaotic countries lying near any strong power commonly do present this danger. If the adjacent power does not control events, some other power may. Repeatedly, such areas have proved temptation to imperial operations. The breakup of nineteenth-century empires after World Wars I and II saw great areas released from previous imperial or colonial control. Too often their governments were unstable, or quarrels among them tended toward chaos. That condition is now marked in the eastern Mediterranean; currently, Israel alone excepted, no stable, well-defended government exists in the huge subcontinent lying between the Persian Gulf and the Sudan, between the Mediterranean Sea and the Gulf of Aden. Absent some order-producing power solution such as world government or world consortium, this is a classic condition engendering imperial adventure.

B. MESSIANIC CONVERSION

Messianism—a mission to save the world—is a second historically familiar impetus toward empire. The theme has repeated itself in history, from Mohammed to the present. Saving the souls or improving the lot of other peoples, combined with development of its own effective power, seems to attract most nations at one time or another. The United States is not excluded. In the nineteenth century, "manifest destiny" had a content of messianism. In 1898, Americans felt impelled to save colonial Cuba from the cruelties of a Spanish regime. In 1917, President Woodrow Wilson felt called on to make a world "safe for democracy." From 1917 on, Lenin and Stalin proclaimed, and their adherents believed, that the Soviet Union had a holy mission to bring about world revolution, liberating the world from nineteenth-century capitalism. The United States, from 1950 on, with lesser intensity, developed a yearning to save "underdeveloped" countries from economic misery by spreading the benefits of modern productive technique.

Pragmatically, a messianic power frequently can (certainly according to its own standards) better the lot of the people whose souls, bodies, institutions, or economy it wishes to save or improve. The nineteenth-century British colonialism balance sheet would probably show that, physically and economically at least, most "natives" fared better under British colonial rule than under their previous chieftains—better, in many cases, than under their own politicians after they achieved independence. Despite current criticism, American foreign aid to underdeveloped countries has been of material assistance and advantage to the populations of those nations, while its educators and technicians have directly benefited many and have offered opportunity to more. But one must always reckon with the formula of Arnold Toynbee: once introduced, any spearhead of an alien culture or social system into a foreign area tends to draw after it an ever greater content of the culture of the sending agent. Unless the two cultures are already commensurate and capable of easy interaction, the result is a clash. The sending power, in any case, favors the agents, official or unofficial, of its own line of thinking and its own material methods; the receiving country resents invasion of its habits. The political sequel may well be an endeavor by the sender to influence and perhaps control the thinking and methods of social organization of the receiving country.

In extreme cases (for example, the mission to organize another country as a Communist state), attempt to exercise political control necessarily follows. To be valid, the resulting government (in the eyes of the sending power) must be "pro-Russian," "pro-American," "pro-French," "pro-Chinese," as the case may be.

C. "A PLACE IN THE SUN"

There is a third, and odd, motive for empire also constant in history. This is the consciousness by the asserting nation of its superiority, engendering self-esteem and a conviction that it is entitled to "a place in the sun." Hohenzollern Germany certainly had that feeling; Nazi Germany had it in exaggerated form. Those familiar with present-day China are unanimous in their testimony that most Chinese feel an inherent superiority about their own culture and qualities. Certainly most, if not all, Chinese, wherever found, feel that the Chinese nation or race is entitled to a position in affairs comparable to that of any other world power. When Chinese armies in the Korean War effectively mounted a successful countercampaign against Americans after the Yalu River was reached, Chinese everywhere—even those opposed to the regime of Mao Tse-tung—got a vast lift from the spectacle of a China capable of asserting itself against one of the greatest of world powers. A generation earlier, Imperial Japan had boosted the self-esteem of every Japanese when it sank a Russian fleet, defeated a Czarist army at Mukden, conquered Manchuria, and established itself as a major Pacific power.

D. ECONOMIC DETERMINISM

The weakest reason for empire, at least in the present generation, is the much-discussed "economic determinism." A nation, it was believed until recently, would automatically move to control areas that provided sources of raw material, afforded large returns on capital investment, or dominated important trade routes. Marxists and Western liberals agreed on the doctrine. Powerful these motives certainly were, notably in the seventeenth, eighteenth, and nineteenth centuries. They are still present, but I believe they have lost much of their earlier force.

Raw materials, though still important, are available by ordinary purchase from so many quarters that their acquisition as a rule need not be assured by conquest or domination of the country of their origin. Many previously "vital" supplies required from abroad are being superseded as modern technology increasingly permits locally produced synthetic substitutes. Modern manufacturers and capitalists no longer find attractive markets in underdeveloped countries. To the contrary, governments of underdeveloped countries today press for, even demand, markets in the more powerful, populous, and developed nations for the materials they produce.

Even trade routes (whose geographic persistence in history is amazing) are becoming significantly less important as technology improves. Cutting the Suez Canal would have had far greater effect in 1910 than did its closing in 1967. The oil trade, at present, finds it cheaper to build and transport petroleum in huge tankers too large to transit the Suez; economies in building and operating the large ships more than outbalance the costs of the long voyage around the Cape of Good Hope. The appearance, already imminent, of huge airplanes and the explosion of the volume of air freight are likely to diminish still further the economic importance of old "lifelines of trade."

Capital still seeks to find areas of high return. To some extent it can do so in northern and central Africa or South America, but the stakes no longer seem important enough to call in the armed forces of the country from which it comes to assure either access to the areas or protection once it is there. Economic influence is still present, still appreciable, and, in some cases, still important. But of the four main impulses toward empire—defense, sacred mission, national esteem, and economic advantage—economic impulses are now the weakest.

4. Forms of Empire

Given the presently existing impulses toward empire, what are the effects?

Ultimate expression of empire leads to conquest in the case of populated countries; and the "population explosion" steadily lessens the number of unpopulated areas. British conquest of India, first by the East India Company and later by the British government, could occur only because "India" at the time of take-over did not exist.[1] It was a geographic conglomeration of greater and lesser states, sultanates, kingdoms, principalities, even tribal areas. The administrative unity of India and even its one common language (English) were the result of the conquest. Once the region was united, it was presently clear that no handful of Britons, however high-minded, devoted, capable of organization, and measurably altruist to a considerable degree (as, contrary to some critics, so many of them were) could maintain sway in a country of 550 millions (present Pakistan included). The required commitment of force would be immense; the cost would be astronomic; the political task would be impossible.

In empty or sparsely settled countries, the trick can be turned. Take-over there can frequently be effected with limited force. Unhappily, unless the population finds the take-over acceptable and is prepared to become a fragment of the taking country, re-

1. "India" as a united nation first appeared in history as signatory to the "Declaration by United Nations," executed at Washington on January 1, 1942.

sults have to be attained by straight colonizing—that is, by exporting population from the imperial power. Bloody conflicts can rarely be avoided; but in thinly settled countries they can be won. Savagely, logic suggests ultimate mastery by genocide, mass expulsion, or through complete capitulation of the natives and their acceptance of a servile or subject state. This is what has sometimes happened even in mid-twentieth-century operations. At the close of World War II, the Soviet Union decided to push Poland westward to the Oder-Neisse line, deep in Germany—an operation accomplished in 1945 by Soviet troops. Much of the area's population was German. These were systematically uprooted and thrust by Stalin's armies into eastern or western Germany. Hardly a German now remains in that area; it is almost purely Polish. The Turkish Empire under Sultan Abdul-Hamid had followed the policy in the first decade of the twentieth century—though he was more given to massacre than expulsion—in the Armenian areas of eastern Turkey. Nascent Israel found it expedient to expel all the Arabs from the tiny state as late as 1950—though it is fair to add that the policy of the surrounding Arab states almost compelled the step if Israel were to survive.

Domination, colonization, and even annexation without such extreme measures obviously can and does take place; but only where the local population either is negligible in number or can be readily assimilated, brought into alliance, or reduced to complaisant acquiescence. The later-twentieth-century world has found it increasingly difficult to achieve the latter.

A weaker form of empire is the establishment of a system of "client" governments. This was indeed the normal method of empire-building up to the end of feudal or personal governments. If a local chieftain, duke, king, rajah, pasha, or sultan could secure his throne by agreement with an imperial power—which included his compliance with its chief desires—he would do so. Because he knew more about governing his people than the imperial power, he was useful to it. Because he kept his own privileged position, the arrangement was useful to him. The King of Pergamum, having (with the aid of Rhodes) successfully got the Romans involved against the Seleucid Empire in Asia Minor, presently discovered that he was *persona non grata* in Rome. His successors, accepting the power reality, became client kings, and finally bequeathed the kingdom to Rome's direct government. But we need not dive into ancient history. Marshal L. H. G. Lyautey's conquest of Morocco for France was directly due to his skill in backing one of the three or four contending dynastic pashas who perennially struggled for power in the country, leaving him to dispose of his (and France's) opponents, as he promptly did. The British followed a similar policy in the weak princely states in India and on its borders.

Client governments are all very well as imperial instruments if they stay "client." Yet there never was, perhaps never will be, a client king, chieftain, or government who did not harbor a desire to tell the patron nation, "Get out," leaving freedom of decision to the local power holder. The desire comes to the surface whenever the imperial government is under attack or stress. Then, the client government endeavors to maneuver. If it guesses right and maneuvers cleverly, it may achieve, at least for a period of time, substantial independence in decision-making, though in the end (as did Pergamum) it may find that it has only changed masters.

Less restrictive, because it leaves more decision-making freedom to both sides, is a system of alliances. At this stage, the difficulty of avoiding empire becomes obvious.

A small or relatively weak state adjacent to a larger powerful country finds its decisions restricted in any event. It cannot, for example, ally with an enemy of its neighbor without risking or indeed expecting military or other reaction. Realistically, its only choice is between inoffensiveness to or alliance with the adjacent power. Its power holders know perfectly well that the neighbor cannot accept a substantial threat to its own safety; it must act whether it enjoys the process or not. If the weaker country also desires market trade or other advantages from the nearby power, it must at least maintain a state of affairs not dangerous to its greater associate. To secure full co-operation, it must become in fact, if not in name, an ally. The oldest and weakest form of empire is a system of alliances, formal or informal, by which neighboring countries, in greater or less measure, contribute to the strength of, or certainly forgo hostility to, the more powerful state.

Canada, sturdily independent as it is, knows quite well that it can scarcely enter into military arrangements with the Soviet Union that might threaten the northern border of the United States. In case of conflict, the United States would have no choice but to take measures excluding Soviet force (however applied) from the region. At this point, in the absence of world government, the inevitability of some version of empire becomes apparent. The United States, whether it wishes to or not, cannot be indifferent to Canadian decisions—or, for that matter, to Caribbean or Mexican decisions—when ultimates are concerned. If stress or threat is extreme, it must inhibit decisions by the nearby countries that threaten its own safety. Politicians in these countries talk about preserving the "independence" of their governments, perhaps not without reason. But if "independence" is construed as freedom to assume positions or favor interests directly hostile to the United States, they have also to assume that the United States will act to protect itself. Ireland, for example, could not undertake to enter into a military alliance with a country whose objective was to destroy Great Britain—and it had the good sense not to do so during World War II. A Cuban government that in 1960 had assumed a position bitterly hostile to the United States (Fidel Castro once talked of dictating "peace" in the White House!) and had invited Soviet troops to the island was wholly unrealistic in expecting that President John F. Kennedy would not react.

The loosest, most transient, but sometimes most effective form of empire is ideological conquest.

If power holders in a nation are convinced (or act as though they were) that their countries should be governed according to the rules of some doctrine dictated from another country, the immediate results are somewhat the same as making it a client government. Stalin succeeded, chiefly by force, it is true, in setting up a series of Communist governments in mid-Europe between the Soviet Union and the Western powers. Thereafter, Moscow claimed the position of "elder brother" in the Communist world and arbiter of the Communist faith. Communist solidarity, while it lasted (from 1945 to the fall of Khrushchev), assured common action. Communist international conferences laid down doctrine; the Soviet dictatorship delivered orders to other Communist countries; their governments acquiesced. The monolith began to weaken with the defection of Yugoslavia and the later, far greater, defection of China. Currently, Rumania, Czechoslovakia, and, to some extent perhaps, Poland tend not to follow the "big brother" lead. Yet for nearly fifteen years, the decisions of the Iron Curtain countries could be dictated in Moscow—and in substantial measure are still so dictated, though Moscow's power to do so seems to be diminishing. At least so far as decisions with respect to Israel are concerned, Gamal Abdel Nasser succeeded in achieving a variety of Pan-Arab ideological empire capable of establishing, at least temporarily, norms of common action. He translated them into mobilization of the forces of most Arab states against Israel in June, 1967. He held the combination together even after defeat of the Arab forces in the Six-Day War.

Ideological conquest, as noted, is apt to be transient. While it exists, nevertheless, it is a force to be reckoned with. It can, within limits, determine and bring about decisions by subject states in accord with or in support of the plan of the ideological leaders.

Again, there is the problem of inevitability. It is not easy for a large and successful country to avoid affirmation of confidence in the ideological system on which its internal power is built. Americans, for example, do have a conviction that their own methods of organized freedom are, on the whole, good. (I except the so-called American "New Left," which proclaims that the system is hopeless; but even they manifest a pathetic confidence that the American system will guarantee their own freedom and their rights of expression and provide for their support.) Most Americans, and certainly representatives of its organized activities, governmental and private, take for granted—and set high store by—the values of American democracy and the apparent evolutionary capacity of its social economics. In a sense, most Americans are missionaries for their idea system, and would like to see it regnant throughout the world. Messianic regimes like the Soviet Union's and China's not only believe in the superiority of their idea system, but also systematically support propaganda, political adherents, and political, and in some cases paramilitary, action looking toward its introduction in most parts of the world.

Can smaller countries, especially if their social organization is not too effective, avoid being drawn into the orbit of one or another of the clashing ideologies calling for action in the mid-twentieth-century world?

5. The Imperialism of Capital

Export of capital by a strong country to a weaker country presents a problem of relations yet unsolved.

Weak and poor countries—not to mention many strong and developed ones—inescapably want foreign capital. Justifiably, they wish to increase their own production. Their businessmen need capital both to expand their enterprises and to gain more profits. Socialist countries wish to develop their natural resources and increase their supply of plants, machinery, and equipment. Unable in earlier stages to process their own raw materials, to manufacture their own machinery, or to produce consumer goods, underdeveloped countries must buy capital goods from abroad.

Highly developed countries—notably the United States—can accumulate surplus capital and can export money, exchangeable for capital goods they can produce beyond their own requirements. To these, other countries have recourse. They try to borrow against their promise to pay interest regularly and eventually to repay their loans. Or they seek "investment"—asking foreigners to buy and operate mines, factories, plants, and the like in their countries, producing, selling, and making profits there.

The twentieth century has seen a refinement. The United States, beginning tentatively with the Good Neighbor policy in Latin America in 1933 and following it, after World War II, with regular foreign-aid programs, developed a policy of making limited gifts of capital to countries appearing in need. By persuasion or example, it has induced other powerful countries to do the same. Demand for gifts of capital is now a regular occurrence in the foreign offices of all powerful and economically developed nations, including those of small but wealthy nations.

Yet the wishes of capital-seeking countries are not unaccompanied by fear of the result if their wishes are fulfilled. When capital flows from one country to another, it produces either or usually both of two effects. Its influx is almost inevitably accompanied by the growth of influence of the financiers, supervisors, and technicians of the sending country. If it takes the form of buying ownership of enterprise, the receiving country's economy becomes the property of and operations in it are directed by foreigners. Dread arises that in receiving foreign capital, aliens will become masters in the economic house of the recipient. Need of and desire for capital obtainable from abroad and for the productivity it can bring squarely conflict with desire to avoid growing economic domination by the sending country.

This phenomenon has been encountered in the Western Hemisphere from Buenos Aires to the Arctic Circle. Take, for example, Canada, a highly developed, well-governed, thoroughly efficient country whose civilization equals the highest in the world, as it splendidly demonstrated in its famous world's fair, Expo '67. The Canadian dilemma is basically due to geography. A population of 21,000,000 inhabits a land area larger than that of either European Russia or the continental United States; territorially, it is, in fact, the second-largest country in the world. Its proved mineral and other natural resources are enormous, though exploration is far from complete. Its problem is that of development, which fairly cries out for capital in amounts larger than Canada can presently accumulate. It has, heretofore, sought and found it in its friendly neighbor, the United States. Commercially, the results have been satisfactory to both. Canadian development has gone on apace, Canadian production has steadily increased, Canadian standards of living have risen. But, increasingly, its manufacturing concerns are coming to be subsidiaries of large

American corporations, or joint ventures in which U.S. capitalists have a preponderant share. Growing amounts of commercial loans and bond issues have been floated in the United States. In the past few years, there has arisen a dread of finding Americans the true owners of Canada. Naturally, it reflects itself in Canadian political attitudes. May not the "independence" of Canada be endangered?

The Canadian example is striking because Canadian civilization is in as good position to maintain and defend itself in all respects other than military as any country in the world. One need not be surprised that tension of the kind existing between the United States and Canada becomes infinitely greater when American capital is sought by and flows into a less-developed country— say, Chile or Venezuela—and that it rises to boiling point in Arabian countries, where foreign capital is responsible for most of their significant economic life. There, one element only need be added: the propensity of other powers to stir up resentment. Competing capital-export countries want the business. Communist dogma and propaganda assume and assert that introduction of foreign capital is merely a stage leading toward subjection of the receiving country to the exporting country. Export of capital is "imperialism," asserts Communist doctrine; consequently, foreign ownership should be seized and foreign debt repudiated. Even gifts from foreigners, it is claimed, must be considered as an entering wedge of imperialist designs.

The difficulties are clear enough. Obviously, Canada could prohibit further entry of American capital, could refuse its people permission to borrow, could outlaw foreign ownership of its enterprises or foreign stockholdings in them. This might eliminate the influence accompanying influx of foreign capital. But it would cut down development of resources and growth of production. It would prevent American directors sitting in board rooms or corporation headquarters in Chicago or New York from exercising the economic power of administration over Canadian enterprises. But there would be fewer Canadian enterprises, less production, less rise in the standard of living.

Even countries like the Soviet Union, which did expropriate

foreign enterprises without compensation and repudiated all foreign-held debt, presently began to seek foreign capital in recondite forms. It bought foreign machinery on credit and bartered quotas of its own products deliverable in time installments to pay for foreign capital goods. Communist Cuba, having eliminated all foreign ownership of its enterprises and having repudiated all its debts, shops in Canada and Western Europe as well as in the Soviet Union for credit to buy the capital goods and current supplies it finds it must have.

The problem of capital flow from one nation to another is not readily eliminated—unless a nation is willing to develop only by accumulating its own capital. That means cutting down the consumption of its people, producing its own capital goods and a margin of goods that can be sold abroad and whose proceeds may be used for foreign machinery. To underdeveloped countries this means growth at a snail's pace—in a world whose developed countries are galloping. The more that foreign capital is excluded, the greater the disparity between those countries and their more advanced neighbors. Underdeveloped countries in the twentieth century face a bitter choice: take foreign capital in some form, accepting its implications, or risk remaining primitive indefinitely. Not even social revolution will eliminate that problem.

Gift capital obviously helps: there is no repayment obligation. But, especially in underdeveloped countries, it is not likely to be sufficient in amount. Further, the recipient wants and needs more than the mere purchasing power of the gift. To make it productive, there must be technical direction and experience available from outside and capacity to accumulate and compound the profit within the country. Foreigners, in other words, must set up and assist in executing any productive plan and leave most of the profit behind.

Capping the climax is the dependence of even the most powerful and most developed nations on receiving "incorporeal capital" in the form of technology and the fruits of scientific research from abroad. Western Europe in 1967 shuddered when it thought it discerned a growing "technological gap" between its highly mechanized countries and the United States. Concern went beyond the "brain drain" occasioned because European engineers, technicians, and scientists, lured by higher pay and opportunity, frequently emigrated to the United States. Enormous emphasis on research, in both pure and applied science, in the United States was thought to have given America a long and growing technological lead. Its capital had translated the knowledge into plants and machinery of ever-growing complexity and efficiency. The question is how to borrow or acquire advanced technology. The problem of concentration of "incorporeal capital" is rapidly becoming an issue greater than that of concentration of money capital or of physical capital goods.

These pages have recorded my own belief that economics does not engender power in its strongest forms. Many of the fears occasioned by influx of capital are unjustified, though by no means all. Yet the aggregated force of foreign capital in another country does exist. It may produce psychological crises like that examined in Canada. It may bring about financial crises, as where conditions prevent repayment of debts or throw foreign-exchange accounts out of balance. How to maintain technological balance—a degree of parity in technology and the resources of trained men—has yet to find adequate solution.

It is the weary problem: In the modern world can the hegemony of the most powerful economic nation be avoided in the territorial areas to which its surplus capital must flow?

6. Preservation and Self-Preservation

The cardinal question is whether empire can be avoided. Can great powers avoid drawing smaller adjacent states into their system? Can smaller states maintain themselves at all except in the orbit of one or other of the greater states? Lacking a world government in which all nation-states are part of a planetary system capable of preventing or reducing conflicts, is there an alternative to some imperial or quasi-imperial organization?

As matters stand, I am unable to say that I believe it possible to escape creation of, or entry into, empire in some form—at least until a minimally effective world government emerges.

To begin with large countries, can they avoid becoming empires? The governments of all of them are subject to one categorical imperative: they must maintain safety and choate order for their own people. They have no alternative. Failure to obey it means their prompt replacement. If chaos arises, the anarchic vacuum will presently be filled—either by new organization of that nation-state or by absorption of its wreckage into other nation-states.

Safeguarding the existence of a people and a nation calls for measures having effect beyond its borders. Weak nearby states can be seized by more powerful and more ambitious countries; this has to be prevented. Pressures are likely to grow more intense. Almost certainly within twenty-five years, many weak as well as all strong states will have atomic bombs and methods of delivering them. One would like to believe this particular threat could be avoided by world agreement, but it seems unlikely that any agreement effectively preventing proliferation of nuclear weapons will be acceptable. Technical improvement steadily makes these weapons cheaper and more available. A wave of messianism or even the madness of a weak local dictator could precipitate massive destruction. Clearly, the interest of countries in their own self-preservation must lead to increased, not lessened, concern with their neighbors' attitudes and affairs.

Occasionally, a small country equipoised between power systems may be able to maintain itself outside any system—as has Switzerland in Europe. Such cases will scarcely be typical. A few primitive civilizations in geographically, militarily, and strategically unimportant areas, needing little if any trade, may survive as anthropological museum pieces. Aside from these, small countries are forced by every current influence, military, economic, ideologic, into some sort of alignment. Nineteenth-century diplomatic agreements neutralizing, like those relating to Belgium before 1914, and demilitarizing areas have proved no guarantee of safety on land, in the air, or at sea. Because small nations are unable to defend themselves militarily, their defense necessarily devolves on greater powers. In case of conflict among these —will they, nill they—the weaker must join, or be joined to, one or other of the contending powers by alliance, appropriately acquiescent policy, or surrender, and their safety must abide the outcome of the struggle.

Geography and capacity permitting, certain groups of weaker states may join with each other, forming a single structure as one nation or a confederation of nations. Were Western Europe to do so, the area would become a truly independent superpower. Conceivably, in the power vacuum presently existing in the eastern Mediterranean and North Africa, an effectively independent Arab state might emerge. The continent of South America might sink its differences and unite. But this is not escape from empire; it is the organization of new empires.

So far as economic considerations determine affairs, economic existence is not, never has been, and never is likely to be "independent." Unless a country or group is so primitive that, like Australian bushmen or pygmy tribes in the African jungles, it neither wants nor needs intercourse or commerce with the outside world, it must live in some international economic system to survive. Small nations, even more than large, are dependent on the exchange of goods with others; they are rarely big enough to be self-sufficient. Of necessity, they must live in some organization of transport, commercial exchange, money and credit, common law and practice, to keep the lines open if their people are to live. Especially if highly populated, like the Netherlands, they find that membership in some such arrangement is essential to keep their population fed. Moreover, their interest requires these arrangements to be uninterrupted. A high degree of conformity must exist within any such system for it to work. Indeed, if governments do not formally enact such arrangements, merchants, carriers, exchange organizations, and financiers will themselves make them.

Even the greatest superpower is not "economically independent." Unlike smaller countries, it would be able to survive alone —but the sacrifice involved would be great. There is always a margin of necessary goods and necessary services—and, more recently, of scientific and technical thought—obtainable only from abroad and exacting a modicum of continuous exchange. Superpowers have considerable range for decision in these matters, but not full freedom. Smaller countries usually have far less. In the economic context in which they must live, a greater part must be made by others. Conformity with and acceptance of this is a fact of their lives, if not a condition of existence. Ultimately, the fact causes development of some sort of alliance, if it be membership only in marketing arrangements.

Behind all, there is a marked and discernible urge whose force cannot be denied. Countries, like power holders and most men, desire to have significance—to contribute to, participate and be important in, the stream of affairs. Isolation contravenes that primordial desire. Like men, therefore, nations seek an area with which they can communicate and in which their contributions can achieve significance.

In combination, the considerations come to a single result. Great nations are driven by motives of defense, of messianism, of economics, and even of common humanity to erect systems within which their weaker neighbors exist. Small nations by compulsion or desire find or are conscripted into, or need and seek position in, some system. At the center of any system there is at least one great power capable of organizing, supporting, defending, and maintaining it. Despite condemnation of empire, some form of it appears demonstrably unavoidable. The nations— Communist China, the Soviet Union—that lead in condemning empire are themselves the most active proponents of empire on their own terms—that is, expansion of their own ideologies and systems. Neither great nor small powers have free choice in the matter.

No wish is father to my thought in coming to this conclusion. It is the devastating answer thrown up at the end of every line of analysis. There will not be international chaos. Absent a world government, the great nations, to the extent of their capacity, will create some sort of order.

7. The "Good" Empire

Let us now clear our minds of semantic associations with a historical word. Nearly a century of thinking has conditioned many of us to believe that empire is inherently unjust, if not positively noxious. Especially in America, liberal thought has been trained to assume that in any form it is a process of exploiting inhabitants of other countries for the benefit of an imperial country; that it is invariably accompanied by economic exploitation of the weak by the strong; that, even where it produces approximate economic and even social justice for all concerned, it deprives the smaller countries of that experience in decision-making by which they develop; that while private enterprise exists and unless all productive property is in the hands of the "people"—that is, of governments—conflicts will exist in which strong nations invariably subjugate and exploit the weaker countries and peoples.

Readers perhaps will by now have escaped imprisonment by some of these clichés. Empires are not created for profit. Converting systems of property into systems of power does not remove economic conflicts. Delete all economic motive, indeed, and empires would still occur. No system has yet been devised depriving the strong of capacity to exploit the weak—but fear, rather than exploitation, propels nations to dominate their neighbors.

The content of empire, however, is not fixed. Its social and economic content can be what the participants in it choose. Imperial countries can be fair or even altruistic. They can accept any quality of institution in associated countries despite their factual capacity to dominate—up to the point where their safety is threatened. Within limits, they can make of any imperial organization what they wish. A Holland or a Belgium, a Nicaragua or a Chile, need not sacrifice its political, cultural, or social independence because it enters a common market. It may, and indeed should, achieve and enjoy a higher degree of political, economic, and cultural participation than if it were nonaligned. A

France or Germany may have power by direct military action to upset the governments of smaller neighbors—but either is less likely to do so when a combined system exists.

Caribbean governments and the capacity of their people to choose them are unlimited so long as they do not threaten the safety of the United States, though they are within the sphere of commercial and economic arrangements of the hemisphere. Co-operating Communist governments there are entirely conceivable, though they would have to forgo "independence" to make military arrangements hostile to the United States or designed to overturn or dominate the regimes of neighboring countries. Development of institutions and free choice of government can be respected within systems today called "empires"—as well as without them.

There probably are limits of action whose violation would not readily be tolerated. Were Mexico to enact a slave system, the problem presented to the United States (its stronger neighbor) and of the smaller Central American states (weaker) would be grave indeed. Were Venezuela to undertake the massacre of Jews or Negroes, it would be graver still. Fortunately, ideological standards are not often transgressed, though they came close to being so in the Dominican Republic during the dictatorship of the late Rafael Trujillo, and again in Cuba during the excesses of the class war of 1959–1962. (The United States has been condemned almost as much for not intervening to overthrow Trujillo, whose tyranny had—literally—commanded acceptance by the Dominican people, as it was berated for moving into that country in 1965 when a threat to Dominican and American safety second only to that of the Cuban missile crisis was directly presented.)

If my regrettably reached conclusion is right—that without world government some form of empire is unavoidable—the discussion must turn to content. What forms can it take? What results does it bring about? Whose standards and judgments are to control? What dialogue must exist between those affected by the system and those able to modify or change it within the ineluctable limits set by modern conditions? I am sure these questions can be so answered and these problems so solved as to provide conditions as nearly satisfactory to populations as can be reasonably expected.

It seems wholly unrealistic to refuse to accept the fact that there are a few large, populous, and highly developed countries whose command of military, economic, and technical resources gives them the capacity to conquer or dominate their neighbors. These must live in a world composed chiefly of smaller, weaker countries, of which there are more than a hundred and thirty. Empire may signify institutions for sensitive and intelligent co-operation quite as readily as for economic and social exploitation. Empire is as empire does. There is no ignoring the hydraulic pressures that force nations into systems, and the relative impossibility of escape from such systems, by either strong or weak. Equally, there is no reason to assume that the systems christened by current nomenclature as "imperial" need resemble older empires that have come and gone.

Until world government arrives, the need is to make the inevitable empires "good."

8. What of the United States?

This is not a book about current politics. Yet it is impossible to resist devoting a few lines to the position of the United States in world affairs. Such diversion is not without precedent. Machiavelli closed *The Prince* with an irrelevant but impassioned plea for unification of Italy and exclusion of the foreign powers that had made Renaissance Italy a cocking main.

The United States is manifestly one of the "polarizing centers" in a system christened in semantic attack by Communist opponents and some West European associates as "imperial." We have already examined the realities. Let us not quibble here about words. Readers of the foreign press, indigenous and American, are struck with the impression it gives of American presence, power, and capacity to determine events in great parts of the world.

(Wryly, one sometimes wishes the United States had the power and capacity attributed to it. Anyone working inside its government knows it does not have a fraction of it.)

Mythology, for example, asserts that the United States triggered "an attack" by Israel against Egypt in June, 1967, designed to set up Israel as its client government controlling the fate of the crucial land bridge between Europe, Asia, and Africa. The complete untruth of the myth is demonstrable. Factually, Israel did not attack; it carried out an effective resistance to an attack armed by the Soviet Union and organized, mounted, and announced by President Nasser. The United States diplomatically endeavored to fend off an armed clash between Israel and the Arab states and failed. The surface evidence suggests that the Soviet Empire may have been guilty of provoking the Egyptian attack. History may prove that Arab emotional fanaticism forced a situation contrary to the advice of the Moscow Foreign Office. Yet, as often happens, the propaganda myth becomes a reality in the thinking of peoples and therewith an element in the struggle for power position between the Soviet Empire, the Chinese Empire, and the United States.

The tentative standstill agreement reached between President Johnson and Chairman Kosygin in June, 1967, had only one effect: neither power entered the hostilities between Israel and the Arab states. Equally, neither renounced action in the region.

The armed conflict between the Arab states and Israel, though dramatic, was merely a surface event in a greater movement of forces. On conclusion of the fighting, Israel's position was strengthened, but the Arab countries were not destroyed. The Soviet Union solidified its diplomatic influence in the Arab crescent all the way from Iraq to Morocco and the Strait of Gibraltar. It used it to establish connections and bases giving it added military capacity in the Mediterranean, and is still doing so. Some American bases were expelled. France had already withdrawn from Algeria, Morocco, and Tunis. The only power presently preventing the Mediterranean Sea from becoming a Russian-Arab lake is the American Sixth Fleet, whose withdrawal Brezhnev, the First Secretary of the Soviet Communist party, had demanded shortly before the Israel affair, on the ground that it was an "obstacle to peace." The Mediterranean nations of Europe—Greece, Yugoslavia, Italy, France, Spain—have not combined, and without combination certainly have not the capacity to prevent Soviet expansion on the Mediterranean's south coast as far as Moscow wishes to push. The possibilities can only be surmised. J. H. Pirenne's demonstration of the effect of Mohammedan domination of that sea is pertinent. It pushed the power center of Europe northward, and in time caused the rise of Charlemagne and of Germanic power.

An American problem is posed by this situation. Can it safely abandon the Mediterranean to Soviet military power? Must it not choose between a withdrawal to the Western Hemisphere and a contest with the Soviet Union, carrying danger of world conflict? Italy, France, and (for practical purposes) Spain have been pushed by Arab nationalism out of North Africa, as in their time Western Europe and Britain pushed the Turkish Empire out of the same littoral. If the United States does not confront the Soviet Union by direct or indirect force, must it not by diplomacy make agreement with Moscow to determine the limits of respective spheres of influence or retreat to the Atlantic?

Any of these choices would materially change the position of the Western European nations. United, they might re-establish the imperial power of Western Europe prevailing before World War I. Divided, each of them must seek alliance with one or another of the superpowers. Their present military position is not strong. The Italian, Greek, and Spanish armed strengths are not impressive. Brave attitudes struck by France conceal the fact that its army amounts to about three divisions, and its naval establishment is not great. Temporarily, Britain's position is equivocal; after being ruled out of Europe by General de Gaulle, its ties are American. Meanwhile, the American-European alliance—the North Atlantic Treaty Organization—can be canceled after 1969; already it has been reduced to paper by the policy of Gaullist France. It is no longer a power factor. The result makes possible, if not certain, a long-range Mediterranean confrontation between Moscow and Washington in which Moscow will hold the principal force cards.

The Mediterranean situation is merely one of several similar circumstances forcing internal and external policy decisions on the president of the United States. He must make and defend them in the unceasing dialogue between presidential power and the Congress of the United States, the American electorate, and American public opinion. In that debate, the questions raised here—Is American "empire" avoidable? If unavoidable, what shall be its content?—are not theoretical, but concrete.

Certain minimal imperatives of decision at least appear unavoidable. Any American president and his government must take measures to assure that the safety and people of the United States are not threatened. The Soviet and Chinese empires are under similar imperative. All three, to the extent of their capacity, must prevent the intrusion of either of the others into certain geographical areas, whether the countries involved like it or not. Rightly, I think, the United States refused to intervene at the time of the Hungarian revolution of 1956, despite the poignant moral appeal of a people wishing to throw out a brutal regime imposed from the Russian side. The Soviet Union need not have forced a Communist regime on Hungary, but it could hardly tolerate a regime that might become a client government of its enemies. In its somewhat warped view, any non-Communist government would of necessity be a client of some power it regards as a potential enemy. The United States is in a similar position in the Caribbean. The declared ambitions of Cuba under Fidel Castro and the Soviet alliance make solid peace presently unattainable. This is not a question whether Cuba shall be "Communist"—Americans can readily accept a regime not based on private enterprise and private property—but whether it shall be a political, psychological, and military ally of a superpower whose propaganda up to now has proclaimed a messianic mission to overthrow any non-Communist government, and especially the United States, when possible—and in the process to subvert the neighboring governments in the Caribbean.

The power holder of any polarizing state thus must indulge the coolest, most basic, and least arguable calculations. Able foreign-affairs men know this and—unless they are prepared to risk war—respect the principle on which their opponents as well as they must act.

Geography used to set up fairly clear lines for a sphere of influence. These lines have been greatly blurred, first by the advent of aviation and air-borne striking power, and now by nuclear intercontinental ballistic rockets. I am less perturbed by these last than most; I think no calculation can ever justify any government in using them. (The situation is capable of technical change if and when defense systems are evolved giving rise to the belief that rockets and nuclear bombs can be used offensively while the reply can be blocked. That time has not—may never—come.) Air-borne striking force is a factor. But it is relatively ineffective except as an adjunct to naval and land forces. By itself, it has been overrated. (This is one lesson of the Vietnam war.) Indistinct but still more or less determinable geographic spheres surrounding each superpower can be discerned, though their limits are open to question.

The minimum need in these areas is to deny the countries constituting them the privilege to decide to enter a combination hostile to their central superpowers. To that extent, superpowers must control certain decisions of the countries within their spheres, though outside their borders. Similarly, the superpower is almost constrained to compel peace within this sphere lest a hostile power mix into local rivalries. These were the real issues in the Cuban missile crisis of 1962 and the Dominican crisis of 1965—issues not yet wholly determined.

If "empire" consists in capacity to compel or inhibit certain decisions by countries within the area, there it is, and little can be done about it. As noted, this form of empire may be co-operative, rather than despotic; the interests of all members of the area are or should be the same. But there is always the danger of a megalomaniac—a Hitler, a Castro, a Guevara—a fanatic, or a dogmatic messianist power holder to whom the rational interests of his people (or even of himself) seem irrelevant. To this extent, the United States, like the Soviet Union, has to accept a power position, whether or not called "imperial." Neither has real freedom of choice.

Spheres of influence automatically emerge from this reasoning. It was, as Professor Arthur Schlesinger, Jr., has pointed out, the hope of Franklin Roosevelt, Cordell Hull, Sumner Welles, and myself to avoid exactly this, as World War II approached its end. No power in the world has desired an imperial position less than the United States; none desires it less today. Its refusal to institute such a system at the close of World War II was based on the hope that the Soviet Union would support the United Nations, developing it as an elementary form of world government. Stalin, keeping his counsel, though assenting to the conception of the United Nations, undertook to build his own spheres of influence by occupying the countries and determining the governments of the mid-European states, and later sought to expand them to include Greece and the Dardanelles. In fairness, it should be added that the United States never renounced its power position in the Caribbean and, to a lesser extent, in Latin America and the Western Pacific.

One would like to think that agreement will be reached on nuclear disarmament (but must not let wish control). I believe that in time either this will come or technical development will make it unnecessary. Neither, unhappily, is a present likelihood. When it does come, its effect will be to increase the range of decision by smaller countries to enter or leave the orbit of some superpower. Increased co-operative arrangements for world marketing and world sharing of essential supplies (for example, petroleum) should reduce dangers resulting from the individual decisions of any government, and chip away at the desirability of spheres of influence constructed merely for economic purposes. More accurately, they already begin to foreshadow a world economic system in which mere economic spheres of influence would become irrelevant. In this field far greater progress already has been made than in the military context. As matters are running, a half-century from now quite likely will see two areas in which an equivalent of world government really does exist: world-wide economic arrangements for money exchange, marketing, and production, and a world-wide scientific and technical policy. In these fields the greatest progress could be made to reduce the inevitability of empire.

Finally (an imponderable of first importance), every country on earth harbors a passionate desire to maintain its individual cultural autonomy. Western Europe rightly and understandably does not wish to look either like the United States or like the Soviet Union. Costa Rica, Puerto Rico, Mexico do not wish to be offset copies of America. Yugoslavia and Poland do not intend, if they can help it, to surrender their special cultural style. The fact that they are not free to make many decisions in military matters or power politics gives rise to fear lest they may be also constrained to conform in economics, social organization, esthetics, and eventually the development of their way of life. Any "empire" that produces cultural conformity promotes resistance—and should. Unless freedom of cultural expression is construed to include barbaric oppression—for example, massacre of Jews or whites, or the introduction of slavery—empire in the cultural field is not only avoidable but also unacceptable.

The last and most dangerous problem facing America is whether it shall use power to endeavor to preserve world balance and world peace—until the golden day of effective world peace-keeping arrives. Had a working agreement been reached between the superpowers, as Franklin Roosevelt proposed, it would have been solved. As between the Soviet Union and the United States (contrary to the opinions of intellectuals like Mr. Louis Halle [2]) peace has not been arrived at, though indications suggest that the Cold War between them can be ended within a decade or so. China's position remains problematic, though ultimately that country must be drawn into some such agreement.

Peace-keeping, meantime, must remain a problem in whose solution use of power may at any time become the final argument of nations. Such a problem was posed in Southeast Asia in 1962, with the equilibrium of the vast Pacific world as the apparent stake. Then, the Soviet Union and Communist China were working together. Chinese troops had occupied Tibet, and were presently

2. See *The Cold War as History*, New York, Harper & Row, 1967.

to move into the border territories of India. "Wars of liberation"
were being prosecuted in Laos, Cambodia, and Vietnam. In the
attempt to maintain a precarious world balance, President John
F. Kennedy reached a fateful decision. He determined not to move
in Laos and Cambodia (these were left to the dubious protection
of understandings for their neutralization), but to dispatch American troops, thinly disguised as "advisers," to assist in defending
South Vietnam. Few, if any, foresaw that Peking and Moscow
would presently quarrel; that Indonesia, through revolution,
would refuse to enter the Chinese orbit; that balance of world
power in Asia would again be dangerously restored as Soviet
force and effort were increasingly deployed to deter or prevent
Mao Tse-tung's armies and infiltrators from entering Soviet-held
Turkestan and Siberia from Sinkiang and Manchuria. Still less
did anyone forecast the huge cost to America in life, treasure,
morale, and good will, though the *status quo* was for the moment
maintained. In immediate event, American power proved the deciding element. The longer-range consequences of its use of power
were—and still are—as always, unpredictable.

A like problem was presented in June, 1967, when the Arab-
Israeli war broke out and fleets of the Soviet Union and the United
States faced each other in the eastern Mediterranean Sea. The
immediate conflict over the very existence of Israel, though great,
was clearly secondary to a greater issue: would Moscow and
Washington decide to enter a struggle for control of the Mediterranean and its entire eastern and southern littoral? Both sides
decided, for the time being, not to act. That decision still stands,
though the Soviet and American powers uneasily face each other's
maneuvers in a chaotic area crucial to the fate of three continents.

Britain used its power, not without success, for a high content
of peace throughout the nineteenth century. Can the United States
escape a similar burden—and its greater dangers—in the twentieth? It will be accused as much for withholding as it has been
for committing its power in such situations. At home and in many
other nations, some of the same men who indicted it for blood
guilt in Vietnam are likely to demand that it move in the Israel-
Suez area—such is the fickleness of emotion in foreign policy.

But as the evanescent results obtained by its intervention in two world wars are reviewed, the probabilities appear to be that in the long run staying out may accomplish very nearly as much as moving in.

Certainly this was true in World War I. I should not have enjoyed Hohenzollern hegemony in Europe, but I cannot say that the French hegemony in the ensuing decades was much more attractive. Neither phase could have lasted long. World War II clearly raised graver issues: Hitler's government had descended below the level of civilized acceptability. Roosevelt's desire to stay out was overcome by the sheer megalomaniac and sadistic lunacy of the allied Japanese and Nazi regimes. On the other hand, has history justified the American policy of endeavoring to limit the Asian ambitions of Imperial Japan in 1938–1941? Is Asia better off in its present state than if Roosevelt had not opposed the Japanese "co-prosperity sphere" (a euphemism for an expanded Japanese Empire)? Is the United States safer? Would not twenty years have reduced this to a local problem or, conceivably, have brought a region into orderly productivity in which freedom could evolve? The might-have-been is unknowable.

Granted that a form of empire, be it sphere of influence, alliance, or tighter grouping, may be unavoidable in limited area, should not the policy of all superpowers—including the United States—be limitation of the principle, rather than its extension? Some commitments and involvements, it appears, must be accepted. Can they not all be oriented toward a slowly developing world government? To the limited extent that new forms of empire may be inevitable, must not American policy, and that of other superpowers, be translation of nineteenth-century conceptions of empire into co-operative arrangements in which a minimum of control and a maximum of co-operative effort are achieved for all the inhabitants of the region?

That was the conception of Roosevelt's Good Neighbor policy as it evolved during his regime; of President Lyndon Johnson's outline of co-operative development for the Mekong Delta and River for Southeast Asia; of United States policy toward the Latin-American Common Market outlined by Johnson in 1967. If empire cannot be avoided, it can be made fruitful. It may even be made to move toward an effective system of world order.

Following that policy, every area of potential conflict may perhaps be converted into a line of communication. Potential confrontation between the United States and the Soviet Union, between the Soviet Union and China, between all three and the Asian nations may be made into opportunities to seek arrangements, perhaps even real understandings. In this greater scope, the United Nations may prove essential and greater use be made of its inherent capacity. As its power and authority grow, the inevitability of empire may disappear.

V

International Power and the Emergence of World Government

Preface

Power in international affairs, as we have seen, rests in the hands of individuals who dominate nation-states. Heads of the greater of these states acquire capacity to direct or influence action of other nation-states by conquest, intimidation, alliance, combination, persuasion, or merely prestige. In any case, they come into contact with other states and their power holders. A rapidly shrinking world intensifies that contact, as modern communication, commerce, and technique increasingly make it one.

Contact between international power holders may produce any of a number of different results. Conflict is one, if one power holder seeks to dominate another or to contain enemies or incompatible rivals. Or it may lead to overt or tacit understandings, setting up spheres of influence or delimiting the scope of action of each power holder. The aggregate of these understandings may produce a system of balance of power. Such a system prevailed during the nineteenth century, and did organize international power. It appears to be re-emerging in the second half of the twentieth.

Conceivably, this intensifying contact now covering the entire earth may result in a supranational organization of power—in brief, a world organization or government—the role once forecast for the League of Nations and later for the United Nations.

In considering the principal organizations, real and attempted, of international power, emphasis must be laid on one continuing fact. Nation-states are still the only continuing effective institutions by which international power has been, and is, held and exercised. This has been true throughout history. It is true today. Analysis based on any other assumption would be self-deluding folly. Yet this fact must be qualified by conditions peculiar to the mid-twentieth century. Those conditions powerfully tend toward change in the position of nation-states. Already they have whittled down and qualified the power of most, if not all, of them. The next generation almost certainly will live in a world of nation-states whose autonomous capacity to use international power will have far less scope than in the past. The potentialities of the growing nucleus of world government exercising at least a minimal degree of world power must not be underestimated.

History, ancient and modern, has seen attempts at world empire, has seen the reality of lesser empires, has witnessed the phenomenon of balance of power; and more recently has seen combinations or groups of nations endeavoring to pool their power. The twentieth century has seen two attempts to organize world government—one of which is still extant.

1. World Empire

Throughout much of history world empire was conceived as a possible institution capable of regulating international affairs by sheer power.

Such an empire never did exist. That of Rome—often and erroneously described as the ruler of the world—never dominated more than a fraction of the earth's surface. The illusion arose from relative lack of contact with northern Europe, with the vast Asian wastes, with India, China, much of Arabia, and all of Africa south of the Mediterranean littoral—not to mention the unheard-of continents of America. Even within the sphere of Roman contact, the Persian Empire remained unconquered and independent. Factually, the Roman Empire collapsed when, in the fourth and fifth centuries, Asian hordes pushed or were pushed one after another across its northern and eastern borders, and by that time the empire was already divided between Rome and Constantinople.

The dream nevertheless persisted. Essentially, it was messianic. Christian doctrine, brilliantly proclaimed by Saint Augustine in *The City of God,* even as the Roman Empire fell, took this as a basic faith: the kingdom of God must come on earth. Such was the messianic idea system. Its proposed earthly institutional instrument was to be the Roman Catholic church, translating itself also into an empire. Later, the Holy Roman Empire—in practice, a union of Germanic states—was one product of this dream. In Europe it almost succeeded as the House of Hapsburg reached its maximum imperial power under the Emperor Charles V about A.D. 1550.

But as Protestantism became established, the Catholic idea system was no longer universal. With the defeat of the Spanish Armada in 1588 by a Protestant, Queen Elizabeth of England, the dream became impractical. It remained only for the bloody stalemate closing the Thirty Years' War to write finis to that project of world empire.

No comparable attempt at world empire has emerged since.

World empire as a method of organizing international power now seems too remote a possibility to merit consideration—at least, at present. In the dim future, a messianic dream—possibly out of China—might develop a universal idea system and forge an imperial instrument powerful enough again to attempt conquest of the earth. Success is highly unlikely, if not downright impossible.

One contemporary philosopher, Mr. H. G. Wells, believed the idea of world empire is evolving into the conception of a world state. He wrote, in *The Outline of History:* "For a time men have relapsed upon these national or imperial gods of theirs; it is but for a time. The idea of the world state, the universal kingdom of righteousness of which every living soul shall be a citizen, was already in the world two thousand years ago never more to leave it. Men know it is present even when they refuse to recognize it." [1] This conception will be examined later.

2. Empire

The vast, romantic, and suggestive word "empire" has many meanings built upon a central idea. Rulership of areas beyond the boundaries of a nation-state is implied in all its meanings. Exact content ranges over a wide spectrum.

Empire, it may be noted, is government by the power holders of one country but effective in others—as Queen Victoria was Empress of India; as power holders in France had the capacity to choose rulers and make laws in Algeria, Morocco, parts of Asia and Africa, and a few West Indian islands in the Caribbean. In slightly weaker form, the king or chief of state of one country might also be king of another—as the emperors of Austria were also kings of Hungary, and titular rulers of a good deal of ad-

1. Third edition, 1921, pp. 797–798.

joining territory. Still looser use of the word connotes overriding power in the hands of rulers of one state—say, Great Britain— over a number of associated but more or less autonomous states —Canada, Australia, New Zealand—as well as direct authority to rule other colonies. The means by which control of regions or countries was vested in the power holders of another are infinitely varied. All have, in common, actual power exercised by power holders of one nation-state over all or part of the affairs of another.

At weakest, the imperial concept and empire dissolve into associations of states which for common safety, profit, or advantage have pooled their interests, combining around a powerful central nation-state. Probably empire ceases when the power holders in a central state no longer have authority to influence choice of power holders in the associated states. At this point rulership changes to arrangements of alliance and grouping.

Empires, until the close of World War II, were the institutions by which and through which international relations were established and their affairs carried on. Until 1918—that is, until the close of World War I—the affairs of the world were almost entirely handled by thirteen empires. In coexistence with a group of associated American states in the Western Hemisphere grouped under the Monroe Doctrine around the United States, these imperial institutions controlled practically all the planet. A few independent nations equipoised between them existed (often happily and prosperously) without alignment. This was true of Switzerland and the three Scandinavian countries—Sweden, Norway, and Denmark. It was the situation of a few Southeast Asian countries, notably Thailand.

The twentieth century has seen these empires fall like dominoes. The Spanish-American War of 1898 ended the Empire of Spain. The close of World War I saw the dissolution of the empires of Germany, Austria, and Turkey. In the years following World War II—that is, after 1945—the British and French empires in Asia and Africa were more or less voluntarily liquidated. Japan's empire was ended with its defeat. Prior to that, Japanese and Russian armies had liquidated the remains of a decadent Chinese

Empire (to revive after 1950) and had made impossible any reconstruction of the Netherlands Empire over Indonesia and the East Indian archipelago. Belgium abandoned its African possessions, almost completing the list. Portugal still retains, though tenuously, substantial territories in Africa and some in the East Indies, but its authority, especially in Angola, is presently under bitter contest.

Vestigial remnants, of course, do exist. They do not impair the point here made. By 1960, the old empires had ceased to be the institutions through which international affairs were conducted. They could not be, they are not, adequate instruments of power. Much of the turmoil and disorder throughout the world, notably in Africa and Asia, arise from the fact that no institutional organization of affairs has attained power enough to replace them.

One other empire—the Russian—nominally disappeared following its defeat and the Bolshevik Revolution in 1917. Disappearance was apparent rather than real. Joseph Stalin, succeeding to power in 1928, promptly restored the Soviet Empire. As one of the victors in World War II, he pushed its limits farther than those of the preceding Czarist empire. This was done by force of Soviet arms, especially in Europe, where he converted the Central European countries, from Poland and East Germany to Yugoslavia, into client states. He could and did choose their power holders and governments, and changed them more or less at will. Twenty years later, even that empire is showing signs of decay. Yugoslavia has successfully broken clear. Some of the Iron Curtain countries show signs of developing a degree of independence. It is by no means certain at present that Moscow can at will dethrone or replace governments in other countries—for example, Poland, Bulgaria, Rumania. The Soviet rulers did do so in Hungary when that nation rebelled in 1956. But the cost was great. It was still greater when in 1968 the Soviet Union, using its overwhelming military power, intervened in Czechoslovakia. Further use of force might cause a mass rising throughout Central Europe. Plainly the imperial structure is weakening.

The remaining instrument—the United States and the associated Western Hemisphere states—is not an empire, but a grouping. It still exists, though weakened by a number of circumstances. One was the successful take-over of Cuba by a Communist government, though that government's capacity to maintain itself depends almost entirely on economic and military support from the Soviet Union. Other countries in the combination discuss and sometimes assert their "independence" of the Western Hemisphere grouping, in which the United States is unquestionably the most powerful. Perhaps because of its very looseness, the association has not broken up. Its advantages are too great to abandon. Autonomy of the constituent American republics is as complete as exists in a modern world where superpowers exist. Short of threatening the security of the United States by association with a hostile empire—as Cuba did when Fidel Castro made it a client state of the Soviet Union in 1960—they have their destinies as nearly as can be in their own hands. This limitation—their inability to threaten the neighboring United States without interference—does qualify their sovereign autonomy. But almost every state in the world is subject to limitations of that kind in greater or less degree. Even so, the Organization of American States—the present instrument of the Western Hemisphere group of countries —is rarely an instrument of power in the hands of the United States, or, indeed, of anyone else. The American occupation of the Dominican Republic in 1965 was due almost exclusively to fear in the United States lest the Dominican Republic be taken over by and added to the Soviet Empire as Cuba had been. That fear corresponded to a feeling on the part of most other American states that the danger threatened them as much as it did their North American neighbor.

Neither the sole remaining empire—the Soviet Union—nor the grouping of nations in the West has yet achieved relationships permitting it to function effectively as an instrument of worldwide power.

Danger as well as hope inheres in this condition. The danger is familiar and ancient: that of chaos. Notably in Africa, the states emerging in the limits of the now dissolved empires are weak, badly organized, ill-equipped to maintain themselves economically or politically. Sporadic or endemic fighting goes on. Disorderly disputes like that prevailing in 1966 between Ghana (formerly British) and Guinea sufficiently exhibit the danger of chaos. Within the borders of many of these states—for example, the Republic of Sudan, the Republic of Congo (formerly part of French Congo), and Nigeria (formerly British)—ceaseless conflicts flare between opponent African tribes and races.

Power abhors a vacuum, and where chaos impends, some power holder is almost certain to fill it. Where more than one power holder seeks to do so, there is risk of conflict, just as European wars developed when chaos began to prevail in the Balkans as the Turkish Empire waned. Fall of the nineteenth-century imperial system did mean the end of a functioning system of order, however unsatisfactory. In great areas—for example, the Red Sea littoral—no substitute order-keeping system has yet become effective.

Hope lies in the fact that chaos cannot last. Danger of it in these and other areas could cause a third world war. It may also prove a powerful motive toward enhanced support of a true system of world order. The earth is clearly groping for such a system. Under strong enough stimulus, it may find one.

3. Combinations of Nations and Balance of Power

With empires or without them, and especially without them, groups of nations can combine their policies for common advantage. The basis of such groups is consensus and agreement on some aspects of the use of their power, and the method of making decisions. In a pinch, the agreement may not hold up. But until it proves wanting, the group stays together.

Empires formed such groups before World War I. Hohenzollern Germany worked out the Triple Alliance with Hapsburg Austria and Italy under the House of Savoy. The understanding was that if one of the three was attacked, the others would join in its military defense. In response, France, Britain, and Czarist Russia joined in the Triple Entente. Although it was less definite than the Triple Alliance, its substance was the same: attack on any one would bring the others to its side. Confrontation came in 1914. Exactly who attacked whom is debated by historians. Factually, Austria moved against Serbia with German approval. Russia considered itself threatened and mobilized its armies. Germany did likewise; its military men were by no means unhappy at the chance to attack France. France at once demanded assistance from Britain under the Triple Entente, and got it as German troops invaded. Italy, summoned to join the Triple Alliance, found excuse to refuse, and presently was induced by Britain and France, through promise of territorial gain, to join the French-Russian-British combination.

Bad as it may have been, this system of combinations—alliances, as they were then called—did serve as an instrument by which power could be used either to maintain international peace or to wage international war. Power holders in London, Paris, and St. Petersburg could and did give orders for common military action. Not only the three countries, but also their imperial possessions throughout the world, were mobilized by their action. Agreement between the alliances meant world peace. Conflict between them at once caused a world-wide struggle.

Dying after World War II, the imperial system was in part replaced by combinations.

The grouping of Western Hemisphere states was fortified by the Treaty of Rio de Janeiro—essentially military in character—and by the Charter of the Organization of American States [2]—political, economic, and social in character. Armed attack by any state against an American state is to be considered an attack against all American states, and consequently "each one of the said contracting Parties undertakes to assist in meeting the attack

2. Members: Argentina, Barbados, Bolivia, Brazil, Chile, Colombia, Costa Rica, Cuba (who has been excluded from participation since 1962), Dominican Republic, Ecuador, El Salvador, Guatemala, Haiti, Honduras, Mexico, Nicaragua, Panama, Paraguay, Peru, Trinidad-Tobago, United States, Uruguay, Venezuela.

in the exercise of the inherent right of individual or collective self-defense." So says the Treaty. Joined in the Organization of American States, the same countries agreed to co-operate in strengthening "their economic structures, develop their agriculture and mining, promote their industry and increase their trade," and to achieve just and decent living conditions for their entire populations, and agreed to co-operate on a number of other matters as well. Before this, a looser group had existed whose chief purpose, under the Monroe Doctrine, had been to prevent overseas empires from extending their systems to the Western Hemisphere. That grouping, though indefinite, had proved effective. Because of it, all American states eventually declared war on Japan and on Germany after Japan's attack on the United States at Pearl Harbor.

Simultaneous groupings appeared elsewhere in the world. Agreement to establish a common market was reached between three small states—Belgium, the Netherlands, and Luxembourg —in 1947. Presently the movement expanded; the European Common Market was established, including not only the three small countries, but West Germany, France, and Italy as well. On the military side, the North Atlantic Treaty Organization came into existence in 1949. Its heart was agreement that if any of its members should be the object of an "armed attack" in Europe, the other members "would afford the party so attacked all the military and other assistance in their power," and, by separate treaty, "an armed attack against one or more in Europe or in North America shall be considered an attack on all." That grouping in time came to include most of Europe west of the Iron Curtain, and eventually Turkey.

Newer countries, emerging from the old empire system, also grouped, though their agreement and organization was looser. The Arab League was formed in 1945, and has since taken in most of the African coast of the Mediterranean. The Organization of African States nominally includes most of the areas that attained their independence from the German, Belgium, French, and British empires. Its primary interest is racial, and its concern is to support the African Negro countries against colonialism—

515

though it includes some countries not necessarily Negro. New African states have not reached an angle of rest from dispute among themselves. Neither the Arab nor the African group is an efficient instrument for the use of power, though either or both may become so.

The Soviet Union has had in fact an empire running from the Oder-Neisse River in mid-Europe to the Pacific in Siberia and south to the borders of Greece, Turkey, and Iran. It might have rested on that, but, as did the Western nations, it preferred to bind the group by a series of treaties. The most important is the Warsaw Treaty Organization, pledging the Soviet Union and the mid-European countries—Poland, Yugoslavia, Czechoslovakia, Hungary, Bulgaria, Rumania, and East Germany—to common military action. Yugoslavia has since withdrawn, and it is far from certain that the others would stay in it if their power holders saw a good chance to take them out. Probably the Warsaw group is held together not by consensus of will, but by Soviet force. Yet, for the time being, it is an instrument by which the Soviet-dominated bloc can and is likely to exert power in case of need.

Smaller, more fragile, combinations exist. It is enough to say here that in some measure the power organizations set up by the old empires and their alliances have been replaced by blocs.

The tensile strength of any of these complexes is open to question. The North Atlantic Treaty alliance—NATO—exists on paper. Its effectiveness has been violently curtailed, if not destroyed, by the virtual secession of Gaullist France. The Warsaw bloc appears to be eroding as East European countries nervously seek freedom of action.

Empires, alliances, blocs, and groupings almost automatically bring into play the principle of "balance of power." Its theory is simple. Each empire or alliance or bloc has to command sufficient force to deter any other from attacking it. It used to be thought that when power was equally balanced, no one would resort to war; the hazards were too great. The system did produce peace for substantial periods, though it broke down in ultimates. Mr. Cordell Hull, Secretary of State of the United States from 1933 to 1944, spent much of his time endeavoring to devise a different system of world organization—as in fact he eventually did when the United Nations was formed in 1945. As the ensuing decades proved, it did not change the system as much as he had hoped. Balance of power still remains a primary principle in world affairs, and the system of blocs has played a part in maintaining that balance. NATO came into being to prevent a Stalinist Soviet Union from moving westward in Europe. The strengthened Organization of American States and its mutual defense treaty arose out of a somewhat similar fear. The African states united (to the extent that they did unite) largely to eliminate remnants of colonialism in Africa and deter any attempt at renewed colonial expansion there.

National policies were likewise affected. Because the United States had atomic bombs and presently intercontinental ballistic weapons, the Soviet Union developed comparable armament. "Massive retaliation" came within the capabilities of both. Each country claims, with substantial reason, that its system will "deter" the other from long-range rocket bombing. Thus far, the deterrents have been effective. At all events, these weapons have not been used, and the impression increasingly spreads that they will not be. Yet each member of each bloc nervously suggests that it cannot be safe without having such a system. Proliferation of atomic weapons is at present an unsolved problem for statesmen everywhere.

Balances of power are readily upset by forces not always foreseeable. Two nation-states, or two empires, of comparable size and armament will cease to be equal if one or the other deteriorates, materially or psychologically. Two blocs of comparable capacity will cease to balance if one of them begins to come apart while the other holds together. Today, both the principal blocs—NATO in the West and the Warsaw group in the East—seem to be disintegrating; neither is reliable as an instrument of power even for the defensive purpose for which each was formed. From that disintegration may result chaos, eventually to be filled by power from somewhere; or it may result in a regrouping. Conceivably, it may result in a higher degree of consensus on a world system of some kind.

Organization of international power throughout the world thus clearly is in a state of growing and very uneasy flux. Because of this, lights burn late in Washington, London, Paris, Moscow, and Peking.

4. The United Nations—Appraisal and Forecast

With this background, the United Nations may be appraised. It is the only approximately universal institution of world power in existence. Forecast for it can, I think, be restrainedly optimistic.

Let us first consider the negatives.

Although a framework exists and institutions are outlined, the United Nations has not lodged continuous effective power in any individual or in any group of institutions enabling individuals to guide events. This means that the United Nations cannot necessarily be counted on to act, however gravely world order and peace may be threatened. In 1966, doubt even existed whether the United Nations could choose a titular head—its secretary-general—though the problem was overcome. The first secretary-general, Trygve Lie, a Norwegian, was opposed in office and his work frankly sabotaged by the Soviet Union and the Communist countries following its lead. His successor, Dag Hammarskjöld, maintained his position chiefly because of his own superb personal and statesmanlike qualities. Upon his death, U Thant was agreed on as a compromise candidate—asserting personal power was not his gift. A Soviet proposal—nicknamed "Troika"—lies inert on the table. It asked that the powers of the secretary-general be placed in the hands of three men, representing different points of view—presumably Western, Communist, and nonaligned. If adopted, what little power the secretary-general has now would be split to the point of ineffectiveness. Dormant at present, the proposal could be resurrected.

No adequate and accepted idea system exists to gird, guide, and support the present framework of the United Nations. Spare parts

—universal desires and uneasy motion toward agreement—do exist, but these have not yet been used. A very large nation, China, is wholly outside the organization, and Germany, a smaller, powerful country, has been excluded. Thus, except in a few areas, not yet is there consensus on ideas and principles. Institutions languish or capsize in that situation. Nations and men are unwilling to trust their fates and lives to them and hesitate to transfer effective power to them and their heads.

Americans remember the fate of the Continental Congress from 1774 to 1787. The American confederation then displayed many of the weaknesses shown by the United Nations now. Whenever there was substantial unanimity, the confederacy could act, but lack of agreement appeared so regularly that it possessed little power. Thirteen years after its organization, it acquired its constitution and was superseded by the federal United States. Europeans remember similar experiences in their own history. The Germanic states from time to time organized diets; these proved ineffective. The constituent crowd of kingdoms and principalities formed an effective power system only when Bismarck brought his German Empire into being in 1871.

Even the United Nations institutions seem shaky. The Security Council theoretically includes all the great powers of the world as well as six minor elective members. But, of the five supposed great powers, one permanent membership is held by France, and eminent and glorious as France is, it is a European, not a world, power. Another permanent member is China, but the Chinese seat is held by a representative of Generalissimo Chiang Kai-shek, who actually governs Taiwan, not China.

Worse condition exists in the General Assembly of the United Nations. Under the adopted principle that in law all states are equal, the vote of Guyana, Upper Volta, or the Sudan holds equal strength with the vote of the Soviet Union, Great Britain, or the United States. No one has extended the principle of "one man— one vote" to representation in the United Nations. Rhetoric, rather than reality, governs the pronouncements of the Assembly; certainly they do not represent power.

Finally, many, if not most, of the newer, smaller nations are astonishingly irresponsible, both in their votes and in their financial contributions to the world organization. On a number of occasions, had the United States withheld its hand, the staff of the United Nations would have gone unpaid; had it withheld its influence, many debates would have been abortive.

In result, no man or group of men in the United Nations, however solemnly authorized by the Charter of the institution, has dependable power to act. Solemn decisions have been taken both by the Security Council and by the General Assembly. The former are rare, because they can be vetoed by any one of the Big Five. Assembly resolutions, resulting in the appointment of commissions of inquiry or calling for enforcement of policy, often have been flouted or ignored.

If one accepts all this, review of the positive side of the United Nations displays a more hopeful outlook.

The United Nations is there: it is in existence. Its heads are men who command the ear and the respect of most of the world. The organization and its representatives are the only alternatives to a chaotic abyss. No single power or probable combination of powers appears capable of meeting the problem. Intercontinental and, presently, space-traveling missiles and satellites carrying nuclear warheads can be touched off at any time. Unlimited and unforeseeable horror could result. No national statesman can give credible assurance to his own people that they will be immune. The imprisoned titans and monsters of chaos are guarded slenderly—but even slender guard is better than none.

Faced with the choice between chaos and power, nations, like men, will always seek refuge in power. The United Nations organization at present may be little more than a framework and nucleus. Its mere existence nevertheless offers more help than a complete vacuum; it could serve as sudden recipient of power in a crisis.

Test may be made by imagining what would happen if one morning the newscasts were to announce the dissolution of the United Nations. Nationalism or empire then becomes the only possible refuge, though these offer chance of conflict at least as much as chance of peace. At once every army would be strengthened; every economy would be burdened with greater development of rockets, space weapons, nuclear air bombs, land and sea armament. Tensions everywhere would become intense. Psychologically, at least, the United Nations is a reality. The men in it have potential, if not actual, power in crisis. Were conflict to follow its dissolution, everyone knows a new world power structure would have to be invented. It was not accident that the federal United States followed hard upon the postcolonial confederacy. Nor was it accident that the United Nations succeeded upon dissolution of the old and impotent League of Nations. World organization is accepted as essential because it is recognizably needed, however slow its progress toward adequate development.

Though it is not yet supported by a philosophy or universal idea system, elements of that system are in being. They are rudimentary but they are strong. A degree of peace is, at present, everywhere considered preferable to the vaster forms of war. The common language of science at once evokes both fear of destruction and hope of progress. Its language is universal and its methods command general acceptance. Some of its dictates have already established world-wide rules, and some of these have survived even through stress of war. Commerce and its underlying economics increasingly engage world-wide examination and establish world-wide habits.

Consequently, it cannot be said that a germinal idea system is absent. By historical standards, world agreement on a central body of principles, though slow in developing, is emerging with visible speed.

Finally, the tenuous power structure of the United Nations has both created and recognized a field of responsibility. It has called into being a rudimentary dialogue between it and holders of international power, be they in the halls of the United Nations itself or in national structures. Organized and formal dialogue exists through discussion in its General Assembly and the debates maintained through several months each year. These are communicated to the vocal elements of the constituent nations from all quarters of the globe—Communist China excepted—and even Communist

China maintains observers. These debates need not be idealized—still less the representative quality of many of the orators. All of them, nevertheless, are formal entrants into the dialogue of responsibility. Each of the delegations in the Security Council and Assembly meetings is speaking, even at its worst, to constituencies at home and elsewhere. Radio networks, journalists, magazine commentators, diplomatic correspondents transmit the substance of the debates to local capitals. In return, comment, criticism, attack, approval, suggestions flow from the farthest outlying countries back to the delegations in New York. Besides official communications, the views of radio commentators, newspapers, private organizations, intellectuals, cartoonists of all kinds are expounded to anyone who will listen, in the hope that they may have effect either on national power holders or on the central organization.

Foundation is thus being laid for a true world-wide structure capable of developing international power. It is woefully incomplete. It might be demolished in any heavy international storm. Yet it is stronger by far than any world organization previously known to history. In its amorphous, hesitating way, the United Nations seems to be attaining, rather than losing, momentum. Granted a few years' time, vouchsafed a few more statesmen of the caliber of Dag Hammarskjöld, given a few first-rate contemporary national power holders inspired to help, and the dream of Woodrow Wilson, Franklin Roosevelt, Cordell Hull, and young Anthony Eden may become reality.

In the area of reality, technical fields already are, and will increasingly prove to be, areas confided to and governed by the power of the United Nations. In these, the technical imperative supplies enforcement. Three such fields have already emerged. The International Civil Aviation Organization, set up in 1947, makes the technical rules by which aircraft travel between nations. The International Telecommunication Union, taken over in 1949, sets up international regulations for radio, telegraph, and telephone service. The World Health Organization, organized in 1948, establishes minimal rules for the control of the more obvious forms of communicable disease. These three "specialized" agencies can govern, quite simply, because without a measure of world government the facilities they regulate could not exist. Any nation can defy their rules—at the price of losing capacity to engage in civil aviation, to communicate with the world, or to be (to some extent) protected from the international march of disease. Their rules are not dependent on sanctions imposed on states that violate them. Sanction is automatic. Departure from the assignment of wave lengths by the International Telecommunication Union would mean that the state involved could not reliably send or receive messages. Assertion of the sovereign right of a state's airplanes to follow their own procedures, irrespective of international rules, would simply mean that its aircraft could not safely land at any field beyond the borders of its state. This is self-enforcing international government.

Emerging rapidly is a highly specialized, immensely powerful agency, loosely affiliated with the United Nations, known as the International Monetary Fund. Ever so slowly, this agency is working toward a variety of world currency. It is also the world's largest source of quickly available international credit. As it increasingly develops media of international exchange for settling international balances of payment, it moves into an area where its decrees also are self-enforcing. Any state may withdraw from it, may refuse its facilities, may violate its rules. But in such case that state cuts itself off from the flow of international commerce, which is requisite, if not essential, to its well-being and perhaps its existence. The two superpowers, the Soviet Union and the United States, conceivably might exist without it. But the superpowers would suffer enormous disadvantage were they to divorce themselves from a world system. Purely primitive states might exist at subsistence level, but primitive states capable of living in isolation are so few as perhaps not to matter.

If the United Nations represents only a fetus of organized international political power, the specialized technical agencies [3] are clearly developing toward giving that fetus arms, legs, hands, and feet.

Everything considered, on fair assessment of chance, I believe

3. None of these were derived from the old League of Nations. Only the International Labor Organization, which has few dispositive functions, remains virtually intact from the League of Nations regime.

the United Nations is more likely to succeed than to fail. Its success will be gradual. Power in smaller matters will be vested in its executive and in its specialized agencies. The areas of power thus held will grow, and in time a structure will emerge.

And if the United Nations fails, it is as nearly certain as anything can be in this field that the specialized technical agencies will survive and that a new political institution will be invented to take its place. Meanwhile, the world will buy time through balance-of-power arrangements between superpowers and grouped powers. The world is not prepared to unloose the titans and abide the results of the ensuing chaos.

5. The World Community: Science and Morals

Glaring gaps in the preconditions needed for organized international power have been set out in previous sections. After giving weight to all, there is nevertheless evident a solid, though small, content of existing international power. There appears to be a trend to its increase. Here is the basis for reasoned belief that international power sufficient to avoid chaos will be evolved in the foreseeable future. Though certainty is impossible, a balance of factors suggests probability.

Military considerations aside, the world scene indicates general agreement in one striking aspect. Almost all nations, and most men and women within nations, want the product and results of modern technical culture. Clamor for industrialization, use of natural resources, transport, communication, greater production is literally universal. A few lonely enclaves may prefer not to have habits disturbed or lives interrupted, and in some great countries religious or other objection prevents the use of many of the new techniques. These situations are exceptional. Consensus of desire for "development" is planetary.

Already this wish has brought two results. One is an outline of a world community. The other is a universal technical language, permitting, even requiring, world organization. The onrush of applied science steadily expands this rudimentary nucleus year by year. Nothing suggests that this impetus can be stopped; only temporary interruption is possible. Technique depends on scientific knowledge. The premises and language of science are virtually universal. Messianists, nationalists, imperialists, racists leave bias behind when they enter technical conferences. They may disagree in all kinds of ways, but if they want the results of science—and they do—they agree on general principles of scientific method and the validity of scientific conclusions. Pure scientists of whatever race or national origin meet on common ground and discuss problems from this common base. Applied scientists—technicians—do the same. Being men, they make mistakes; they disagree in detail, and fail in their estimates of importance. But their communication never breaks down.

Secretary of State Dean Rusk, on January 10, 1964, made an accurate summary:

World community is a fact
—because instantaneous international communication is a fact;
—because fast international transport is a fact;
—because matters ranging from the control of communicable disease to weather reporting and forecasting demand international organization;
—because the transfer of technology essential to the spread of industrialization and the modernization of agriculture can be assisted by international organizations;
—because modern economics engage nations in a web of commercial, financial, and technical arrangements at the international level. . . .
So, while nations may cling to national values and ideas and ambitions and prerogatives, science has created a functional international society, whether we like it or not. And that society, like any other, must be organized.[4]

It is all very well to discern the existence and growth of organizations wielding international power based on scientific development. There is hope in the fact that these converge and increasingly cluster around the political institution of the United Nations. Yet, as I see it, science and techniques are not enough.

4. *Documents on American Foreign Relations, 1964*, New York, Harper & Row, pp. 373–374.

If we are realistic in our analysis, we must discover a more adequate idea system or philosophy, likely to hold a world apparatus together. Does any such idea system exist?

Fragments of it do—but the system is incomplete. The chief discernible imperatives, as noted, are scientific. Science does indeed set up a philosophical system—as far as it goes. Its method is to work from hypothesis through experiment to proof, and then to construct new hypotheses, arriving at new proofs, continuing toward the unreachable goal of the infinite. Thereby science increasingly explains the material world, and increasingly brings physical forces under control, putting them at the disposition of men. As this is accomplished, it increases man's capacity and his range of choice. A philosophy born solely of science does not, however, tell any man *what* choices to make. It outlines a vast map. In time it may—in tiny measure it perhaps does—indicate the place of mankind, possibly even the place of each individual, on that map. It may suggest directions in which he may most advantageously move. *What it cannot do is tell him what he wants to be.*

Science does not (outside its own range) set up a value system. If survival is the foremost value, it can (within great limits) tell him how this can be achieved. Yet at all times in history men have decided that under some circumstances they would rather die than live—for example, that they would not relinquish their freedom or their religion merely to survive. The greatest scientists acknowledge this limitation. Denmark's great physicist Niels Bohr considered that there were two world descriptions: the physical or statistical description of science and the philosophical description in terms of ethical values and the free will of men to choose them. Bohr believed the two were complementary, although each must be restricted to the aspects of life to which it properly applies. I have found no better analysis than Professor Bohr's. I do not see that a scientific idea system can either replace or include an ethical idea system. Science need not be in conflict with religion, theist or rationalist, but neither can it replace it or substitute for it.

The brilliant editor of *The Bulletin of Atomic Scientists,* Dr.

Eugene Rabinowich, commented (all too briefly) on this question in the November, 1966, issue. He had before him Konrad Lorenz's penetrating study *On Aggression*. Lorenz's point was that groups, animal as well as human, had strong group attachments, but also had "intra-specific aggressions," inducing attacks by some within the group against other members of it. By evolution, Lorenz believed, other instincts developed, modifying and controlling these "intra-specific aggressions." These aided the group to survive. Lorenz, accordingly, was optimistic, expecting like evolution to bring into being instincts controlling the aggression against each other of human beings, within the group known as "man." Science, he considered, consequently was one of the strong supranational forces in human affairs. To this, Rabinowich replied: "For mankind to move toward more civilized intergroup (international) relations, all societies must move at the same time. Otherwise the lagging groups will pull the more advanced ones down rather than the other way around." Faith in evolution hardly covers the case. Lorenz himself believed evolution favored survival of those whose free decisions were for the good and the beautiful, not the bad and the ugly, but this was an act of faith rather than reason.

Rabinowich's argument is unanswerable, and my own conclusion follows the line of Niels Bohr's thinking. Parallel, indeed superior, to any idea system built on science, there must be a complementary idea system dealing with moral judgments. Science can guide in matters of physical necessity. It can extend and maintain life. Moral philosophy is needed to indicate what life ought to be. On this no universal consensus, such as exists in the scientific field, has emerged. It is not accident that the most promising areas of supranational organization and power thus far work only in the physical field.

Hope, I think, need not be abandoned on that account.

In our long journey, we have observed that power and its institutions were invariably paralleled and guided by a philosophy. We have no evidence proving that either preceded the other. We do not know. It is quite possible, and I believe that existence of a power apparatus in and of itself generates an idea system. Zeus needed Athena at once when he gathered his forces to bring the brood of Chaos under control. The mere fact of supranational organizations brought into being by scientific and technical thought suggests to me a simultaneously emerging, if not a pre-existing, philosophy beyond technology. The International Tele-communication Union and the International Civil Aviation Organization, for example, assume that communication and fast transport are "good things" for reasons other than the pleasure of observing radio transmission or jet planes. Yet these are more than toys with which men play. They spring from the stated or unspoken desire of men to have contact with others far away. If one accepts that value, it becomes a bad or unbeautiful choice to reduce contact, a good and beautiful choice to foster it. Here is a value judgment not dependent on technical or scientific premises. A good case can be made for the proposition that organizations either express an existing or create their own philosophy as well as are supported by it.

The United Nations and its system of tributary organs seem to me to be doing exactly this. The organization and its satellites came into being because substantially all nations wanted some or all the advantages they offered. Appreciation of their real values was probably vague, nevertheless. The fact that an assembly meets each year and that subsidiary institutions are continuously in session makes their values more definite with each passing year. In aggregate, a substantial body of value judgments has already been produced. More will emerge as time goes on. The organizations and their meetings are, among other things, an intensive education in values for the men who take part. Annually, they produce a grist of men more or less appreciative of these values, and send them back to the ends of the earth. Partly because of that fact, the United Nations' tensile strength is vastly greater than that of the predecessor League of Nations.

In political and human aspects, the imperatives of the United Nations are definitely not scientific. Its value judgments are taken on moral grounds. Slowly the gap beyond science is being filled. The thesis of a world under law flung out by Woodrow Wilson, maintained by Aristide Briand, repeated by Franklin Roosevelt, advocated by Anthony Eden, and painstakingly forwarded by Dag Hammarskjöld is stronger in 1969 than it was in 1945—and infinitely more real than the Versailles paper formula of 1919. True, the United Nations has yet to produce an individual capable of restating its values, or a statesman capable of giving them greater degree of reality. Dag Hammarskjöld, an intensely religious man, had that stature. Fate denied him time; his death in an air crash on a mission of peace was a world tragedy of the first order. But other men can and will arise.

My conclusion is that the cause of world government will survive, will strengthen itself, will continue to develop a choate moral philosophy of world-wide impact. The process will be slower and more costly in every way than any could wish. Yet it will be more rapid than permitted by any previous condition of history.

6

The Decline of Power

I

The Forces of Erosion

1. The Ruined Acropolis

We began our study of power at the altar of Zeus on the high acropolis of Pergamum. All the surrounding indicia of power were there: temples, countinghouses, palaces, fortresses, libraries. The ruler was king, commander, priest, administrator, teacher—from time to time, god. In their brief but brilliant era, the rulers of Pergamum gave order and law to most of Asia Minor and doctrine and learning to much of the world of history. All aspects of Pergamese power had been concentrated on that rock cap, today a majestic mass of ruins overlooking an insignificant Turkish town. Comparable meeting of power cannot be had in the twentieth-century world, certainly not in the most powerful single nation, the United States.

There is no acropolis in contemporary America. The directing officers of its power institutions are scattered throughout the country. Here, as elsewhere, king-gods are gone. The nearest substitute is the occupant of the White House—a political figure with few autocratic attributes of personal command.

Implacably, it seems, the balance of twentieth-century currents undermines the possibility of concentrated power. Power exists, as it always has, but fragmented, lodged among men administering all manner of diverse institutions—political, commercial, military, educational—and is subdivided among and within each of these. Yet strangely and paradoxically, never has power been more urgently invoked, perhaps, than at present.

Above all, it is sought most passionately by those who attack it as an undefined "power structure," when their desires or ideals are frustrated, their grievances unattended, their possibilities unrealized. Intellectuals cry out against it even as they silently cherish (and sometimes express) their wish that a locus of power may come into being whose fiat will make their dreams real. Humbler people, finding life difficult and unfair, demand that an abstraction, the "state," legislate more gracious and tolerable conditions. Rarely, perhaps, has there been such yearning for a center of power to which appeal can be made, and that is capable of making changes in conditions and altering the course of events.

In virtually half the world, Communist revolution has overthrown property and its individual control because the results were unjust, and its supporters have precipitously fled to regimes in which dictatorial power was the only reality. Even in that complex, the power system is already beginning to disintegrate. There is no longer a Communist world, but a number of quarreling schismatic states. Within all these states, not least the Soviet Union, dictatorial power is plainly being eroded, if not fragmented. In the late twentieth century, desire for power does not bring it into settled existence.

The notable fact of contemporary history is that power finds ultimate embodiment in men directing states—this means in heads of political institutions. But these chiefs, principal bearers of power, have sunk from rulers to administrators. They must devise, plead, and persuade more often than they command. As always, men seek and enjoy power when they can get it. Having it, they nevertheless work in a climate of conditions essentially adverse to power holders. Current thinking considers power instrument rather than end; power holders are neither kings, priests, nor gods, but managers who occasionally prove able to make themselves also accepted as architects, artists, teachers, or spiritual leaders.

2. The Fallen Temple

That senior power now lies in politics, conferred by revocable mandates rather than by entrenched position, tells a great deal about the later twentieth century. It evidences world-wide change from the days when the ruling philosophy took an omnipotent god for granted, when within each country some institutional group was accepted as his mouthpiece, and when some human attempt to reconstruct his will was the proclaimed idea system underlying the institutions of power and validating the will of their heads. The terrestrial religion called "Communism," it is true, does seek to control opinion and attitudes somewhat as popes and ecclesiastical councils controlled Catholic thought and action in medieval times. Yet the nineteenth-century decline of authoritarian religion continues in the twentieth and is evidently paralleled by decline of modern authoritarian Communism. The twentieth century apparently will not vest in any group of doctrinaire interpreters, transcendental or materialist, authority to prescribe dogma for unquestioning acceptance.

Religions and philosophies are, of course, everywhere present. Probably a large majority of the human race believes, somewhat vaguely, in an omnipotent god, and professes and practices some religious faith, including the nontheistic doctrines of Marxism-

535

Leninism. The missing factor is any propensity to believe that current power holders ever were, now are, or in future will be unassailable authentic bearers of a mandate from these gods or faiths. Anyone can ask questions and expect answers. Men now make their own interpretations; they do not take them from power holders, priestly or political.

No other institution or apparatus has taken the place of the demoted priests, religious or lay. Rulers are no longer flanked by a power-holding priesthood. Unlike monarchs in older generations, they could not and cannot take over the ecclesiastical position. That phenomenon probably has contributed more to the changed position of power than any other identifiable historical force.

Though power holders did not and do not replace prophets, popes, priests, or philosophers, another group in some measure now occupies part of the ecclesiastical territory. These are the scientists and their children, the technicians. They, beyond question, have set in motion currents of events changing the face of the world more dynamically than the decrees, fiats, and constructions of any previous power apparatus. But they refuse to represent either god or state, though they may believe in the former and sometimes serve the latter. Their studies and learning developed the postulates, the principles, and the language of science today, but the resulting resources promptly became, not guarded temple mysteries, but available to every individual capable of using them. Inventors and promoters of automobiles have altered the physical contours and the social habits of the earth more than the armies and conquests of Alexander the Great or the engineering of Roman legions and administrators. My former schoolmate Norbert Wiener pioneered cybernetics, and the unnumbered technicians and mathematicians who followed brought computers into existence. Their results may well shift human habits in the coming half-century more than did Roosevelt, Churchill, Stalin, and Mao Tse-tung combined. As the sense of being ruled by viceroys of God on earth disappeared, it was replaced by consciousness of (not to say faith in) the pervasive and implacable effect of applied science.

The result was not power in any conventional sense. Rather, it was a diffusion of capacity among uncounted millions of individuals. We have solid reason to think the range of possible results of unlimited use of applied science has barely begun to appear. The scope transcends the wildest imagination of fiction writers. Because the myriad applications of steadily widening scientific discovery cannot be controlled, but only transitorily guided, by any known power organization in this phase at least, they erode the idea as well as the practice of power itself. They introduce widening areas in which individuals cannot readily be made to conform to the will of others.

Behavioral sciences, tentative, amoeboid, undisciplined, unsystematized as they are, could one day show themselves even stronger. Sigmund Freud, a modest Viennese doctor, never held power of any kind. Yet his theories caused the disintegration and change of social institutions in the space of a few decades; until they are disproved, replaced, or carried forward to another phase, they remain a force driving away at basic conceptions of responsibility, family relations, and social judgments. The science of genetics points a wavering finger toward control of the nature of man itself. Clearly, power in the next era must traverse deeper waters even than at present. Monopoly of political, spiritual, and intellectual resources. is now impossible. No prospect exists of its being reconstituted. Legendary Zeus may have sensed his downfall when Prometheus stole fire from the gods and brought it to men. Prometheus could be chained, but fire was irrevocably loose among men, for each to make of it what he chose.

Scientists—modern successors of Prometheus—have not become, and, I think, are not likely to be, power holders. Not unnaturally, many of them have speculated on the possibility. Given their achievements, scientists can hardly be blamed for aspiring to power positions. Yet the precise qualities that make a scientist make him incapable of the political role. Conclusions dictated by reasoned observation admit of no compromise. Reached by theory and verified by experiment, they cannot be traded or bargained with to work out arrangements acceptable to enough people so that the bargain will be accepted. A scientist may indeed be-

537

come powerful, but while getting and staying in power, he cannot be scientist, but must be politician. It will not be his science, but quite other qualities, that will enable him to appreciate, choose, and use his power to seek human goals for which the scientific resources and tools he has forged shall be used. Nor can he canalize human emotions and assent by mathematical formulas. A generation of scientists with the companion capacity for political leadership may later arise. Such a group in future generations may come to include the men on whom power eventually devolves. But that world lies far ahead.

Meanwhile, the religions, the philosophies, the idea systems on which power institutions have been based cease to have that passionate hold on the minds and hearts of men which reinforced the older power systems. Science has increased the individual and collective capacity of men and societies. It has yet to express the aims and call out the emotions and loyalties by which, apparently, human beings must move and be moved.

Each power holder must therefore choose—or develop—his own philosophy, and attain acceptance of it as best he can. In the modern world neither religion nor science can be relied on to supply the lifeblood of the institutions through which he must act. He must mobilize elements of both, giving them personal expression. If he has the quality of attracting men—charisma—the personal loyalties he sets up may carry him far, though not for long. Firmer institutional base is needed. So each power holder constructs or adopts or at least professes his own philosophy or religion, necessarily drawing heavily on the inheritance and tradition of the nation he governs, the corporation he runs, the school he administers, or the family he guides.

Plato dreamed of a civilization in which philosophers would be kings and kings philosophers. Surprisingly, it has in a measure arrived—with the sardonic twist history often gives to realized ideas. The twist of our time is that the political leader is not a king, except occasionally; that he is not a philosopher, but is conscripted into being one; that he must accommodate his philosophy to his politics, instead of the reverse.

3. The Tamed Countinghouse

Neither in nor away from any American acropolis do we find the headquarters of those agencies of economic power which in the previous century made their owners and chieftains supreme. Banks, manufacturers, merchants, and utility operators have not disappeared. They are present in more highly developed organization than ever. Their head offices are scattered throughout American cities; many of them control far-flung enterprises within and beyond the American continent. But they cannot be determinative unless they can become monopolies or attain control of the state itself. This, so far, they have proved unable to do.

From my window as I write I can see a great white tower cleaving the view of New York Harbor. It was built in the year 1929 by the then largest commercial bank in the country. If economic power then resided anywhere, it resided there, not only because the bank was at the time the largest in the United States, if not in the world, but also because its relations with Washington were such that it came close to choosing the personnel and directing great functions of the government itself. Yet in February of 1933 that bank, despite its enormous architectural, financial, and organizational façade, came close to being—perhaps actually was—insolvent. I then had the ear of the President-elect. Through my tiny office a file of unhappy men, power holders in that and other institutions in similar plight, passed in wearying line, all seeking help. They reckoned that only statist power could rescue them. They were right and they were rescued. Today, these banks are strong again, many times wealthier than in 1933. Yet their power has been limited and its base has changed. Their strength was restored and they could be undergirded because a determined man, Franklin Roosevelt, had become president and took and used power to bring order out of financial chaos. By the laws he caused to be enacted, banks were backed by new institutions created by the federal government and authorized to use its power over currency and credit. These granted them a great but subordinate place in allocating its use. Their present position and the substantial measure of power it creates they hold now by a concession from the state, in trust to perform certain functions. They are vassals, not sovereigns.

Men heading these institutions, consequently, are really limited concessionaires of the statist power. Three-quarters of a century ago, the institutional heads of these banks were able to influence, if not control, the state itself. This is true no longer. The days are gone when, as happened in 1929, the president of the National City Bank could defy the Federal Reserve Board and insist on lending money for stock speculation against its will. Gone, too, is the time when no one would trust the government of the United States to organize a bank itself; today, such a measure might not be considered desirable, but if desired would be feasible. In New York, there remains an archeological artifact—No. 23 Wall Street—once the head office of J. P. Morgan and his legendary banking house. It was the acknowledged seat of concentrated private, virtually uncontrolled, and final economic power, exercised through a country-wide system of instrumentalities of banking and finance. A one-and-a-half story building sunk among skyscrapers, it is today a branch of Morgan Guaranty Trust Company, kept as a memento of past position, like the coat of arms of a famous ancestor. No man, no financial institution, no group has succeeded to the power it once had.

Nor is there any commercial enterprise holding power comparable to that of the Morgan or the Rothschild families of a century ago. Several hundred enormous and powerful corporations do exist. They are annually listed, with asset and income figures, in *Fortune* Magazine. Within each, their salaried executive heads can make decisions and give orders—until the day when their retirement comes and they suddenly become gentlemen of leisure. But none dominates the field. The several hundred of them do not and cannot form a guild whose chief can aggregate the power and influence of the group. Individually, each holds a fragment of economic power. All—or at least most—of them know that they cannot aggregate these fragments. Only their emergence as a political controlling force could do that, but wielding political power is at once beyond their desire and beyond their capacity. The steel industry discovered that fact in 1962 in a tangle with President John F. Kennedy—an occurrence foreshadowed when, campaigning for the presidency in 1936, President Roosevelt said of the great corporate noblemen that in his first administration they had met their match; in the second, they would meet their master.

Several hundred centers of economic power formed by the corporate organization of banking and business are still in being, still vital, still enjoying fragments of economic power. Their enterprises are not in ruin, but prosperous. Their advertising and public-relations departments are rampant, thanks largely to the new electronic mass media. But their essential charter of continued existence lies not in their power, but in their capacity to supply—perhaps stimulate—the growing and manifold wants of a population affluent by all previous standards of comparison. As long as corporation managers are able to satisfy these wants, they are safe in their particular niches. As long as they observe the inchoate law that markets must be supplied, that employment must be continuous, their prices at least acceptable, and their technical progress maintained, they are safe enough. Economic power used for these purposes is tolerated, respected, even admired. Used beyond these limits or for other purposes, very likely they would be political targets to be eliminated from the scene and replaced by some other system.

Tangible, though unexplored, potential exists in the state to substitute itself—and thereby enormously increase its power—for the nonstatist corporations by which American supply and commerce are carried on. When there is breakdown in any really needed economic service, the state in fact does step in. If the American railroad system continues to disintegrate, it is entirely possible that government ownership will result. In 1933, the greatest expert on that subject in the United States, Interstate Commerce Commissioner Joseph Eastman, said in substance that, bad as the situation was, he advised against government ownership; it would locate so much power in political Washington that danger might result. Today, that argument would not hold much weight. Instead, it is said that if the French government can run an admirable railroad service, the government of the United States can also find a way to do so.

Private economic power there is—fragmented, co-ordinated, helped, checked, valued, and to some extent guided and subsidized by Washington. As an independent force aside from politics, it has yet to achieve more than secondary importance.

4. The Uncertain Sword

The most powerful single institution in Washington is the Department of Defense, often called "the Pentagon." It spends almost one-tenth of the entire national income of the United States, directly or indirectly, on wars past, present, or possible in future. Under its direction are fleets and forces, bases and garrisons from Vietnam and Guam in the far Pacific to Western Europe, the eastern Mediterranean, and Turkey. It develops and draws on all the resources of science for its weapons, and fortunately can and does make available their by-products for civilian use. When directed, it must make war. It is a formidable, complex machine —so complex that few, if any, understand all its motions or can interpret all its signals.

It has popular support in the country and in the Congress that, in ultimates, might even be opposed to that of the president of the United States, nominally its commander in chief. When military operations are forward, its staff can lay down a most devastating barrage. Its experts can say, "If you wish the safety of the United States—or the success of this military operation—you must take these and these measures. Otherwise we can take no responsibility for results." Few in the United States, whatever their official position, care to meet that deadly argument. In 1944, I opposed the policies of the contemplated conference later held at Yalta in February, 1945, and decisively lost the debate. It seemed to me the result might cast the peoples, liberties, and self-determination of mid-European countries from Poland to Yugoslavia and Bulgaria into the uncontrolled hands of Stalin. His real intent, I believed, was to bring them under the Soviet imperial system—as he later did. Many elements entered into President Roosevelt's Yalta decision, but one—and I think not the least—was the opinion of the Joint Chiefs of Staff of the United States. Their position was that once the German armies were destroyed, they wished to redeploy much of the American force from Europe into the Pacific to drive the Japanese back to defeat in their mainland archipelago. (The atom bomb was then uncompleted; it became available only after Roosevelt's death.) They wanted Stalin to enter the war against Japan—as he had agreed to do after the Germans were defeated, and were anxious not to give him any excuse for nonfulfillment. I think the argument of the Joint Chiefs of Staff may have determined the issue. So American force and power were not permitted to go beyond the Iron Curtain line that now divides Europe. Assistant secretaries of State may influence, but certainly did not and do not now overrule, the Pentagon.

Today there is under discussion acceleration of the armament race by creating a huge antimissile defense system matching a similar system said to be under construction in the Soviet Union. The president and the Congress can say, "We do not wish this." But the Pentagon and the Joint Chiefs of Staff can say, "This is your choice—but if you so choose, remember that in our honest and expert judgment" (it is both) "we consider the security of the United States against attack by the only other serious atomic power—the Soviet Union—and the potential future atomic power —China—requires this measure." This is peacetime military power—no question about it.

On examination, it may be somewhat less pressing than appearance would indicate. Again, the scientists have both enhanced and eroded the basis of military power, muting the trumpet and blunting the sword.

For one thing, atomic destructiveness, combined with capacity for world-wide missile delivery, has created a situation in which that kind of war cannot produce predictable results. More accurately, its only predictable results are unacceptable—be the technical military verdict victory or defeat. Though the enemy might be wiped out, the survivor would be so decimated and his economic and social organization so shattered, that victory would be meaningless. No one knows this better than the military men themselves. I am sure Moscow understands this as well as Washington, though, perhaps, with less conviction. So will Peking if and when that government attains comparable missile capacity. It is not accident that in more than two decades since the atomic bomb was dropped at Nagasaki in 1945 no military use has been made of it. Technical proliferation of atomic weapons has intensified, rather than changed, the terror equation. In blunt fact, the ultimate weapons are weapons no one desires to employ.

This will continue to be true even when, as seems possible, many nations not superpowers come to control a measure of these weapons. The smaller the country, the more it will realize that any use of atomic weapons by it will mean immediate national suicide. Military power in this ultimate aspect cannot be used. For that reason, it could, and perhaps will be, abandoned by world-wide agreement, though apparently such agreement is presently unlikely. Mutual deterrence is the apparent, but perhaps adequate though expensive, alternative. Yet in either case, the result limits the use of military power and, by consequence, the individual power of those charged with it.

Missiles and atomic bombs aside, lesser military power still exists, and the men having it in their control influence, if they do not take, decisions. But their capacity diminishes. They now are controlled by the need of a continuous moving source of supply. Particularly in World War II, the field armies were essentially grinding edges of a huge machine comprising transport and supply lines, leading to munitions factories and supply organizations, which latter were kept in running order by politically organized governmental economic mobilization of entire nations. So no general could carry his operations beyond the geography and objectives determined (and limited) by the capacity of his political government to motivate and organize continuous flow of men and matériel toward the fighting front.

Contrast this with the operations of Julius Caesar, or even of Napoleon I. Their armies, living off the country, could go as far as they would, making and unmaking kings and governments as they went. They needed little help from home. In Korea in 1951, General Douglas MacArthur could not disobey orders not to extend his operations even by air to China. His government had ordered a "limited" war. In Vietnam in 1967, the American armies under command of General William C. Westmoreland could enter North Vietnam only through preventive operations by air. And the Pentagon could not, against the will of the President and the Congress, carry out a decision to do otherwise. In the end, civilian government controls military power—unless the military can take over the government.

The result has been to eliminate the general-king, much as science and education have eliminated the god-king. As we find the politician in place of the priest, we also find him in place of the field marshal. Nations may and can organize and make armies. Armies, as a rule, cannot organize and make nations. Occasionally they can seize governments, but rarely for long and even more rarely in a "developed" state. In any case, it is not a danger in the United States.

A measure of lesser power unquestionably does lodge in the high command of armies in the United States, but it is subordinate. It has not the power to choose a president or cabinet or to take decisions contrary to the will or without the solid cooperation of the political state. It will be said that generals commonly emerge in politics *after* they have been successful military leaders. Marshal Foch directed French policy, for all practical purposes, during the years immediately following World War I. General Eisenhower became president of the United States eight years after his victory in Europe. The difference in the positions of the two men is striking. Fifty years ago, a Foch, or perhaps even a Ludendorff in Germany, could direct the policies of the state because of his capacity to use the force of an army. No comparable figure emerged after World War II. General Eisenhower owed his popularity to his military career, but certainly was not elected because he could cause American military force to help him take over the American state. Nor, for that matter, could General de Gaulle have become virtually dictator of France (as he became) by relying on the support of French troops. Many of them were his worst enemies during World War II, and when he assumed headship of the French state for the second time and withdrew the armies of France from Algeria, they opposed him to the point of near-rebellion. Politics, not battles or bayonets, led to the emergence of these military leaders, and political, not military, forces remained the basis of their power.

A twentieth-century fact is that military organization cannot prevent or bind chaos, certainly not in the United States. A military idea system cannot bring about that loyalty on which the institutions of national scope essential to the country's operations can be effectively maintained. Particularly in Washington, where there is no tradition of military-political power, the Pentagon holds, at best, a subordinate position. It has its own idea system and its own values. But these ideas, these values, are so limited that the Pentagon leaders cannot command or induce the nation to organize itself for their realization. So they must have the politicians. They can help or hurt politicians up to a point, but they cannot either make them or break them. The Pentagon is powerful, but not decisive.

5. The Shrinking Palace

Pergamum's acropolis was crowned by its palace. Its kings, who were also generals and high priests, and sometimes its gods, created the most splendid dwelling in Western Asia. Even when Eumenes II's vast gamble in calling in Rome to fend off the Macedonians had failed, reducing him to client king, its splendor was legendary. The cards, it is true, were badly played; twenty-seven years later, the last Pergamese ruler bequeathed his kingdom to Rome, perhaps because he realized the game was over. Eumenes and his successors nevertheless in those years brought

Pergamum momentarily to the highest development of luxury, art, commerce, and military organization in the Mediterranean world. For a historic moment the power illusion was complete. The palace held all threads.

Is there such a palace in the United States? If anywhere, it would have to be the White House. Symbols of temple life there also are, though in modern reality they are subject to it. There is a noble congressional library—one of the greatest in history and in the world. There is the Smithsonian Institution—many things besides its natural and physical history exhibits—dominating a great mall. The National Gallery of Art vies with the great treasure houses of the world. A small volume would be needed to list the varied institutions of all kinds functioning in Washington and subject to the president. Yet the palace is not the epitome, or even the source of guidance of these institutions, each of which has its apex in the marble buildings in Washington. The president must act and is limited by laws enacted by the Congress. His influence (apart from his power) is chiefly interpreted by their institutional bureaucracies. It is the work of a lifetime even to know them. The president's term, except in case of death and vice presidential succession, is limited to eight years.

The scope of a modern capital in a superpower today is so great that each institution can, does, and, in fact, must acquire a life of its own. Each can, and as a rule will, accommodate the expressed policies of the president. It will obey his direct orders, though a great deal can be done to change or shift them by "interpreting" them. Their effect can be minimized to the point of invisibility, or perhaps magnified to permit the institution and its bureaucracy decisions beyond those intended. But the opposition of the head of any of these institutions to presidential policy or even a presidential order can be formidable. Combined opposition of a group of them can cripple his ability to cause the Congress to pass measures he desires. Aggregated, they may even endanger his re-election, or the success of his party. So the palace becomes a place where conflicting interests are resolved, rather than where orders are given.

Occasionally, it can be the launching pad for new measures

and new ideas. In each case, the proposal of a new course entails a risk to the power holder. If, on the whole, more like than oppose the new course, the power holder gains. If opposition is stronger, he loses. This is true whether he moves in the field of the arts, of education, of foreign affairs, or of domestic policy. Unless he has a flair for martyrdom, preferring to be right rather than president, he estimates the pluses and minuses before he acts. Contrary to the crude idea of some journalists, he thinks less in terms of votes at the next election (though these are important) than in terms of whether his proposals will be realized or will fail. He has a strategic position from which to exercise "leadership." In terms of American power, leadership is no better than the extent of followership it excites.

Perhaps this always has been true; the difference may be one of degree. But it is an important difference. The king-god-priest of the acropolis or the Babylonian fortress had a far higher factor of command. Because it was his will, most of his subjects accepted his decisions to make war or peace, to exact taxes or to remit debts, to authorize trade or refuse commercial relations. Even so, it was dangerous for him to propose changes contrary to the accepted ideology or religion of the time. In these fields, he had to seek support, rather than command.

In our time, and in America, the command factor is low in all fields.

As one element, the power of the palace in America is qualified by widespread information, accurate or misleading, available to and received by the public. Everyone has access to some, whether by way of news reports and pundits' essays in daily papers, or even books, or gained from broadcasts, newscasts, interpretation by radio commentators, or chance impressions derived from television. The knowledge may be illusory. Returning from spectacular situations in foreign countries, I always suffer a shock on discovering the wide difference between popular impression here and my own picture derived from observation on the ground.

In lesser theaters of power a somewhat similar condition prevails. Often the head of a corporation has one view of the conditions and dynamics of his plants, his local managers another, the surrounding public frequently a third. Any reader who has seen a news account of something in which he has figured knows how far afield the report strays from the fact. An American power holder, engaged in dialogue with the people his decisions affect, is constantly struggling against their opinions based on their information—or perhaps their misinformation. Many people at once develop ideas on the rights and wrongs, the supposed motivations, the possibilities and impossibilities of each situation. Some of their ideas are well based, some uninformed, some absurd. These ideas, aggregated in public opinion, ultimately determine whether and how power to act can be developed and used. As Fiorello La Guardia used to say to his colleagues, "If you have to correct or explain, you are lost." The power dialogue, based on mass information, or perhaps mass misinformation, and the views it engenders increasingly limit palace power. Freedom of the press, in America, is designed to accomplish precisely that limitation.

Nor is it possible for the American (or perhaps any other) palace now to know enough about all the myriad fields for whose condition it is held responsible. Other men must accumulate and estimate the knowledge; on their summaries the power holder must decide. A political commentator, David Lawrence, proposed [1] that the White House convert itself into a Presidential Council of twenty outstanding persons, most of whom should be general managers in various departments and institutions and counsellors of the president in their respective fields. Cabinet officers and the nominal heads of departments would devote themselves to the more obvious problems; the managers, appointed for terms of fourteen years, would operate the power institutions. This would permit each to develop complete knowledge of his field, including the functioning of his department. Meeting twice a week, they could advise the president, who visibly has a job too large for any man to handle. This suggestion (it has been made in other forms) amounts to setting up an unchanging "second

1. *U.S. News & World Report,* July 17, 1967.

government" in America like that which for years has existed in France, functioning through the French administrative bureaucracy and its permanent undersecretaries. The proposition has merit up to a point. If ever carried out, it would mean reducing the president to ceremonial head, rather than power holder. Factually, political power itself is so subdivided that any central power holder increasingly loses direct contact with the problems he is supposed to solve.

Greatest presidential power lies in foreign affairs. A president can commit the United States to war—as did Woodrow Wilson in 1917, as did Harry S Truman in Korea in 1950, as did the Kennedy-Johnson administration between 1962 and 1964. His pronouncement may assume the force of a "doctrine"—a title accorded the declaration of President James Monroe in 1823 insisting that the American continents were henceforth not to be considered as subjects for colonization by any European power, and in 1947 (perhaps wrongly) to President Truman's declaration that the United States would combat Communism in the eastern Mediterranean. Survival of palace power in foreign affairs is not illogical. Essentially, the international world has been anarchic. It may be emerging from that condition in the later twentieth century, but chaos is always visible over the horizon. In default of international order, the course of affairs is inherently unpredictable. Conditions may require—or be thought to require —swift, drastic action, and an American president's power in that field is accepted. As world order in time emerges—and it eventually must—the president's power will be increasingly limited. Until then, the power of the United States wielded by him will remain.

And yet, obstinate human instinct seeks to find and trust a man in any major emergency. That instinct has not changed. In millions of Americans it emerges, seeking, creating, placing, and finding almost unlimited power in its chief of state, at least during any period of perplexity or danger. Americans expect him, as personal leader, to avert impending chaos, to interpret events to them, to act. They hold him responsible for the outcome. Though the acropolis is dispersed, the palace is not extinct.

II

Epilogue in America

1. The Seeking of Zeus

My book written, but with the fascination still upon me, I made a new rendezvous with Zeus.

The task proved more difficult than finding him on the acropolis of Pergamum. There is no Hesiod to guide through the mists and currents of the twentieth century. Power, organizing composite and complex elements, is everywhere present. Search for an assignation is a lifetime odyssey, filled with strange adventures, some worthy of record, some not. In every encounter the reality was not power, but a man—and the man proved more interesting than his power. He was not power; he held it—or, perhaps, it held him. Some, like Woodrow Wilson, had sought it. More often it had devolved on them as a natural development of their lives. Opportunity opened; they stepped in. They fought chaos in some small situation and emerged victorious. The institutions of their time then sought them, often for complicated and inconsistent reasons; they took advantage of the opening. Some, inspired by a messianic drive, beat at the gates of every situation they found, claiming power and, fairly or falsely, proclaiming conceptions or dreams to whose fulfillment men and events must be coerced. The panoply of men has included all sorts and conditions of people in every conceivable occupation.

Twentieth-century kings are rare. Those enjoying the title as a rule have not, and know they have not, much more than ceremonial position. High priests are few; this age accepts religion but grants it little faith. Scientific thought, its real religion, has no unchallenged popes or caliphs; still less, fixed rules and inflexible institutions. Bankers and businessmen are controlled by affairs rather than guide them.

At long last—such are the detours of a lifetime—I find myself in a modest office. From it a door leads into a luxurious ceremonial room equipped with desk, papers, and chairs for entertainment, with anterooms guarded by secretaries and receptionists, keeping at bay a changing group of suppliants and hangers-on. It is in the modest room behind the ceremonial office that power really resides.

Invariably, in the twentieth century, it is a political office, since ultimate power lies in the hands of politicians—in heads of institutions of government.

This fact by itself tells much about the twentieth century. There were times in history when the word of a priest was stronger than that of a king. A pope's interdict could paralyze a realm; the proclamation of a holy war could set armies in motion. Little of that now exists. In scattered areas, occasional survivals of priestly power remain. Messianists in the Communist system still talk the language, as did Leonid Brezhnev, General Secretary of the Soviet Communist party, when he sought to impose Marxist unity at a conference of Communist parties held in Czechoslovakia on

April 24, 1967. But Brezhnev's plea had little more effect than the contemporary exhortations of Pope Paul VI for an end to all war. In any case, Brezhnev was a Russian politician and power holder, as he was to prove a year later with 600,000 Warsaw Pact troops in an unannounced occupation of Czechoslovakia.

In my youth, I had seen and talked to power at the White House in the office then occupied by President William Howard Taft. I have repeated the scene in that same office many times with different characters. In sum, power is a tired politician on one side of the table with a trusted friend on the other—this is the reality. The rest of the panoply is outline only. In Europe, in Latin America, and a little in Asia, in camps and courts, though personalities vary, the essence is always the same.

Unsurprisingly, just such an office had to be the place of any twentieth-century assignation with Zeus.

2. The Frontier of Power

I opened. My question was elementary: "Do you exist?"

"I do," Zeus stated. "Why ask?"

"Because," I said, "you are assumed to control events. You say, 'Go,' and men go; 'Come,' and they come. You can arrange, within measure, that armies take or leave the field. In extremes you can say, 'This man may live; that man, die.' You achieve a measure of order, for that is the condition of power. But I do not see that events follow your will. Drawing on the work of men who died before them, a few adventurers develop a machine called the internal-combustion engine and presently come motorcars. Whereupon, in the space of my lifetime, the physical characteristics of cities and entire countries change beyond imagination. Your power did not do that. The habits of men evolve most improbably, and you cannot change them. Was this transformation of half the world any determination of yours?

"Einstein suggested to Roosevelt development of an atomic

bomb to defeat Hitler; a group of scientists brought about a nuclear explosion in 1945, and armories of nuclear bombs ensued. They forced surrender of the Japanese Empire—but the entire world now lives in fear of them. A chief of this operation, Robert Oppenheimer, perhaps more than any single man, brought about the result. Did you or he hold the power of that thunderbolt?"

"I did—not he," Zeus answered. "In historical fact, a committee of eminent but not too intelligent Americans advised President Truman to drop the bomb and end the Japanese war. Truman had power; he, not the scientists or his committee, made the decision. Like your automotive friends, scientists brought into being new resources. Power alone could say how they should be used—or, perhaps, prevent them from being used at all. Any resource of nature brought under control of men can and will be used. After Prometheus stole my fire, no act of mine could control it. Momentarily, power can determine what occurs next—little more. During its moment, only it creates reality. Never has power on this earth held control beyond the moment."

"You give yourself a scant span," I commented.

"Not at all. Power is less important for what it does than for the forces it releases. It can foster the creative and hinder the destructive. Truman decided to loose the atomic bomb as a weapon of war. I am certain Roosevelt would not have done so except for demonstration; he was an odd, imaginative, tender man. But once that bit of fire had been filched from nature, neither he nor Truman nor anyone else could have prevented its translation by human beings into a weapon, both of war and of peace. Have you forgotten that Stalin's spies informed him day by day of the progress of those experiments by which the atomic bomb was created—and at once he was able to duplicate the results himself?"

I fell silent. This was true. My own knowledge of the atomic bomb had been prematurely derived from FBI counterespionage reports intercepting information on its way to Moscow, which, at the time, I saw officially. I had no ready reply.

"Your difficulty"—Zeus grinned at my discomfiture—"is that you take power more seriously than it deserves."

"I agree it has limits," I answered. "But when power used by Hitler can order extermination of 6,000,000 Jews in Germany, or used by Stalin can direct starvation of 5,000,000 Ukrainian peasants, or used by Mussolini can kill a Matteotti, or used by a Southern governor can exclude Negro children from state schools, I suggest its subjects have a right to take it seriously indeed. Even tiny bureaucrats in government or corporation offices can wreck the careers of subordinates. Power may have only momentary effect, but it can determine that these men live or die, are free or bound, succeed or fail."

Comfortingly, Zeus agreed; he was in a good mood. "You have," he said, "an answer to your question. Power exists. At any given minute, any given man may be completely in its grip. Or, for that matter, kingdoms or continents. When I say you take it too seriously, I mean you assume its lasting effects can be willed by its holder. This is illusion.

"Have you forgotten Pergamum? My pupil Eumenes did not like to coexist in an Asian empire set up by Alexander's old general Seleucus. So he accorded with some Rhodians to ask Rome to dispatch an army to invade Greece. It did, and crossed to Asia Minor. The Roman army, under command of Lucius Scipio (his more famous brother, Africanus, was his junior officer), met the Seleucid armies at Magnesia. There Eumenes brought up the Pergamese cavalry, reinforced the fleeing Roman legions, and that day destroyed the Seleucid Empire. So he got what he wanted. But the Romans undertook to control Asia, and less than thirty years later Pergamum's last king willed the kingdom to Rome. It became a minor province of Asia. The acropolis you visited in your prologue dwindled and now lies in ruins. Eumenes signed Pergamum's death warrant when, at the zenith of his power, he gained that victory at Magnesia. He could determine the immediate event. The forces he released destroyed him."

"You are," I said, "implying that power can determine what happens to events, men, and perhaps nations, for the moment.

Beyond the moment, the results of exercise of power are uncontrollable and unpredictable."

"I am saying rather more," Zeus patiently explained. "I say power controls immediate events—but forces other than power determine their results. With your infernal inquisitiveness, you will next ask what those forces are. A Russian scribbler named Tolstoy asked that question in a novel called *War and Peace,* but he provided few answers."

"I think he believed in destiny," I answered. "If so, there would be little point in power. It would be comfortable to believe that destiny would supply order, would liberate men for creation, would prevent them destroying each other, would make life livable, and so forth. But men have never accepted the government of destiny. They always do want to control events. Not unnaturally, I think, because a great many events are extremely uncomfortable for them, and some threaten their survival. They will always seek of power that it procure their immediate safety and their possible comfort. And they have an obstinate desire not only to be safe and comfortable, but also to believe they and each of them are significant. So they accept philosophies and set up institutions and allocate power to someone—and hope for satisfactory results. As indeed may happen, for some—at least for a time. Can power go farther?"

"Well," Zeus commented, "men have always believed it can. They continuously try to devise ways and means to that end. Some of them are surprising. You are, however, changing the subject. Your real question concerns not the existence of power, but its use."

3. Success or Failure

The ensuing passage was complicated. It was carried on against a rapidly changing panorama of pictures. They were the instruments of power—sublime, disgusting, ridiculous, a vast spectrum.

Great music; great universities, where teachers develop strong and tender relationships with many students; great libraries with treasures of learning and art, some familiar, some esoteric, some unexplored. Schools, great and small; musicians; splendid orchestras; scribblers in tiny towns, and orators on street corners. Impressive offices, mobilizing science for destruction, but tossing out by-products for civilian use. Police, guarding communities, but simultaneously conducting horrible cruelties in back rooms. Courts and lawyers, redressing wrongs, committing them. Prisons, with all the perversions engendered when men's bodies are placed under control of others. Vignettes of palaces in Istanbul against a fortress prison with a killing post, where successions of men have died by executioners' bullets. Glimpses of cities whose greatest institutions are balanced by their meanest, whose achievements for richer life are matched by the sordidness of the ghettos.

Zeus explained. "The positives are always flanked by negatives. Some think the balance is invariably even—that power always creates as much misery as it alleviates. Others, that power is negative only—so down with it; its armies scatter bullets and fire, its policemen's clubs and its instruments freeze injustice into permanence. In fact, everything you would call 'good' and 'beautiful' they consider came from revolt against power. That is the case against me. Well, you have seen the twentieth-century world, and something of men in power. Did they call these negative horrors into existence for their pleasure?"

"On balance," I replied, "no. I am not altogether sure in three cases: Adolf Hitler, Joseph Stalin, and, in lesser rank, my old acquaintance, that Dominican dictator, Rafael Trujillo. They liked pain for their people, power for themselves."

Zeus assented, tolerantly. "They were all good pupils," he mused reminiscently, as a teacher recalls students whose work had interested him. "They were all different. They all met chaos. They conquered it in their countries and in their times. Their methods, you might say, were crude. You will agree, nevertheless, they came to power, stayed in power, and governed while in power."

"All of them," I commented, "ended badly. Mussolini, a lesser killer than any of the cruel trio, was murdered by a mob of his own people in a little town by Lake Como. Hitler was defeated, died by his own hand in a Berlin bunker. Stalin, if not murdered, was allowed to die without help in his Moscow palace. Trujillo's assassins are today heroes in the Dominican Republic. In point of fact, most of them died because their own people feared more experience of their power and, therefore, ended it."

"Does that matter?" queried Zeus. "Death ends power in any case. Can the holding of it be judged by the few days or hours of its end? Would the verdict have been different had they died peacefully in their beds?"

"If nothing else," I countered, "their end suggests that they failed."

"You have a regrettable habit of misapprehending the subject," Zeus answered. "A power holder succeeds or fails, you think, not by whether he attains and holds power, but by whether he accomplishes his intended purpose. By those standards, few power holders really succeed. Mussolini's dream of a Mediterranean empire fell to pieces; Hitler's European system, which was to last a thousand years, ended miserably. Stalin, however, aimed to establish and advance a Russian empire, using Communism as his nominal philosophic system and its institutions as his power apparatus. The empire, philosophy, and apparatus have already survived him for more than a decade. Trujillo's children have no power, but he got for them, though exiled, wealth beyond the dreams of most men. For all you know, Hitler may secretly have thought, as Napoleon once did, that his system would die with him, and that power was for his personal adornment only. More than one pupil of mine has had that idea. Power for its own sake, without other forethought or afterthought, is attractive, especially to those who know little about it. True, their span of possession is likely to be short—but then, possession of power is always short, limited by a life span, if by nothing else.

"Was the power of Roosevelt vain because he died before victory came, giving him no chance to realize his dream? Was Churchill tragic because, immediately upon victory, the institutions allocating power in Britain threw him out? Power's end is always tragedy—it can have no other. Why judge by the end? Stalin killed more men in peace, perhaps, than any power holder in history. Perhaps he died badly, yet more of his work survives than that of Churchill."

"And Roosevelt?"

"A different case. He was not a good pupil of mine. His conception was less a plan to do some particular thing or accomplish some particular result than to give a generation of people freedoms—especially four—to act according to their will and choice, for better or worse. In that he partially succeeded. Americans, individually and collectively, have had greater opportunity than any population on earth to act wisely or foolishly. They have used this opportunity, in both ways, with gusto. You are confusing two subjects—the existence and maintenance of power, on the one hand, and, on the other, an estimate of the use to which it is put. The first is my business. The second is, more properly, the affair of my daughter Pallas Athena and my son Phoebus Apollo—both extremely difficult children. Now that they are grown up, they insist on passing judgment on their father. So presently I shall turn you over to Athena. Before leaving, you will perhaps permit me a comment.

"Power is no judge of values. It acts instinctively against chaos and to maintain itself. Automatically, it will create a degree of order, if only because no order exists without power and no power exists without order. This I arrange every minute of the day, every day of the year, and every year in history. What the order signifies, what its control of immediate events does with and to people, not excepting my power-holding pupils, is, whether good or bad, really not my business."

"But," I persisted, "the creation and maintenance of order, which, as you say, is essential to power, must involve doing those things that conduce to its continuance."

"Earlier in this conversation you yourself observed," Zeus replied with irritation, "that the results of any act, especially acts of historical significance, were unpredictable. You even made the impolite point that no power holder could know enough about probable results to judge intelligently. So a power holder will, in your absurd modern phrase, 'conserve options,' meaning that he tries not to bind his future actions—as though he could ever foresee what they might be. What he wants, what he ought to want, what results he hopes to get turn on considerations outside power. So he tries to think. Thoughts are developed by philosophers—odd individuals who rarely become kings, and, if they do, usually handle the job badly. My former mistress Metis would have understood them—she did nothing but think. Regrettably, she left decisions to me. She invariably quarreled when I made them as best I could. To a thinker, you see, everything is possible. He is lord of his own mind; there, every line can be followed, every dream can be indulged. If a power holder in action behaved as a thinker does in his mind, he would be thrown out at once."

"You then assign yourself," I said, "a low position. It seems to me you become merely a strong but somewhat undisciplined laborer in someone else's garden. You make yourself at best a jobber and contractor doing what has to be done, letting thinkers set the tasks."

Zeus yawned. "Perhaps. I give power to men, and men are curious animals. They work on two levels. In power, they try to do what has to be done. But also, they obstinately keep on thinking. There, I cannot help. I somewhat limit their thinking because they must do what has to be done, and in doing so usually become more interested in the process of their power than in the results of their thought. Still worse, when they think, they usually battle their own power instincts. I concede that thought at long last can bind power itself. Your old friend Hesiod thought as much, and so did Metis, and so I had to destroy her. As you recall, she survives in my daughter Athena. Probably I do work for Athena and Apollo, though, I regret to say, they do more thinking than acting, making me unlimited trouble. If that makes me nothing but a jobber and contractor for them, perhaps you are right.

"But never forget one fact: their thinking and that of their pupils would not exist or have expression or have meaning were it not for me and the order I set up. Now, with your permission, I shall send you to Athena, lest in irritation I blast you to catch a few moments' sleep."

4. The Library of a Great Lady

The scene shifted, much as Jean Vilar used to change his stage settings at the Théâtre Populaire in Paris.

Columns of light gently moved, blended, separated themselves, regrouped. Their movement in swift succession suggested a temple, an eyrie, a stately museum, and settled at length into a noble library, measureless in space and height, the light centering on a scholar's desk illuminated from above.

You met Athena, great lady that she is, in Athens. She had not changed. She courteously took the initiative.

"Be welcome, for my father's sake and your own. My father, as I have come to realize, has great qualities. In ultimates, they are decisive. But I have never thought he had any brains, and he may not have been kindly to yours."

"He seemed to think," I stated, "that power justified itself by being, that its existence alone was enough, but that its purposes and results, when such were sought, were your affair rather than his. So he turned me over to you."

Athena nodded. "He probably said, with his usual disarming honesty, that power rarely knew what it was doing. So it sought the views of thinkers and artists and occasionally followed them. In any case, without the order he creates, thought and feeling could not very well be pursued. But power does not pass judgment on itself. You and I have to do that. If power holders were gods like my father, they would indulge no self-criticism. Since actually they are men—creatures of thought as well as of instinct—they do pass judgment on the uses of their power. In fact, they often ask me and my pupils to what use they can put their power. More often than not they find the advice inconvenient. Frequently, the best use of power may be not to use it, or sometimes not even to have it—a view that hardly can please a power holder."

"Let me," I proposed, "come to the main problem. I have learned that power is essential to order. If that were all, a graveyard would be its soundest expression. Plainly, this is not the

561

answer—that form of social statics would be singularly unattractive to human beings. So within its living order, power must choose either to do or prevent something or to permit or deny something. Criteria for these choices, one appreciates, lie in your jurisdiction. Control of immediate events, even without foreknowledge of their long-term results, can tend in one direction or another."

Athena warmed to her own approach. "The real function of power and the order it creates," she affirmed, "is the liberation of men and women to think and be and make the most of themselves. That means liberation in all senses. They should not be bound by misery or want. They should not be paralyzed by fear of their neighbors, of other nations, or even of power itself. They should not be frustrated by ignorance or by inability to learn and use the techniques of knowledge and thought. They should be allowed to discover the resources of the arts my brother Apollo cherishes on Parnassus. That is the true use of power; in fact, its only significant use. The order power enforces is to set up that liberation."

"Paradoxically," I commented, "this liberation of men seems to run counter to the principle of power, perhaps even of order. Men and women given the instruments of life and production and thought will be able to refuse allegiance or obedience to power."

Athena smiled. "Any woman understands that paradox. Do you suppose when she conceives and gives birth to a child, that she wants the child to be a mere doll-plaything, able to act only by her will and consent? The essence of creation is that the thing created, be it child or idea or work of art, is independent of its creator; strong enough, indeed, to defy or even deny him. Else there would be neither creation nor liberation—merely endless manufacture of marionettes."

"Then the true use of power is to liberate force capable of its own destruction?" I asked.

Athena assented, as to an obvious banality. "Power always can destroy itself without help and return to Zeus, who gave it. If it has no purpose, its owner goes mad, and self-destruction ends it. If its holder's chief purpose is to deify the power holder, disintegration is even more rapid. But when it liberates men and women, each develops in himself a measure of power. They contend with themselves, with each other, and with their power itself. So it is the business of the power holder to call in my pupils. Those philosophers my father holds in such low esteem cause men and women to do surprising things. Not least of their tasks is to cause men to choose to agree on values—on notions of good, which should be pursued, and of evil, which should be avoided. Men and women play ape to their dreams of a good life. Power is most safely held when it fosters and gives effect to these dreams and makes possible their pursuit."

"You suggest," I pointed out, "that power at this point ceases to be blind. It can create conditions and institutions for realizing these notions."

"Some of them," agreed Athena. "The order it creates, in any case, cannot bind any man's dreams. You were unhappy at negative use of power—a terrible and dangerous capacity. Yet the dreams of any one man coupled with ability to use technique to destroy or impede those around him may call for just those negatives. Power must maintain institutions by which in endless dialogue dreams can be discussed, debated, assessed, accommodated, and on which consensus may be reached. Your democratic institutions attempt to accomplish this. So they must foster, defend, and enlarge institutions by which knowledge can be made greater and choices wider and more certain. My library here is one of these, and not the least. Power must even devise and maintain political institutions capable of changing power holders themselves—an idea not widely accepted until recently, and not happily accepted in many places even now. Then your dreams of the quality of order and of the good life it should engender can supplant older dreams as they become restrictive and outworn."

"You have set a large task for your father and his pupils," I said, "including that of creating machinery for their own dethronement. Indeed, you require power to enter every field. In economics, it must foster production sufficient to free men and women from want. It must handle production so that it will be adequately distributed to everyone—these are the raw materials of life. You ask that power shall arrange for teaching, so that knowledge, when assembled, shall be available to everyone to the measure of his capacity. You want it to make available limitless methods of human development in thought and in the arts. You are asking for institutions that will not only allocate power but also guide it and change its holders if they do not live up to this task."

Athena nodded. "This is what I say to Zeus when he asks and is in any mood to listen—as he usually is not. I know—and so does he—that power is not the producer, is not the merchant, is not the teacher, is not the painter, is not the musician. It can only command my pupils and my brother's disciples to go to work."

"Even to do that must he not give them a measure of power?" I asked.

"He must. In fact, he does. All of them—you, the curator of this library, the writer of your book—have a tiny grain of power. They and you, not Zeus, best understand that power is a tool only. If you go to your classroom, or my curator to his office, or the scientist to his laboratory, seeking power, you all fail. Holding your minim of power is futile unless it is accepted as subordinate to its result. Men and women being what they are, some will transgress and violate their trust. Certainly, they will make mistakes. But their passion and desire and hope must be realized, not in minor power positions, but in the measure to which they give resources for greater development to those with whom they have contact."

"And if they do not?" I asked.

"They fail. In time, they are displaced. If the structure of power fails to achieve this result, the undirected thought of men will presently develop explosive force, invoking chaos, liquidating old power structures, and, in time, building new ones. You call that revolution. The new structures may be little improvement on the old; that depends on the ideas that inspire them. In any case, they must pick up the burden of order and once more attempt the liberation of men and women in all aspects of life."

Athena looked down the long dim corridor of the endless library, musing, as the light quietly faded.

5. The Streets of the City

Broad daylight of a spring afternoon made the crowded street a brilliant though unsurprising impressionist picture. Invariably, the street is the next stop after palace or temple—a fact that often has struck me on leaving either the White House or Columbia University. Great buildings make the backdrop, commonly masked by trees and flanked by arched gates and walls. But the theme is always the same: inside dwells power; outside flow passing crowds.

Specifically, it was a May afternoon in New York. The street was Broadway; the gates were Columbia's. At the moment, they might have been those of any university—in Paris, Warsaw, Rome, Stanford, Berkeley. For that matter, many of the palaces of Zeus were in similar state. This afternoon the crowds were not disparate individuals, each busily going his own way. They were masses, more or less held together by jerry-rigged organizations whose leaders carried placards, distributed throwaways, chanted slogans. "No class today, no ruling class tomorrow" perhaps illustrated the indistinct emotion whose appeal gathered considerable numbers for indeterminate purposes. Police guarded the gates; admission was allowed only to pass holders. From inside the walls, waves of folk-rock music and occasional chants drifted between buildings and through the trees to the street, where a lady of indeterminate age and great beauty confronted a very tough old man. Both were familiar.

"Why are you not inside creating order?" asked Athena.

"Why are you not inside making this thought creative instead of destructive?" asked Zeus.

"Those are your votaries," she replied, pointing to a strike committee leading the demonstration. "They are demanding power."

"Those are your pupils," Zeus said, grinning and waving a hand toward the students and their followers. "They say they are seeking a philosophy of meaningful life."

Athena became visibly angry. "My father," she accused, "these people want power. They do not know why; they have no settled plan, hardly even a purpose. But they want your tools. You will allow them to clear the way for some undisclosed follower of yours who will promptly seize it. Your new favorite will take over. Raw power will make order; the crowd here will be discarded, tenderly or, more likely, brutally. The old cycle will begin again."

Zeus tossed a remark in my direction. "Your doctrine of power giving liberation seems to have limitations," he observed.

Athena refused the interruption. "These boys and girls are not being liberated. They are in the process of being enslaved."

"So?" said Zeus. "Perhaps a little servitude would do them good."

Both turned on me.

"Out of courtesy to Athena," said Zeus, "I allow you to defend yourself. From this university, from that palace in Washington, in twenty places you have worked, American-style, at your doctrine of 'liberation under power.' When they are liberated, this is what men do."

Athena rejoined, "For years you have insisted that power must always control to give order, and that liberation fostered under order would protect and nourish restrained power institutions to defend and maintain the liberated. Are you right?"

I said, "You make me the judge, though either of you can destroy me. At least you should listen. Fifty years ago, the grandfathers of most of these youngsters were poverty-stricken proletarians. All their working hours were spent filling their bellies, putting clothes on their backs, getting crude shelter over their heads. That was their life from birth to grave. Thirty years ago the balance shifted. My generation did not destroy. We fostered production. Using crude economic tools we guided a portion of it to the poor, and can guide more. The result lifted half of America's population from the brute servitude of poverty to tolerable living. They became free in some measure to choose how they should live and how they should think. Political power coupled with economic power achieved this in one generation. We asked help from Zeus, some from Athena, and we used our own heads. The grandfathers and most of the fathers of these students could not have gone to any university—they had not the means, and, in any case, there were not sufficient universities to receive them. Today, half the population of university age is entering universities. Is it surprising they also seek power?"

"No." Zeus nodded. "But giving power to any of them means denying power to most of their fellows. So a few of them must dominate the rest—unless, in impatience, I set up a dictator to rule them all. They fight what they call the 'Establishment' because, in fact, they wish to be the 'Establishment.' These fellows will not succeed, because from my daughter they have accepted no philosophy by which they can construct institutions of power. They are helpless in the grip of their own unthought-out desires. Yet Athena complains that I give them no order—and is afraid I may do so."

"No," Athena answered. "They think they are fighting an establishment. In fact, they are fighting themselves. They ask my father for power for the purpose, they say, of finding a meaningful life—as though he could give that or had ever given it. All the wisdom of earth is in that library within the walls some of them have just desecrated. But they have not looked there."

"Then give them a philosophy," Zeus commanded. "So far as I am concerned, I can settle this affair with a whiff of grapeshot or a well-placed bomb ordered by a dictator who has a few ideas, probably bad ones. You can give them a philosophy capable of remaking a society—perhaps even what you call a 'free society.' "

Athena considered for a moment. "I can," she said sadly, "offer them everything and give them nothing. This generation, beyond any in history, has and has had freedom—to read, to study, to think, to 'do their own thing,' to conclude what conceptions give meaning to life. Behind this disorderly affair there are half-formed ideas. There are libraries full of plans to build these youths into a living social organism. You cannot say that because they are liberated from the slavery of poverty and the dead order imposed by it, they cannot construct a greater order. But that order must be of their making, not of yours or mine."

Somewhat wearily, Zeus agreed. "They had best do so swiftly. Otherwise, using the services of the police, who, I am glad to note, are in evidence around these gates, I can construct order of a sort. Whether it will satisfy our aging author-visitor here, I am inclined to doubt. Tyrannies are not popular today. Cities are too big and rhetoric is too cheap, as your friend Aristotle observed some twenty-two centuries or so ago. To be satisfied— to be happy, if you like—these people must want more than power giving them permanent management of others, which is my precise business. As that Aristotle person claimed, the design of the gods of the universe is to give life that is at once self-con- tained and in a state of external activity. Neither the one nor the other seems likely to emerge from this noise. So I suggest we leave talking, gather a few recruits, and go to work."

He offered a courteous arm to Pallas Athena. They moved gently toward the great gate. The guards saluted and stood aside.

"It is time, Father," she agreed. "Little as you liked my mother, you pondered marvelous schemes in your heart to bring into being men who would defend against destructive gods. . . ."

I was left outside. A group came up the street chanting, "Black Power"; another, "Student Power"; another, "Power to the Poor"; still another, "No Ruling Class." From within the police barricade Zeus waved at them. "I'll send you a master," he called genially, and a mustachioed and brown-shirted ghost floated across the afternoon shadows. "I will send you a thinker," said Athena. "You will need him soon." A faint vision of St. Augustine mistily moved across the plaza fronting the library. A young engineer and five workmen manning a wholly unghostly truck hauled up by the curb. He gave an order, and his crew set about repairing an overhead electric-wire system. The engineer grinned at the demonstrators. "While all this racket goes on, somebody has to make things work," he shouted to me, laughing, through the noise. "All these characters need lights."

Bibliographical Note

This volume is an attempt to distill theory and conclusions from personal experience and observation of men, events, and history rather than from books. Since power is, I believe, a universal experience, almost any reading brings some fish into the net. References have been made in the text to some of these fish.

In place of conventional bibliography, I here note some highlight experiences of my own in the world of books, encountered along an intellectual journey continuing from World War I and its concluding Versailles Peace Conference to the present day.

Allegories of Chaos and Power

No poem of power's origin rivals that of the *Theogony* of Hesiod (Hesiod: *The Homeric Hymns,* with an English translation by Hugh G. Evelyn-White, M.A., Cambridge, Mass., Harvard University Press, revised edition, 1936). According to standard Greek mythology, Chaos brought forth Earth. Chaos lay with Earth and produced Heaven (Uranus). Uranus lay with Earth (Gaea), producing twelve Titans, headed by Cronus. He promptly assumed rulership and imprisoned his brother Titans. Cronus lay with Rhea (again, Earth). Their youngest offspring was Zeus, whom Cronus sought to destroy, but who was saved by Rhea's cunning. In time, revolting against Cronus, Zeus liberated the imprisoned Titans from captivity, but they, Hesiod says, "with bitter wrath were fighting continually with one another at that time for full ten years, and the hard strife had no close or end for either side, and the issue of the war hung evenly balanced" (p. 125). Whereupon Zeus makes peace with three of his cousins, enlists them as allies, wins the war against the Titans, and confines them "in a dank place where are the ends of the huge Earth" (p. 133). Of interest are the alleged attributes of Zeus—all children of Pallas Athena. They were: Emulation, Victory, Strength, and Life-force. These "have no house apart from Zeus" (p. 107). The Titan monsters were the seed of Earth and Heaven, all proceeding from primal Chaos. The warfare of Zeus with them is, I am certain, an allegory of the subjection of the attributes of chaos to power.

The first chapter of the Book of Genesis is simpler: an earth without form and void, darkness on the face of it, succeeded by the Lord's decree giving light and order. But in it there is, naturally, little human interpretation until Adam and Eve appear in later chapters.

My choice of Pergamum as take-off point is arbitrary—any of several citadels would have done as well. The literature on Pergamum is substantial, though chiefly written for historical specialists. For general readers, Pergamum's historical importance and, particularly, Eumenes II's intrigue leading to the intervention of Rome and the fall of the Seleucid Empire is best set forth in a fascinating volume, *Rome on the Euphrates: The Story of a Frontier*, by Freya Stark (New York, Harcourt, Brace & World, 1967).

Power in History

Take it wherever you strike in, most history chronicles the aspiration to power, its seizure, the uses to which it was put when attained, and its downfall. The great histories compel meditation.

Foremost must always be Gibbon's *Decline and Fall of the Roman Empire*, whether or not one agrees with his detail or his theory. For years, Gibbon's superb drama has driven the night away for me in hours between bedtime and sleep.

More analytic is a modern volume, *Oriental Despotism: A Com-*

parative Study of Total Power, by Professor Karl A. Wittfogel (New Haven, Yale University Press, 1957). He attempts to trace the origins of despotism and its organization to the monopoly of water achieved by local chieftains in Asia Minor and to derive from these experiences the organization and development of power in modern managed societies.

An interesting world study is Jacques Henri Pirenne's *Panorama de l'Histoire Universelle* (Paris, Editions Albin Michel, 1963), a condensation of the seven-volume *Les Grands Courants de l'Histoire Universelle*, written by his father, Jacques Pirenne. Conflict between liberalism (freedom) and authoritarianism is one of its principal themes. For me, the unpredictable results of acts of decision-making power were underlined by reading Pirenne's dry summary of the result of the Roman Republic's decision to intervene in Asia Minor—though fifty similar illustrations could be drawn from the volume. (Some of the Roman pronouncements at the time of the excursion against the Seleucid Empire diabolically resemble some American declarations of foreign policy since 1947.) Intervention by the Roman Republic in Asia Minor even more than the Carthaginian wars unpredictably launched Rome on its course of conquest toward world empire. The Soviet Union's imperial intervention in the eastern Mediterranean—or possibly intervention by the United States in opposition—could have similar results for either one or the other in the next few years.

More generalized, though not less interesting, is a monumental book by Professor William H. McNeill, *The Rise of the West: A History of the Human Community* (Chicago, University of Chicago Press, 1963). I particularly commend his conclusion, "Dilemmas of Power." His closing suggestion, perhaps overoptimistic, is that the elaboration of power structures in our time may be moving to a climax. "The globe is finite and if the rival political-social-economic power systems of our time coalesce under an overarching world sovereignty, the impetus now impelling men to develop new sources of power will largely cease" (p. 806). Outstandingly, McNeill recognizes the modification of power effects resulting from the imperatives of art and search for beauty.

Finally, I acknowledge a prejudice for and admiration of H. G. Wells's *The Outline of History: Being a Plain History of Life and Mankind* (New York, Macmillan, 1920; later revised). Wells tells a majestic story, considers history a long search for world unity and world government, and says, "Unity must come or else plainly men must perish by their own inventions" (p. 1087). He wrote that line a quarter-century *before* the advent of intercontinental missiles and nuclear bombs.

Wells states as fundamentals of the coming world-state: a common world religion; universal education; no armies, navies, or classes of unemployed people (either wealthy or poor); world organization of scientific research; free literature of criticism and discussion; direction of affairs responsive to the general thought of the population; private business enterprise as servant, not robber; a world currency safeguarded against abuse. There are plenty of ambiguities in all of these; we have not yet got there. Yet it seems to me that for the first time in history the preconditions are appearing, giving rise to sober hope that organizing world order may not be impossible.

American history is an epic in itself, brilliantly covered by Samuel Eliot Morison's *Oxford History of the American People* (New York, Oxford University Press, 1965). Preceding Morison's saga is Edward M. Channing's famous six-volume *History of the United States* (Boston, 1905–1925). As the Columbia Encyclopedia (third edition) observes: ". . . it is generally considered one of the finest histories of the United States ever produced by one man." Whereas Channing's is primarily history, Morison's volume (no less authoritative) reads like a novel.

Literature of the Communist empires is naturally recent; the evidence is not in, and will not be until Chinese and Soviet archives open up their data. Two books are outstanding: Jan Librach's *The Rise of the Soviet Empire: A Study of Soviet Foreign Policy* (New York, Frederick A. Praeger, 1966), and, for the period since World War II, Louis J. Halle's *The Cold War as History* (New York, Harper & Row, 1967).

Theories of Power

All processions, as older generations used to be taught, are headed by Aristotle.

The "Politics" of Aristotle (edited and translated by Ernest Barker; reprinted New York, Oxford University Press, 1962) certainly heads books on this subject. Book VII ("Eternal antithesis between power and might," an attempt to relate power to ignorance) and Book I, Chapters V and VI strike us today strangely. When slavery, says Aristotle, rests merely on superior power, it is unjustified; when master and slave are in the respective places they merit, it is allowable. Compare this with Friedrich Nietzsche's *Beyond Good and Evil* and *Thus Spake Zarathustra* and his insistence that the will of the conquering superman makes its own right. Nietzsche was an immoderate columnist-commentator as well as philosopher. (The present generation is just discovering how vastly it has underestimated the irrational attraction demonic neurasthenia like Nietzsche's holds for many people.)

Of more recent books, one of the most thoughtful is *The Quest for Community*, by Professor Robert A. Nisbet (New York, Oxford University Press, 1953; republished in 1962 as a Galaxy Book under the title *Community and Power*). Nisbet's discussion of Jean Jacques Rousseau (pp. 140–180) ought to be required reading for those currently attracted by the thinking of Herbert Marcuse (*The One Dimensional Man*). Rousseau had some idea of ethics, whereas Marcuse professes none. Rousseau's "General Will" (contained in his "Discourse on Political Economy") led straight to Marat, Danton, Robespierre, and the Terror of the French Revolution, and also to the absolutism of totalitarian states and the horrors they created. By accepting the power of the state, Rousseau points out, one "participates" in the "General Will." He is credited with insistence on popular sovereignty, which thus helps to free the civilized world from despotism; but participation in (subjection to) the General Will leads right back to totalitarian despotism, equally derivable from another great

573

treatise on power, Plato's *Republic*. The result Rousseau did not get but may have hoped for was, in Nisbet's words (p. 157), "freedom, equality, brotherhood, virtue. It is community." (Rousseau is both angel and devil; unfortunately, his theory of mass power as mass freedom has proved a ghastly lure for everyone from Marat and Napoleon to Stalin and Hitler.) Totalitarian governments are not always in conflict, says Nisbet, with the desires of the masses—they always are preceded by mass movements. They are not irrational; rather, as Hannah Arendt has pointed out in *The Origins of Totalitarianism* (New York, Harcourt, Brace & World, New Edition, 1966), totalitarian tyrants offer a seemingly logical escape from mass despair. Professor William Withers' *Freedom through Power* (New York, John Day, 1965) tries to strike a balance. He believes, as do I, planning is essential in a modern state; planning implies power; careful use of that power can, indeed, give greater measure of decision-making—that is, freedom—to the individual; but, as always, power can be abused.

A major philosophical attempt to analyze the problem of power is by Bertrand Russell: *Power: A New Social Analysis* (New York, Norton, 1938). This was written before Russell, more logician than political philosopher, had lapsed into his final passionate phase. The book is valuable, though it does not come to grips with the fact that power invariably lodges in individuals whose intellectual and emotional make-up at once thrusts into the power process.

Perhaps best among the more modern books is that of my old friend Robert M. MacIver: *The Modern State* (London, Oxford University Press, 1926; reprinted as an Oxford paperback in 1964). He draws sharp distinction between economic and political power, as I do; but he wrote before the breakthrough that gave economics some at least of the attributes and manageable applications of a real science.

The most ambitious recent attempt to discuss power is included in a highly academic work, *Man and His Government: An Empirical History*, by Professor Carl Joachim Friedrich (New York,

McGraw-Hill, 1963). Part II, "The Dimensions of Power and Justice," and, more especially, the two chapters on power and leadership and rule and rulership are interesting, logical analyses in classic scholarly form. Friedrich's bibliography is as complete as any student might wish.

Institutions Transmitting Power

No study of power is valid without taking Max Weber into account. I think he was less interested in power than in the machinery by which it was transmitted—but this can be only an interpretation. He spent an immense amount of time on the study of comparative civilizations, as witnessed by the *Protestant Ethic and the Spirit of Capitalism*, and his sociological analyses in *The Religion of India* and *The Religion of China* and *Ancient Judaism*. He was preoccupied with status groups, including the effect of moral ideas proceeding from them. For our purposes he is perhaps more relevant in his examination of bureaucracy, largely contained in his essays. Some are not available in English. I recommend an excellent summary by Reinhardt Bendix: *Max Weber: An Intellectual Portrait* (New York, Doubleday, 1960), especially Chapter XIII, both for its analysis of bureaucratic structure and for its recognition that anyone who has achieved the position of power holder must then struggle to control the institutions of transmission, namely, the "apparatus." Weber's *Theory of Social and Economic Organization* (New York, Oxford University Press, 1947) and his *Essays*, particularly Chapter VI, "Wirtschaft und Gesellschaft" (which deals with structure of power), and Chapter VII (which deals with bureaucracy), are perhaps most interesting in our exploration.

Political Power

Classic in this field, as one might expect, is Niccolò Machiavelli's *The Prince*, with which must be bracketed his *Discourses. The Prince* is a "how-to-do-it" power manual, never equaled. Rightly, on his tombstone is inscribed the briefest epitaph: "No eulogy could equal so great a name."

Of endless scholarly commentaries on him, I recommend *Machiavelli,* by Giuseppe Prezzolini (New York, Farrar, Straus & Giroux, 1967), a translation of his Italian volume *Machiavelli Anticristo* (Rome, 1954). Thought-provoking is Prezzolini's conclusion: "Contemporary conflicts can be understood better if we consider them as conflicts between nations and not between ideologies" (p. 349).

Of equal importance as analysis and perhaps of greater causative effect is Vladimir Ilyich Ulyanov's (Lenin's) monograph, *What Is to Be Done?* (1902)—a pamphlet on the theory and method of revolutionary seizure of power, though almost all his political works deal with the same subject. A handy selection of Lenin's writings may be found in Stefan T. Possony's *Lenin Reader* (Chicago, Henry Regnery, in conjunction with the Hoover Institution of Stanford University, 1966). For present purposes, the collections contained in Chapter IV ("The State") and Chapter VII ("Organization") are perhaps the most interesting. Lenin is an intellectual blood brother of Machiavelli. Adolf Hitler's *Mein Kampf* (English translation, New York, Reynal & Hitchcock, 1939), bad, but unhappily causative, is essentially bastard Leninism.

As offset to Marxism-Leninism and its by-products, I recommend two books by a brilliant scholar at the University of Michigan, Professor James H. Meisel: *The Myth of the Ruling Class* (Ann Arbor, Mich., University of Michigan Press, 1958; reprinted as a paperback, 1962) and *Counterrevolution* (New York, Atherton Press, 1966).

Everyone owes a great deal to a book describing the interrelations between economic and political power (the two now are not always distinguishable) by Milovan Djilas: *The New Class* (New York, Frederick A. Praeger, 1957). No answer has yet been made to his argument that every dictatorial regime creates such a "class." Mr. Djilas has expanded and refined his thinking on power in a new book, *The Unperfect Society* (New York, Harcourt, Brace & World, 1969).

Economic Power

We are barely coming to understand (if we do) the realities of economic power. They are far less impressive than current mythology supposes, and will become increasingly less impressive as economics continues its progress toward becoming a usable science. Economic power more often than not reflects political power; essentially, it is instrument, not cause. With Dr. Gardiner C. Means, I explored the principal modern expression of that power in *The Modern Corporation and Private Property* (New York, Macmillan, 1932; revised edition, New York, Harcourt, Brace & World, 1968). Bertrand Russell draws somewhat on its conclusions in his *Power,* referred to above. The most ambitious recent exploration is that of John Kenneth Galbraith in *The New Industrial State* (Boston, Houghton Mifflin Company, 1967), though he is indefinite in his conclusions. Compare it with Robert L. Heilbroner's *The Limits of American Capitalism* (New York, Harper & Row, 1966). Heilbroner agrees that the limits of business power within American society are shrinking, but I believe he still overestimates its capacity in the past and possibly also today.

Obviously, the intellectually great analysis of economic power is that of John Maynard Keynes: *The General Theory of Employment, Interest and Money* (New York, Harcourt, Brace & World, 1936; reprinted in paperback in 1965). Leaving aside its clear technical worth, the transcendent value of the study lies in his Chapter 24, "Concluding Notes." Underlying them is his reasoned conviction that economic disparates can be controlled, that the state can and must exercise a guiding influence on consumption and investment, that who "owns" the instruments of production is less important than the central control of what they do; and that, ultimately, the social philosophy of the state will determine its economic results.

We are, I suggest, on the eve of a truly scientific theory of economics, making possible controlled use of its instruments of money production and distribution to produce desired results. A book on that has yet to be written. When it arrives, politicians, rather than entrepreneurs, will be seen to be the managers of the great machine. They will be held accountable for its results, and these results (and the politicians as power holders) will be judged by the opinion of the immense mass of individuals comprised within the field of economic responsibility. Dialogue between politicians and the field of responsibility, at present disorderly, will then become an integral part of economic government.

Corporate Power

The change of the nonstatist corporation from private business enterprise to public institution and now to political institution is being fairly traced by historians. The most comprehensive American study of the subject is *The Business System: Readings in Ideas and Concepts,* edited by Clarence Walton and Richard Eells (New York, Macmillan, three volumes, 1966, under the sponsorship of the Columbia University Graduate School of Business). The evolution of modern corporations from owner dictatorships to institutionally organized bureaucracies with staff and line formation is well documented in *Strategy and Structure: Chapters in the History of the Industrial Enterprise* by Alfred D. Chandler, Jr. (Cambridge, Mass., The M.I.T. Press, 1962). My own *Power Without Property* (New York, Harcourt, Brace & World, 1959) and *The 20th Century Capitalist Revolution* (New York, Harcourt, Brace & World, 1954) deal with aspects of that evolution. The modern corporation, oddly enough, is an unintended revolutionary instrument. It has transformed, and still is transforming (I mean, literally, "changing the form of"), capital, property, production, and norms of ownership in measure and qualitative depth undreamed of by nineteenth-century socialists and barely appreciated even now.

Poetry and Power

Power is personal. Consequently poets, especially dramatic poets, have interpreted its interplay with men through the ages. I here note only some favorites of my own; all literature is full of the subject.

The First and Second Books of Chronicles and the First Book of Kings in the Old Testament (I prefer the King James version) come high on my list of intellectual experiences. They relate the fall of the last two great judges in unorganized Israel, Eli and Samuel, and the rise and fall of Israel's first king, Saul, succeeded by David. They record the emotional crises of the men as well as the external events (note especially David's relations with his general, Joab). My friend the Reverend Douglas Krumbhaar, of St. Paul's Church, Stockbridge, Massachusetts, tells me that the portions dealing with King David appear to be surviving contemporary record—history perhaps, but informed with poetic insight, raising it to high art; history is itself an art form.

But there is no question about Shakespeare. His historical dramas are poetry all the way through. Reference has been made in the text to a few interesting passages only. Regretfully, I have omitted many more. Take, for example, the evolution of Macbeth from well-meaning field commander to murderous police-state dictator, leading to loss of touch with reality and consequent downfall. It could be paralleled by the history of several contemporary Caribbean dictators I have known—for instance, the late Rafael Leonidas Trujillo, of the Dominican Republic; see Robert D. Crassweller's *Trujillo: The Life and Times of a Caribbean Dictator* (New York, Macmillan, 1966)—or, for that matter, by the chronicles of contemporary European dictators. Interplay of personality and power is constant; perhaps the best education a power holder could have would be solid acquaintance with Shakespeare's plays.

Also on my list would be Johann Christoph Friedrich von Schiller, some of whose plays outstandingly reveal the emotional life of power holders as they encounter the uses of their might. These are *Don Carlos* (a play about the court of Philip II of Spain) and the dramatic trilogy *Wallenstein*, though the elements are not missing in others of Schiller's plays. (He never finished a contemplated drama whose central character was to have been the Comte d'Argenson, Louis XIV's chief of police.) Schiller violates history—the historical Don Carlos (son of Philip II of

Spain), far from being the romantic idealist portrayed by Schiller, was more likely a mentally retarded idiot—but one must take an artist's interpretation from the artist's own choice of historical premises.

Finally—a personal taste—I consider an exquisite experience the reading of Books XX and XXI of Sir Thomas Malory's *Le Morte d'Arthur*. The legendary King Arthur's chancellor was Sir Gawaine. Cognizant of the love affair between Sir Launcelot, Arthur's general, and Guinevere, Arthur's queen, Gawaine, to hold the kingdom together, steadily prevented the inevitable quarrel from erupting. When it finally did explode and the Queen was rescued by Launcelot, Sir Gareth, Gawaine's favorite brother, was killed by Launcelot in the fighting. Gawaine's statesmanship gives way; demanding vengeance, he encourages the King to make war on Launcelot, and is mortally wounded in an ensuing battle. But news comes that Arthur's illegitimate son, Mordred, is in revolt and is about to seize the kingdom. On his deathbed, Gawaine renounces his quarrel, calls Arthur, urges him, despite all, to make peace with Launcelot and seek his help. The state's safety outweighs all personal quarrels, however justified. Arthur sadly accepts the advice, asks Launcelot for help, and returns to fight for his kingdom, though Launcelot, following swiftly with reinforcements for the King, arrives too late.

Malory perhaps was an artist by default. Actually, he was a feudal bandit writing in jail (where he died) and translating and adorning books for Caxton, England's first printer, to while the time away.

Every reader, however, will find his own illustrations. Literature is full of them. What power does to men is an unlimited source of drama.

International Power

The literature is endless; every morning's newspaper adds to it. I know of no good general book in the field. Observing and reading history is the best tutor.

Index

Index

210; interaction with corporations, 197; as lawmaker, 286–288; monopoly of force, 288–292; power of, 267–273; as repository of ultimate power, 285–286; rise of the government bureau, 194; slow innovation by governmental organizations, 211, 213; spending, 324

Great Britain: and the Balkans, 42; cabinet ministers, 310; ceremonial function of the monarchy, 307; child labor in, 167; control of economics in World War I, 181; conquest of India, 481, 483; culture of, 425; economic understanding in the 1930's, 178; emergence of as a manufacturing country, 174; equivocal position in world affairs, 498; and the European Common Market, 462–463; evolution of democracy in, 97; gold crisis, 323–324, 414; and imperialism, 443, 448, 510; industrial poverty in, 172; and Ireland, 484; judicial system and public administration, 399n; labor conditions in the nineteenth century, 225; and the Munich crisis, 417–418; as a naval empire, 473; Parliamentary defeat and power withdrawal, 77; *pax Britannica*, 503; peace with the United States (1783), 447; rise of Socialism in, 184; and the rule of law in international affairs, 442, 443; and the Soviet Union, 89; student revolt in, 253; successful colonial record, 478; and the Triple Entente, 514; and the Turkish Empire, 498; under Elizabeth I, 473; unemployment in, 182; and the United Nations, 443, 519; and the United States, 498; and the Versailles Treaty, 427; wealth and political power, 218; weavers' strikes of the 1850's, 255; and

World War I, 514; and World War II, 150

Great Currents in Universal History (Pirenne), 25, 571

Great Depression. *See* Depression (1930's)

Greece, 498, 501, 516; ancient Greece, 57, 106, 555

Green, John Richard, 174–175, 184

Gregory IX, Pope, 453

Grey, Sir Edward, 425

Gross National Product, 197, 349

Guam, 542

Guaranteed income, 350

Guatemala, 514n

Guerrilla force, 474

Guevara, Che, 500

Guided missiles. *See* Rockets and guided missiles

Guinea, 513

Guinevere, Queen, 580

Guyana, 460, 519

Haiti, 514n

Halle, Louis J., 502, 572

Hammarskjöld, Dag, 518, 522, 529

Hanna, Mark, 153

Hanoi, 76

Hapsburgs, 453, 508, 513

Harbrecht, Dr. Paul, 377

Harding, President Warren G., 50, 276

Harlan, John Marshall, Justice of the Supreme Court, 356, 357n, 358n, 359, 359n

Harlem, New York, degradation in, 172

Harriman, Averell, 218

Harrison, President Benjamin, 300

Harrison, President William Henry, 300

Harvard Law Review, 352n, 368n, 382

Harvard University: Annual Report (1966–1967) quoted, 253; and the class structure, 278; develops into a "national university," 129; Graduate School of Business Administration, 93, 93n; Littauer Center, 129; Political Science Department, 129; research fellowships, 81; School of Edu-

cation, 129; School of Public Administration, 129; and World War I, 424

Hatshepsut, Queen, 14

Hawaii, 280, 290

Health, universal rules, 411

Hearst, William Randolph, 220

Heaven (Uranus), 569

Heilbroner, Robert L., 577

Helena, Montana, 282

Helicon, Mount, 5

Henry II, King of England, 164

Henry IV, King of England, 78–79

Henry III, King of France, 305

Henry IV, King of France, 305

Henry V, King of England, 78

Hephaestus, 9

Hera, 10

Hercules, 9

Herrera, José, President of Mexico, 422

Herrin, Illinois, labor unrest at, 225

Hesiod, 5–6, 7, 8, 10, 11, 12, 49, 551, 560, 569

Historia regum Britanniae (Geoffrey of Monmouth), 74

Historical laws, 25–26

History, oral tradition in, 13

History of Plimoth Plantation (Bradford), 85–86

History of the United States (Channing), 572

Hitler, Adolf, 58, 86, 88, 120, 126, 182, 259, 414, 417, 425, 432, 433, 439, 443, 447, 457, 458, 468, 476, 477, 500, 504, 554, 555, 557, 558, 574, 576

Ho Chi Minh, 432

Hodgson, Richard C., 93–94

Hoffa, James R., 154, 223, 223n–224n

Hohenzollerns, 425, 479, 504, 513

Holinshed, 74

Holland. *See* Netherlands

Holy Roman Empire, 508

Homer, 5, 10

Honduras, 514n

Hoover, President Herbert, 54, 185, 303

Hopkins, Harry, 186